COMPULSION

by Robin Moore

PITCHMAN

THE DEVIL TO PAY (*with Jack Youngblood*)

THE GREEN BERETS

THE COUNTRY TEAM

FIEDLER

THE FRENCH CONNECTION

COURT MARTIAL (*with Henry Rothblatt*)

THE KHAKI MAFIA (*with June Collins*)

THE HAPPY HOOKER (*with Xaviera Hollander*)

THE FIFTH ESTATE

DUBAI

COMPULSION

ROBIN MOORE

with psychiatric analysis by Dr. Robert L. Custer

Compulsion

1981

DOUBLEDAY & COMPANY, INC., GARDEN CITY, NEW YORK

"Little Boy Blue" by Eugene Field from *With Trumpet and Drum* courtesy Charles Scribner's Sons, New York.

Library of Congress Cataloging in Publication Data

Moore, Robin.
Compulsion.

1. Hodges, Joe Henry. 2. Gamblers—United States—Biography. I. Custer, Robert L., 1927–
II. Title.
HV6713.M66 362.2 [B]
ISBN: 0-385-13322-7 AACR2
Library of Congress Catalog Card Number 78–20028

Printed in the United States of America
First Edition

To Nancy—who'll never know
how very much I love her.

Joe

PROLOGUE

The journey Robin Moore takes you on in *Compulsion* is a strange one. It may seem like a dream. It is a nightmare. And it is true.

This essentially is a story of survival. It's vicious, but bloodless. It's painful, but gripping. There is risk-taking, fear, and danger. It's a story of an individual who has remarkable ability to cope with dangers while lacking the ability to control impulses which precipitate these very dangers. It shows how excitement can be an end in itself—even worshipped. The excitement makes the stress and distress of life disappear and nullifies the basic needs of affection, sex, safety, hunger, and sleep. Then, in turn, it generates agonizing, unbearable pain.

Some will see this as the story of an adventurer, a rogue, or a madman. It is none of these. What it reveals is the euphoria and the anguish of the pathological gambler—the compulsive gambler. The metamorphosis from recreational gambler into pathological gambler is subtle. It can be compared to a man in a canoe that is floating gently beyond the periphery of a whirlpool and then drifts leisurely into the outer whirls. At this stage, the water is calm and seems safe. But there has been a change: the man no longer controls the canoe's direction. The canoe picks up speed, slowly at first, then with frightening rapidity, and the man is carried toward his doom.

The disastrous course he is taking is totally unrecognized by the compulsive gambler until it is too late. His cries for help have not been recognized, understood, or responded to until recently. Friends and relatives recognize his predicament long before he does but seem too scared or bemused to react appropriately. Perhaps this is because what first seems like innocent recreational activity passes to the irrationality of compulsion too quickly or too secretly. But the pathological gambler has been misunderstood most by society, which considers him a degenerate pleasure seeker, and the courts, which consider him criminal. He is neither, although one has to admit that he is destructive, both of himself and others.

The life of Joe Hodges is being lived by thousands upon thousands and to them this journey will be familiar. Some will survive, many will not. To most of us nonpathological gamblers, this story will be almost incredible or, at the least, baffling. These are expected reactions to what we don't understand. Yet irrational behavior only appears mindless because some of the pieces are missing or not recognized. All the pieces are present in this story by Robin Moore and will be identified and organized in the epilogue to show how the unreasonable can be reasonable, or at least understandable.

Robert L. Custer, M.D.

COMPULSION

CHAPTER 1

That certain quality of unreality pervading the Sahara Hotel casino seduced Jonathan Alan Roberts the moment he entered. Like all the other gambling casinos in Las Vegas, this one was a world to itself, and like them a combination of French baroque and Miami Beach, with a hint of Hollywood and the Wild West. It was furnished with thick carpets and walnut tables and ornate chandeliers which broke the light into innumerable sparkles and prisms.

Bar girls came through swinging doors with free drinks for the men and women at the green felt gaming tables. There were no windows or clocks to break the spell. Everything had been done, at a cost of millions, to produce the illusion of opulence that would give the gamblers a false sense of their own invincibility. And the psychology was sound. The casino owners had discovered long ago that the guests must be fed on fantasy if they were to bet against the house advantage day and night until the last dollar they could lose was gone.

So the operators in Las Vegas provided for their customers the most surreal ambiance they could conceive. Jonathan Alan Roberts, a scarred veteran of twenty-five years battling the casino odds, still experienced a surge of excitement when he walked into one of these rooms. Suddenly he was absorbed in a special, eerie microcosm that instantly severed him from the actualities of life. All things became possible. He felt charged, authentic, at the center of the universe.

Jon Roberts wanted desperately to separate himself from

humdrum actualities and was now hugely relieved to be back at last in the other world, the world of gambling. The tension built as he contemplated the big win that he just knew, as he always did, lay ahead. Once again he was young, omnipotent, able to overcome all odds in his quest for victory over the hated casino bosses.

"Hello, Jon," "Hi, Mr. R," greeted him as he stepped up to a crap table and put down fifty $100 bills. Smoothly the pile of assorted technicolored chips was slid across the garishly marked-up green felt surface toward him. He began to throw. The opening roll was an eight. He must shoot another eight before he rolled a seven or he would lose. It did not matter to him that it was mathematically easier to shoot a seven, which would favor the house. Ignoring what he knew to be the truth, he placed $600 more on the eight and $600 on the six.

Jon knew the statistics and had long since memorized the probability tables. He had as swiftly forgotten them. What did it matter that they favored the house? With what he believed to be his consummate skill and a little luck he would overcome. He rolled again. The six came up. He put $600 more on the eight and $500 on the nine. Again the six appeared.

He told the stickman to press it, to double the bet and put $500 on the five. When the nine appeared and was followed by another six, Jon's concentration on the dice became intense. He was a quiet shooter with a style all his own. He covered the dice, the top of his hand on a parallel plane with the table. The dice seemed to squirt out from under his hand, past the small finger and streak across the table in one abrupt motion. While a croupier piled chips on the numbers Jon had bet, the stickman rolled the dice back and again Jon's hand covered them for a moment before making the sudden throw.

Perhaps inside he was talking to the dice and addressing himself to the fates, asking that he be favored above others. But his face was expressionless as the dice flew from under the palm of his hand pressing down on the table.

Word was spreading around the casino that the dice were hot at table two and more spectators and casino officials gravitated toward Jon's table to watch him. He was wagering $500 on four numbers and in addition was betting that he would win the eight the hard way with a pair of fours. Every throw of the dice brought him additional hundreds. There may have been considerable reaction among the spectators but he seemed not to notice it. He was in the tunnel of his crap game, a tunnel that enclosed himself and his dice and the chips, excluding all else. Soon he had made his point and more chips slid toward him. He racked them into the trough of the table in front of him and started anew. They sent the cocktail waitress over and he recalled hearing her soft voice ask him if he wanted something to drink. Without turning his head he told the voice that he would appreciate a malted milkshake. Already his stomach was grinding under the tension.

The croupier was retrieving the dice with his hooked stick, impassive and observant. The pit boss and his assistant, a perfectly matched pair, stood watching his every move. He could sense vaguely that they were slightly disturbed. He had won $8,000 already and intended to win much more. He deserved it. He willed it.

Jon was running full throttle now, throwing the dice faster and making his points. He changed his drink from milk to bourbon and then to black coffee. He played on and held on to Lady Luck, riding her upward as the chips accumulated. Around him he could feel the crowd pressing in. It included one Praying John who whooped up strange incantations every time Jon threw. If he threw a nine the man would shout: "Strychnine!" If he threw an eight the man would cry: "Eighter from Decatur." When he threw a five the man chortled: "Phoebe!" And when nine reappeared he came out with: "Ninah from Carolina!"

Dimly, as Jon threw the dice, he was aware of the crowd roaring its approbation of his shooting. Again he made his point and the croupier stacked the chips his way. His heart began to pound. He could walk away right now a big winner, but he was being touched by the elusive Lady and he kept playing. What else could he do? To play dice is to ride the tiger. There is danger for him who rides, but he who gets off too soon is a fool. Jon was certain he could ride it to the end.

As his hand ended he redistributed his bets, eyeing the next shooter. He came up winner again. Suddenly Jon sensed a dangerous twist coming. He withdrew everything but three hundred dollars from the table, which he placed on the "Do Not Pass," and watched a shooter frantically shake the dice and cast them violently down the table. Double three. The point was six. Next throw. Six and one. Seven. The shooter lost everything on the table. Impassively the croupier raked in the chips for the house. Jon congratulated himself for having finessed that play. The next man was also a loser, Jon decided, the kind that can't throw a winning roll. It defied logic and mathematical probability but such men did exist and did come to Las Vegas. They were doomed to lose and he felt sorry for them. He waited.

Now it was his turn with the dice again. He threw a four. He must throw a four again without rolling a seven to win. For the briefest second he realized the odds. *There are six ways to throw a seven and only three ways to throw a four. The odds are six to three in favor of the house. You are bucking odds of two to one.* But he was sure he would win. He noted these odds, conceded that they were true but gave them only passing attention. He was sure that there was such a thing as *momentum* on his side, a momentum sufficiently forceful that it would prevail against odds of two or three or even four to one.

He continued to win now, sensing the crowd was cheering him though he was not listening to their exhortations. On an impulse he put down a side bet that his next roll would come up double sixes. He lost and placed the bet again. That too he lost but on the next throw he doubled the bet and rolled a third time. The dice bounced down the felt table—he was throwing hard now—knocking chips in different directions, bouncing against the restraining wall around the table. The two sixes landed softly to the accompaniment of delighted cries from the players surrounding the table.

He did not stop to count the chips that the house gave him, estimating he was approximately $20,000 ahead of when he had entered. The casino manager was looking at him the way matadors look at bulls: quietly but with unmistakable intent. Jon ignored him and continued. He had to keep going.

"For heaven's sake, stop. Go away, go away."

He could not tell who was talking to him. It was a woman's voice. There were many people around the table and from his vantage point behind the dice they all seemed to look much alike. All in all, it surprised him that anyone would think $20,000 was such a good win that he could walk away satisfied. It was so little compared to all he owed. What does $20,000 mean to someone who owes hundreds of thousands? And how could an intelligent man walk away from a winning streak?

He was throwing fast and well now; calm, controlled, deliberate.

The adrenaline was pumping and, despite his overweight and near fifty years, he felt resurrected. It was as though he had left home and his myriad troubles behind forever and had returned to the days of early youth when life was full of magic, when wishes were commands and you could tell the dice to come up six-five. He was in a mental world where nothing is forbidden and rules are not imposed. He was master of his domain. There was no one who seemed better than he or more able than he. The clocks had been turned back, or rather they had been eliminated and destroyed. The windows to the outside had been sealed off. The pain and disappointment of the last two decades were washed away, negated utterly, at least for the duration of the contest.

CHAPTER 2

Joe Hodges was frantic. His bankroll was not where he had left it. He had hidden his gambling money in different places before and had never misplaced it. Had he really forgotten where he stashed the money? or had Nancy discovered it and secreted it somewhere else?

The more he searched, the angrier he became with her, though he had to admit she was justified.

Even if he were going to stop gambling, he needed that money; he needed to go to Las Vegas that weekend and he needed to win. He owed too much money to too many people around Houston to stop now.

He stumbled through the house, limping on his bad left leg and cursing under his breath. He had gone through the drawers of her bureau and ransacked their closets. He had inspected the kitchen shelves and even probed through the containers of sugar and flour. It just was not there. Eleven thousand dollars and it was gone.

He hurried through the kitchen and bumped his bad leg against the counter. It hurt and he exhaled slowly and stopped. He sat down and poured himself a bourbon and water. A gentle Texas breeze wafted through the curtains. Although it was early in the day it already seemed late and he felt tired. Why was he so tired? Perhaps the strain of living two lives at one time was becoming too much for him. To maintain his business and family on the one hand and an addictive passion for gambling on the other kept him in a constant state of siege. Too much was demanded of him. He had to present a calm demeanor to the world and move about Houston as if God were in his heaven and all were right with the world. Yet all the time he had to plot and finagle, inventing the most Machiavellian schemes to get the money to finance the next trip to Las Vegas.

A killing at the dice tables—the big win? No more exhilarating flight to the heights was imaginable. Joe Henry Hodges would then be authenticated: he'd be a man of worth, a man of substance and character who could and would redeem his notes at the banks and pay off his debts, contribute to his church, provide a good home and the other amenities for his family.

With the big win comes love from one's family, approbation from bankers, businessmen, and friends—and prestige. Even thoughts of gambling and winning, which were always in the forefront of Joe's mind, like sex in the mind of an adolescent who has just discovered girls, gave him a foretaste of that high that only comes with gambling and winning. Today, as he searched for the missing bankroll, his frustration and anger rose as he thought of the creditors out there waiting for him to make good. Of course each one assumed that he was the only creditor and knew nothing of the other nineteen. One was chairman of the board of his church and another was his dentist. Two more were friends from college days. They were all fine, overly trusting people who had had confidence in him. And why shouldn't they trust him? He was going to pay them back. He only had to find the $11,000 and catch the morning flight to Las Vegas.

He had less than an hour to find the money. If it took him any longer he would miss his plane and that stunning lucky streak he felt coming on. A dazzling run of fortune lay ahead if only he could find the $11,000 and be on his way to Vegas.

If Nancy hadn't hidden it, what had he done with it? Joe poured himself one more drink and put the bottle away. But he did not take the drink. He was lost in the labyrinth of his thoughts. Had he put the money in the attic? That was unlikely, it was too hard for him to get up there. In the kitchen or living room? Certainly not in the bathroom. Then where? Slowly and deliberately he eliminated every room in the house—*except the laundry room.*

He left the drink on the kitchen table and moved down to the laundry room. Carefully, confidently he began to rummage through the pyramid of clothing on the table. Suddenly his mind clicked. He had hurriedly put it behind a container of bleach on the shelf when Nancy arrived home from school the day before. He clutched the stack of $100 bills with a half-amused expression on his face. If she really had secreted it he never would have found it.

Although he regretted taking this money which rightfully belonged to his family, it was certain he would win that day and replace it. The first $11,000 of his winnings would go right back into the family coffers to meet household and other obligations—and soon!

Now that he had found the money he was relaxed for the first time that day. He went upstairs and walked over to the telephone. He was exhilarated at the thought of the waiting casinos. His limp would disappear. He dialed the office he shared and told the secretary he would be out on business calls all day. He started to dial the school where Nancy taught to leave a message for her, but he stopped in mid-dial and decided not to call. Instead he wrote her a vague note saying he had been called out of town on business for a couple of days. Then he drove directly to the airport and climbed aboard a plane.

He strapped himself into his seat and studiously ignored the chatter of the stewardess. As the plane roared off into the sky he reveled in anticipation of the big win and then of the second exhilarating high, going to the people he had borrowed from and paying them back.

A few yards ahead the stewardess was laughing with the flight steward over something that had occurred the day before. It seemed that some drunk had walked into the Houston terminal and asked for a ticket to hell. The man behind the counter had handed him the schedule for flights to Las Vegas.

Joe did not think it was funny but then he was not in any mood for humor. He began to scan the faces of the other passengers on the flight. There was a pack of laughing business conventioneers and there were at least two other recognizable gamblers on the flight. They were experienced players whom he had seen before at the green felt tables at the Flamingo Hotel.

For a moment he made eye contact with them, but swiftly all three averted their glances. Why was it that they were embarrassed with each other? Because they all knew the reason they were going to Las Vegas? They would never have been embarrassed if they had met *in* Las Vegas. But on the plane it seemed irritating somehow. Perhaps it was because they were still in the outside world and chagrined over what they were doing.

Fleetingly he cast one final glance at the two gamblers. He felt sorry for them. *They are going to lose, they are both going to lose,* he thought with pity. But he was secure in the belief that he was going to win and that no one else would score like he would this weekend. It did not matter that he had lost heavily on his previous four visits. Those were sporadic bursts of bad luck which he was now going to reverse.

For the second time in five minutes he checked to ensure that he had his bankroll safely distributed in his pockets. It was still there of course. He wondered in the back of his mind how much he might have to lose before Lady Luck turned his way. Instantly he blocked out the thought. Probably he would lose almost none of his bankroll. The first roll would be a winner. He looked forward to a marvelously fulfilled weekend and began his mental game deciding in what order he would visit (and beat) the casinos. Well, there were the Desert Inn and the Dunes to try. Let's see . . . Desert Inn Dunes–DID. I did it! That's the right order.

After running over the names of the casinos he came up with another acronym. The Desert Inn would be a longer cab ride. How about the Sands, the Sahara, and the Tropicana. SST. Supersonic transport. Yeah! That's the way to go!

Despite the protesting stewardess, Joe was on his feet while the plane was still rolling into the Las Vegas air terminal. He was the first man off the plane when it taxied to a stop. The other passengers and the stewardess might have been surprised or annoyed but they couldn't know how badly he needed to get to the first casino. He hit the pavement running, not even bothering to enter the terminal. He cut across McCarran Airport directly to the highway and flagged a taxi.

"Sahara Hotel, please!" He controlled the impulse to add, "hurry." In Las Vegas he invariably preserved a calm demeanor.

Within ten minutes Joe was paying the driver and getting out of the taxi. He was no longer limping. He was moving fast and as he entered the casino a wondrous transformation began to come over him. As he emerged into the gambling hall itself, all his worries and preoccupations dropped away. Like a professional soldier in battle he was now in his element, and he realized that he had missed it more than he had thought possible. He walked down the arena steps.

They saw him coming and recognized him immediately. He told himself what they had to be thinking: *Here comes a player, watch out for him.* He spelled danger and they acknowledged the threat at his approach. It was high noon and Joe Henry Hodges was ready for them.

CHAPTER 3

Joe Henry Hodges was born under the sign of Scorpio on November 1, 1928, in Beaumont, Texas. His father had worked all his life for the Magnolia Petroleum Company refinery in Beaumont which today is part of Mobil Oil. When Joe was born his father was making $80 a month and when he retired in Beaumont after forty years of labor his salary had risen to $586 a month.

Joe's father was not the most ambitious man in the oil industry and out of the three thousand employees at the Magnolia refinery he was always the first out of the gate after his shift. His chief interests in life were his home, his family, and odd little hobbies that he developed.

Joe's mother, Florence, was a schoolteacher in Beaumont and for forty-two years did her part in supplementing the family income.

One of Joe's fondest early memories went back to when he was seven or eight. It was then that his father and mother, after a number of years living in rented houses, finally built a $5,000 home they had designed themselves. They had actually worked on building the house and finishing the interiors. It was the first place Joe lived in that he could remember. It comprised a large living room with a fireplace, a dining room, a den, a spacious kitchen, and three gracious bedrooms with two bathrooms, and it was on a large lot of land.

Joe even kept a horse in the backyard and he and his mother raised chickens out there in the summers. Joe Henry Hodges, Sr., and Florence had many friends in Beaumont, all of whom were far wealthier than they. There was, however, one outstanding advantage to their undeniable lower-income status. The Hodgeses did not have to engage in the old middle-class American game of keeping up with the Joneses. They couldn't do it and nobody expected it of them. Nevertheless, Florence couldn't help being aware of their circumstances and seldom let Joe Sr. forget it.

In second grade at the Averill School in Beaumont, Joe had his mother as a teacher. The classes were divided up into A, B, and C students and all the A students went to Mrs. Hodges' class. Although Joe's grades were always A's, his behavior was not the model his mother might have wished it to be and Mrs. Hodges herself frequently administered corporal punishment to young Joe in the coat closet at the back of the classroom.

As Joe progressed triumphantly through the school from year to year he developed a more than healthy amount of conceit and got into almost daily fights with other boys as a result. The fact that his mother was teaching in the school he attended gave him an additional feeling of superiority over the other students, even a special sense of power.

When Joe and his peers left Averill and went on to the town's junior high school, Joe felt a sudden loss of importance. This was complicated by an incident that happened in the Boy Scouts.

He went out with the other boys on a fourteen-mile hike, and they spent the night in pup tents. Two boys shared each tent and Joe was disappointed that he and his close friend, Jimmy Moll, could not be together. After the scoutmaster ordered lights out, Jimmy Moll, thinking he couldn't be heard, started talking in low tones to his tent mate, but his voice rose in pitch as he talked and carried to the next tent.

"Joe Hodges wanted to be my tent mate tonight," Joe heard. "He's a good friend, you know, but he thinks he's more important than he is just because his mother taught at Averill. He's really kind of—not up to the rest of us."

When Joe was still only eight his father took him on a trip to New Orleans where in the lobby of a hotel a dice game was going on. Joe watched as his father was drawn to the excited crowd around the crap table. His eyes widened as his father lay a $1 bill down on the table and he pushed forward to watch the shooter. The dice came up seven on the first roll, the shooter won and Joe's dad picked up $2 and they walked away.

Just like that, Joe thought to himself. You go to a dice table, put $1 down, and walk away with $2. He was awed by what he had seen. It was like a magic trick.

Equally mystifying was the business of drawing checks. When Joe's father said he didn't have any money to indulge his son in some desired luxury or plaything, Joe would tell his father to write out a check. That was all there was to it as far as he could see.

For seven summers Joe greatly enjoyed a boys' camp in Kerrville, Texas, known as Rio Vista, which overlooked the Guadalupe River. The summers were divided into two terms of six weeks each. Sometimes he would go for the entire twelve weeks. In high school he was maintaining an A average and becoming increasingly interested in girls. He and his special friends Jay Crager, Jimmy Moll, and Reed Quilliam started the second six-week term at the camp after their sophomore year at high school.

Unfortunately, a boy from Laredo with an undiagnosed case of polio also arrived for the second term. Within two weeks thirty-nine of the two hundred boys in the camp contracted polio. The parents flew out to the camp to retrieve their sons.

Upon returning home Jay's dad, Dr. Crager, warned all the boys who had been at the camp not to exert themselves for at least three weeks. Most of them obeyed the doctor's instructions. One came down with flu which kept him in bed. Jay was a heavy youth and not given to athletics anyway. But Joe paid no attention to Dr. Crager's advice. He had become virtually a compulsive athlete and immediately found a berth on a local baseball team. In one day he played two vigorous games at Stewart Stadium, a minor league field. That same evening he went to the bowling alley and bowled fourteen games, which completely exhausted him.

The next morning Joe fell to the bathroom floor. His mother

contacted Dr. G. P. Stevens, an orthopedic specialist, who came to the house immediately and examined Joe. He did not diagnose the problem as polio but said the boy was probably suffering from some sort of spinal disease. Joe's fever went to 104 and his body twitched all over. It was not until his breathing became labored that the doctors realized he had polio and rushed him to an iron lung.

After two days Joe's breathing eased, but from his left buttock to his left foot he was paralyzed. The fever lasted for almost two months and when it was over his left leg had already begun to atrophy.

Joe's parents took him to the John Sealy Hospital in Galveston, Texas, where he was outfitted with a brace from his left hip to his foot. When he returned to Beaumont he found that bowling was the only sport in which he could participate.

The brace did not inhibit him and indeed he frequently pulled his pant leg up to show his friends the apparatus he was wearing. Nevertheless, the expenses mounted as new treatment was sought to normalize his use of his left leg.

The Hodgeses sent Joe to the Ochsner Clinic in New Orleans, Louisiana, where it was felt his leg could be brought back to normal again with daily treatments. Joe was consumed with guilt because of the soaring costs of his medical treatment. He was miserable when his parents had to sell the house they had designed to pay his medical expenses. He was well aware that if he had followed Dr. Crager's instructions and stayed at home, resting, he would not have contracted the disease. None of the other boys, all of whom had carefully refrained from tiring themselves after their exposure to polio, had come down with the dread affliction.

Joe's mother and father drove him to New Orleans and went with him to the Ochsner Clinic where they met the therapists and the doctor who would oversee Joe's treatment. Then they took him to the YMCA where he would stay during the months of the treatment.

Florence and Joe Sr. went up to the dreary little cubicle which would be Joe's home for the better part of a year. He was missing his junior year at high school and he dreaded the thought that his mother and father were going to leave him in the little room upstairs at the New Orleans YMCA. He'd kept hoping something would happen so he wouldn't be left behind there. Alone. It was 1943, World War Two was raging, and he felt insecure and worried. Joe wondered who slept in the other beds, but there was no time to ask and no one to answer.

Florence Hodges smiled tentatively at her son. Not a real smile. It was more like a Methodist Church Sunday morning smile when she was in a hurry to get home after the service and didn't want to stop and visit with anyone.

She patted his shoulder. "Now you be a good boy, Joe, and do everything Dr. Caldwell says." Her eyes fell on the heavy brace he was wearing and the smile faded.

Joe's father waited silently for his cue to utter an exit line. "Well, son"—he cleared his throat nervously—"be sure and write your mother, hear?" He too eyed the monstrously clumsy brace. "We'll be going now. Why don't you lie down and get some rest? And let us know if you need anything . . ."

Joe nodded, hoping he wouldn't cry. *If I need anything,* he thought. *What I need is to get in the back of the old Chevy with you, like always, and go home to Beaumont. I didn't want to come down to this clinic in New Orleans. I don't want to be left here in this crummy room . . . Oh, mother, don't leave me here alone . . .*

He'd known all along it was going to be the way they said. The way *she* said.

At home he'd had his own horse, his friends and school. He loved school. But here he was, and here he would stay until his leg got better.

He walked haltingly to the window of his small room in the YMCA where he could see his mother and father getting in their car, headed for Beaumont and home. Home . . . a gasping sob strangled him, but just for a moment. He called out to them. "Goodbye . . . drive carefully. Oh, Mother, please don't leave me . . ." But she didn't hear. She was saying something to Joe Sr. as they drove off.

He heard the elevator door clang open, then voices and footsteps.

The door was flung open by two older men. They looked at least eighteen or twenty. Sailors, Joe knew instantly because of their uniforms.

The taller of the two shoved his snowy white cap back on the brightest red hair Joe had ever seen. He grinned, holding out his hand.

"You gotta be Joe Hodges. Name's Gus Hendricks. This here is Andrew Barrett Noble II. His dad's an admiral. He's gonna get us on a battleship to fight this man's war."

Joe stood as straight as his brace allowed, wondering whether to salute. It was unbelievable luck that these two good-natured sailors were to be the occupants of the other two beds in his room. Andy left no doubt about it. He flopped horizontally on the corner bunk, landing flat on his back.

"Goddamn right! My old man's in the submarine service, so I've put in for a battleship. You ain't getting me two inches below sea level."

The one with red hair winked at Joe. "Yeah, this here sailor can pick and choose. Sends a daily poop sheet to Nimitz, but somehow he don't get no replies back from CINCPAC thanking him for his suggestions for beating the Japs."

Joe had recovered his aplomb. Maybe these guys would go bowling with him. But maybe they were too busy with the Navy base to take time for a kid. "Say, how'd you know my name?"

Andy and Gus squinted at each other, then at Joe. "We heard you were some kind of a bowling expert, so we asked the manager if you could bunk in here with us," Gus said.

"Yeah," Joe affirmed happily. "That's me. But how—?"

"Never mind, kid," said Gus. "Go wash your face and let's the three of us go out for some chow. And then—and *then* we're gonna step around the corner to the Acme Lanes and see what kind of a champeen we got us for a roommate!"

It wasn't going to be all that bad, after all, Joe decided.

He was due at Ochsner Clinic at ten the next morning. The brace was hard to manage and he had trouble getting on and off the streetcar. The conductor was about to yell at him to step up but then saw that nobody wearing the ironwork that bulged through the boy's clothing could step anywhere very fast.

The doctor was appalled. "Who rigged this thing up, son? We're throwing it out—now!"

"But, doctor—" Joe protested. "My folks—I mean, it cost several hundred dollars . . ."

Two days later, Joe was walking well on aluminum crutches. No more brace, not ever, the doctor said. The physical therapist was brunette and patient and Joe was hopelessly in love with her within the first five minutes. The exercises were painful, blindingly so, but Joe insisted he felt no pain. He was walking better every day, tossing his crutches slyly in the air as he rounded corners and nimbly catching them.

"See, Miss Tompkins. No hands!"

She smiled enigmatically. "Won't be long before you're doing the jitterbug, Joe."

But even though she was right—Joe did become a fine dancer as the years went by—it was so long, so long, before he could go home again. Nevertheless, he studied his correspondence courses diligently so he could stay with his class for the senior year and that helped time go by.

Florence and Joe Sr. saw their son only twice that year he was in New Orleans. It cost too much for them to make the trip, Joe guessed. They wrote, or rather his mother wrote, sending love from Dad. But it wasn't quite the same as having them come to see him. Christmas was very lonely, though he got lots of mail from girls in Beaumont and a few boys. One wealthy father of a friend of Joe's, Carroll Conn, sent him a letter and enclosed a $5 bill. "Spend this on something you really want," Mr. Conn wrote. That $5 was special. The money his mother supplied every week was for food, not for luxuries, so he splurged by taking Andy and Gus to the movies.

It was January 7 when Andy and Gus left New Orleans for duty aboard ships somewhere on the New England coast—the end of the world, it seemed—and Joe would have done anything on earth to be going with them.

Once he overheard them talking in the room. "You can say what you want, but Joe is too young a kid to be 'way down here by himself. It ain't right. It just ain't right."

Then Gus said, "Oh hell, there's worse things than this. His folks are doing all they can. Still, you'd think his mom could have got a little place here and stayed with him—"

The remark hit Joe hard, and he limped quietly away from the door. He felt the same way. She *could* have done that. But she hadn't. Why? . . . Well, for one thing, he told himself, she had to work, teach school to help earn enough money to send to this stupid YMCA and pay Ochsner and the doctors and therapists. So how could his mother have lived here in New Orleans to take care of the son who got himself polio just because he was bullheaded enough to play on the new baseball team and bowl fourteen games on one of the hottest days of August?

He was shaking, trying to hold back the tears that always came too quickly. I wish I wasn't so emotional, blubbering like a baby, he thought miserably. He pushed open the door of the men's room at the end of the hall, listening to see if anyone was inside. Empty. He limped quickly inside and leaned his head on his arm against the tile wall of the lavatory. Oh God. I wish I was home. Then he drove his fist against the cool tiles. Anger dried his tears as quickly as that silly uncontrollable emotion had brought them.

I'll never let this get me down, never, never, never. I'll laugh and laugh and everyone will think it doesn't bother me. Actually, it *doesn't* bother me. Anybody would be homesick, that's all. It's not the polio, it's being away from everybody that hurts . . . But the letters—some people do care about me, do think about me. Yet it would be different, seeing them. You don't want to get letters from your friends, you want to be in the same town with them. You should get letters just from aunts and uncles. And your mother and dad ought to be where you see them every day, not writing letters.

CHAPTER 4

Joe lived at the New Orleans YMCA from November 1943 until August 1944. He had kept up in his studies, and it was with great joy that he finally returned to Beaumont in time for his senior year at high school.

After the long therapy he was able to walk easily with a cane, which he would discard a year later. His mother and father were happy to see him come home to the garage apartment they had rented. These rooms helped rekindle Joe's guilt about the financial problems the polio caused his parents, but his mother and father were so glad to have him home that the guilt was less intense.

When Joe was back in high school he found that the polio had stripped him of certain adolescent satisfactions for which he tried to find substitutes. He was reluctant to parade around in the locker and shower rooms naked in front of his peers or in short-shorts at gym classes when all the other boys were in their cutoffs and the girls in leotards. At the sexually conscious ages of fifteen and sixteen he was denied the high of cavorting with the boys and girls, wearing swim trunks while the girls revealed their budding figures in bathing suits.

Still, Joe was as anxious as the next youth to authenticate himself and feel important despite the embarrassment of his physique. He felt he was no longer an acceptable sex object when sex was the principal topic of conversation among his classmates. Unable to immerse himself in sports, which had once exhilarated him, he sought other means to instill in himself a sense of worth.

The urgent need to win—at anything—was now the driving force in his psyche.

Soon he was dating a girl he had been fond of before going away, Sue Ellen Jenks. He had liked Sue Ellen's mother and used to play bridge with her and her friends, several of whom were the mothers of other girls he dated. He had played excellent bridge even as a high school freshman and he enjoyed conversing with these women as much as he enjoyed the games. Sue Ellen's mother considered Joe one of the nicest young men her daughter was seeing. Perhaps the polio and the cane gave him a deceptively trustworthy mien. In any case, Mrs. Jenks was convinced that Joe's interest in her daughter was strictly platonic. As well as rejoining this bridge circle, Joe regularly attended the First Methodist Church. The minister was Joe Z. Tower, whose son would later become a senator.

Joe covered his embarrassment about his atrophied leg, which had been strengthened by the treatments in New Orleans and the cane with which he walked. The leg and the cane were even his badge of courage, at least when he was with his peers. When he was with his parents they were a constant, nagging reminder that he had cost them their home and their savings.

Now, at sixteen, he had found in Sue Ellen a comfort and solace he badly needed. He had reached the age where he also wanted to possess her sexually and Sue Ellen seemed amenable to eventually satisfying his needs and undoubtedly hers as well. He was convinced, when she finally succumbed, that it was not because she felt sorry for him but because she was deeply attracted to him.

The slightly withered leg in no way seemed to repel her. Sue Ellen and Joe walked to high school almost every day together. One fall morning when he came by to pick her up she was not downstairs waiting. Her mother, late for an errand, told Joe to go up and hurry Sue Ellen along so they would not be late for school. Joe went up the stairs to Sue Ellen's room and pushed the door open to find her half undressed, waiting for him. No words were necessary. She lay back on her bed and without further encouragement Joe quickly took off his own trousers and underwear, lay between her legs, and in the excitement and thrill of the moment pressed his virginal maleness into her. Her delight in their newfound pleasure thrilled him more than any sensation or event that had ever occurred in his life.

They dressed hastily and casually walked downstairs, calling goodbye to her mother in the kitchen before starting off for school.

The following morning Mrs. Jenks greeted Joe. Sue Ellen was once again not ready, and Joe said with a grin, "I guess I'll have to go up and hurry her along." She was waiting for him and this time they prolonged their lovemaking.

For the next weeks it became almost a routine: Joe having to "hurry" Sue Ellen so they would not be late for school, snatching delectably libidinous moments before leaving.

Despite these happy experiences, Joe's awareness of the catastrophic financial burden he had placed on his parents never quite left his mind. The proceeds from the sale of their house had gone to paying his medical expenses, and now Joe's attendance at the University of Texas would continue to bleed them financially just as they were trying to recoup from the loss of their assets.

Sue Ellen and Joe were always good friends, although both of them dated others, and when in the fall of 1945 Joe moved to Austin to start college, he had made other conquests and so had she. They were growing apart from each other as they entered a new and more adult world.

While still in high school Joe had become adept at all types of gambling. He'd started with pinball where, once he'd learned to beat the game, he could win three nickels for every one he put in. In his senior year, now that his athletic endeavors were severely limited, he became interested in dramatics and singing. Despite the polio, he even became a good dancer and was voted the best dancer in his senior class.

In Beaumont, Joe and his friend Jay Crager discovered a gambling joint fifteen miles outside of town called Jack Thompson's, which had a crap table, a blackjack table, and roulette. The patrons drove around to the back where their cars could be hidden. The doorman, upon recognizing a patron, permitted him inside what looked like a contemporary brick house. The crap table was professionally staffed and the dealers were said to be as good as any in Las Vegas.

Future judges, congressmen, lawyers, doctors, accountants, and businessmen from Joe's class frequented Jack Thompson's. Liquor was served and a $1 minimum bet imposed, with a $100 maximum.

During that summer Joe was awestruck by a new girl in Beaumont, Eugenia Betts. She was his age and also entering college for the first time in the fall. Her dad was the new president of the American National Bank of Beaumont. She was a beautiful girl with a regal bearing, honey-brown hair, and an engaging smile. She was tall, five feet six inches, and he had always been attracted to tall girls. But more than anything else it was her obvious fine breeding and her outgoing personality that attracted him.

Joe was a little nervous around Genie Betts and he made it a point to be charming to her mother, whom he greatly admired. That fall Genie went to Randolph-Macon Woman's College, in Lynchburg, Virginia. Joe saw her off before traveling to Austin for the fraternities' rush week.

At the University of Texas, Joe was rushed by several fraternities. He wanted to be asked to join Phi Gamma Delta, the fraternity his friend Jim Moll had already committed to quite early in the year. It was Jim Moll who had made that remark years ago to the effect that Joe Hodges wasn't quite up to the rest of them socially, a sentiment he suspected many of his friends harbored and which still cut him deeply.

He was invited to many rush parties but was only asked to join one fraternity, which was not the one he wanted. Crushed, he took a small apartment with two other students on Wichita Street near the campus and ate at the big college cafeteria known as the Commons. He watched his money carefully and prided himself on eating for less than a dollar a day and buying one pack of Camel cigarettes every other day.

Joe studied conscientiously and was virtually a straight A student. He made good grades because he knew how to play the grade game and win. Math came easily to him and he liked

English. He could memorize history, dates, causes and effects. He hated French but nevertheless made the requisite A.

A girl in his French class, Kathy Spence, began dating him steadily and helping him with his French.

In Joe's second semester, in January 1946, he was thrilled when Jimmy Moll and other Phi Gams were able to secure a bid for him to join their fraternity. Once he was pledged to Phi Gam, Joe's life on the university campus seemed complete.

In his first term at the university he had placed his first bet on a football parlay card for $1. He picked the winners of four football games being played that week and for his $1 bet got $9 back. Nine dollars was a lot of money to him and the excitement of the parlay cards continued from week to week as he bet $1 or $2 each Saturday thereafter, though without ever winning another card. He was caught up now in betting. It didn't absorb him, and he didn't bet more than he could afford, but he enjoyed it. It was fun.

In the spring of 1946, he was a Phi Gam pledge dating sorority pledges. He was also steadily seeing Kathy, who continued to help him with French. Near the end of the term, at the Phi Gam Old South formal ball, he and Kathy arrived at the fraternity house in a horse and carriage, Joe dressed as General Robert E. Lee and Kathy as the southern belle from Houston that she was.

Once pledged, he spent much of his time at the fraternity house, eating all his meals there, enjoying the camaraderie and learning the Phi Gam songs. In May of that year Phi Gam won the fraternity SING SONG, and Joe was one of the stalwarts of his fraternity's singing group.

Getting straight A's was of great importance to Joe. His problem area was English, particularly creative writing. Assigned to write a short story of about five hundred words, he was at a loss as to how to begin. He went to see his cousin Joan Yawn, who was also at Texas. Joan agreed to do his assignment and wrote a sensitive little piece about her father. The story received an A-plus from Joe's teacher, who unwittingly embarrassed him by having him read it in front of the class.

In his first year at Texas, Joe did little serious gambling. Bridge was his primary card game, and he had honed his skills considerably since contracting polio.

In the summer of 1946 he went back to Beaumont and took a midnight shift job at Mobil where his father still worked. Eugenia Betts was home and he wanted to spend as much time with her as possible. He also saw Sue Ellen. The intensity of his feeling for Genie was such that he still hadn't kissed her or made any serious overtures toward developing a more intimate relationship with her. He was in awe of her, in love from afar.

Jay Crager and Joe were kindred souls when it came to gambling and that summer they spent a lot of time at Jack Thompson's place and sometimes drove all the way to the Louisiana border where gambling was more wide open than in Texas. They played for increasingly high stakes, sometimes winning or losing $100 or $200. By summer's end Joe had earned about $800 and was hoping not to have to use the $100 a month his mother sent him when he returned to college.

At Texas University one of Joe's best friends at the Phi Gam fraternity was Paul Smith whose father was the president of the State National Bank of El Paso. Paul and Joe visited back and forth between Beaumont and El Paso on vacations. But Joe's best friend over the years was Jimmy Moll. They were as close as two boys could be and had even shared Sue Ellen's affections.

Since his last year at high school Joe had become increasingly aware of his father's love and devotion. When he entered college his dad bought an old Chevrolet standard shift sedan and adapted the clutch with pulleys so that Joe could engage it by hand. It meant a lot to Joe to have a car at the University of Texas. Joe Sr. and Florence both enjoyed coming down to see their straight-A student son, but Joe Sr. wanted nothing but the best for him. Therefore, although Joe got along fine in the reconstituted, if somewhat decrepit Chevrolet, Mr. Hodges worked out a loan with the help of one of his wealthy friends to buy him a special present.

On one festive fall weekend, he and Florence appeared in Austin along with another couple whose son was at the university.

To Joe's delight his parents presented him with a brand-new automatic-drive Ford convertible. It was a thrilling moment when Joe, his parents watching proudly, took a group of his Phi Gam friends out on his first drive in the new car.

Joe Sr. was as pleased as his son at the ease with which young Joe could drive the new convertible without having to shift gears. Speeding around Austin with his friends in the bright, peppy new automobile added greatly to the zest Joe found in his sophomore year.

Sadly, he had only two months to enjoy the classy little convertible. Just before the Christmas holidays he took his eyes from the road to reach for a pack of cigarettes and smashed his car into a tree beside the road. Nobody was hurt but his beloved convertible was totally wrecked. Again he discovered how indulgent his father was. Joe Sr. arranged all the details of the insurance payments and scraped together enough money to put Joe back behind the wheel of another car with an automatic shift.

Christmas was a time to see Eugenia Betts again and even though Joe dated several girls at college, he always considered Genie his number one girl, secretly believing he would marry her someday.

With the spring term Joe blossomed forth in concert with the season. He decided to stop pining for Genie and to develop deeper relationships with girls on campus. He was winning at bridge and also took up poker and blackjack. He worked at various jobs as well to avoid using the $100 checks his mother sent him every month.

Joe found a boring job at the local supermarket candling eggs, holding them up to a light and looking through them to see whether they were fertilized or not. He also found a job at a girls' dormitory waiting tables. He took the job mainly, however, because he wanted to be around the girls.

Joe had by now discovered a gambling house in Austin called Maureen's where he occasionally went to escalate his gambling activities. Just as he and Jay had become regulars at Jack Thompson's between Beaumont and Port Arthur, so he now frequented Maureen's where he was beaten more often than he won. But he liked the fast action of craps, which he had learned at Jack Thompson's, and Maureen's was the only place where he could roll dice.

A number of students played gin rummy, bridge, and poker, and among these Joe was a consistent winner. Still, his friend Paul Smith didn't gamble, and since much of Joe's recreational time was spent in Paul's company, his gambling kept within bounds.

He spent the summer of 1947 at the University of Texas, but because Genie was in Beaumont for the summer, he made frequent trips home to see her. When he wasn't seeing Genie in Beaumont he was going out to Jack Thompson's to shoot craps or else to another gambling house, the Grove, in Louisiana. Though both establishments were illegal, the local law officers made little effort to discourage their operations and Joe became acquainted with a number of gamblers from the Beaumont, Port Arthur, Galveston, and Houston areas as well as from Louisiana.

Back at college in the fall, Joe was making numerous telephone calls at $6 each to Genie in Virginia.

At the end of the year, he was elected to Phi Beta Kappa, a distinction of which he was justifiably proud. He was also proud of the fact that for a year he had not cashed any of the checks his mother had sent him. The college gambling games and his various jobs supported him entirely.

Both Joe and Paul Smith, who was now president of the fraternity, decided to go to law school. Joe applied to the University of Texas Law School and was accepted in the fall of 1948, having received his B.A. degree in January. However, he had always heard that Harvard had the finest law school in the nation so he applied there for a full scholarship.

With a straight A average and a Phi Beta Kappa key his chances seemed good. But there was a fly in the ointment. During his last year at the University of Texas he had taken the full course in accounting which was required for law school and, to his chagrin, earned himself a D. Distraught, he went to see the accounting professor whose mark had blotted an otherwise straight A record. "I can't have any D on my record, I can't imagine why you gave me a D," Joe opened the discussion.

"Because you wrote a terrible paper and you didn't understand the course," was the logical reply.

Privately Joe agreed. He didn't understand the accounting course. Nevertheless, employing his considerable powers of persuasion, he explained why he couldn't have a D. He told the professor about his straight A average and of course he was wearing his Phi Beta Kappa key. He lay heavy stress on his application for a full scholarship to Harvard Law School. It would be a great honor to both the university and himself if he were accepted. He was alternately aggressive, indignant, and supplicating. After the professor had studied Joe's total college record he finally agreed to change his grade from a D to an A, giving him a perfect record.

Upon graduating from college in January, Joe had time on his hands. He was still living in the fraternity house and, since he'd finished with his undergraduate work, he studied, gambled, played golf, and took graduate courses. To his amazement, in the spring of 1948 he received a letter from Harvard awarding him a full three-year scholarship to the law school. All his expenses would be assumed and he only had to pay his transportation to Cambridge.

During his last year at college and the freewheeling summer that followed, Joe had gambled because he could thereby always win the money he needed to live on, not because he was hooked on gambling. If he could have afforded to maintain his romance with the young woman of whom he was particularly enamored and live the way he liked, he would not have gambled at all. It was just a means to an end.

The spring and summer of 1948 were fine for Joe, what with women, golf, the interim courses, and winning at cards.

He visited the beach cottage of one of his girls and in Beaumont saw as much of Genie as he could, although his relationship with her never attained the heights of some of those delightful sexual bonds he forged with the girls at Austin.

Inevitably fall came and everybody had to get back to school. It was Genie's last year at Randolph-Macon in Lynchburg and she and Joe decided to take the train together from Beaumont to Lynchburg via New Orleans. Joe would stay aboard all the way to Boston to begin his first year at Harvard Law School. The trip was an exciting prospect for both of them.

They talked all the way to Lynchburg about what they were going to do with their lives, and yet the intimacy Joe had hoped to establish on the long train ride didn't come to fruition.

He said goodbye to Genie and they confirmed plans for him to come down from Cambridge for a visit and maybe even go to her Senior Prom. Then it was overnight to Boston where a bewildered Joe Hodges, late of Austin and Beaumont, stepped off the train. He was nineteen and he was going to Harvard Law School—and once again he was alone. Because he had wanted to make the train trip with Genie he was ten days early for law school registration.

From South Station, Joe made his way to Cambridge, hanging on to his heavy suitcase, and checked into the Commander Hotel.

What am I doing here at Harvard, what the hell am I doing here? he asked himself. What would he do for ten days in this strange eastern environment?

Since polio had prevented him from playing an active part in most athletics, he had developed a keen interest in spectator sports. So now he took a subway every day to watch the Boston Red Sox play at Fenway Park, and if they played at night he went to the night games. He ate alone at cafeterias. He tried to acclimatize himself to the atmosphere of Harvard which seemed rarefied after the open, warm, friendly one at Austin, but he was always lonesome. There was an austerity, a reserve about Cambridge that was alien to him. He was thinking of Genie and also of several girls in Austin whose warmth and tender compliance he missed. He had loved the Phi Gams and missed the fraternity terribly. There was no fraternity house in Cambridge where he could find companionship. He made no friends and nobody talked to him. He might as well have been a Trappist monk for all the communicating he did with his fellow Harvard students.

Eight days after he arrived in Cambridge, Joe abruptly picked up the telephone in his hotel room and called home. He had cashed the $500 check his mother gave him and purchased a plane ticket back to Austin. His mother and father were so shocked at hearing their son's sudden decision to quit before he even began, they were unable to argue. They should have raised hell with him, Joe knew, but they didn't and he caught the plane to Austin. When he got off the plane he hastened to the registrar's office and enrolled at the University of Texas Law School. In Cambridge he didn't register at the law school, didn't go to the first class, and made no attempt to contact any Harvard officials. He never even notified Harvard Law School he wasn't going to attend, nor did he ever write a letter of explanation after he returned to Texas.

Joe quickly settled into the old comfortable ways. He was back with his Phi Gams and those special girls he loved. Law school was stimulating—and when Joe was stimulated nowadays, he found his mind turning to gambling. He began to gamble extravagantly.

He learned that when he needed money to get into a big poker game it was possible to cash a check in Austin on his Beaumont bank and then, when he made a strike, hightail it back to Beaumont to put the money in the bank before the check hit. Little did he suspect that this knowledge would prove to be his Achilles' heel.

CHAPTER 5

Jonathan Alan Roberts displayed none of the elation he felt as, with at least $40,000 over and above his original bankroll in front of him, he savored an overwhelming sense of vindication. He could take his money and leave right now, a big winner and a man of accomplishment and ability. He could go home and pay off friends and business associates, boosting any flagging confidence that might have developed among them. He had told himself that when he hit $80,000 he would indeed cash in his chips and head for the airport.

Again he hit a winning hand. He knew he would win the quota he had set. Although his face and movements showed no sign of the adrenaline coursing through his blood, he was in the midst of a mental and physical high that only another compulsive gambler could possibly understand.

It was his turn to throw the dice again. He moved up to the vacated place at the head of the crap table. For a moment his concentration was interrupted by the sight of a man he recognized from the plane who was walking away from the next crap table toward the casino exit. He knew this man had probably lost his entire bankroll. Such was the tragedy of others, people who should have known better. But Jon knew he would win because he wanted to win.

He placed a stack of chips on the pass line in front of him and with that sudden abrupt movement of his right hand shot the dice across the table. They came out six and two, an eight, an easy point. Now he covered all the numbers and threw again. With a spasm of surprise he saw that he had thrown a seven and lost $3,800. The dice passed to the next shooter. Then Jon played again, and lost $4,000 more.

The stinging shock of the loss was apparent to none of the crowd watching him. He was still sure he was going to win big on this trip. What did it matter if there were a half million people coming to Las Vegas every month with the same conviction? What did it matter that the money they lost ran yearly into billions? He was certain of victory. He had been up and down several times already. He could see in his mind's eye the immense winnings that he would take home in triumph. Already he could visualize himself repaying the people who had trusted him. To him that vision had the force of a fact, and it was a fact toward which he was working his way.

The dice were falling against him now, descending like some executioner's knife. The bar girl came by and he asked for a bourbon on the rocks which she brought instantly. Soon he asked for another and he poured the remnants of the first drink into the second glass. Then he changed his mind and asked again for coffee which she quickly brought. In the chill of the air conditioners and the solitude of the game he drank the hot black coffee.

The punishing losses mounted, tempered with few winning hands. He could not understand why luck had turned against him. Perhaps he *should* have cashed in his remaining chips and walked out a winner. But he dismissed the thought as quickly as it occurred. He would stand there and take it. He always knew his combat with the casino bosses was a battle to the death.

He was becoming unsteady on his feet after five—or was it six or even ten?—hours of hard gambling. Contrary to the regulations of the house, he asked for a stool. They brought him one and it helped somewhat. But his throat was getting dry; it tasted like gravel. Panic and nausea were coming at him in heavy waves, sweeping over him and cascading down, then withdrawing silently.

He looked at his chips. It was hard to calculate how much he had because there were various chips of different values and only the black chips, which were worth $100 each, stood out conspicuously. He figured that he had about $1,300 remaining. This was a tenth of the sum he had possessed when he arrived and a fortieth of the sum he held when he was riding high. He was inexorably losing and should have stopped. Had he been an alcoholic, he would have had to stop drinking at such a point. When an alcoholic drinks heavily he is getting closer and closer to his body's limit for the day. For a gambler the habit and compulsion are different. There is no limit for the day and there is no physical limit to the experience except death. It is like drinking salt water to relieve one's thirst. *Gambling creates its own continuing need.*

Now he had to place his bets more carefully. He had to nurse his remaining money and make it grow, talk to it, encourage it. It was all he had; this time he had to make it work for him.

The dice seemed to be favoring the sixes and the eights. There came a six, seven, three, eight, four, six, eight, seven . . . He waited until he felt certain of the pattern and then bet $300 on the eight and $120 on the six. The dice rolled to a six. He received $140 but then withdrew all his bets. The dice rolled to an eight. He cursed inwardly. He would have won $350 if he had had the courage of his convictions! Carefully he placed $300 on the six and eight spots. The dice rolled seven and the croupier took everything for the house.

Now Jonathan Alan Roberts had only $700 remaining. The downturn was persisting. Theoretically he could leave the game, but subconsciously he knew that the moment he did he would relinquish the wondrous feeling of being involved, of being caught up in the action. He would lose the tension that is the beginning and end of all gambling. Even for the loser, gambling is the fountain of youth; it brings him back to the days of wonder when the world was his and nothing seemed to block his way. How could Jon leave willingly? If he did he would have to begin thinking again about home and a wife who was waiting for him there and—

He took the dice and began to throw. He won a single bet, a mere $100, and tried again. It doubled to $400. He redistributed and won again. Now, despite his air of dispassion, sweat was pouring down his back. He began taking wider risks and won $300 more. For a passing moment he suspected the tide was turning. Then it plunged.

In nine more minutes he had lost everything.

CHAPTER 6

Joe Hodges thought of his addiction to gambling as of a fever, but it was a fever that at first rose imperceptibly. If normal body temperature be 98.6° F., then maybe by the time Joe graduated from the University of Texas he had a gambling fever of 98.8°. However, in law school his temperature had risen to over 100° by the time he graduated and he had had his first inkling that his commitment to gambling was becoming an addiction.

At law school he was once again seeing his special flames at the University of Texas, one in particular, and still telephoning Genie in Lynchburg. Genie was talking about going to the University of Texas herself when she graduated from Randolph-Macon in Virginia.

Joe took an apartment with his high-flying Phi Gam friend Doc Kiel. Doc always had money and Joe borrowed from him when he was short, paying him back after a successful poker session. Joe avoided getting into head-to-head gambling games with Doc but he was enough of a barracuda that if Doc was losing a lot of money in a game with him and several others, Joe didn't hesitate to win his share. Doc liked to drink whiskey, more than Joe, which further contributed to his gambling losses.

Directly across the street from their apartment was the Austin municipal golf course with manicured greens and fairways which Joe played almost every day. Doc was still trying to get through his undergraduate courses while Joe was finishing his first semester at the law school. Halfway through his first semester Joe's midterm grade was 86, considered high in law school.

Perhaps this grade gave him a false sense of confidence for by the end of the term his barely passing grades were 66 in contracts and 65 in torts; 65 was a pass, 70 was considered good.

Joe was shattered—these were his lowest marks in all his scholastic career. His professor told him he'd have to try harder the next semester and Joe realized that he had been too involved in "pokering it, golfing it, girling it, Phi Gamming it."

The son of Joe Sr.'s best friend, Carroll Conn, Jr., known as C.W. to his friends, arrived at college as an undergraduate and Joe arranged to get him into the fraternity. Joe still remembered the $5 C.W.'s father had sent him in New Orleans and regarded C.W. as a special friend.

Joe's parents sent him checks regularly, although he tried not to cash them. After all, he had given up a full Harvard scholarship and come to the University of Texas with no scholarship whatsoever. During his first year of law school he paid the majority of his expenses by gambling. He failed no courses, maintaining a respectable average of 72. Once in a while, when he hit a turn of bad luck at Maureen's or one of the professional games, he had to cash a check from his mother, but most of the time he got by very comfortably on his gambling winnings.

By the summer of 1950 Genie was ready to attend the University of Texas to take a master's degree, purely because Joe was there.

It was during that summer at home in Beaumont that Joe got up the nerve to kiss her. Although many of the other girls at the university went "all the way," Joe never could bring himself even to suggest such a thing to Genie whom he still had ideas about marrying.

Genie was a mature young woman by now and she and Joe were rapidly falling in love.

Besides the awakening of his infatuation with Genie, Joe was also discovering the Beaumont bookies and spent too much time in their betting places watching gamblers wager on the major league baseball and football games. Second-by-second results came in on the Western Union ticker tapes. When Mickey Mantle hit a home run they knew it at the bookmaking joints in Beaumont before the crowd sat down again at Yankee Stadium. On the gambling scale Joe's temperature was over 100°. Furthermore, he was finding that his sex drive was being channeled into betting.

In some ways dating girls was more of a matter of habit than desire for Joe. On one occasion, now that he and Genie were together steadily, he felt compelled to put on a little act and go after an old high school girl friend in front of her when Paul Smith and some of his other friends were in Beaumont visiting. He made a play for this other girl just to exercise his power over Genie. It was a cruel gambit and in his heart he didn't mean it.

By this time Genie thought she was in love with Joe and he of course felt he was in love with her. She was beautiful, much prettier than the girl he pursued for effect. But Genie was so crushed by this macho display that her love for him, undoubtedly more infatuation than love, began to dissipate.

Genie had accompanied Joe to the Grove where they played bingo and she watched him shoot craps; she also went to Jack Thompson's with him several times. Of course she couldn't recognize his almost trancelike posture at the crap tables as a sign of things to come. Somebody who understood compulsive gambling would have realized the extent to which Joe had slipped into its toils, but Genie thought it was just fun and that the fine meals served were the real reason for going to Jack Thompson's.

During his final year at law school Joe moved out of the apartment with Doc Kiel and into a graduate house. Genie was now at the university and they dated regularly, although the incident of the summer was not completely forgotten.

Inexplicably Joe's affection became less intense. He'd now captured her completely. Her sorority at Randolph-Macon, Pi Phi, had a chapter at the University of Texas and as president of the sorority her last year at college, she was in the midst of all activities at the University of Texas Pi Phi house. She took Joe as her date to the formal ball and then to the big costume party where she went as a nurse and Joe dressed as a baby in a winter nightgown with lots of ruffles that she had bought for him.

In December, Joe and a casual girl friend double-dated with one of Joe's fraternity brothers and his girl, Nancy Hippard from Houston. The date was for an afternoon intramural football game between the Phi Gams and another fraternity. Joe and his date arrived and there was his fraternity brother with a striking, dark-haired girl in a tight-fitting yellow plaid skirt and a plastic raincoat. She was the cutest girl Joe had seen on campus, nothing like Genie in appearance but really cute.

At eleven o'clock that night when the dates were over Joe called the Tri Delt house where Nancy was a member. His opening line was, "Guess who this is?"

Nancy replied, "Joe. I don't remember your last name."

They talked for a long time that night and when Joe hung up he realized that he had a new chase on his hands.

Because Joe was trying to study hard for this final year at law school, his first date with Nancy was to go to the law library where she sat with him while he studied until ten o'clock; afterward they went out for coffee and conversation.

Of course Nancy was seeing other men, including Joe's fraternity brother who had introduced them, but at Christmastime Joe hinted that he would like to go to Houston, and she encouraged him to call on her over the holidays.

That festive season Joe divided his time between Genie, with whom he had long-standing dates, and driving eighty miles to Houston to see Nancy. They were both going to the Cotton Bowl, he with Genie and she with Joe's fraternity brother. Joe found out that they were going to attend the same party the night before the Cotton Bowl game. It was at the home of the Thompsons, one of the richest families in Texas.

At the party Joe found out from Nancy where she would be staying that night in Dallas and made a late date with her. At twelve-thirty on New Year's Eve he took Genie home and then went back to where Nancy was staying and picked her up. It was in the early hours of the morning that they kissed goodnight.

The following morning Joe had to go back and pick Genie up and take her to the Cotton Bowl. By now he was so infatuated with Nancy that he told Genie during the first half of the football game he was violently ill and had to go back to Austin. Nancy was staying in Dallas, so it wasn't to see her that he drove back to Austin; it was just that suddenly he realized he wanted out of the relationship with Genie.

By eight o'clock on New Year's night, after the game, Joe had returned to his room in Austin and was in bed. The telephone rang. He snatched up the receiver and called into it eagerly, "Nancy?"

"No, this is Genie," came the cold reply. "How are you feeling?"

Joe felt really sick. He did not want to hurt Genie who had been so close to him for so long. This wonderful person was being hurt because he was such a heel. But he couldn't help himself. He was captured by Nancy. They talked for a short while and Joe tried to cover up, but the damage had been done.

The next day Genie came back to Austin and it took five days before Joe finally got up the nerve to go over to her sorority house and tell her that he didn't love her.

"Is it Nancy?" she asked.

Joe denied that vehemently and left her.

Shortly afterward Genie married another suitor. But Joe would always find it painful to recall that discordant ending to what had been a beautiful friendship and romance.

From the time Joe met Nancy until the end of his law school career, she was the only woman in his life. Nancy fitted in with his Phi Gam friends naturally. She got to know Joe's best friend, now Paul Smith, and recognized him as an unusually good person. It pleased Joe immensely that Nancy admired Paul to the extent she did.

Nancy learned to enjoy spectator sports with Joe, going to golf tournaments in San Antonio and Dallas and Houston with him. All this time Joe continued playing poker.

There was one incident which perhaps should have been a warning to Joe. During the last half of his senior year at law school he and some other students were shooting craps at a dice house when the police raided the place and arrested eighteen University of Texas students.

The entrepreneurs of the game made arrangements for the students to be let out of jail and pay a fine and that was the end of the legal consequences. But Joe had to appear before the university disciplinary committee. Paul Smith was the chief judge on the student court and Joe had been appointed attorney general in the fall by the president of the university's student body. He was retired from this position as a result of the raid and sentenced to probation for the rest of the term which meant that if he missed a single class he would be expelled.

Since Joe never cut classes anyway, this did not bother him, but it was highly embarrassing and he was nervous about it for the rest of the term. However, a raid does not deter a gambler and within a week he was back shooting craps again. By now his betting fever was around 101°.

Every Sunday Joe went to the University Methodist Church and seldom during the entire time he was at Austin did he miss a Sunday service. He had been a sincere believer since boyhood and religion meant much to him, even though he frequently offended against its teachings. Nancy now went with him.

Nancy was the first girl to whom Joe presented his Phi Gam pin and he and she became a serious couple. Nobody was prouder of Joe than Nancy when he was awarded his Bachelor of Law degree and passed the bar examination with a commendable 76. Now that he was a full-fledged lawyer, Joe and Nancy first discussed the possibilities of getting married. Joe seemed to get along well with Nancy's father, George Hippard, and her mother, Frances.

In the summer following his graduation from law school Joe went home to Beaumont and began looking for a job. He was interviewed in Houston and Austin by the large law firms. Unfortunately, new law graduates were not much in demand at the time.

Joe's greatest desire was to be taken into the Beaumont firm of Orgain, Carroll and Bell, one of the most prestigious law firms in Texas. He submitted his application, along with a résumé and a transcript of his record, to Cleve Bachman, who was Will Orgain's son-in-law. There were ten lawyers in the firm of whom five were partners. They dealt with every type of law but were specialists in defense matters. Y. D. Carroll, the father of Joe's good friend Bill Carroll, was one of the senior partners.

Joe launched a low-key campaign in Beaumont to get himself accepted and anxiously awaited the decision of the five partners. The day they voted on Joe he waited nervously by the telephone at his parents' home.

Toward the end of the day the decision was reached and Joe notified. The partners had voted three to two against hiring him. It was a monstrous blow to his ego and aspirations. Vowing he would never go through the humiliation of subjecting himself to rejection by another law firm, he immediately stopped looking for a position and decided to hang out his own shingle.

The Orgain, Carroll and Bell turndown was traumatic. Never before had Joe been so crushed, and the anguish of this repudiation would remain with him as a stinging memory. His ego, at its highest when he graduated from law school, would never completely recover from this stroke. On his graduation hadn't his minister at the First Methodist Church in Beaumont intoned from the pulpit, "Joe Hodges is more important to this world than Doak Walker will ever be"? Doak Walker was the all-American Texas football player, one of the most famous college football players of all time.

In times of deep trouble Joe would analyze his college career, particularly his law school days. He felt he had not learned how to practice law. It was not that the University of Texas hadn't taught him well, or tried to, but it seemed he had learned only how to make grades. He had learned form, the art of passing examinations, but had not acquired substance.

To be a Phi Beta Kappa you have to have either substance or form, he reasoned. He was long on form and short on substance, by no means an intellectual.

And so Joe Henry Hodges had made his first sally into the adult world, still a little self-conscious about his body because of the polio, persuasive to the point where it would be easy for him to become a con man, sincere when it served his purpose, an adept manipulator and self-salesman—and yet unable to persuade Orgain, Carroll and Bell to buy him. It had never occurred to him that he might not make that sale.

Joe wanted to earn a living but he had no overpowering desire to make big money. Rather, he wanted to be a prominent part of the society in which he lived. He wanted to work, he was not lazy, but prestige and acceptance were his goal. He worked at increasing his contacts, making friends with prominent and potentially important people in Beaumont and its environs.

Joe had a number of friends who liked to gamble. There was Carroll Conn, his father's crony, who blew five hundred dollars at the table without the blink of an eye, but then probably wouldn't go back to the tables again for two or three months. The others were pretty much the same way: tightfisted businessmen who nevertheless loved to bet football games and throw dice—occasionally.

CHAPTER 7

By midsummer of 1951 Joe had rented an office in the American National Bank Building on Beaumont's Orleans Street, one of the main downtown streets. He put new carpet on the floor, bought a desk on time from a furniture store, and arranged to share a secretary with another lawyer. His overhead was $450 a month. He picked up scraps of insurance business but basically found himself going nowhere. In September, Nancy went back to college.

During the summer Joe had gone out to Jack Thompson's to gamble and had also discovered the Liberal Club, a domino hall across the street from his office where he played a game called "moon," similar to bridge but played with dominoes. Also there were the Commodore, the Texas Club, the Cue Club, Rich's, and Johnny Venza's Yukon Club, making a total of six domino parlors all within five blocks of Joe's office.

The big players could win $100 or $200 a session. Joe quickly learned how to play moon at the Liberal Club. One day between twelve noon and one-thirty he won $40 at a time when he was worried about paying his overhead. The next day he went back and won $80. There were a number of variations of dominoes, all of which Joe mastered. Then he began betting on the major league baseball games and the professional football games.

Out at Jack Thompson's one night he lost all the money in his pockets—about $200. He borrowed $100 from a lady playing there whom he knew slightly. After losing that $100 he was broke and now in debt to the tune of $100. At this point Joe went to the American National Bank to make his first loan. Genie Betts's father, Frank Betts, was the president of the bank, but Joe didn't go to him—he went to a vice-president, Henry Simpson, and asked for the loan. The vice-president asked him how much he needed and Joe said $100 for ninety days.

Henry Simpson handed Joe a note which he signed and the loan was made. Joe took the $100 and immediately tripled it gambling; then he paid the $100 to the bank and another $100 to the lady who had made him the loan in the first place. Out of this experience he learned how easy it was to go to a bank and get a loan. Joe was a little awed by the whole business of borrowing from a bank. At the same time it was marvelous. What an invention a bank was. A person could just go in, sign a piece of paper, and walk out with cash.

Joe was picking up more insurance business and also getting involved in damage suits, domestic relations, and child custody matters. Occasionally a small estate case came to him. As his meager practice increased, so did his gambling. Finally he got his first murder trial. A black man named Abbey Mouton killed an eighty-six-year-old blind man, also black, for $2 in an old sock. Joe was appointed defense counsel by the court.

Abbey was about twenty-six years old and the police arrived on the scene just as he was burying the eighty-six-year-old blind man who was still alive. The victim had been shot twice and finally died. Joe pleaded insanity as a defense. He made an impassioned plea to the jury on behalf of his client but the verdict was guilty, and Abbey Mouton went to the electric chair. Joe, as counsel, witnessed the electrocution early in 1952.

Joe had been glad to be appointed to the case although he thought it was a crime in itself to appoint some "jackleg lawyer just out of law school who didn't know his ass from third base."

Joe's fortunes rose and fell with his gambling. When in late November of 1951 he took another loss out at Thompson's he went back to the bank and this time borrowed $300.

Henry Simpson was as accommodating as he had been the first time. So, with $300 at 7½ percent for ninety days, Joe went back to moon, Thompson's, and the bookies.

His "fever" was over 101° and he was betting $100 a week on football parlays, which meant trying to pick three teams that all had to win. If he bet $100 and won his parlay he would get back $550. All the money Joe was making at his small law practice was now going into betting. It seemed that he was losing more than he was winning but that didn't stop him. Gambling, which had been an avocation for a number of years with him, was now becoming his vocation.

In his law office, when there was nothing to do, he studied football and baseball records in an effort to increase his odds on winning. Most weekends he drove to Austin to see Nancy, and during her final college year she and Joe spent only two weekends apart.

As the losing continued and it became difficult if not impossible to go back to Henry Simpson at the bank for a further loan, Joe took to dropping by the school where his mother taught, telling her some lie to get the $200 to $300 he needed to continue gambling. He would tell her he had some fees coming in on a case he was working on but that he wouldn't get them for about two weeks and his rent was due and his telephone bill was "just atrocious" and he was scared not to pay it.

Joe's mother believed him. She asked no questions and gave him what money she had. Usually he borrowed $200 to $300 from her but on at least one occasion he had to ask her for $800 to pay off a gambler and a bookie.

Nancy graduated from the University of Texas in June of 1952, and in the fall, just as she found a job teaching school, Joe formally proposed to her. When they announced their engagement, her father suggested that they wait until Nancy finished her first semester teaching before getting married.

On December 27, 1952, a large and lavish wedding was given for Joe and Nancy by her parents. He had ten groomsmen and Nancy had eight bridesmaids. They were married at the Trinity Episcopal Church on Main Street in Houston, Joe's father being the best man. A huge reception was given at the Junior League afterward and several hundred people attended.

Ten days before the wedding Joe's mother and father had given him a wedding present of $1,000, all of which Joe lost in one night shooting craps at Jack Thompson's. It was just fortunate he had already paid cash for the wedding ring but now he had to figure a way to pay for the honeymoon.

On December 23, two days before going to Houston for Christmas with Nancy, Joe went out to Vidor, east of Beaumont, and visited a crap game run by Joe Tortorous, an Italian big-time bettor and bookie. This was not a first-class place like Jack Thompson's but Joe found the action he wanted and won $400 with which he prudently left the game.

The wedding included a rehearsal dinner Friday night before the Saturday ceremony and another luncheon at the country club in Houston on Saturday hosted by Joe's parents. Joe's friends came from all over southern Texas and he put them up in the new Shamrock Hotel. The entire dining room of the Hippards' house was loaded with wedding presents.

Joe had rented a small apartment in Beaumont and Nancy resigned her short-lived teaching position. They enjoyed the wedding reception tremendously, staying late and then, after they made their exit, showing up at another party that the groomsmen and bridesmaids were having at the Shamrock Hotel.

Sunday morning Joe and Nancy said goodbye to their parents and started off on their honeymoon which they planned to spend in Hot Springs, Arkansas, a resort and wide-open gambling town. The first night they drove as far as Fort Worth. At noon the next day when they had planned to start driving to Hot Springs, Joe was feeling sick and suffering from stomach cramps. He didn't know it until later but he was having an appendicitis attack. He and Nancy decided not to drive on to Hot Springs but to remain in Fort Worth and take it easy. So they stayed in the Dallas–Fort Worth area and on New Year's Day went to the Cotton Bowl and watched Texas beat Tennessee.

Joe had a $500 bet on Texas and so the big moment of the honeymoon was the Cotton Bowl game.

The next day they drove back to Houston and loaded up the car with their new belongings to take back to their apartment in Beaumont. Nancy and Joe were happy to get back to Beaumont and the law practice. He was making more money as a lawyer now although he could never make enough money to feed the gambling habit he had acquired.

Joe was earning $1,500 a month in 1953, just enough for two or three bets. But from a gambler's viewpoint, you might lose $250 in a day playing moon or craps, so what good is $1,500 a month?

In the spring of 1953, when they'd been married only a few months, Joe had another attack of appendicitis. This time he had to have his appendix out and he went to the hospital at 8 A.M. for the operation.

Late that same afternoon he was back in his office raising the money to pay a persistent bookmaker, afraid Nancy would find out about it if he didn't pay off. After some judicious phoning he found the money and, straight with his bookmaker once more, returned to the hospital for the night.

At the age of twenty-five Joe may not have been mature but he was able to realize that a psychological shadow was falling over his adulthood. A second personality was very definitely intruding upon his psyche. He didn't as yet comprehend the power of this dark entity that was battling for control of his conscious thoughts, but he tried to keep its existence a secret from everybody else, particularly Nancy. He must have been largely sucessful since even his friend Jay Crager had no inkling that it was there.

In the meantime, Joe attempted to maintain a normal home life, but in vain. An alcoholic becomes incapacitated at the bar and can't even motivate himself to go home; the drug addict becomes oblivious. Not so the gambler, who becomes neither. Nancy was not a prude and certainly did not object to Joe going out with his friends C.W. or Jay or John Powell, but she had no idea how serious his gambling really was. She simply did not classify her husband as a gambler—at least not yet.

As the first year of their marriage progressed Joe frequently didn't get home evenings until seven or eight because he'd been playing dominoes or cards.

By now he had used up most of his excuses, the flat-tire stories as he called them, and his alibis had become as lame as his polio-weakened leg. Quite reasonably Nancy would ask him why he couldn't have picked up the phone and called her to say it would be eight o'clock before he got home. Joe couldn't explain to her that a gambler couldn't just leave the game at any moment and make a phone call. A gambler doesn't even go to the bathroom; he knows he's going to win the next hand. Just one more game, so why stop to call? Joe was being devoured by his gambling and he was powerless to do anything about it. When he was playing he couldn't look at his watch because that would make him gamble carelessly. Time pressure on top of all the other strains of gambling puts the player at a big disadvantage.

There was no way he could explain the situation to Nancy. If you get up, somebody else may quit; and maybe you're losing and you don't want them to quit—so you don't call your wife.

But when a gambler's wife starts scolding him for domestic absenteeism and he is thinking about a crap game he could go to that night, and when she continues to scold him but he goes to the crap game anyway, without saying he's sorry, then he knows he is one day closer to the destruction of the marriage. Who is to say, though, whether the fault lies more with him or with that penumbral being he has allowed to grow inside him?

CHAPTER 8

It was a horrifying losing streak and Jonathan Alan Roberts could not help thinking what a sorry spectacle he presented. To him the most unjust aspect of it all was that he could certainly have ridden through the downturn if he had begun the game with a sufficient bankroll.

If I had a million dollars I could go to Las Vegas and win, win everything, he told himself illogically, ignoring the ineluctable house odds. *My problem is that I never have the bankroll I need to do it. I can only get $10,000 or $20,000 for the bankroll. Maybe $50,000 once in a while, but even that is not enough. That's why I can't win. But if I had a million dollars I could come out here and ride out all the defeats they could throw at me, turn it around and beat the casinos out of their last dollar.*

On his way out of the casino he told the pit boss that he was now ready to check into his room. The pit boss, who had known him for years and who had seen him drop hundreds of thousands of dollars on his tables, was willing to "comp" him, put him in a free room, a gesture extended automatically to the heavy gamblers who flock to Las Vegas.

"Certainly, Mr. Roberts, I'll have your room key for you in just a minute. Please come this way. And give me your plane ticket." High rollers like Jonathan Alan Roberts were given the cash value of their round-trip plane tickets to Las Vegas.

Jon, still numb from his losing streak, handed over the plane ticket he had used on National Airlines. The manager took the ticket from the pit boss and scurried off. The pit boss, who seemed faceless, droned on with good wishes and pleasant chatter and then walked over to the registration desk to help Jon check in. Everyone was being polite, almost gentle. The manager returned and had the audacity to wish Jon luck as he gave him the envelope.

He took the elevator to the room the management had given him. It was a full suite decorated in modern Wild West style with fake gas lamps and satin wallpaper. Beside the circular bed covered with a red velvet spread there was a control panel for the stereo system and television. He lay down on the bed and looked up at the mirrored ceiling.

Lying beaten and bedraggled on the bed, which seemed just right for orgies, he saw a dazed expression on the face looking down on him. *I look like someone who's trying to find the car that just hit him. Is that me?* He realized he needed a shave and a shower and clean clothes, but that it would take more than that to restore him to himself.

He opened the envelope. Three hundred and ninety-eight dollars. The price of the round-trip ticket.

He reached for the console and turned off the lights. The mirror image disappeared instantly and the room became filled with a deep rich darkness. But he knew there would be no sleep until he evolved the plan. He had $398. Not enough to do any real good. Still, it was something. The obvious solution to his problem was to obtain another bankroll. He turned on the light and looked at the envelope again. It was not much of a beginning. He grimaced to himself, thinking how difficult it would be to build it up again.

He rolled off the bed and went to the bathroom to wash, shaking as he splashed the water on his face. He told himself he needed a good meal, a thick lean steak. He had not eaten all day. He had only been drinking countless shots of bourbon interspersed with coffee and orange juice. His stomach felt like the inside of a garbage truck.

For a brief second he contemplated eating a good meal; after all, it would be on the house. But he didn't have the time. He needed to create the new bankroll first. Within minutes he had left the hotel and flagged a taxi to take him to downtown Las Vegas. He was realistic enough to know he didn't have the money to fight it out at the large hotels like Caesars Palace and the MGM Grand: he would begin again down in the center of town in the area known as "Glitter Gulch." There he would find the second and third echelon hotel casinos where he was now certain he could rebuild his shattered fortune.

The taxi let him off at the beginning of Glitter Gulch and he walked down the avenue toward the Golden Nugget. Garish yellow and orange lights blinked at him, summoning him to a game where he could start with a few dollars a bet and work back up to the $1,000 and $2,000 a throw games that were necessary to make the real killing.

He wandered around the Golden Nugget casino stopping to spend a few moments watching the poker game that had been going on there for eighteen years. Some thought that the continuity was fascinating, others considered it merely bizarre, but all concurred that there was a ghostly quality to a game going on so long that the earliest players were dead and buried. In some ways it was an experiment in perpetual motion. As indeed was everything in Las Vegas.

He was feeling better already; he should have come here and not have tarried in his hotel room. Hotel rooms had a way of bringing the past swooping upon him like some bird of prey. They were good for sleeping but otherwise to be avoided.

He cradled the remaining $393 in his hand and anxiously purchased chips for the crap game. Almost shyly now he inched his way to the tables. Instinctively he chose a table at the back of the casino. No longer did he feel himself the high roller. Deep in his mind he felt convinced that he was destined to win but he now acknowledged that there were pitfalls in his way and he would have to maneuver carefully around them.

A huge-chested woman with mascaraed eyes was throwing the dice upon the table and impulsively he bet the number four, despite the fact that there are only three ways to shake a four. The odds against him and in favor of her shooting the deadly seven before the four appeared, however, were two to one. He bet $10 nonetheless and breathed more easily when double twos came up and he was paid $18. He moved $12 to the six, and another $12 onto the eight spot. The six appeared. The adrenaline was moving through him again and he felt sufficiently in control to order himself a drink. When it arrived he drank it down straight, ordered another, and placed $35 in bets along the board.

The grotesque-looking woman continued to throw and win. If it's true that ill luck seldom comes alone, the same should be true of good luck. Soon he had won the heartening sum of $540 and he felt a winning streak coming on. What did it matter that he had lost more than $10,000 that afternoon? Those losses were past and were forgotten.

He doubled his bets, won, then pulled his chips back. Like those American Indians who could sense when they were being hunted, he divined a special danger that was threatening him. It was therefore no surprise to him when the woman threw a seven. She looked at him, wondering how he had known, but he said nothing.

Silently, as a new shooter stepped up, he began placing his bets again. He was no longer thinking about home, or mounting problems that might soon get him into serious trouble with the law—they were all blissfully absent from his mind. He felt omnipotent again, younger. He had come home. As he played and they slid the chips to him he realized that this world was his reality. It seemed natural to him that there were no clocks or windows to reveal whether it was day or night in the outside world, that drinks and food could be summoned by a snap of the fingers, that he could anticipate winning thousands of dollars.

Soon he was feeling rich and powerful, basking in a glow of strength, with more than a thousand dollars' worth of chips in his tray. The dice were in his hands and he was burning up the table with them. The crowd was three deep around him and cheering; they were with him and nothing could slow him down. He felt he could go on forever. Then this fragile rush toward victory was interrupted when a young blond thing placed a $2 bet too late and his dice hit her hand and bounced off the table. He was annoyed, and when they had trouble finding the dice under the table, he angrily called for new dice. They gave him new dice automatically but the run of luck seemed jarred. Finally he threw again, cursing under his breath, and the dice came up seven.

The spell was broken. Palaces were changing into pumpkins. He wanted to scream aloud to the crowd of well-wishers, to ask the casino manager if it would be possible to take the throw over again. But he said nothing. He did not explain and he did not complain. Instead he bet again and again. But his luck was turning now, beginning to plunge against him. The wonderful $1,000 which he had so heroically won began to dwindle. As with most declines, it was swifter than the rise had been. Within ten minutes he was down to his last $100. When he lost $40 of that, he stopped, not so much from prudence as from shell shock. He moved away from the table, stumbled through the casino past the slot machines, and turned around to survey the frenetic activity he had just left.

A pair of tourists came by and stopped in front of him, then burst into laughter and went away. He glared after them. *What are the bastards laughing at?* Then came another spectator who also exploded in laughter. Joe scowled at him. But he wondered how they could see that he had been so badly defeated. Wasn't it a secret?

He finally noticed the cause of the mirth. To his left was an old slot machine of uncertain vintage and upon it some discontented wag had written in lipstick the words:

IN CASE OF NUCLEAR ATTACK
STAND NEAR THIS MACHINE.
IT HASN'T BEEN HIT YET.

He had to read it twice before he understood it and realized they thought it funny. How could anyone joke about something as serious as gambling? Gambling was the most serious thing in the world.

CHAPTER 9

Well before his first year of marriage was completed Joe Henry Hodges was in debt $3,800. Already he was an expert on pumping money. Out of necessity, a compulsive gambler becomes inventive and a convincing liar.

Joe's father-in-law, George Hippard, did business with General Finance Corporation through a Mr. Irion, who was its owner. Using his father-in-law's name Joe had Mr. Irion introduce him to Kenneth Fisher who was running GFC's main office downtown. He borrowed $2,000 over a month's time from GFC and then went on to develop other "spots." It was like playing gin rummy. If you're holding a hand, how many opportunities do you have to gin? If only one card in the whole deck will gin you, you're not in very good shape. The maximum number of "outs," or cards that can gin you, is nine. Five or six outs is very good. Joe applied the same principle to borrowing money. He kept developing spots where he could make loans. He had GFC now and the American National Bank, from both of which he frequently borrowed money and then repaid it. He had also developed the First National Bank through a friend of his who was an officer there.

Toward the end of 1953 he had fifteen reliable spots including his mother, an automatic but limited source. His mother was always low on funds. Still, when he couldn't think of another out he could always go back to the school and get $200 or $300 to pay an irate bookmaker or to lay down on the table at Jack Thompson's. Whether or not his mother believed the numerous stories he invented about why he needed the money was unimportant. She gave it to him, usually without question. Her easy compliance made him feel acutely guilty, but guilt was as nothing against the weight of his need.

He was betting $200 or $300 a day on baseball games and still visiting the domino halls. Most of the older gambling men Joe knew maintained a separate account. Carroll Conn kept his gambling money in a cigar box at his Conn Appliance Company.

It was in the summer of 1953 that Joe cashed his first hot check. From his old friend Doc Kiel at the University of Texas he knew about a bank in Wichita Falls called the City National Bank and merely wrote a check on that bank to himself, J. H. Hodges, Attorney, and scrawled an illegible signature on the bottom of it. The check was for $800. Then he went to the teller with whom he had begun doing business at the American National Bank, Dick Peabody. Peabody knew Joe, of course, and his mother and father. He also knew that Joe kept an account with the bank. Of course the president of the bank, Frank Betts, knew him well, but Joe did not want to go to Genie's father directly when he needed money to gamble.

Joe was surprised and impressed when Peabody took his spurious check and cashed it. "How do you want this?" Peabody asked.

He was asking whether Joe wanted it in hundreds, twenties, or whatever, but he caught Joe, surprised to be receiving anything, off guard. Nevertheless, Joe mumbled an answer and walked out of the bank with $800 cash, trying to appear cool and nonchalant. He had his briefcase with him and was able to rummage around in it while he regained his presence of mind. From then on he always carried a prop of sorts that he could use to divert the attention of bank tellers or officers when he was cashing bad checks.

After receiving the $800 he walked over to say hello to B. B. Henderson, a vice-president of the bank who also played at the domino hall. Joe had grown up with Henderson's daughter, Dottie, and had been good friends with her all through school. Henderson was smoking a cigar at his desk as Joe walked by. Joe was fully aware of the gravity of what he'd done, but he was confident he could handle the situation before trouble arose. He wasn't getting the money to pay somebody or reduce his bills; he was simply without a bankroll to gamble with and had to have one.

In two days he had lost the $800 and now knew he was in bad trouble from which he had to extricate himself. The hot check would be bouncing back in a matter of days and he would be liable for criminal charges. He was $3,800 in the hole now, a staggering debt structure for that time in his life, married only eight months and twenty-four years old.

At home sitting on the toilet, the only place where he could find privacy from Nancy, he went over his debts on neat little note pages and wondered what to do. It was in the bathroom that he studied the sports pages of the daily newspapers—his *Wall Street Journal*—to see how his bets were falling and to plan new ones. He also listened to the radio there, picking up the scores and tabulating his wins and losses.

Joe worried about debts. He had watched his father pay the bills the same day they came into the house, writing the checks that very evening and sealing them in an envelope, stamping them and getting them ready to go out the next morning. It was an emotional requirement for Joe to pay his debts. His need to meet his financial obligations was always a driving force within him.

So now, coming into the fall of 1953, with one hot check outstanding, Joe reviewed all the possible people he could go to for help. He thought of Frank Betts but ruled him out and finally decided to approach A. D. Moore, a well-known lawyer. He represented some of the very wealthy estates and families in Beaumont and was a deeply committed Christian who, along with Frank Betts and Will Orgain, was a pillar of the First Methodist Church. These men, whom Joe so respected, made him proud to be a member of that congregation.

Although Moore was well-to-do, $4,000 was a lot of money to ask from a stranger in 1953. Joe only knew Moore from his church work and his reputation. He had never shared any business interests or worked on any law cases with the older attorney.

Joe was nervous when he went to A. D. Moore's office, closed the door behind him and sat down. He still had pride and in a way it was degrading to go to this solid and respectable man to ask for a loan. But Moore was gracious. "I'm so glad to see you. What can I do for you?" he opened the meeting.

Joe figured his actual debt was $3,800 so he decided to ask for a loan of $4,000. He wanted $200 for himself. He wouldn't even admit to himself what he was going to do with the extra $200 but he didn't want to make a loan for $3,800, pay it all out and have nothing left.

"Well, sir," Joe began, "I'm afraid I've got myself into some trouble."

His one-man law office was not doing well, he continued, thinking perhaps he could solicit a little sympathy from the established attorney for a young struggling lawyer. Since he had never made any secret about his visits to the domino halls or Jack Thompson's, he felt it necessary, in a self-deprecating way, to touch on the fact that, yes, of course he had done a little gambling but had certainly learned his lesson.

Moore, a man in his mid-fifties, listened patiently as Joe went on with his story. As Joe talked he took notes and wrote down the amount of the loan Joe wanted on a legal pad. Then he asked Joe to come back the following morning.

When Joe came around, Moore had arranged a loan for him from the Rothwell estate which he managed. He wrote out the check for $4,000 to Joe H. Hodges and Joe signed a note to repay it at $100 a month with interest.

"You must try to be careful now, this is important," Moore admonished as he handed Joe the check. Of course there was no doubt that Joe intended to continue gambling. What else had he been thinking about when he borrowed $200 more than he needed? Besides, how else could he repay the loan? He walked confidently out of the office, his weighty financial obligations comfortably consolidated.

Nancy had started to teach in Beaumont at Longfellow elementary school and had her own bank account. She was earning about $450 a month and was no financial burden on Joe. The $4,000 gave him a feeling of power. The worry and tension over his debts and the hot check on the Wichita Falls bank, which was still in the air, began to fade.

It was, of course, principally the hot check that prompted Joe to approach A. D. Moore for the loan. Already the gambler's mentality was telling him that the other debts could have waited. But when you have a hot check out, your permissive powers increase in geometric proportion to the time you have left before the hot check hits.

Once Joe had deposited the check he went to Dick Peabody and casually said, "By the way"—he always prefaced a particularly sticky confession with this opener—"you remember last Wednesday when I cashed that check for eight hundred dollars?"

Peabody allowed as how he guessed he remembered the check and then asked, "Why?"

"There's a chance it may come back. The guy called me saying he'd made a mistake with his account and the check may be returned. But there's no problem. I'm just putting this four-thousand-dollar check into my own account."

Joe was covered. Peabody knew who A. D. Moore was, of course, and the check was on the Rothwell estate account so he had no concern about an $800 check coming back. Joe learned something that day. A $4,000 transaction raised him considerably in the esteem of the bank.

Joe did not get emotional about business or about hot checks. He did not get emotional about gambling either. He always knew what he was doing and approached his goals calmly and deliberately. Yet his reaction to depositing the $4,000 he had borrowed was ambivalent.

While he saw it, fleetingly, as the possible prelude to larger transactions, the more important thought that swept through his mind was that it wouldn't be necessary ever to do it again. Never again would he write another hot check or get into trouble, he promised himself.

Now he began to wonder how to use the $4,000. He didn't absolutely have to pay off all his debts; but his father-in-law knew about the GFC loan so he paid that right away, and by so doing opened the spot again for a subsequent loan. Then, after some reflection, he made himself liquidate all his other debts before he could be tempted to bet the money and perhaps lose it.

Getting out of his difficulties, at least superficially, did not change Joe's habits. Nancy soon learned to tell when he had been gambling at the domino hall because he had a pool-hall-type smell about him that she was able to recognize. He couldn't wait to wash his hair and get the smoky musty odor out of his clothes—but often he wasn't quick enough. Something he learned about her was that when he won and counted out $800 or $900 in front of her she was unimpressed. When he told her he'd earned $500, she might say matter-of-factly, "Oh, that's good." But the knowledge of what he was actually doing had not yet penetrated her consciousness.

Joe in fact paid off the $4,000 loan plus interest to A. D. Moore at $100 a month and, when he had the money, at an even faster rate. He was proud of the fact that he never missed a payment.

By the time they were approaching their first wedding anniversary, Joe was going out to Jack Thompson's to shoot craps once or twice a week, arriving about seven-thirty in the evening and coming home about eleven or even midnight. He played the sporting events regularly now, sweating out the results each morning when the newspaper arrived. Playing baseball games was actually more taxing than working in the office. It was not enjoyable—but winning was bliss!

Some psychiatrists of gambling aver that a gambler enjoys losing. Joe did not enjoy losing. As far as Joe was concerned there was not one iota of truth to the legend that the gambler is masochistic and wants to lose. Joe always wanted to win.

One rainy night his compulsion forced him to turn his car in the opposite direction from the apartment where Nancy was waiting for him and head for Jack Thompson's.

As the rain pelted the car and the windshield wipers worked at full speed Joe wanted nothing more than to be home with Nancy. Why was he doing this? he asked himself. Well, the rent on his office and apartment were due and he needed money for a number of things, he answered, knowing he was lying to himself. The truth was he felt he couldn't lose tonight.

That persistent alien spirit, which now seemed to be riding his shoulder, made him speed along despite the hazardous road conditions. He went into dangerous skids as he turned corners or stopped for a light. The sensation of being controlled by a force outside his will frightened him, until he simply gave in to it. Then he felt relaxed.

Finally reaching Jack Thompson's, he ran through the rain and hardly noticed his wet clothing as he made for the crap table. He swiftly laid down the first of a stack of $10 bills and started throwing the dice.

Not until he had lost every dollar did he notice it was eleven o'clock—Nancy would be worried about him on this rainy night, wondering if he had met with an accident. Nevertheless, relief rather than guilt was uppermost in his feelings as he drove home. He had done what he had to do: he had gambled hard and lost despite his best efforts. He had assuaged his need. Now he must manufacture a plausible lie for Nancy and figure an answer to the inevitable question, "But why didn't you at least call me?"

CHAPTER 10

For Christmas of 1953 Joe gave Nancy a membership to the Beaumont Country Club. It was really a present to himself but Nancy was thrilled on Christmas morning to find the membership card for Mr. and Mrs. Joe H. Hodges hanging on the tree. It was not easy to become a member of the Beaumont Country Club but it was looking for new, young members and Joe had been able to find four other attractive, eligible couples who would join with him. Their junior memberships cost $500 plus $40 per month dues.

Joe was elated that he and Nancy were allowed to join this very beautiful country club. It offered congenial company to play gin rummy and bridge, and Joe began golfing three or four times a week. There were also poker games, although the club did not approve of high-stakes card games.

In the club's first gin rummy tournament after he became a member, Joe's skill at cards was still unknown. The tournament was a Calcutta and when the pool opened for bids the gin champion, Leonard Stone, was bought by a syndicate of old members for $1,000. Joe bought himself for $50.

The Calcutta pool paid $5,000 to the syndicate that bought the winner and the runner-up paid off his buyers with $2,500. Joe's well-honed skills at gin saw him win his way to the finals in the tournament but he was then beaten by Stone, whose buyers received the $5,000. Joe, having bought himself, made $2,500, a fantastic win in the circumstances.

Nineteen fifty-four was a relatively happy year for Joe and

Nancy. She seemed content and Joe's gambling was done in the daytime, much of it at the Beaumont Country Club. He loved daytime gambling because he got home on time and it facilitated his task of keeping his betting excesses a secret from Nancy.

Professional gambling was rife in Beaumont and wide open. The Kayla brothers from Port Arthur financed a gambling shack affixed to the back of Deloti's service station on the edge of downtown. Between the dice shooting and the football and baseball parlays, Joe got deeper and deeper into debt as the year progressed. He went into 1955 owing $9,000 around Beaumont.

He was spending more and more time in the underground crap games, playing at Deloti's service station or wherever he could find a game. The Beaumont gamblers would take a card table, shove it against a wall and put a blanket on it and some boards around it. Presto! They had their crap game. It was quite a contrast for Joe to go from sweaty, smoke-wreathed crap games where he would sometimes shoot between $200 and $400 a roll to the urbane gambling at the Beaumont Country Club. But the ring-a-round games, as they were called, with local gamblers were beginning to absorb more and more of his attention.

Finally, hating himself, he had to ask Nancy to lend him her diamond engagement ring. Reluctantly, wide-eyed with worry, she withdrew it from her finger and handed it to him. He pawned the ring for $200, raising another modest bankroll for the ring-a-round games. Nancy was far more distressed at the fact that Joe pawned her ring to get gambling money than she was at the actual loss of it. Although he lost the bankroll from the ring, he later scored a big-enough win to redeem it and return it to her.

The gambling became more frenzied and the search for a bankroll more frantic. Remembering that his father saved dimes and wrapped them up in stacks, Joe, who had the key to his parents' home, went there and found his father's dime collection, $40 worth. The dimes evidently brought him luck because he won and ran from the game just in time to get to his parents' home before they returned from work. It was with a deep-drawn sigh of relief that he slid the dimes back under the socks in his father's drawer and went home to Nancy with his winnings.

A week later he helped himself to his father's dime collection again, and with the same results.

The third time he had to resort to the dime collection he was not so lucky. He lost it all. His inability immediately to replace the dimes in his father's drawer hurt him badly. It was one thing to owe banks and gamblers, but to take and then lose his dad's little collection of dimes was a distress of another order. A few days later Joe located another spot where he borrowed enough money to get into a ring-a-round, which he won.

With his winnings he rushed to the nearest bank, bought $40 worth of dimes and carefully wrapped them in the brown paper his father used. Feeling like a man suddenly released from damnation, he replaced the stacks of dimes in his father's drawer once again before they were missed. These desperation moves to keep gambling did little for his self-image.

Joe was now bowed down under a debt structure of over $14,000. He had already exhausted his credit line at the banks and the finance companies. Various individuals loaned him $2,000 or $3,000 and even Will Orgain, of the prestigious law firm which had turned down his first job application, loaned him $1,500. Joe could sense who would loan him money and who would turn him down and seldom approached the latter.

Although his parents were hard-pressed financially, they provided their son a comforting base of solidarity. Joe Hodges, Sr., had held the same job for forty years and Joe's mother had been teaching at the same school for almost as long. Now Joe had to go to his parents for money again, this time for a substantial loan. Before approaching them, however, he made one last loan of $2,500 from Cy Williams, a knowledgeable oil man and gambler with whom he maintained a sincere friendship. But every week he had to make payments to his debtors and at least call on those he could not pay. He was like a juggler keeping six or eight plates spinning in the air at once on top of precarious sticks.

One method of keeping the plates spinning and repaying the $500 on Monday that he'd borrowed on Friday was to write and cash checks against insufficient or nonexistent funds. Fortunately for Joe, Beaumont was a small town where everybody knew each other and he received the benefit of the doubt when his checks threatened to bounce. He always had a story and somehow managed to cover one hot check by writing another and cashing it at a new spot.

Finally the Jefferson County district attorney, Ramie Griffin, called Joe into his office. "I've been hearing a lot of disturbing things about you, Joe," the D.A. admonished the young lawyer.

Joe admitted he might have made some mistakes, leaving all reference to gambling out of the conversation. Using his considerable powers of persuasion he proceeded to talk his way out of this confrontation with the district attorney and no charges were filed against him.

Joe Hodges, Sr., had $700 in the bank when his son shocked him with the news that he had to have $7,500 immediately. Limited though his resources were, he went to his friends, including Carroll Conn and Dudley English, a doctor. With three friends as endorsers he approached the First National Bank and borrowed the $7,500 which he undertook to pay off at $150 a month plus interest. Now Joe had the $7,500 and with his stature in town fast crumbling, he took $6,000 to his most urgent creditors—to pay off the heat, as he termed it.

From the money borrowed on his father's standing in the community Joe kept $1,500 as a bankroll. This semi-bailout by his father, however, did not for a moment stop Joe from gambling. He had taken to placing $200 or $300 a day on wild baseball parlays at Johnny Venza's betting parlor and his $1,500 bankroll was fast being dissipated.

One night, with the heat inexorably increasing, he bet $800—everything he had left—on a wild six-game baseball parlay. If there is such a thing as sensible gambling, this long shot certainly was not it.

The next morning Joe was standing on the sidewalk outside his apartment waiting for the newspaper to arrive. At six-thirty he took his paper directly from the delivery boy. He didn't tear it open to get at his "*Wall Street Journal*" sports page. To have suddenly been confronted with the results of his parlay bet in one stroke would have been too much of a shock. He carried the newspaper still folded back to the apartment and went into the bathroom, closing the door after him. Then, sitting on the toilet seat, he carefully unfolded the paper to the sports page and slipped his hand over the scores.

Slowly he moved his hand down the page uncovering one score at a time. The first sports headline read: Yankees 2, Baltimore 1.

"Won that sonofabitch!" he exclaimed jubilantly.

He continued to move his hand down the page uncovering an article slugged: ROBIN ROBERTS SHUTS OUT THE CUBS. 1–0. Another win. Sweating out each score as he sat in the bathroom Joe allowed himself to discover he had won three games of the parlay. Trembling, his hand begrudged another score. Four wins! Then five! Finally, in unbearable suspense, he lifted his hand from the paper and read the score of the sixth game. It was a miracle! He had hit the parlay! Won all six games. He had hit Johnny Venza for the biggest win in his life—$16,000.

It was a gloriously agonizing morning that Joe had to wait through until he could get Johnny Venza on the phone at noon, and it was not until the next day after the bookie had assembled the $16,000 that Joe collected his money. It was the most exhilarating day of his life. Not just because of the win, but from relief that he was going to be able to pay off Cy Williams and all the other individuals and institutions from whom he had borrowed money. It was the big win.

Paying off his debts was the monumental orgasmic ego boost of Joe's existence. It didn't take long for the demimonde of the Beaumont sporting world to hear about Joe Hodges' big win. Johnny Venza was telling everybody how "that fuckin' Hodges" really murdered him. But Joe felt magnificent as he went around town paying off the men who had loaned him money. Life was manageable again.

Joe's phone rang. Today he could answer without trepidation. Whoever was dunning him, he could promise to pay him forthwith. Unfortunately, it wasn't a creditor. The voice on the other end of the phone told him there was going to be a big game that afternoon behind Freddie Deloti's service station. Al Kayla, the professional from Port Arthur who it was widely believed paid for the architectural addition to the rear of the garage, was coming up from Port Arthur to back the action. Joe had hardly hung up before he was on his way to the game. He had $8,000 on him but he knew he wouldn't lose it. You couldn't lose that much money in a game behind Deloti's.

In just two hours Al Kayla beat Joe out of every penny of the $8,000 left from the big win.

It wasn't until some years later that Joe realized Al had cheated him, using shaved dice, throwing a little "edge work" into the game. The six and one, the murderous seven, would spill out slightly more often, giving the house, in this case Al Kayla, a decided mathematical advantage. Had Joe known all the angles of cheating at dice he might have had a pair of calipers with him to make sure the edges of the dice were true.

The loss to Al Kayla, just at the moment when Joe had his life almost straightened out was devastating. He never told Nancy about the big win followed by the big loss and continued to make loans where he could to keep up the ring-a-round games in town.

Joe's gambling was of two distinct kinds. There was the sweaty, smoky, back-alley betting in such places as Deloti's service station and then there was the genteel card playing, adorned with golf, out at the Beaumont Country Club.

He was constantly striving to build respectability and to open spots to feed the rapacity of the gambler that shared his psyche. He helped form, and became president of, the Beaumont Duplicate Bridge Club to which the most respectable bridge enthusiasts in Beaumont belonged. At the same time he was gambling with the most disreputable, virtually criminal, element in the Beaumont–Port Arthur area.

As the heat increased and Joe was spending more and more emotional energy soothing the individuals and institutions to whom he owed money, he took a drive one afternoon down to Port Arthur, Beaumont's sister city twenty miles to the south. He had developed a new technique to raise a bankroll and used it to good effect on this trip. Between Beaumont and Port Arthur he stopped at every large grocery store on the way. The grocery stores always had a lot of cash on hand.

He stopped at the first supermarket he came to, walked in and went up to the courtesy booth. Telling the cashier he was a lawyer in Beaumont and showing his driver's license, his credit cards, and his Texas Bar Association card, he explained that he needed to wire some money at Western Union to a client and didn't want to go all the way back to his bank in Beaumont. He hit the first grocery store for $250.

At each grocery store along the route the procedure was the same. He was wearing the dark three-piece suit of the professional man and his suave tongue and authoritative manner gave added force to the image he was presenting. Furthermore, it was early in the afternoon and the cashier could easily have called lawyer Hodges' bank to determine whether the cash was indeed there. He was so convincing that on that trip to Port Arthur not a single grocery store cashier bothered to call his bank. Had they done so, Dick Peabody would have realized much sooner than he did that in Joe Hodges he was handling a commodity dangerous to bankers.

As Joe approached Port Arthur he had $700 in his pocket and decided it wasn't enough. Visiting two more large grocery-chain stores on the outskirts of town, he cashed a check for $500 and then another for $300. He arrived at the Port Arthur bookmakers' place with a $1,500 bankroll. It was a domino-type hall with the tickers clacking out the sports results from all over the country. Bets were taken not only on the major league games but on the Texas league games as well.

For the rest of the day and into the night as games were played around the country, Joe was covering every game and sweating out the results on the ticker. It was a punishing exercise but by midnight he had swept the boards, won every game, and walked out of the place with $7,000 in his pocket. He had desperately needed the win. It would cover a lot of holes, pay off a lot of heat.

When the Beaumont bank opened at nine, Joe was there to deposit enough money to cover all the checks he had cashed at the grocery stores between Beaumont and Port Arthur. Then he had a discussion with Dick Peabody and took care of the other hot checks he had written to himself on out-of-town banks which would be floating in within the next day or two.

After the bank Joe called on the individuals who were pressing him hardest to repay loans and also on the finance companies who were expecting him to make overdue payments.

Again he was building up the respectability and solidity which the demon within would plunder. The Beaumont Duplicate Bridge Club was lending considerable prestige to the name of Joe H. Hodges and the women bridge players of Beaumont delighted in playing with him. He played with the members of the club once or twice a week. He was also president of the University of Texas alumni association in Beaumont, known as the Texas Exes.

Frequently he would come in from the back-alley games sweaty and disheveled and smelling of smoke, then quickly shower, shave, change his clothes, and go on to a meeting of the Board of Stewards at the First Methodist Church. He and his father were both on the board. Every Sunday Joe sang in the choir, which he loved to do, and although by now there was considerable whispering behind his back in town, his own solid façade of respectability was barely cracked.

Joe's ambivalent life-style taxed his physical and mental capabilities to the utmost. The Duplicate Bridge Club, the Texas Exes, the one-man law office, the church meetings and choir practice were, taken together, extremely demanding. At the same time there was the constant financial juggling: the banks had to be appeased, the finance companies visited, the creditors assuaged. Then of course there were the unceasing ring-a-round games, Jack Thompson's, the gin games and golf at the club, and the sports pages of the local papers, all hammering for Joe's attention. Worst of all was the exhausting business of constantly borrowing money, not only a drain on his time and his resources of ingenuity, but a weight on his conscience.

Choir practice had become particularly debilitating for Joe, almost a charade. The other members of the choir had long since come to the conclusion that he must have contracted diabetes and kidney problems along with his polio. Two, three, even four times during practice he would excuse himself, ostensibly to go to the men's room, and use the telephone in the vestry to call his bookies to put down bets on the baseball games and ask for the results of the games he had wagered on.

How long, oh Lord, how long? he asked himself. Something

had to change. Some way he had to start a new life for himself and Nancy.

If he could just get into a wholly different environment, and find something that would supplant the gambling, he was certain he could extricate himself from his problems and liquidate his debt structure which was now like a constant, painful thorn in his psyche.

CHAPTER 11

Early in the fall of 1955, with the baseball season coming down to the wire toward the World Series, Joe's well had run dry. Neither individuals nor institutions would lend him any money. He had almost destroyed his meager law practice, abusing a small but steady source of income to the point where even it had dried up. Insurance companies hired him to file lawsuits at the local courthouse, sending him the $15 fee required to register the suit. Since this was a rather inconsequential legal activity with which most firms did not want to bother, Joe received twenty or thirty such requests a month. But instead of filing the suits he diverted the $15 checks to his own gambling needs, and before he was through they added up to $3,000.

Joe was desperate to extricate himself from the dire situation in Beaumont. He had no money at all and only Nancy's salary as a teacher kept them going. She bore this financial burden without complaining, attributing Joe's indigence to his lean pickings as a novice lawyer.

During his period of heavy sports betting Joe had become an avid major league baseball enthusiast. He had always had a passion for the game and had played second base himself before polio struck him down. He explained to Nancy that if he could get a job somewhere in the administrative or business end of major league baseball, perhaps he would find new meaning in life and an excitement in his work that would take the place of

—yes, he had been disingenuous enough to confess he did some —his gambling.

So, in September, with $10 and a Texaco credit card in his pocket, he climbed into the old car he and Nancy had been driving and started out on an odyssey whose objective was to inject himself into the world of big league baseball. He had convinced himself that being involved in the real thing would be all the excitement he needed and would make gambling superfluous.

On his way through Lufkin, Texas, he stopped in to see an old friend, Tom Adams, and asked for a loan of $50. Tom let him have $5. With $15 in his pocket twenty-six-year-old Joe now headed for Cleveland, Ohio. He had never been north, except once to visit his mother's sister, Kathleen, in Toledo, and the brief visit to Boston. But Hank Greenberg was in Cleveland.

Hank Greenberg had played minor league baseball for the Beaumont Exporters in the early thirties, along with such venerable players as Rudy York and Schoolboy Rowe, Joe's boyhood heroes. Beaumont was a Detroit farm club and the Tigers had always been Joe's favorite team because some of the players he had watched in Beaumont in their minor league days were there.

In 1955 Hank Greenberg bought the Cleveland Indians. Joe therefore reasoned that his best chance to get a job in big league baseball lay with Hank Greenberg, who would know Beaumont and undoubtedly have a feeling of nostalgia for the Texas town.

It took three days for Joe to get from Beaumont up to Cleveland, proceeding from one Texaco station to the next. He filled up his tank, asked the attendant to put a used tire or some other item on his credit card and while he was at it give him $5 cash and put that on the card too. The Texaco stations were amenable to $5 or $10 cash being charged onto the credit card, which gave Joe the money to eat as he went north.

It was on a Thursday at one-thirty in the afternoon that Joe drove into Cleveland. Cleveland was scheduled to play Washington in a twilight doubleheader. Joe went to the offices of the Cleveland Indians at Municipal Stadium, first stopping at a service station to freshen up and put on the pressed suit he had saved for the big city.

He marched up to the receptionist at the Indians' office and asked to see Mr. Greenberg, please. He handed his card—Joe Henry Hodges, Attorney at Law, Beaumont, Texas—to the secretary and then sat down to wait for his audience. It was a busy place and Joe was awed to see in person players who had hitherto only been names to him. Al Rosen was playing and Bob Lemon and Bob Feller. They all walked through the reception room in the two hours Joe sat waiting for the opportunity to see Hank Greenberg.

The first game of the doubleheader was scheduled to start at six-thirty and at four o'clock a big hulk of a man walked into the main office. Joe knew who he was immediately. Hank Greenberg. He watched Greenberg walk on through the reception room and disappear into his own office. Fifteen minutes later he reemerged into the reception room and, though there were several people waiting to see him, called out in a commanding almost belligerent tone: "Who's Hodges?"

Joe identified himself.

"What do you want?" Greenberg asked gruffly

"I need to see you, Mr. Greenberg," Joe almost pleaded.

"And what's it about?"

"Could we go back to your office to talk?" Joe asked.

"Can't you tell me what you want right here?"

Then Joe blurted out, "I've driven up here from Beaumont, Texas, because I want to go to work for you." Hank Greenberg stared at him incredulously. "I'm a lawyer. I've got no money and I want to work for you in major league baseball."

The forthright statement seemed to catch Greenberg's fancy. "Come on back here a minute and let's talk," he invited, leading the way to his office.

Seated in the sumptuous office of the new owner of the Cleveland Indians, Joe explained that he was bored with the practice of law, that he loved baseball and wanted to get into the business end.

"You don't have any place to go?" Greenberg asked, a kindly note coming into his voice. "You want to see the games?"

"Yes, sir, I'd certainly like that."

Greenberg scribbled out a note and handed it to Joe. "You're hungry, aren't you?" It was really a statement.

Joe nodded. "Yes, sir."

"You go up to the Wigwam on the top of the stadium. Give Sammy at the door this note. Help yourself, I'll catch up with you later."

Joe took the elevator to the top of the stadium, presented his note to the manager of the restaurant, and was shown to the buffet where he helped himself to shrimp and roast beef and sat down at a table overlooking the stadium. He ordered a bourbon and water and sat there, already in the big leagues it seemed to him, mesmerized by the scene. He recognized Tris Speaker and Rogers Hornsby, who were behind him at the buffet and sat with him at the club table along with other sports celebrities. Genially they asked Joe who he was and he identified himself as a friend of Hank Greenberg's. Then Greenberg himself showed up and sat down at the table. He told the others that Joe Hodges, a lawyer from Beaumont, had driven all the way up here to Cleveland to see him. As Joe had hoped, Greenberg lapsed into nostalgia for the days he played for the Beaumont Exporters, telling stories of minor league baseball in the early thirties.

Joe sat blissfully listening to the conversation until the great man pulled him out of his trance. "Let's go to the game. Come on, Joe."

The owner's box hung in midair over the upper deck of the stadium. Hank and Joe, followed by others, climbed into the gondola where they sat and watched the doubleheader. Joe was captivated. Hank Greenberg had just traded for two new players and Joe basked in the obscenities he poured out when the new players made two errors. Hank was both general manager and owner and he wanted his ability as general manager to be respected.

After the game Greenberg put Joe up at the YMCA not far from the stadium. Joe stayed in Cleveland five days at Greenberg's expense and felt he had really come to know the baseball celebrity. During this time he went to all the games and had several conversations with Greenberg and his executives about the possibilities of his getting into the administrative end of baseball.

Greenberg called several of the farm teams to see whether they needed any help. There were no openings. Finally he advised Joe that he should get some background in baseball and suggested that he go to the baseball administration school in Florida and then get in touch with him again.

Being impatient and impulsive, Joe, though grateful for his five days with the Indians, was not satisfied with the outcome. He didn't want to have to do anything preliminarily. He wanted to get right into the action. He thanked Hank Greenberg for his hospitality and advice, promising to contact him again when he had finished the course in Florida, which he had neither the resources nor the inclination to attend. Then he climbed into the old car and headed for Detroit. He arrived the next day and drove up to Briggs Stadium, asking to see Spike Briggs. Joe now had about $25 in his pocket. Spike Briggs was not as accessible as Hank Greenberg, however. In fact, Joe didn't get to see him at all.

One hour after arriving at Briggs Stadium he again climbed into his car and headed for Chicago. He found a room at a lodge near the stockyards, which was also close to Comiskey Park. At nine-thirty the next morning, a Sunday, shaved and showered, with his city suit on, he checked out of the motel and went over to Comiskey Park. A big game was coming up that afternoon at one-thirty between Chicago and the New York Yankees. Joe asked to see Mr. Comiskey. After waiting for thirty minutes Chuck Comiskey, Jr., stuck his head out of the back office, slid the door open, introduced himself to Joe and asked him to come in.

Chuck Comiskey was not as gruff as Hank Greenberg had been at the beginning and Joe made the same pitch to him as he had to Greenberg. Like Greenberg, Comiskey was gracious. He arranged for Joe to stay at a motel and for three days Joe went to all the White Sox games while Chuck Comiskey called Indianapolis and some of the other White Sox farm teams. Comiskey did his best for Joe but there just were no openings for a lawyer no matter how knowledgeable about baseball. Joe enjoyed his stay in Chicago, particularly his meetings with the people who milled around the hierarchy of the White Sox. As he had hoped, being in the middle of the real thing, with baseball excitement all about him, drove away all impulse to gamble or bet on sports. But there just wasn't a job for him.

He left Chicago and drove to St. Louis where he managed to see Frank Lane, general manager of the St. Louis Cardinals. Lane listened to his story sympathetically and introduced him to Bing Divine, a young man in the Cardinals' administration who was going places. But the story was the same as it had been in Detroit and Chicago. Divine even suggested that Joe go to the baseball administration school in Florida.

Joe thanked him for the advice, watched a game, and then headed for Kansas City which had just been admitted to the American League. The city had a new team and perhaps would need an administrative assistant who was also a lawyer. But there was no place for Joe Hodges in Kansas City either. Finally he began to think about going home. The two-week sports odyssey was over.

From Kansas City Joe drove back to Beaumont. He reappeared on the scene as quietly as he had left it, disappointed at his inability to make the big leagues but content that he had given it his best effort. Nancy was happy to have him home and his law office was still open.

The dismal cycle of borrowing, betting, and covering hot checks resumed. Joe had to go farther afield to make loans, opening up spots in Houston and even Dallas. But still his world seemed to be closing in on him as the football season progressed and he bet wildly on individual games and parlays. Vaguely he knew things couldn't keep on going this way, yet try as he would he couldn't seem to break out of the devastating pattern that was destroying his and Nancy's life and his parents' piece of mind.

CHAPTER 12

Thanksgiving of 1955 marked a decisive crisis of spirit for Joe. His debts had mounted to over $25,000 and he desperately needed a big score. But it was traditional for him and Nancy to drive from Beaumont to Houston for Thanksgiving dinner with Nancy's parents and for that his financial worries had to be pushed out of sight.

On Thanksgiving Day there were some college games played around the country, not the full slate of scheduled professional and college contests. Normally Texans think of football in terms of the Southwest Conference, the Big Ten, the Southeast Conference, and the Pacific Coast Eight. These are the only conferences they consider worth betting on. In Texas gamblers seldom bet Ivy League games or those of other colleges in the effete East.

On this Thanksgiving there were six games being played around the country on which the Beaumont bookmakers were taking bets. Making the rounds of his borrowing spots Joe was able to get $100 from his mother, $200 from Nancy, and another $200 scrounged up from a friend he had recently repaid. With his $500 he went over to Joe Tortorous and bet it all on a six-game parlay. If he picked the winner of each of the six games the payoff would be almost forty to one, $20,000. Again it was a desperate effort to get himself financially clean, even ahead. Texas and Texas A&M traditionally played every Thanksgiving. It was the big grudge battle of the year and Joe would have bet it anyway. Texas was an eight-point favorite.

In the East, Penn was playing Cornell, a meaningless game to Joe but he had to bet it because he needed it to fill out the parlay. Virginia Tech was playing VMI, Virginia Tech being a fourteen-and-a-half-point favorite. Oklahoma was playing Oklahoma State and, again back in the East, Brown was playing Columbia, an impossible contest for a Texan to pick the winner of.

Further complicating the parlay, the winning team, if it were favored, had to win by more than the number of points by which it was favored.

On Thursday, with everything riding on the Thanksgiving Day football parlay, Joe and Nancy arrived at the Hippards' home for the big get-together for family and friends. They even brought their dog Pepper, a Chihuahua. Joe went through the opening phases of the Thanksgiving scene with flying colors. He was affable and relaxed and smiled for the camera like everybody else.

At family gatherings when children were discussed, Nancy found it difficult not to become morose, and she was having trouble keeping her spirits up now. She and Joe had been wanting to have a child from the first days of their marriage and she was bitter about the fact that she had yet to conceive. Pepper was their only "child."

George Hippard was a football fan and both Nancy and her brother Jim had gone to the University of Texas so they turned on the Texas–Texas A&M game. The first game in Joe's parlay was Texas over Texas A&M by eight points. Thanksgiving dinner was scheduled to begin immediately after the game.

Late in the fourth quarter Texas was six points ahead of Texas A&M and it looked as though Joe would lose the whole parlay on the first game by two points. His appetite for Thanksgiving dinner deserted him. He had been certain he was going to win the parlay and all his troubles would be over.

Then, miraculously, with two minutes left in the game, Texas got within field goal range and the kick split the uprights for three points. Joe had won the first game of the parlay by one slim point. He was one down, five to go as they sat down to the table. Joe had hidden his little transistor radio in the upstairs bathroom. In the East it was one hour later and Joe excused himself from the table to go upstairs to the bathroom. He turned on the transistor radio and got the final on the Penn–Cornell game. He had picked Penn, and Penn won by almost twice the number of points Joe had given the bookmaker. That was two down and four to go.

Joe tried to concentrate on the table talk and give the impression that he was having fun. But the moment the family stood up from the table, he was racing back upstairs to the bathroom for the Oklahoma–Oklahoma State score. Again he won. Three games out of six; three more to sweat out.

Downstairs with the family once more he succeeded in carrying on an animated conversation. Then he stole away from the group long enough to turn on the television set in the next room in case another score came across. Lurking by the television set, but pretending not to notice it, Joe strained his ears for some indication of how his other three teams were doing. At that point Nancy walked in and noticed the set was on.

"Why is the TV on?" she asked sharply.

"I didn't turn it on," Joe replied. "Maybe Jim turned it on. Maybe your dad wanted to get some football scores. It's not up to me to turn it off." Nancy shrugged and Joe pretended to follow her back into the next room where the family were still conversing. From the television set he heard the score of the Brown–Columbia game. Columbia won and so did Joe. Four down, two to go. Then from the Southeast came a fifth score. He had won again and the adrenaline started coursing through him. He had five games out of the six. It was as though sexual climax was approaching and all he needed was to win the Virginia Tech–Virginia game for the final pulse-pounding release. Virginia Tech was a heavy favorite; surely he couldn't lose this one. Even giving fourteen and a half points seemed like providing himself a comfortable margin.

Nonchalantly he carried on a conversation with Mr. Hippard as Nancy and her mother talked at the other end of the room. It was getting time for them to drive back to Beaumont. At six-thirty the sports news came on the television set. First the announcer gave what to Joe was an excruciatingly detailed recap of the Texas–Texas A&M game.

Get on with it, get on with it, he shouted inwardly. All the scores he had already heard were repeated and the sports news was just about to end when the announcer said, almost as an afterthought, "Virginia Tech smashed Virginia today—thirty-three to nineteen. That's all the news of sports today. Now for the weather."

For moments Joe's head spun as he tried to determine whether he had won or lost. In the anxiety it took him moments longer than usual to do the simple arithmetic. Virginia Tech had won by fourteen points. Joe had given fourteen and a half points. The blood rushed to his head as his mind tried to cope with the fact he had lost by half a point—Virginia Tech had won by fourteen points exactly. Twenty thousand dollars, his salvation, had just flown out the window for one half a point.

As he drove back to Beaumont he was utterly silent, in a daze. At first Nancy tried to converse with him but he couldn't answer her. He was literally incapable of speech.

Beaumont, the town Joe was born and brought up in, the town where he had all his friends, where he belonged to the country club, where he was a steward of the church and president of the Duplicate Bridge Club, Beaumont now represented a burden too heavy for him to carry. He owed twelve lending institutions and thirty-five individuals from whom he had obtained loans amounting to almost $50,000.

He had tried to get a job that would take him out of his little one-man law office and pay him well and keep him busy. For a while he thought that his gin rummy partner at the club, Julius Gordon, a millionaire theater owner, might hire him. But instead Julius hired another young lawyer.

A few days after Thanksgiving Joe went up to visit bookie Johnny Venza who was the proprietor of the Yukon Club and also had a crap game out at the Spindletop Motel on the Port Arthur highway. Joe had been betting with Venza for years and despite the memorable win had lost a considerable amount of money to him. Joe made up his mind he would take one last shot at trying to rebuild his crumbling life and career in Beaumont. He told Johnny Venza he had $8,000 worth of hot checks floating around town and that the district attorney, despite his personal regard and friendship for him, would soon be forced to close in.

In his most eloquent manner Joe stressed his need for an $8,000 loan. He strongly implied that if he was arrested and indicted on bad-check charges, Venza would be dragged into the case. After all, Joe had lost many times $8,000 betting at Johnny's place either on the sports events or at the crap tables.

The threat was veiled but unmistakably there. After talking to Venza for two degrading hours, Joe got the reluctant bookie to return to Beaumont with him and sign a note at the bank for $8,000 which he then handed over. Johnny had stubbornly resisted making the loan for the first hour and a half. Just the same, when Joe had the $8,000 in hand he really believed that Johnny made the loan because he liked him, not because he was afraid the district attorney might be looking into his own gambling activities if he didn't.

Joe had nowhere near $8,000 in outstanding bad checks, but there were many short-term loans from people he desperately wanted to repay.

Finally and irrevocably Joe made up his mind to leave Beaumont. He had to get away. Thinking back over the years since his graduation from law school had become a form of self-inflicted torture. So many mistakes, all because he had had to get a bankroll and gamble.

There was the time in 1954 when John Ben Sheppard, a bright young star in Texas politics, was running for attorney general of the state of Texas, an office almost as important as that of governor. Joe H. Hodges of Beaumont was recommended to him as campaign manager for Jefferson and Orange counties and Joe went out and collected money for the Sheppard campaign. Compulsively, he used $2,000 of contributions to gamble instead of turning the money into the campaign. He lost it all.

There was the land deal with Carroll Conn, Sr., his father's close friend and the father of Joe's friend C.W. Joe, working at the time for a substantial real estate promoter, made a deal with Conn to lease for ninety-nine years a choice piece of Conn's land in Beaumont on which a motel would be built, financed by local investors. He went to the investors in the motel venture and then converted their money to his own gambling uses. Fifteen thousand dollars went out to the bookies and over the crap tables on that deal. Somehow, just before the promoter of the motel found out, Joe was able to replace the money. The same had been true in the Sheppard campaign: frantic borrowing made it possible to replace the funds before Joe's larceny was discovered.

By December the troubles Joe could handle in Beaumont had reached the saturation point. The desperate borrowing had debilitated him and deeply distressed Nancy. Twice in the past Nancy had gone with him to borrow money from her father and brother. George Hippard had the good sense not to grant a loan but the experience had been an upsetting one for Nancy. Her patience and unceasing diligence to make their marriage work amazed Joe, at times even provoked him—since they were premised on her ignorance of the awful power of the demon that was driving him, an ignorance that of course he had to try and keep inviolate. At the same time the demon resented her for her role as good angel.

In order to get away from her for a two- or three-day gambling spree, Joe would pick a fight over some small thing and then indignantly walk out on her without apologizing. Sometimes he would disappear for two or three days at a time, missing her, wanting to come home to her yet compelled to keep gambling until he made the big win or was broke again.

When he was lonely, yet couldn't come home, he would go back to the apartment at night and peek in the window to see how she was. Then he would drive around to his mother and father's house, park some distance from it, walk around to the back of the little bungalow and peer in at his parents. Some measure of Nancy's commitment to their marriage was evidenced in her deep desire to have a child and her sadness at being unable to do so. Perhaps if they had a child, Joe would change, she persisted in thinking. The gambling would no longer be a necessity to him.

Joe's decision to leave Beaumont was made entirely by himself. Nobody ran him out of town; in fact, most of the people who knew him would have preferred him to stay around. Beaumont had been Joe's womb all his life and only a set of the most adverse circumstances could make him leave. This was, indeed, the most momentous decision he had ever made.

The one thing he felt thankful for as he drove to Houston in early December for the purpose of resettling himself and Nancy outside Beaumont was that he had no criminal proceedings outstanding against him.

Still, Houston would provide a new life, and it was comforting to reflect that he was not running out on his myriad debts, every one of which was tabulated on a card he always carried with him, merely looking for breathing space, an opportunity to start afresh and somehow earn enough money to pay off the debts. Breaking into these sanguine thoughts, however, was his gnawing awareness that he had left his father stuck with the $7,500 note and an obligation to pay it off at $150 a month out of his small salary from Mobil Oil.

Joe had no appointments awaiting him, no contacts that might help him in his quest for a job, but he had been reading about a corporation in Houston with widespread subsidiaries called the Tennessee Gas Transmission Company. Less than ten years old, the company had skyrocketed into importance by building transmission lines carrying the natural gas of Texas to the Midwest and the East. It was a fast-developing company and was listed on the New York Stock Exchange.

Such a growth enterprise might just be looking for a young lawyer willing to travel anywhere on the company's behalf, Joe reasoned. And once again his persuasiveness and restrained panache stood him in good stead. He found the corporate headquarters in downtown Houston, walked up to the receptionist and asked to see the executive who handled the hiring of lawyers. He was sent into the legal department where he met one of the corporate attorneys. His first interview was at eleven o'clock the next morning. It seemed to go well and after it he talked to the personnel department and then went back to the lawyer he'd first met.

By three o'clock Joe had been hired as a company lawyer and assigned to the field office handling the state of Ohio, working out of Zanesville. That same day he was given a brand-new car, a Chevrolet, which he drove back to Beaumont, leaving his old car in Houston. His starting salary was $900 a month and on top of that he was to receive a $6 per diem for food. His living expenses in Zanesville would also be paid.

In a state of high excitement, he arrived back in Beaumont. Nancy, his mother, and his father all saw this turn of Joe's fortunes as a good omen. The job was a great opportunity for him, what he needed most in the world, and his little family rejoiced. Nancy would finish teaching December 20 so she would stay in Beaumont until then, letting Joe drive on ahead to Zanesville in the new company car.

CHAPTER 13

Joe set off in excellent spirits, eager to take up his new duties. It was a three-day northeasterly drive from Beaumont to Zanesville, Ohio, fifty miles east of Columbus.

On the afternoon of December 5 he arrived outside the Tennessee Gas Transmission Company office in Zanesville. It was snowing. Yankeeland for sure, he told himself. The buildings downtown were soot-covered, and the snow was dirty before it hit the ground. Joe prayed he would find a better welcome from the headquarters group inside the office.

The welcome by the Zanesville field office staff, which was concerned with the acquisition of pipeline rights-of-way, was in fact a hearty one. Babe King, head of the office, was a warm, outgoing man. Probably pushing sixty, Joe figured. Of average height, he was balding, overweight, and obviously well-liked around the office. Within minutes he and Joe were friends.

"Joe, let's get the introduction crap over with and then I'll take you to the bank so that you can meet John Murphy, the president." Joe had arrived with two company checks: one to cover salary, the other for expenses. "Then we'll have us a drink and get some lunch," he went on genially, calling for the office staff to gather around.

Alice Watson, the secretary, was an angular, squint-eyed woman who made it plain she still thought the brass in Houston was crazy to have transferred Joe's predecessor back to the home office when he was so badly needed in Zanesville. Maybe it was a promotion for him, but it was a disaster for the Ohio office to lose him. She disliked Joe on sight, and Joe, who had never worked with an office staff before, made a fatal mistake in failing to realize how important her good will could be under certain circumstances. By and large, however, the office staff was glad to see Joe and made him feel wanted.

As the only lawyer in the office, Joe was stepping into a position of responsibility. The fact that he had not the slightest idea of what the work was all about didn't bother him. He was confident of bluffing his way along until he found out what he was supposed to know.

After Joe had been greeted by everybody in the office, Babe took him down to the First National Bank of Ohio, Zanesville branch. It was a dirty old town they drove through, the two main industries being coal mining and pottery. But if Zanesville, with its population of thirty thousand or so, presented an unappealing aspect to the visitor, its centrality in the state of Ohio made it ideal for the transmission company's field office personnel.

As the new lawyer for Tennessee Gas in Zanesville, Joe was warmly greeted by Mr. Murphy, president of the bank. Murphy, in his sixties, personally opened a bank account for him and deposited his Tennessee Gas checks. A spare, even dour Yankee type, Murphy was not the sort of banker Joe really liked dealing with. The old bankers have all been up and down the road too many times to have any of the milk of human kindness left in them, Joe felt, unlike those still on the youngish side.

Murphy was most solicitous of Joe because the gas company kept a large float of money in the bank to facilitate paying out thousands of dollars a day to landowners for pipeline rights-of-way. Babe King was an important person to Murphy and that made Joe important too.

After the banking business had been completed, Joe and Babe King had lunch and drove back to the office.

When they arrived, Joe noticed a visitor waiting to see Babe King. The man didn't look as though he belonged in the office, Joe thought. He was wearing a hat down over his eyes and had a cigar butt clenched in his mouth. Nothing about him suggested a client coming in to discuss the gas business.

"Who's that?" Joe asked Troy Quimby, the accountant who was showing him his office and helping him get settled.

"Him?" Quimby asked, looking after the man who arrested Joe more than anyone he had seen that morning. "Oh, he's just a friend of Babe's. Not a business friend." Troy Quimby gave Joe a wink. "He runs the Ace Club down the street. His name is Akers. Jack Akers."

A bookie, Joe thought. He would have bet on it. Whatever resolution Joe might have had about not gambling ever again now left him. At 3 P.M., during the coffee break, he went out on the street and quickly located the Ace Club. It was upstairs over a store, with a bar, and Jack Akers was dealing blackjack. A $5 and $10 game, not the sort Joe played.

Joe introduced himself to Akers and told him he worked for Babe King. The two men struck up a conversation and Jack introduced Joe to the bartender. Akers allowed as how he did take bets, but his specialty was cards more than bookmaking. As a favor he'd take a bet but lay off the action with other bookies.

"Who does book around here?" Joe asked.

"Go up and see Carl, at Carl's Cafe. It's about two blocks down the street. You can't miss it."

Promising to come back for some cards and a drink, Joe went downstairs and back onto the street. He found Carl's Cafe just a half block off Main Street. Carl was pleasant-looking, about forty, a big, husky man with an engaging smile. As Joe entered the hash house he received a friendly greeting from the owner. After a little conversation Joe discovered that Carl was a regular bookmaker who laid off his bets in Wheeling and Parkersburg in West Virginia as well as Cincinnati. He dealt with a number of other big-time bookies and assured Joe that he could take care of any action the new man in town might want to lay.

Before Joe left to go back to the office they were discussing how Carl could fit into Joe's gambling picture. Carl's idea of a big bet was $10 or $20 on a football parlay. Joe liked to bet $50 to $100 and before he left that afternoon he wagered $50 on a basketball parlay. With the football season over except for the bowl games and baseball four months away, basketball, Joe's weakest sport, was all he could bet on. Basketball was a treacherous game for bettors. Often small schools had very good teams, schools like St. Bonaventure, St. John's, Xavier, Loyola, Dayton, and such. With his $50 down, Joe went back to the office. Already he had accomplished a lot. He'd met a banker and two bookies and put down his first bet, all on his first day.

Babe King took him to the local hotel where he checked in for the night. The next day Joe moved to a comfortable rooming house and began looking for a home for Nancy and himself.

Dropping by Carl's he found, not to his surprise, that he had lost his $50 bet and tried to put a $200 bet down on a parlay. Carl didn't want to take a $200 bet, saying he didn't get into stakes that high. However, he gave Joe the name of yet another bookmaker and promised to locate more for him.

Ten days later Joe flew to Beaumont and picked up Nancy. By now he had found them a house on Cemetery Street, an ominous name if he'd thought about it, and Nancy had shipped the furniture ahead of them to their new residence. Actually the house on Cemetery Street was a large garage apartment. Nancy and Joe made the three-day trip in two days and arrived at the house on Cemetery Street at night tired but in fine fettle.

Together—yet not quite together—they celebrated Christmas. Perhaps they were lonesome for Texas, but a new life seemed to be opening up for them and they were content. They visited Babe King and his wife Lucille on Christmas afternoon and also Troy Quimby and his wife with whom they met another congenial couple, Tom and Ellen Mitchell.

The day after Christmas Joe was in the office working over condemnation proceedings and suits aimed at farmers who balked at having pipelines across their land despite the law which gave a pipeline company the right to lay them there.

Between Christmas and New Year, Joe dropped in on Carl every day to place a bet.

"You just can't seem to hit the baskets, can you, Joe?" Carl said sympathetically. "Maybe you'd better wait until the baseball season starts."

But Joe was not to be deterred. He owed money back in Beaumont, over $50,000, and he wasn't going to be able to repay it on his munificent salary of $900 a month. His luck would have to turn, he told himself.

New Year's Eve, Joe and Nancy celebrated with the Kings, the Mitchells, and the other new friends they were making in Zanesville. Nancy was precariously happy. It seemed to her that Joe really was making a new life for them away from the bookmakers and crap tables in Beaumont.

By January 20, Joe had lost $9,000 betting on the basketball games. All his expense checks, his salary, and the generous extra living allowance had gone to the bookmakers, as well as three loans from local financial institutions. Finally he had to tell Nancy. She looked at him uncomprehendingly that evening. "You—you're broke? Oh Joe . . . The rent is due tomorrow. What are we going to do?"

Nancy went to the school board the next day, got a list of schools where there might be a vacancy or where substitute teachers could apply. She began teaching immediately, full-time. When her teaching salary wasn't enough to pay the bills she went to work at Penney's, rushing from school at four so she could begin her job there at five, working until nine-thirty at night. By the end of February, Joe owed $14,500 in Zanesville, money he had borrowed from the Mitchells and other friends. And there was still the $50,000 outstanding in Beaumont. Almost every night he went over his debt structure, sending $10 here, $20 there from such winnings as he occasionally made.

"Just one good week . . . even one good day, and I'll have it under control," he told himself. Nancy wouldn't listen to this sort of talk and begged him to stop throwing his money away with the bookmakers. Here they were living in a garage apartment so large that it looked like a good-sized house. Their furniture was good and to all outward appearances they were comfortably off.

The winter was colder than anything they had ever experienced before. Joe and Nancy hated the freezing sleet and deep snow. Sometimes Nancy would get stuck in the drifts and wouldn't get to school on time and then Joe would have to bring out the chains and try to get them over the back tires, cursing them and the weather. They ran out of money for the gas heating bill in the apartment just as a deceptive, balmy early spring thaw set in. Joe decided to cut off the gas completely and not make the overdue payment.

The following week, one of the worst freezes of the season hit Ohio and they had to huddle under blankets just to stay alive.

One morning, while Nancy was heating a pan of water on the stove so Joe could shave, she began to sob uncontrollably. "I can't take it, Joe . . . I've never been so miserable in my life." Joe went to her, put his arms around her and tried to comfort her.

"Let me see what I can do, darling," he said.

That evening he stayed out all night shooting craps in the next town. He lost, and remorse overwhelmed him. Afraid to go home to Nancy and confess, he still had to know that she was all right. So he parked a block from the apartment and walked through the snow to the storeroom under the garage. Quietly he propped a long rickety ladder against the siding and climbed up to the window where he could look in at his wife. She was huddled in a chair reading and he saw her glance at the clock.

The tears stung his eyes, freezing on his cheeks before they could run down his face. He wanted to hold her, comfort her, but he could not go inside until—until—

The next night Joe returned home exultantly. He had beaten the game, he was a winner. They had weathered Zanesville's worst winter in years and things were going to be all right after all. They clung to each other, young enough to smile, old enough to wonder if the smiles would carry them through.

Joe worked on land deals, acquisitions, rights of eminent domain—all the paperwork to do with getting the gas pipelines shooting across Ohio. He was bored but grateful for the paycheck, and the baseball season was coming up. Joe just couldn't hack basketball. At baseball he knew his way around and felt that with just the least luck he could pay back the finance companies and banks that he now owed in Zanesville.

At the Zanesville branch of the First National Bank of Ohio, Joe wrote a $500 check on an inactive account he had down in Beaumont. He got lucky on the baseball bets and was able to wire the money to his account two days later, just in time to cover the check so that it wouldn't bounce back to the Zanesville bank.

This was a dangerous game to play and as he continued to write checks on his inactive account, he had to call Beaumont on more than one occasion and beg a friend to lend him the money to cover the check before it bounced. In addition to his Beaumont indebtedness, he now had to keep the Zanesville plates spinning.

One night, after borrowing more money from the Mitchells, they all went to a drive-in movie together, Joe and Nancy in the back seat, the Mitchells in the front.

Despite the debts and gambling, Joe and Nancy were happy over the fact that she appeared to be pregnant. She had not taken any tests but they hoped for the best. Then, as they were watching the movie, Nancy had a miscarriage. She flooded, suddenly bleeding all over the back seat of the car.

Guilt tore at Joe. What he'd done to her devastated him. He was not so selfish or so insensitive as to be unaware of her feelings. Then why didn't he do something about them? he asked himself. He couldn't answer the question.

In the office of Tennessee Gas, Joe took his bookie sheets listing the games he would bet on into the men's room where he could study them privately. He had an office with a door but to shut the door would give the impression he was doing something secretive. So he had taken to planning his betting for the day in the men's room. He was constantly in the bathroom with the newspapers on the floor, studying the line sheets, planning longshot parlays, and then going down to Carl to place his bets. Occasionally he talked Carl into taking credit bets, but always he had to pay the bookie before he could get on the boards again.

With the baseball games being played all over the country Joe was beginning to have a few wins, not big ones but enough to keep him betting. In May 1956 he had $4,500 worth of bad checks outstanding and was struggling to cover them.

He was sitting on a stool at Carl's diner, musing over a cup of coffee on whether he could wire a Phi Gam friend in Texas for one more loan, when he felt someone tap him on the shoulder. He turned.

"Your name Hodges?" A burly man in a gray gabardine suit and crumpled felt hat was looking at him, his face inches away. Beside him was a younger man whose shoes and clothes spelled cop and whose eyes meant business.

"Yeah, I'm Hodges," Joe confessed.

"You're under arrest," said gray gabardine, and the two men hoisted him firmly to his feet. Joe knew exactly what had happened without being told. His checks had bounced at the First National Bank and the president, John Murphy, who had been so affable and accommodating when Joe first met him, was now putting it to him without giving him a chance to straighten out the matter. All his life Joe had lived in Beaumont where people knew him and where, no matter how much he owed at a bank, he would at least get a phone call to come down and see if things couldn't be set straight. But not in Zanesville where nobody knew him or about him except that he was a gas company lawyer, not with Mr. Murphy of the First National Bank.

At the jail, which was three blocks from Carl's place, Joe was hustled into the sheriff's office. Yes, he was right. Murphy had not only filed a complaint about the bad checks but had rounded up all the others Joe had given to bank customers. The district attorney was already in action.

"You want to make a call, Hodges? One call and here's the dime." Joe took the coin and wondered what to do. He couldn't call Nancy out of her classroom at school. He hated to call Babe King at work. Finally he decided to call Carl at the diner. They were friends, maybe he would help. Carl was naturally upset when Joe had been hustled out of his place earlier and on the phone he sounded uneasy as Joe begged him to call Nancy when she got home. Bookmaking, of course, was illegal and Carl wondered whether somehow he might become involved in Joe's troubles himself.

"Just call my wife," Joe said, trying to sound as though the whole problem was some little misunderstanding that would quickly be put right. "Ask her to let my dad know what happened."

"You sure you don't want me to phone your boss instead of her?"

"No," Joe said emphatically. "Don't do that. I don't want them to know. Not yet anyway . . ." It hadn't occurred to him yet that it was all over. He thought that if his dad could get him the money to cover these checks, maybe Babe King could keep the news from getting around and let him stay on.

The afternoon paper dashed any hopes he might have had in that direction. A front-page story with a banner headline above his staring picture fixed him in the eyes of Zanesville. "Local Attorney Arrested" spelled out the fact that his future in that town with Tennessee Gas didn't exist.

When Nancy called Joe Hodges, Sr., that evening from Zanesville, he thought for a minute she would be saying that she and Joe were planning a trip to come down and see them. Yet there was a kind of trepidation growing in his heart as he hadn't heard much from his son all winter. Every time he let himself get depressed, wondering if Joe was really making it up there in Zanesville, hoping to God he was, he'd get indigestion over his lunch at the Mobil plant. Then somebody would say, "Is everything all right, Mr. Hodges?" He would grin quickly, lower his head so the others wouldn't ask him how his son liked his great new job and keep his dark thoughts to himself.

Over the years Joe Sr. had done a lot of bragging about his boy. There were not many Phi Beta Kappas around the Mobil plant. Not many sons going through law school, having a big society wedding, playing golf at the Beaumont Country Club. He wanted the best for Joe and Nancy, wanted it almost passionately, but deep down he knew there was going to be trouble all the way through Joe's life.

Joe had married a fine girl, his father thought. He ought to do right by her. At the same time, though he himself knew little about psychology, he was convinced in his own mind that whatever trouble Joe found himself in was an outcome of the polio. He and Florence had tried hard to make it up to Joe after he became crippled, but now he felt incumbent on him as a father to continue helping his son to get through his problems no matter how bad they were or how long they lasted.

On the phone Nancy tried to sound calm but there was an unmistakable edge to her voice. "Dad, Joe has been arrested. He's in jail. He wants to know if you can get the money to cover some checks he wrote. I—I hate to tell you this, but . . ."

"Yes, I'll try," Joe Sr. replied wearily. "How much will it take?"

Nancy sighed and a sob escaped her. "Well, it's four thousand five hundred dollars. Joe said—"

Forty-five hundred. Joe Sr.'s face felt as if it had turned to concrete. He was already paying off a $7,500 bank loan from the last time and now . . . Maybe he could go to his friend Frank Betts at the other bank. He never had kept an account there but he could give it a try. "Now, Nancy, don't you worry," he soothed. "I'll get it some place and be up there as quick as I can. You tell Joe to take it easy. We'll get the money paid back and he'll be out of jail."

Joe Sr. dreaded asking the next question but he knew Florence would expect an answer. "Does this mean his job?"

Nancy's voice sounded far away and so alone. "Yes, I'm afraid so. There was a story and his picture in the afternoon newspaper."

He tried to keep the dismay out of his voice. "Well now, Nancy, you just try to get some rest. And don't worry. We'll get the money somehow." Nancy put the phone carefully back on its cradle, her hands shaking from a surge of anger mixed with pity. Poor old man, poor old Dad. It was as though she had just delivered an aging father a death message. Only this message was worse in a way because it did *not* spell the end, it spelled humiliation—contempt, and no doubt pity, from the eyes of friend and stranger alike. That Carl, for instance. Joe had never mentioned him to her. He'd called her just as she had gotten home from the Wilton School.

"Listen, lady, your husband's in jail. What do you want me to do about it?"

Then he had come to the apartment on Cemetery Street, looking for all the world like an undertaker in car-washing clothes. His sad, pudgy face was a study in sympathy, sympathy for a fellow gambler now languishing in the county jail, with just a hint of curiosity as to the grieving wife's reaction.

Nancy admitted him, feeling a rush of gratitude for what he had been willing to do so far. "I do thank you, Mr.—uh—I don't believe you told me your last name."

"Carl, just Carl. Name's Stedd, but nobody calls me anything but Carl."

She swallowed and smiled. "I do thank you, Carl, for getting me on the phone. You see, Joe had these checks—and I guess maybe a deposit didn't get to his account in Beaumont—and—"

Carl was nodding his head in agreement even before she could stammer the lame alibi for Joe. "Yeah. That's what I figured happened. But, see, this D.A. we got. Jeez, what a hard-nosed jerk! He puts the rap on folks, *then* tries to find out the facts. He's one of them guys that truly loves to see people behind bars, lookin' out at the lawmen." Carl apparently decided he was not on the firmest of ground, and waited for Nancy to take the conversational ball from him.

She was one hairline from hysteria. "I know," she said with unnatural calm. "There are people like that . . ."

Carl breathed more easily. "Yeah, sure are. Now, it seems like if Joe's father brings the forty-five hundred and can post another fifteen hundred bail—"

"Oh my! You mean the forty-five hundred won't cover everything?" Nancy had turned white. "I told Joe's dad that was all it would take—" She stared at Carl, her dark eyes desperate.

Carl touched her shoulder anxiously. "Listen, little lady, I thought you knew about the bail . . . Listen, don't cry, now. I can put up the money for that, if the old gentleman can't."

Nancy faced him, feeling wretched for disliking him even a little. "No, no. You mustn't do such a thing. I—think Dad will manage somehow. But I appreciate all you've done." Would he go now? she wondered, wanting nothing so much as to close the door on the world and cry herself sick. Her own parents would have to know. Soon. But before she could steel her nerves for that encounter, she would have to let go with the tears demanding to be wept.

Carl backed toward the door, nodding, even though there was nothing to pin his nods to except Nancy's unspoken agony. What a tragedy this had to happen to Joe. He seemed like such a good guy. Fun. Sharp as a straight-edge razor. A lawyer and all, why didn't he have the goddamn sense not to write hot checks? And those bets! None of the nickel-and-dime stuff for him. Oh no.

Always it was: Carl, can you place two hundred for me on this game or that game? Poor fellow couldn't even pick a winning college basketball game for chrissake. Well, he must be sick . . . it just didn't make any sense to bet the way he did, unless there were big demons riding him. Big demons, and maybe some big debts from the past.

Carl wondered if the Tennessee Gas Transmission Company had looked into Hodges' background, checked him out. Sometimes these big business types are stupider than owner-operators of a luncheonette, he mused wryly. I always get references for my dishwasher and cook, so didn't they for God's sake find out where Hodges had come from? Find out his gambling history, if any.

He would put up the bond money, just as he had said. He knew Joe would appear in court and the bail be returned to him.

Joe sat on a rough bench against the wall of the tank. Jail was hell, all right, less because of the company than the body stench which fought the urinal's odor for supremacy. Heavy chlorine fought both smells, combining with them in a stomach-turning effluvium. Two drunks slumped against each other in one corner among the twelve inmates of Zanesville's palace of incarceration.

Joe sat straight, head held high, eyes on the end of the corridor whence his deliverance would eventually come. If it ever came. The scene was alien, having nothing to do with Joe Hodges, attorney-at-law, native of Beaumont, Texas, and erstwhile legal representative of a large gas company. Damn, if Murphy had only had the common courtesy, *decency*, to call him on the phone—why, he could have convinced him that it was all a big mistake. A deposit that was supposed to have been made for him hadn't arrived in time. It was just that simple. Nothing to get a rash over. Then Joe would have called his father, had him wire the money, and tomorrow it would all be forgotten. But Murphy had called in the cops . . . and Joe Hodges was sitting here in this tank for drunks, crooks, and murderers where he most assuredly did not belong.

Joe was friendly toward the poor slobs beside him. "I'm a lawyer, myself," he hastened to say. This revelation earned Joe instant respect. They wanted to talk and he listened sympathetically, bestowing advice on all who asked.

Finally, a deputy ambled toward the large cell tank and mur-

murs went through the slumped and dispirited group, enlivened by a few obscenities.

"Hodges, step over here. Somebody waiting to see you."

Well, thank the good Lord, Joe breathed silently. It must be Nancy. Too soon for Dad to have arrived.

He searched Nancy's face as she sat primly in the waiting room near the sheriff's desk. Her eyes were bright, but red-rimmed. She wore white cotton gloves and a blue dress sprigged with little white flowers. Her hair was glossy, neatly cut in a short pageboy that framed her pale but expressionless face. There was a little nervous tic in one cheek he had never noticed before.

He felt a stab of acute pain but said briskly, almost cheerfully, "Hi, honey. Now, we haven't got much time—so tell me what's going on!" The old Joe. In command again, and laying it down. He saw the shock run through her body. "Honey—I should have asked how you are. I'm sorry—" He meant it more than his tone implied.

"Never mind, Joe. You're right, we haven't much time for the —amenities. Your father will be here as soon as he can raise the money and get here. I didn't know you would need bail money, so I told him four thousand five hundred dollars. Your friend at the diner, Carl, said he would put up the other." Her voice was cool and firm now, even a little icy, Joe thought.

In a few minutes she was gone. It wasn't a satisfactory conversation, but given the setting and the subject, how satisfactory could he expect it to be? He was relatively at peace now, there in the stinking tank waiting for the day, the happy day when his troubles would all be over. He would pay his debts in full, put money in Nancy's bank account, buy a good house for her, yes, he would surely do that . . . and he could stop worrying about losses. Everything would be wins.

He felt better just thinking about paying off what he owed. It wasn't all that bad . . . maybe $60,000 or $70,000 total. The list showing his debt structure was in his desk drawer at the office, and he frowned. Babe would take care of sending him the other stuff from the desk. Nothing much there he cared about except that list, which he would take with him to the john and go over meticulously. He snorted, imagining what the chief accountant would think if he saw the debt tabulations. Joe knew exactly how much he owed, how much he had paid off, and he rotated the most urgent debts into front position when he won a few thousand. Gamblers are payers, he often told himself. To him paying debts was not only a point of honor but the final spurt of joy that came with a big win.

Jail, while peaceful, was unutterably boring. Joe's restless energy welled up within him, and he looked at the shabby bench where rumpled comic books lay discarded.

A young guy of about twenty sitting near him pulled out a limp deck of cards and looked around to see who might want to play hearts. His eyes met Joe's, then moved away.

Three days later Joe's deadly tranquillity ended. His dad and Nancy were sitting in the sheriff's office when Joe, dressed and shaved, was brought in by a lanky bailiff.

His father was bent over the desk carefully signing papers and didn't see his son enter the room. Nancy ran to him, looking rested, almost smiling. Still, she was awfully quiet, he thought. Carl stood apart, his eyes cool as he nodded at Joe. It was an act of friendship, Carl's putting up the bail. But after all, Carl had taken plenty of cash from Joe these last few months on losing bets. Joe tossed him a brief greeting, not coming undone over Carl's magnanimity because he sensed it was qualified. Then as the elder Hodges finished signing the documents that would free his son, Carl's face changed completely, softening into affection and respect.

"You're a lucky damn man, Joe. Not at betting ball games, but having a dad like you've got. He went around town paying off your bad checks. He even talked Murphy at the bank into getting the D.A. to drop all charges against you so you walk out of here clean. Not many dads that would do that."

"I know, Carl," Joe agreed.

It was over in minutes. Joe drove Nancy's old car to Cemetery Street. "You and Dad go on in and wait for me," he said. "I'm going to sell this car for whatever I can get and we'll go back to Beaumont on the train."

When he returned in a cab an hour later the Mitchells were standing on the step at the door to the apartment. Tom Mitchell heard the taxi stop and yelled, "There he is—we got here in time after all!" He marched toward Joe, his lips drawn tight. Behind him, Mary Mitchell looked as if she was ready to break down doors to get at him.

A deputy sheriff appeared from the side of the garage. "Look here, Hodges. These folks got a lien on your furniture and you ain't moving one stick of it out of town till you pay what you owe the Mitchells."

Joe said nothing, opening the door and motioning them inside. He prayed that by the time they reached the top of the stairs he would have figured out a palatable pacifier for the Mitchells.

As he entered the second-floor apartment he began his plea. "Listen, Tom—I know I owe you two thousand five hundred dollars and I intend to pay it. But—you know what's happened —I can't do it now. But when I—"

Mitchell glowered, ignoring Nancy and Joe's father, who gaped at the visitors in the horror of realization. *It isn't over. Something else is about to happen . . .*

The elder Hodges narrowed his eyes at Mitchell. "What's wrong? What's this all about?"

Mitchell was shouting. "What's it about? It's about money he owes us, and I'm holding the stuff in this dump until it's paid, that's what it's about!" He was breathing hard as if he'd run half a mile to catch up with his quarry.

His father turned to Joe. "You b-borrowed two thousand five hundred dollars from them?"

"Yes. I had to. Last winter. He knows I'll pay it—"

The old man looked down at his hands intently, unseeing. "You'll have your money tomorrow, sir. Now would you leave us alone?"

The Mitchells succumbed to this higher authority and left Joe alone with Nancy and his father.

At last they were on the train from Columbus, Ohio, to Houston. Joe didn't ask his father where he was able to get the money to satisfy the lien. Probably from his Mobil pension plan . . .

Anyway it had come, by wire, and in two days their furniture was packed and on the moving van heading home to Beaumont. On the way home Joe Sr. managed to smile about the devilish snow and driving sleet that had apparently caused his "children" so much trouble the past winter. There'd be none of that in Beaumont, he chortled. Nancy was not smiling at anything, nor was she angry or unresponsive. She was simply quiet.

When the train reached Houston she said, "Joe—I'm going to get off here and see the folks. It's been a while, and Mother insists—"

He looked at her quickly. "Honey, how long do you plan on staying? I thought we'd get right on home to Beaumont and talk about things a little bit."

She pulled on her gloves with care. "I don't really know how long. I—well, I just need some time to think, that's all."

When Nancy hung up the phone after tearfully telling her dad and her mother what had happened in Zanesville, George Hippard's fury was unbounded.

"Frances, this is it! Goddamn fool doesn't deserve a girl like Nancy. I won't have her messed up in a thing like this. Now, you've got to back me up. I called your sister in L.A. this morning and told her you and Nancy would be out there in a few days for a long visit. Tell her you need her to go with you—that you aren't feeling well. Or something. I don't give a damn what you tell her, but see to it that she goes to California with you." He poked the air to emphasize every third word or so, his face flushed, his voice rasping.

Frances agreed with him on all counts, plus others she hadn't discussed with him. Somehow she had the feeling that Joe was not as good a husband as Nancy was a wife. It was a subtle thing—one certainly couldn't flatly ask one's daughter about a subject like sex—but Frances was almost certain she was right. Whatever it was, Joe Hodges cared more for *something else* than he did for his marriage. It wasn't his work. A blind man could see that. Joe wasn't excited about the law. No lights flickered in his eyes as he talked about his meager caseload.

Frances doubted that it could be another woman. Foolishness! Joe very obviously loved her daughter, enjoyed her company—

no, there was a siren wooing Joe that none of them had identified or recognized. What could it be? Or who?

Her daughter had made some mention—very little—of gambling. An occasional glancing reference to betting on a team, or the odds in a dice game. Such things. Frances understood nothing of sports, much less gambling, and had paid no attention. But now . . . Zanesville.

Nancy's voice had been tight, stricken, as she explained over the phone that Joe had lost money gambling. Checks that "couldn't be covered in time"—her mother didn't understand that very well either. One could always get money into a bank account. But Joe had lost his job, been thrown in jail, and his father had been obliged to fly to Ohio with money for restitution. Yes, Frances had felt for a year or more that Nancy had not married well. Now it was time to speak out about Joe, insist that Nancy get a divorce and reconstruct her life while she was still young and attractive. She wanted children—they didn't really think Joe cared whether he had an heir or not—but who would wish a jailbird father on any child!

George Hippard peered out the front window waiting for Nancy's taxi to arrive. Turning back to his wife, he said, "Now don't forget. You *need* her to be with you for a while. Then, after a few months out in the sunshine, in L.A., we'll see. We'll see."

Frances looked up at him from her needlepoint. She was not an intellectual woman but she was canny. She had never liked Joe, nor stood up for him when she and George discussed their son-in-law. "Yes, I hear you. This time I think she'll see it our way," she said quietly, waiting for George to calm himself. If he blurted out his feelings to Nancy, she would like as not turn around and go back to Joe.

He shook his head slowly, almost in sorrow. "Damn fool . . . a likable cuss, too. Got everything and doesn't know it. You know what I think? I think he's substituting *gambling* on baseball and football and stuff, for playing." Hippard scratched his thinning gray hair absently. "Yeah, he can't play those things on account of his game leg. So it makes sense that he's learned every batting average, every major league player's record and—"

Frances tossed her needlework aside impatiently. "Oh, George, I'm not sure we can figure it out so let's stop trying."

When Nancy got home she fought with herself to keep from crying. She did not want to break down. "It was so—so awful. I feel lost . . . ." Her parents nodded to each other above their daughter's head.

There would be no trouble getting Nancy to go to California.

Joe and his father took the bus to Beaumont later that afternoon.

The older man lapsed into reverie, watching Houston's spring-green trees, flower patches, and long, low industrial buildings slide by the window. The exhilaration of the last four days had buoyed him during the train trip from Columbus, but now the heavy humid air of the Gulf put a pall upon his spirit. His moment of triumph had ended. He had gone to the rescue of his only child, only son. Now it was over. The Mobil plant awaited Joe Henry Hodges, Sr. Daily lunches gulped from the scratched tin box with its mended handle. The same conversations, all without meaning. Just the grinding dullness of the job ahead. Wearily he turned to Joe. "Didn't you think—wasn't Nancy awful quiet when she said goodbye?"

Watching Joe's troubled frown he regretted saying it. No use making things any worse than they were. Anyway, God knows, she had a right to feel let down, he thought. A wave of anger swept through him. There ought to be some way of getting Joe to play fair with his wife, with himself and Florence, for that matter. He thought of his wife still teaching school. If it keeps on, we'll never have two dimes to rub together.

Joe straightened in the mohair seat, shifting his left leg slightly. It always ached when he was under stress, but until now he hadn't thought about it. "Well, I don't know," he said. "Maybe just tired. And she hasn't seen her folks since Christmas. If she wants to stay a few days in Houston, what's wrong with that?"

Joe's father touched his arm apologetically. They never touched each other except to shake hands, and the unusual gesture surprised them both. "I didn't mean that anything was wrong, exactly. She just seemed—quiet."

Joe resumed reading the *Chronicle* he had bought at the station. "No. Nothing's wrong. Nancy is just tired. Maybe a little homesick . . ."

Nancy and Frances Hippard left for California three days later with new summer clothes, new luggage, and new hairdos. Mr. Hippard drove them to the airport in the gayest mood he had exhibited for months, tucking four $50 bills into his daughter's purse when he got there. "Take care of your mother now." And they were gone.

CHAPTER 14

Nancy Hodges was now firmly under her parents' control. In Beaumont, Joe went to a friend of his who sang in the choir and was with the Lincoln Life Insurance Company, and arranged to sell insurance on a commission basis. He hit on opening up the Negro market and soon was earning up to $2,000 a month in the insurance business. By now his gambling had ebbed considerably, perhaps to an occasional $50 bet. He was still a lawyer but now preferred to concentrate on insurance.

Selling insurance, however, became increasingly irksome, chiefly because people didn't come to his office, he had to go to them. He went out to the Mobil plant where his father labored and sold insurance to the employees; in the evening, when people were home from work, he made calls on husbands and wives. He was selling a good product and up to a point he was content. He was also bored.

When Nancy came back from her trip to California with her mother, Joe began opening a dialogue with her. Since George and Frances kept her on a tight leash, she had to sneak out to visit with him. Finally, now that Joe was no longer gambling and was doing well selling insurance, Nancy agreed to come back to him. Although there was no formal agreement reached, a tacit understanding had been arrived at that Joe would stop gambling.

The understanding was soon betrayed. Once Nancy had returned to him and they had rented a new apartment and got their furniture out of storage, Joe found himself slowly slipping back into the old pattern of gambling and borrowing to support the habit. He was like a swimmer who has just made the shore only to be sucked into the water again by the strong undertow of the receding tide.

Joe's old creditors in Beaumont were constantly confronting him, and soon after Nancy came back he realized he would have to get away once more, at least until he paid substantial sums against his debts. He was still betting through his friend Sammy Coco, and that was another trap he hoped to elude by getting out of town.

He had heard that Union Oil Company of California might be looking for young lawyers to secure oil leases. The company had offices in Midland, Texas, and he made the long drive there for an interview on a Thursday morning. Without checking on his background, the land development department of Union Oil hired Joe at a salary of $1,000 a month plus an expense account, starting Friday morning. Joe asked if he could start on Monday and was told he could.

On Thursday he checked into the Scarborough Hotel, found a first-floor apartment in a dingy row of flats for $200 a month, paid a month's rent to begin on Monday, and called Nancy. She was happy to hear of his new job away from the temptations of the raffish gambling element which, as she now knew, had taken such a hold of his life and agreed to take the bus to Midland the following Monday.

Also on Thursday, Joe found the local domino hall where he met a hulking, bald bookmaker known as Egghead.

Then on Friday he did something he'd been thinking of doing for several years. He went to Las Vegas. There were no nonstop flights and it took him seven hours to make the trip. He had seen advertisements for the Riviera Hotel, so from McCarran Airport he had the cab take him there. He checked into a room, then went straight to the casino, poised, tense, on the edge of power, insurance policies and oil leases wiped from his mind. He began playing craps, his favorite game, pulling the bills out one by one. He played conservatively—he knew the game well—and babied his bills, keeping mental track of how many were left in his pocket as he went along.

At six in the morning he pulled out his last $100 bill. By now he had lost $1,100. But he'd lost it slowly and was still in the game. Within forty-five minutes he had run his last $100 bill up to a rack of chips which he cashed in for $5,600. With this win Joe hit a new high, one he would never cease trying to recapture. He had entered the whirlpool, he had beaten the odds, he was straight with himself and as good as straight with the world. The shabby events of the past fell away and were as though they had never existed. His take-home bankroll was $4,400 more than he had arrived with.

Between seven and eleven in the morning, after he had put his money safely in his pocket, Joe watched a suave well-dressed gambler playing at a crap table alone. The house will, on occasion, allow a player to have a crap table all to himself. As Joe watched the dude play he noticed that he was betting against himself. Thus when he crapped out, or after throwing a six got a seven before another six, betting himself to lose, he picked up the chips. In the time Joe watched, the gambler won $178,000. This made an indelible impression upon him. It showed him what could be done in Las Vegas.

After going upstairs, cleaning up, resting for a while, Joe went over to the Desert Inn. Gordon MacRae, one of his favorite entertainers, was featured, and Joe looked forward to the big show. So far he'd seen nothing but the casino at the Riviera in the twelve hours he had been in town. The matinee was scheduled for two-thirty.

Half an hour before the show he wandered up to a crap table. He watched a player step up and throw the dice. Joe bet $100 that the player would lose. The shooter missed and Joe won. He decided to continue playing the "don't" line and, shocked, watched the next shooter make thirteen passes in a row. In thirty minutes Joe lost the entire bankroll of $5,600.

This was the end of his first trip to Las Vegas. He forgot the show and, leaden-hearted, went back to the Riviera where he had just enough money to pay his room and cab fare to the airport.

He arrived back in Midland on Saturday night, brooding over his loss. Vaguely he wondered if his mother and father and Nancy were right when they said he was sick. To please his parents he had gone to two psychiatrists when things were at their worst in Beaumont before Zanesville, but he had put the unpleasant memories out of his mind. The second psychiatrist, Dr. Graves, was with the State Department of Health. After forty minutes of consultation he had agreed with Dr. Titus Harris that there was absolutely nothing psychiatrically wrong with Joe. His problems were based on stupidity and greed.

During the short meeting Graves displayed an attitude toward Joe that seemed close to sheer disgust. He said Joe cared nothing about his mother and father, or others generally. The only satisfaction Joe got from paying the doctor's fee was that he had been certified not mentally ill. Just greedy, stupid, inconsiderate, and unwholesome.

On Sunday morning Joe found his footsteps leading him inexorably back to the domino hall. Egghead was there, and after some preliminary conversation Joe asked the bookmaker if he could make some bets on the day's baseball games around the country.

"Sure, kid," Egghead agreed. "How much cash you got to bet?"

"I start work tomorrow for Union Oil," Joe said. "I've got a couple of thousand dollars my wife's bringing in on Monday and I'll have the money by ten a.m. if I lose," he lied.

Egghead shrugged. "Okay, I'll take your action, kid. But I'll be calling it into Cincinnati and if you lose I gotta have the money first thing Monday morning. You hear, now?"

Joe knew he wouldn't lose. "I'll have it," he assured the formidable-looking bookie. He bet $3,000 on an elaborate series of baseball parlays which could win him over $23,000 if his teams came through.

That afternoon he sweated out the games on the ticker tape in the domino hall and, as Egghead gleefully followed the results, lost every bet. "I'll be around to see you at ten tomorrow morning at the hotel," Egghead reminded him when he finally left the hall. "You better be there with the money," he added menacingly.

At 8 A.M. Joe reported for duty at Union Oil's offices and was given a briefing on the oil leases and mineral rights the company was trying to acquire. At ten he left the office to meet Egghead in his hotel room. He didn't have the money, of course, and didn't want to meet the bookie but he was afraid not to. He would have to give him some story to hold him until he could raise the money to pay off.

Egghead was waiting in the lobby with a sullen companion and they followed Joe up to his room.

"Look, I don't have the money right now," Joe began, "but I'll get it in a few days."

"I told you, kid," Egghead roared, "I called that bet in to Cincinnati and I have to get them the money like *now!*"

"I'll have it this week, maybe even—"

A sudden ham-fisted blow to the side of his head abruptly terminated Joe's excuse and another shot to the face broke his glasses, the glass grinding into his cheeks under the blow. Then the bookie's goon hit him in the stomach, bending him over, and another jolting blow to the side of his face laid him on the floor of the hotel, gasping for air, trying to brush the glass from his face and eyes.

Balefully Egghead stared down at him. "That's just a sample. We don't get the money quick we'll kill you, and mess up that wife of yours while we're at it."

With that Egghead and his enforcer stalked out of the room. It was some time before Joe could stand up and go into the bathroom. He washed the blood from his face, retching as he leaned against the sink. There wasn't much time to clean up, change from the blood-streaked shirt and suit into fresh clothes, and get back to the office.

Joe explained to his new boss that he had clumsily tripped on the curb of a sidewalk and fallen down, breaking his glasses and scraping his face. His limp gave the story credibility. Union Oil would have a special assignment for him the next day, he was told.

Joe met Nancy at the bus stop. She had two big suitcases of clothing and also a television set, ready to make a home for them out of the dingy apartment. Despite the surroundings the young couple were happy to be reunited and laying the foundation for a new life for Joe.

On Tuesday morning at the office Joe received the not unwelcome news that they were sending him for ten days to Roswell,

New Mexico, to acquire oil leases throughout that area. It would be a relief to get away from Egghead, he thought, although poor Nancy, just arriving at Midland, would now have to shuttle off to Roswell and some motel.

On Wednesday, Joe and Nancy drove to Roswell and Joe reported to the field office where he was given maps and charts and the names of the landholders with whom he would negotiate. They found a motel and once again settled into strange surroundings. Nancy had determined she was going to stand by Joe, be supportive and make their marriage work.

Joe, for his part, tried to shield her from his worries about Egghead. At some point he would have to go back to Midland and face the brutish bookmaker. He had to pay off. He was sick at the thought of anything happening to Nancy. There was only one answer.

He went to Western Union and wired Sammy Coco in Beaumont most of the money he had been given in advance by the company, placing bets on a baseball parlay. The next morning the sports pages told him the dismal story. He had lost. Before his first negotiation of the day he stopped by the local dry goods store, introduced himself and cashed a hot check for $400. He immediately went to Western Union and wired the money to Sammy Coco with his bets on the games that day. In the afternoon he went to the grocery store and cashed another check, for $250. His appearance and story were credible. He was a lawyer on assignment to Union Oil and the company hadn't paid him yet.

Each day he sweated out the results of the games. He was in a dire losing streak. The disastrous cycle had caught him again. He had to keep cashing hot checks with local merchants, wiring the money to Sammy and sweating out the results of his bets. It wasn't Egghead worrying him now. It was the need to pay back the druggist, the grocer, the clothier, and the others before the checks came back. In nine days, while negotiating the local oil leases, he had exhausted all the possibilities of cashing checks and was desperately contemplating his next move.

A sharp series of knocks at the door to their motel room startled Nancy and Joe just after he had come in from the field office. Joe opened the door and found himself staring at two uniformed sheriff's deputies. He was under arrest for cashing hot checks.

Nancy struggled to hold back the tears of fear and dismay. Joe was brusquely taken from the motel room to the local jail, leaving her alone, with no money and nowhere to turn for help.

"You'd better call Dad," he said hoarsely as he was hustled away.

Sitting in the Roswell jail Joe was helpless. He had to depend on Nancy and his father again. The psychic pain that assailed him this time was unbearable. And there was nothing he could do to relieve it. He could only wait.

As before, Joe Henry Hodges, Sr., was forced to contact his friends and the retirement fund at Mobil Oil after Nancy's despairing call. Nancy determined that there was a total of $5,000 in bad checks with the merchants of Roswell and she hired a local lawyer, Glen Stiff, to represent her husband. It was the second severe shock she had undergone in a short space of time, just when she was recovering from the Zanesville catastrophe.

Joe Sr. duly arrived in Roswell with the $5,000. He paid back all the merchants and hoped that making restitution would save Joe once again from prosecution. But this time it didn't.

The local district attorney put him on trial. As a lawyer Joe faced the prospect of prison and certain disbarment. But he pulled himself together and strode into the courtroom proud and strong, determined to fight it out. With Nancy, his father, and Glen Stiff beside him, he pleaded guilty to illegally taking the $5,000 but stressed the fact that he had already repaid the money. This seemed to impress the judge. But then the words rang out: "I sentence you to five years imprisonment." Joe swayed as the judge paused and went on. "I suspend the sentence because you made restitution." Then the judge reached for his gavel and was about to conclude the case when Joe jumped to his feet.

"Your Honor, may it please the court—*you can't do that!*"

The judge, the stenographer, the bailiff, the deputies, and Glen Stiff, who had argued for his client manfully, all stared in astonishment as Joe told the judge, in the most polite terms, why he could not do what he was doing. Joe explained to the hushed court that any sentence at all would cause him to be disbarred automatically. He was an attorney; the practice of law was his livelihood which would be taken away if this sentence were allowed to stand.

He then launched into an impassioned explanation of all that the law meant to him and what losing his profession would do to him and his family. His words had wings. He spoke of how he had studied law as a youth, dilated on his work in law school and his admiration for the profession. He pointed out that under the law even a bankrupt man may not be forced to lose the means of his livelihood. "You cannot take away the tools of a carpenter or the brushes of a painter; he needs them to live and the law understands that."

Joe asked the judge to understand and realize that his tools as a lawyer were dear to him. He acknowledged that his gambling was a problem, a problem with which he must inevitably cope. But the money had been repaid. And he had spent several days in jail which, he respectfully assured the court, did constitute additional punishment. For all these reasons, he declared, he hoped the court could see its way clear to letting him keep his livelihood. This he asked for himself and his family.

Glen Stiff was openmouthed at Joe's effrontery. He could have been sent to prison for five years. He was getting a suspended sentence and yet he was complaining and appealing. It was daring or lunatic, his lawyer could not decide which.

The judge seemed to find the logic compelling. The law did not wish to take away a man's profession and make him and his family wards of the state. Nor did the law wish to punish a man who was trying to rehabilitate himself rapidly. With a certain amount of malaise the judge reversed himself. He turned to the court stenographer and told her to strike both the sentence and the suspension. Because of the restitution, he pronounced, the case was dismissed.

Outside the courtroom Joe Hodges, Sr., pulled a handful of quarters from his pocket and walked over to a phone booth. It was hot and he mopped his brow with a handkerchief as he fed the change into the box. Finally he got through.

"I got him out, Babe. He's okay," old Joe said to Florence. "I'll be back home soon as I can make plane connections."

After hanging up he turned to his son. "Have you got any money, son?"

Joe shook his head. Speech was too painful.

His father reached into a pocket and pulled out some bills. "Here's fifty dollars. It's about all I've got. Go on, take it. You and Nancy will need it," he added when Joe hesitated to reach for the folded bills. Joe nodded and took the money. He and Nancy watched as the old man wearily climbed into a taxi for the start of his arduous plane-hopping journey back to Beaumont.

There was no need to check in with the field office of Union Oil. Joe knew he was fired. He and Nancy drove from Roswell back to Midland where they rented a U-Haul trailer and returned to the apartment which they had used for such a ridiculously short time. Still there was the television set and all the possessions Nancy and Joe had brought to Midland. If he had given the situation more thought, Joe realized, he wouldn't have bothered to go to Midland, but at the moment their meager wardrobes and the TV seemed important.

They drove the old car and trailer around to the back of the apartment, and by now it was night. Nancy at first didn't understand why Joe wouldn't turn on the lights. They packed their things in the dark.

Suddenly a thunderous pounding on the door shook the whole apartment. In terror Nancy threw her arms around Joe and he held her tightly to him.

"We know you're in there, Hodges," Egghead was shouting. Joe thanked the Lord he had parked his car in the lot behind. "We'll stay here until you open up," he yelled. Nancy looked at Joe in horror but he shook his head, gently placing his fingers over his mouth. "You better let us in, Hodges!" Then, after five minutes of hammering and obscene epithets, the noises stopped.

"The sonofabitch will be back," they heard Egghead cry to the goon with him. "And so will we."

Nancy shook and trembled in Joe's arms as they waited five, then ten minutes before hurriedly finishing their packing, slipping out the back door and filling up the trailer with their possessions.

In the dead of night they cautiously drove out of the parking lot and soon were on the road—for where they didn't know, and it didn't matter. They were leaving Roswell, Midland, and Egghead behind. They had made their getaway and were floating down the highway with $56 between them, Joe feeling lucky to be alive. As for the gambling, it was over. Joe had lost all desire to make another bet.

CHAPTER 15

At first they merely drove through the night following the highway east. Then Joe began to formulate a plan. They had to find some direction in life, starting now. He saw a road sign shoot by, reflected in his bright beam: Dallas 254 miles.

"Let's give the Big D a whirl, Nancy," he suggested.

"Whatever you think, Joe," she acquiesced.

"It's straight ahead. Might as well. We should get there before dawn."

All through the night Joe drove, Nancy dozing fitfully beside him, and finally came to a motel on the outskirts of Dallas. Wearily they checked in, not bothering to take anything but essentials out of the car, and before sunrise they were asleep. After a few hours rest Joe woke up and calmly prepared to find a job. They didn't have much time for him to start making money.

Nancy brought in Joe's best blue vested suit from the car, brushed and pressed it with her portable iron, and laid out his best white shirt and pale tie. When Joe, resplendent in his finest wardrobe selection, was ready to go out and seek their fortune, Nancy kissed him and wished him good luck. She had been badly jarred by the episode at the apartment but by now she had recaptured something of her normal resilience.

Wearing a confident smile and carrying his briefcase full of résumés, Joe caught a bus downtown to the office of the County Bar Association in the Dallas courthouse. If he had worries or self-doubts, they didn't show as he introduced himself to the chief clerk, a relaxed, friendly man in his late sixties.

"I'm Joe Henry Hodges from Beaumont," he announced, handing his Texas Bar Association card and his business card to the clerk. "My wife and I have decided we'd like to move up north to Dallas and I thought you might know a firm looking for a lawyer with wide general experience."

The clerk looked through his files, trying to be helpful yet apologetic because he had no openings listed. Then, as if as an afterthought, he turned to an elderly lady seated behind a desk.

"Myrtle, wasn't there something came through a couple of days ago?"

"Irving," the woman called back.

The clerk turned to Joe. "Oh yes. Seems that out in Irving they're looking for a city attorney, or were last time we heard."

"Where is Irving?" Joe asked.

"The town between Dallas and Fort Worth. It's only about twelve miles from here. Why don't you go over and check the town hall? The job might still be open."

Joe asked directions and was told where to catch a bus to Irving. He went over to the terminal and bought a ticket, paying out three precious dollars. In Irving nobody in the sleepy town hall seemed to know about the job opening and all said that only the mayor, Dr. Paul Laird, could help. Joe found a telephone booth, looked through the Irving yellow pages under lawyers and found the name Adrian Carter whose office he called. The attorney sounded affable over the phone and invited Joe to walk over to his office and discuss the possibilities of the city attorney job with him. Maybe he could help.

Joe found Adrian Carter a genial young lawyer, a few years younger than himself, with considerable knowledge of the local scene. An immediate rapport sprang up between them and the Irving lawyer suggested that Joe just go on over to Mayor Laird's office, introduce himself and ask for the job.

"Paul's a fine doctor and damn good mayor," Adrian asserted. "He'll be glad to see you. Not much older than me, in his mid-thirties I'd guess. Solid type, you know. No funny business with him." Adrian grinned broadly at the lithe, full-bosomed young redhead sitting at a desk in his office. "That right, Dotty?"

"I wouldn't know, Adrian," she smiled back. Joe instantly

sensed that Adrian and his secretary had a relationship that transcended office work.

"You go see Paul, and call me, let me know how it comes out." He handed Joe his card and scribbled a number on it. "Most likely I'll be here late tonight. If not, here's my home number."

Mayor Paul Laird was not at his office as it was Wednesday and his day off. Joe caught a taxi to his home and found him outside his comfortable-looking bungalow, standing barefoot in the driveway washing his car, old khaki pants rolled up above his ankles. Joe walked up to the young doctor and stuck out his hand.

"I heard you were looking for a city attorney and I took a chance you'd talk to me at home." He paused. Then: "Of course, if it's not convenient I could come back tomorrow. My wife and I are staying in Dallas." The mayor was surprised. Usually people saw him only by appointment, but now this husky young man was standing in front of him and shaking hands and asking about the new position with no formality whatever.

Laird laughed and invited Joe into the house where they drank iced tea and talked. The mayor was impressed by the Phi Beta Kappa on Joe's résumé and taken with the spark in the young lawyer's eye. On an impulse he decided he would convene a special meeting of the city council immediately. He put out the phone calls and within forty minutes the various members of the council filed into the mayor's living room to meet Joe. They went over his credentials and ideas and talked with him, laughed with him, joked with him. All the while they seemed to be scrutinizing him searchingly.

Joe knew he had to impress them sufficiently so that they would not bother to verify his references and thus learn about the hot checks and the trial, or get wind of his general reputation. That would end any chance of landing the job. So he talked earnestly, occasionally joking, going over his qualifications and asking questions about the new position.

After an hour they sent Joe from the room so they could debate his merits. He went into the kitchen and pulled out a cigarette. He felt hoarse and weary but confident about the decision. The mayor's wife, a lovely and understanding woman, came out to the kitchen to ease his tension by offering him more tea or coffee, but he declined. He wanted the job so badly he could hardly speak to her.

After what seemed many hours but in reality was no more than ten minutes, the mayor came around the corner of the kitchen entrance and invited him back to the meeting. "It seems you are the new city attorney of Irving, Mr. Hodges." He smiled warmly. "Can you start Monday?"

Within days Joe was being introduced all over town as the new city attorney. Nancy was proud of his rehabilitation. One night they were hiding inside their darkened home while gangsters pounded the door trying to collect their gambling debts, and two days later he was socially reinstated, the new city attorney of Irving, Texas. He had a respectable salary, he had a good position, he had his life in order—all within the space of forty-eight hours. It was a *tour de force*. Last week he was facing prison and disbarment. This week he was on the right side of the law and carving his place in his community. It was more than impressive, it was phenomenal. The newspapers were carrying photographs and articles about him and everyone seemed impressed.

There was a near-tragedy when some well-informed crank wrote an unsigned letter to the city council suggesting that they look more carefully into the past record of Joe H. Hodges because in it they would find an interesting tale of bad checks, embezzlements, and a trial.

The members of the council panicked and called an emergency meeting. They were frantic, wondering whether they were responsible for bringing a criminal into a position of power in the city government.

Joe asked to be permitted to come talk to them and naturally they allowed it. It was a tense situation but he decided on a brazen approach. He felt he could bring out the best in them and he made a try at it. He told the council members that the charges were true but added that he was repaying all his debts. He noted that he had gone to trial but that the case had been dismissed.

All this was in the past, he avowed, a dusty memory and nothing more. The debts were being taken care of, the work he was doing for the council was proceeding well; he felt pleased with the work and honored by their trust. He intended to live up to it, he said, provided that they gave him the chance.

He stood up well to their icy stares, their protestations at being deceived, their suspicions. He was so calm and friendly they found it impossible to consider him evil; they couldn't imagine that he would betray their hopes in him. Toward the end of the meeting one of the members asked him politely why he had not warned them about his previous gambling. Why had he not told them when he applied for the job that he had that on his record?

"Let me put it this way, sir," Joe replied, making a last attempt to dispel the tension and bring an air of levity to the proceedings. "If Marilyn Monroe asked you to make love to her, would you then stand up and announce that you weren't that good at making love?" Everyone laughed and admitted that he would not.

After forty minutes of exchanges Joe realized he was winning. The councilmen were relaxing, leaning back in their chairs. Joe reassured them again that the gambling debts were being paid. Someone began smoking a cigar and he offered one to Joe. Interrogation gave way to discussion. Before the hour was out he was free of all investigation. He ended by declaring he was certain everything would work out well for all of them.

This was a great victory, second only to getting the job in the first instance. It reassured Joe as much as the first accomplishment had. On the other hand, it may have brought him dangerously close to complacency.

After almost two years of making himself part of the community, establishing a Sunday school class, singing in the choir, forging strong relationships with the prominent local citizens and a close personal and professional one with Adrian Carter, Joe was in firm control of his life.

Nancy enjoyed teaching school, and as respected members of the community she and Joe were intimately involved in the mainstream of life not only in Irving but in Dallas where Joe was increasingly working with law firms and banks in transacting the city's business. For the burgeoning city it was a time of tranquillity, and so it was for Joe. Both the senior Hodgeses and the Hippards visited the contented couple, rejoicing in the new life they had made for themselves. Yet Joe did not forget the past. Every two weeks, when his paycheck came in, he sent out as much money as he could afford to repay the old debts. First it would be checks to Beaumont, then to Midland, then to Zanesville as he steadily made restitution.

For Joe that other, painful era of his life was over. Making good his debts helped reinforce his resolve never to let the destructive personality that lurked within him reassert itself. Nancy thought of this two-year period as the happiest of their lives.

The gambling began again innocently. It started with no intent on Joe's part to harm anyone or change his status quo. One of his business acquaintances, Al Kramer, asked him if he shot craps. Vaguely, as if he were answering from across a great distance, Joe answered that sometimes he did shoot craps. If he were interested, Al suggested, there was an afternoon game that went on in a parked van at a nearby construction site.

It was described merely as "a friendly game" and Joe went off to observe it more out of curiosity than anything. He was certain there was no harm in doing so. He had so little money on him that he could not lose much, if indeed he decided to play. And there was the possibility that he would just watch and not venture to join the fray. Besides, there was no pressing work at the office, only a mass of ordinances and regulations and zoning restrictions that he could go through the next day. The afternoon was bare of interest or challenge.

Later, when he would think back to that day, he speculated that it was his need of challenge that prompted him to go to the game; but he discerned another element, the one that had led to the downfall of the ancient Greeks, namely hubris. He had been too sure that he would not renew his gambling cycle, too convinced that this was only going to be an isolated and friendly game. After all, for twenty months he hadn't even contemplated so much as a friendly wager or the purchase of a charity lottery ticket.

Joe entered the smoke-filled van to find a circle of men playing around a makeshift table amid much laughter, groaning, and gnashing of teeth. The names were reeled off as he was introduced. There was Everett Veech, Tide Ole, Hank Larson, Idus P. Ash, Sid Wright, and Joe Butcher. Joe was introduced as the city attorney of Irving and they all nodded pleasantly. Then he moved up to the table.

It was the return of the old days the moment he picked up the dice. It was an incipient surge of power and glory that harked back to his youth. It was like the period before he contracted polio and could play baseball. It was like the time he was going out with lovely Genie Betts before he mysteriously sabotaged their relationship and sent her away. It was like the days when he felt his parents were proud of him. He had the old assurance that his wishes were orders. If he wanted a six then the dice would come up six. If he wanted an eight the dice would come up eight. All that he desired was available simply because he desired it.

When he walked out of the game that evening his pockets were crammed with money and the other players were in a daze. He was hard put to conceal the high that this victory gave him and he remembered how his previous wins had always seemed to authenticate him as a person. An exhilaration, a feeling of *physical* invincibility that few people experience or can understand swept him up and lifted him to the top of Mount Olympus.

Someone called after him to please come back soon and another voice laughed, "Not too soon!" Joe struggled to temper his joy. He had cleaned them out. As he eased himself into the seat of his car he began unloading his pockets. They were stuffed with \$5, \$10, and \$20 bills. He counted them all and found the total was some \$1,020. It was a magnificent win, it brought in extra money at a time when he needed it (or believed he needed it), and in its sinister way it proved to him that he had nothing to fear from a harmless bit of crap shooting. After all, he had won, had he not? There was no danger in that.

When Kramer phoned to ask Joe if he'd like to shoot again the following day, Joe tried to conceal his delight.

"My God, d'you guys play *every* day?" His laugh boomed over the phone, giving him a chance to cover his excitement. "Yeah," he said, "I'll stop around. That is, if I get through some stuff here in the office."

In truth he had been busy that morning, but not on the city's affairs. After depositing all but $300 of his winnings from the day before, Joe experienced the second emotional explosion of the big win as he made payments on debts in Midland and Zanesville, with accompanying notes to his friends. He still had a debt structure of $35,000 remaining in Beaumont, but nobody was rushing him on that, and he was paying on it with regularity.

The ability to pay off loans from friends was in fact the ultimate emotional high for Joe. Gamblers are payers, he told himself, and he relished repaying even more than he did winning.

So, driving to the seedy motel where today's game was going on, he felt a swell of triumph equaled only by the long-past baseball parlay in Beaumont when he won sixteen thousand dollars from the bookie Venza. He breathed deeply, and every now and then laughed aloud. With the men he would be playing with, he thought, another win was a cinch. Any time he was matched against ordinary doctors, dentists, plumbers, or whatever, Joe knew he could outmanage them. And he fully intended to do it again today.

Hank and Tide were there, a little sullen, but eagerly awaiting Joe's arrival. Both men could walk into the Irving Trust in Dallas and borrow $100,000 on their own names. Forget the collateral, they were good for it. But let them lose a few hundred in a crap game? They sulked.

Joe was right. He won another $1,300 within an hour and, accurately assessing the situation—the money around the table was getting thin and it wouldn't be long until somebody was borrowing—he said gaily, "So long, be seeing you fellows."

Again, that exquisite joy as he wrote more checks, clearing more personal loans. Not all, of course, but enough to substitute a sense of relief for the guilt that nagged at him. He was experiencing expiation of a sort. I'm not a bum, not a thief, not a con man. I hate myself less today than yesterday. Tomorrow will be better. He did not repay his father. The blood tie was of course a stronger, deeper commitment than the tie made to a casual acquaintance, but his father was a fixed figure in his life, unchanging, always there. When he made a real score, his dad would get it all back. And much much more. Meanwhile Joe needed to nurse his tiny bankroll against the next gambling situation. Without it he felt naked, vulnerable, helpless if opportunity presented itself.

Opportunity was not long in coming.

Kramer phoned again. "Listen, lawyer, I got a real game going this afternoon. One you hadn't ought to miss . . . How about it?"

When Joe arrived, he couldn't believe his good fortune. Only Hank and Tide and Idus and Sid were familiar faces from the other winning days, and the six men lounging around a smartly appointed table were a different sort, shabbier-looking, apparently easy marks.

Buddy Bramlet sat at the end of the table and appeared to be inebriated, almost hidden by a rumpled stack of $20s and $50s, barely missing the heap with his cigarette which dangled alarmingly in his fingers. As Joe entered and introductions were mumbled, Buddy scooped another riffle of money toward himself, giggling foolishly. "Oh—did I win?"

Kramer wasn't playing, but Joe thought nothing of it, concentrating on the business at hand. This ought to be fast and fun, and very rewarding.

Thirty minutes later Joe was broke. True, he'd thrown a few wins, but somehow at the crucial play the dice seemed to roll over on command, blanking him out just as a huge win looked possible.

"I guess I'm through," he muttered, sweating over the loss of his $400 bankroll. It was just bad luck, he told himself. His fingers had run over the edges of the dice to verify their sharpness. Nothing wrong. Couldn't be. Just a tough break.

Sid looked up, his face bland. "You need some money?" It struck Joe that this offer was out of character for Sid. They hardly knew each other, and Sid guarded his cash as a violinist guarded his bow arm.

Buddy Bramlet reached to the floor and hoisted his bottle of bourbon, taking a four-gulp swig. "Come on, let's get the show on the road!" he mumbled, shaking the dice in an extravagant gesture, muttering imprecations as he prepared to throw.

Joe quickly took the $500 Sid offered him. Then another $500 and another. At the end of the game he was $3,500 down. He couldn't wait to leave. His clothes reeked of perspiration and defeat. "Sid, I'll see you first thing Monday morning. Okay?"

Sid nodded impassively.

Bolstered by Dr. Jekyll's position as city attorney, Joe's Mr. Hyde had no trouble borrowing from two banks in Dallas. So with $4,000 in hand, Joe met his creditor at the domino hall and handed it over without a word. Sid grinned. "You kinda took a bath there, didn't you, lawyer? Jeez, from the way you was going Wednesday and Thursday, I figured you'd really clean old Buddy out. Him drunk and all . . ."

At least Joe had found the right way to borrow from banks. No more installment payments. Much better to take out ninety-day paper. He knew he could win back more than enough to pay off in that length of time, so why shackle himself with regular tabs that ate away his salary?

There were moments of anxiety and depression in the next few days, but Joe quickly confronted his own position. Confidence—that was his bulwark. Knowing and believing that the next bet would be a winner—that was his straw in the maelstrom of mounting debt.

Joe, as he had before in Beaumont, in Zanesville, and in Midland-Roswell, gravitated toward the gamblers and grifters as well as to the civic leaders and staunch citizens and churchgoers. Adrian Carter had to go to the city attorney frequently on behalf of his clients, and he and Joe became fast friends. Adrian was a man of magnetic charm, vital, entertaining, the kind of man who can tell a risqué joke in front of women and get away with it. Although, as Joe suspected from the first, he was a dedicated womanizer, he also maintained a solid home life and Joe and Nancy were frequent guests at his house.

Idus Ash and Sid Wright were gambling companions with whom Joe shot craps, played occasional card games, and bet on sports events.

Joe discovered a crap game in Arlington, a town beyond Irving toward Fort Worth, and went to great lengths to meet Boston Smith, a courtly old gentlemen with a thick thatch of white hair who made book at the Fort Worth stockyards. Boston was known as the most honorable (and the biggest) bookmaker in Texas and he only accepted bets from men he knew and trusted. To become a client of Boston Smith was considered quite an accomplishment among the gamblers in any part of Texas.

Each day Joe sat in on various games and placed bets on baseball as the season opened. He increased his bets, even playing moon for high stakes—and kept losing.

He played gin with Buddy Bramlet and never seemed able to beat him. Buddy ran a fish market and sold the best bait in Irving, his reputation with the serious fishermen to whom he supplied minnows being as solid as it was with the gamblers. But Buddy was not really serious about selling catfish and bait; it was more hobby than means of livelihood. His real money came from gambling, though he was neither a professional nor a compulsive gambler. It was a consuming occupation, not a consuming drive.

The fish market, so called, kept him in touch with the kind of men he liked, and it was a headquarters—a place where he could be reached. Behind the front section was a comfortable office which would accommodate gin rummy games—Buddy's specialty—or whatever kind of gambling the occasion called for.

Two or three times a week Joe would pump up $600 or better and bring it to Buddy Bramlet's fish market where they played gin in the back room. After Joe had lost his cash, Buddy continued to let him play on credit. Buddy was always such a sloppy player, seeming to be drinking as he played, so loose and casual Joe couldn't understand how he was losing.

One day after Joe had lost another $500 cash to Buddy and almost $1,000 in markers, he threw down his cards. "How much do I owe you on the markers, Buddy?" he asked. "I'll bring you some money tomorrow to pay down on it. I shouldn't be playing gin with you anymore."

Buddy looked across the table at Joe alertly and pulled the markers out of his pocket. "I don't know what they amount to, Joe." Joe figured it was approximately $2,500. "But it don't matter." With that he tore up the markers and threw them on the floor. "Now you come on back and play any time you like."

Joe, of course, understood the ploy. Here he was bringing cash in to Buddy at the rate of maybe $1,500 a week and the professional gambler was too smart to kill the goose that was laying the golden eggs.

"Joe, I want you to come over to my place, meet my wife Dorothy and my little girl, Cindy. I've been telling them about you being a lawyer, the city attorney, an upstanding citizen in town. I promised to bring you around."

Buddy's house was just plain Texas tacky. In a run-down neighborhood, it was the least of its peers and needed paint, a new roof, and weeding around the edges. Inside, it was a different story. Television sets in every room, electric appliances to gladden the heart of a gadget nut. Cut velvet in a startling shade of magenta covered the living room furniture, and equally "elegant" carved matching credenzas, dining table with four leaves, and a dozen chairs filled every foot of floor space.

"The best," Buddy said, laconically gesturing at the appointments as Joe looked around. "I like things right."

Dorothy Bramlet was a dyed blonde, a friendly woman, well filled out, Joe couldn't help noticing–pleasingly plump as they said in Texas. A former Miss Fort Worth, her beauty queen days were obviously long gone but her personality was warm and she made Joe feel almost part of the Bramlet family as she introduced her daughter Cindy to him. Cindy, at twelve years old, already showed signs of developing into a fetching beauty queen of the full-blown type herself someday.

"Cindy is studying piano," Dorothy offered.

"Well, Cindy, please play something for me. I used to study piano myself when I was about your age."

Cindy smiled and went over to the piano and sat down. Joe walked over and settled himself beside her on the bench. "I used to play *Clair de lune*," he told her jovially. "Have you tried it?"

"My teacher has me working on it now, Mr. Hodges," she said. "I haven't really learned it yet though."

"Well, let's try anyway," Joe cajoled. "I might remember the notes and help you."

As Dorothy beamed, watching Cindy and the city attorney play the piano, Buddy nodded at her and smiled. He knew that most of the people he brought around the house were not what Dorothy hoped would be the company their daughter kept when she grew older.

After Joe and Cindy finished at the piano, Dorothy served tea and Cindy voraciously questioned Joe about the world beyond. It was obvious that Buddy and Dorothy weren't going to keep Cindy satisfied with a dull existence in Irving.

Finally Joe said he would have to get back to the office before he went home and took his leave of the Bramlets. "Next time you come to see us, Mr. Hodges, we'll be in a new home," Cindy cried excitedly.

"Well, I'll look forward to seeing your new house, Cindy, and don't you call me Mr. Hodges. I'm Joe."

Buddy walked out to the car with Joe. "Glad you could come by. We'll do it again. You sure made a hit with Cindy. Dorothy's got her thinking they don't meet any of the real people in Irving. Don't know who the real people are but I guess you're one. Coming out for some gin tomorrow?"

"You still getting your money together for that new house?" Joe chuckled.

"It's all bought and paid for. You'll see."

"Well, I'll be out in a few days, soon's I can get a bankroll together."

That night at home Joe couldn't keep his problems from Nancy. She had seen the signs before and knew that he was gambling again, going through the old cycle: borrowing, losing, and borrowing more. She made herself keep off the subject of money though she couldn't help asking, "Joe, do you think I should go back to teaching? I don't have much to do at home and I might as well be working."

Subtly she was expressing the two great disappointments in her life: Joe's gambling and the fact they had no children.

"Well, why don't we wait on making that decision," Joe replied evasively. "By the way, I was talking to Hope Cottage this morning—that woman, Miss Fly."

Nancy looked up eagerly. "What did she say, Joe?"

"Right now all the babies are spoken for. But there'll be more for adoption and we're close to the top of the list."

"I hope so, Joe," Nancy breathed, her mind turning from the familiar symptoms of Joe's gambling she had learned to dread.

CHAPTER 16

Aimlessly walking the street in downtown Las Vegas, Jonathan Alan Roberts wandered into the 4 Queens coffee shop. Eschewing the ubiquitous slot machines and gaming tables, he sat down at a counter. He didn't really want a cup of coffee but he had to pay for the space he was taking up. Brooding, he went over in his mind who he could telephone. Of one thing he was certain. He had to get a bankroll so he could return to the tables and make that big win. He felt it out there waiting for him.

He glanced at his watch. Eight in the morning. That would make it 10 A.M. back home. Hank would be in his office writing out company checks. It was Friday, and Hank always got the checks out by noon. The mental image gave him new life and he sprang to his feet, leaving a dollar to cover the coffee he had barely sipped.

He pulled out the rest of his money, $50, and obtained $10 worth of quarters from the girl in the slot-machine change booth. Finding a pay phone away from the jangle of the casino, he put through the call person-to-person. The phone rang and he identified himself when the secretary answered. "Put Hank on, please?" he asked.

Soon he heard the perennially cheerful voice. He chatted with the wealthy executive a few moments. Then, "Hank, I'm out here in Las Vegas." He paused and laughed sheepishly at Hank's comment. "You called it. I'm broke. And I've got those fellas coming in from New York on the real estate deal. I gotta entertain them right if we're going to put it across. Can you send me ten thousand by Western Union? I'll get it back to you as soon as I get home."

Jon listened to the ensuing blast and then meekly replied, "I understand, Hank. Be in touch with you later." He hung up and began to ponder the other possibilities. A thought came to him. Once more he direct-dialed a number and fed the stream of quarters into the coin box.

"Hello, Mr. Staples. Yes, I'm out here in Las Vegas on that real estate deal. Look, do you think the bank could advance me another ten thousand dollars on that loan? I'm sure to make the deal before the end of next week and I'll be able to extinguish the whole loan." He paused, listening, his face reflecting for whoever might be watching the tenor of the banker's reply. "Yes, sir," Jon concluded lamely. "I'll be by to see you next week."

Struck out again. There was one other possibility. Call old Three Finger Pat. All the money he'd lost to the bookie, the least he could do was advance Jon ten grand now that he needed it. Jon dialed the number and it was busy. He cursed. Three times he dialed and fed in the quarters only to find the line busy. He hung up and the pay phone disgorged the change in a rush. Finally, on the fourth try, he made the connection.

"Hey Pat, this is Jon Roberts. Yeah, I'm in Vegas. Yeah, broke. And look, I've got those guys coming out from New York on the real estate deal out on Paradise. You know the spot, I showed it to you when I brought you out here with me." He laughed suggestively. "Hey, remember those girls we had? Sure, I'll look her up for you. She really liked you."

Jon was working his pitch hard. "Look, Pat, I gotta get ten grand out here right away. Can you send it to me Western Union? I'll be able to let you have it back next week." He listened a moment. "Gosh, Pat. The checks are on my desk. I'll have the money for you soon as I leave here. But I need the ten now."

Jon listened to the inevitable lecture. "I know I still owe you from last week. Five thousand, right. Look, Pat, send me five and I'll pay you the whole ten next week. Okay?" He didn't want to sound as frantic as he was, but he had to have the money so he could get back to the tables.

As Jon sensed old Three Finger weakening, he kept up the

plea, subtly reminding the bookmaker of all the money he had taken to him and the times they had enjoyed in Vegas at Jon's expense.

"Thanks, Pat," Jon gushed when the gambler agreed to send the money. "Look, I don't have my I.D. with me so send it with a code. Middle name Alan, spelled A-L-A-N. Okay? Will you do it right away, Pat? Please. I'll be waiting at the Western Union office. Five grand."

He breathed a long sigh of relief as he walked away from the phone. Five grand was coming in. All was well now. He'd be back at the tables soon. Knowing that the money was coming, he walked over to the El Cortez with the $40 he had left. What the hell, he might as well get some action. The casino was around the corner from Western Union. He'd build his $40 up to $5,000 before Pat's money arrived, he thought happily.

Jon played conservatively, running the $40 up to several hundred in an hour. But this wasn't the kind of action he was looking for. He wanted to put the big bets down. He cashed in and walked across to Western Union. An old white-haired man was sitting behind the cage wearing a green eyeshade.

"Anything for Jonathan Roberts?" he asked. The clerk shook his head.

"Should be here," Jon muttered as he walked out. Back at the El Cortez he went to the crap tables and started buying numbers recklessly. That was the only way to make a bankroll out of a few hundred bucks. In ten minutes he was down to $50 and on his way to Western Union once more.

A woebegone young woman, obviously not a hooker—yet—was pleading with the clerk to look again, but he shook his head and she stepped aside.

"Anything for Jonathan Alan—"

"Not in yet, Mr. Roberts," the ancient cut him off.

As Jon cursed and walked away, he threw a curious glance at a desperate-looking man with shirt and tie askew, suit badly in need of cleaning, the smell of smoke and whiskey clinging to him, who was making his way to the cashier's cage.

Again he returned to the El Cortez and began to work on improving his meager bankroll. It didn't matter since he knew the money from Pat would soon be in and he'd be going big time again. He upped and downed the $50 and finally, with $5 left, went back to Western Union. Briskly he pushed his way through the derelicts and approached the cashier.

"Not yet, Mr. Roberts." The old man shook his head emphatically. "Why don't you just sit down and I'll let you know when it's in."

Now Jon didn't have much choice. With only $5 in his pocket there wasn't much he could do. Hell, the money would soon be in and the big time was waiting. But he couldn't stand the dreary atmosphere at Western Union, or the uncomfortable feeling he got from the sleazy characters waiting for $10 or $20 to come in. He walked out and went around the block again.

Six hours after Jon had called Three Finger Pat the bookie's money arrived. For a moment the dour-faced Western Union clerk allowed the trace of a smile to appear at his lips. "You have your I.D., Mr. Roberts?"

"Isn't there a code?" Jon replied.

"Sure is. You got it?"

"Middle name is Alan, spelled A-L-A-N."

"That's correct. Here's your check."

"Can't you cash it for me?" Jon asked.

"They'll cash it at the El Cortez."

"I don't have I.D.," Jon confessed.

"I'll call the El Cortez for you and tell them you own the check. You had the right code word."

Jon nodded and walked back to the El Cortez for the fourth time since he had called Pat. Jonathan Alan Roberts was jubilant. He had five big ones. There was no way he was going to do anything but win big. He had already put yesterday's huge loss out of his mind. That was in the past. He had his fix, his shot. Back to big-time playing. He entered the El Cortez and walked over to the cashier's cage, the Western Union check firmly in his hand.

CHAPTER 17

Tiny Meeler was a Methodist Church stalwart in a Sunday school class with Joe before the 11 A.M. service. He was a civic leader in Irving and a well-to-do land developer and builder in the small city that was growing fast just twelve miles from Dallas. Joe decided to give Tiny a shot. He had worked out his pitch and went around to see Tiny in his office on Monday.

"What can I do for you, Joe?" Tiny greeted the city attorney. "I might be needing a favor myself. Cousin Charlie Wyche is getting into a speculation here that might need your attention since it's within the town limits."

Joe had heard of Charlie Wyche, an eccentric buyer and seller of real estate worth many millions of dollars and somewhat of an embarrassment to his conventional relatives. Charlie lived in a rundown place on the edge of town where it was said his wife washed his clothes in an old fire-blackened pot outside the house.

"Tiny, I got myself into a big piece of trouble. A friend from out of town gave me a check for eight thousand dollars on a debt he owed me. I put the check in the bank and drew against it. But that sonofagun so-called friend of mine gave me a bad check. The bank got after me, real serious, and what did I do? You'd think a lawyer would know better but that bank was going to take legal action against me."

Tiny listened to Joe's story sympathetically, nodding in understanding. Joe paused and went on. "So I covered the shortage at the bank by writing checks on an account I don't have any money in. They'll all be coming back this week. This bank is covered but now I've got hot checks out all over town and I have to cover them."

"How much is involved, Joe?" Tiny asked earnestly.

"Seventy-eight hundred dollars," Joe replied. "I know it was stupid of me to write those checks, but I just couldn't figure any other way out and I didn't have much time. I'll be able to repay you in a short time, maybe a month."

Without further ado Tiny pulled the checkbook from a desk drawer and wrote out a check to Joe for $7,800.

"Tiny, I really do appreciate this," Joe said warmly. "I was in real deep trouble. I know you'll keep this just between the two of us."

"Oh, you can count on that, Joe," Tiny assured his friend. "I guess we all get into these bad situations at one time or another."

Joe took the check and, thanking Tiny again, left the office. He would have to go to Tiny's bank, cash the check, and then speed over to Fort Worth to give Boston Smith $5,000. The other $2,500 he'd take to the game in Arlington on the way back and try to win a big score at the crap table there.

Before he went to bed that night Joe had lost the entire $7,800. Although discouraged and depressed at first, he had a plan that had worked once and would work again. He had to hit it lucky at some point.

Friends and strangers bought the story about his "trouble," and Joe accumulated enough cash to pay the most pressing debts, gamble heavily, and dash from bookie to bookie, paying off losses and collecting a few wins, all the time trying wildly to keep up the appearance of conducting the legal affairs of the city of Irving.

He was always at work early, always left the office last in the evening. Soon after arriving each morning he grabbed his sagging briefcase and hustled off "to the courthouse." He had mastered his perfunctory duties so well that they were performed in a few minutes, and he could then speed from bank to bank, bookie to bookie, cashing checks, placing bets, listening to baseball games on the car radio. He discovered a hilltop in Irving where he could park his car on a heading of northeast and pick up the ball games being broadcast from the East. When he lost, he would stagger back to his office to regroup his energies against the morrow. Another "spot" and another $7,800 had to be found. Somehow it was.

Of the more than $200,000 debt structure he had run up, $170,000 represented losses at craps. Only $30,000 went to bookies. He understood the reason for this imbalance, but even so couldn't control his compulsion to shoot craps. A gambler had an advantage—or more protection against his own folly—betting on baseball or football games with bookies than playing craps at a casino, simply because games ended, bookies closed up shop and went home. The crap tables never ceased play and even when a gambler was thousands ahead, he had come for action and stayed to play. Sometimes the smart money went home a winner. But more often than not, the temptation for another big win was too strong—and the hoped-for win became a grueling loss.

Joe was in a House of Mirrors. Two steps inside was not so frightening. But with the third and fourth step, the mirrors became distorted, concealing any exit. Joe's disorientation became complete once he had reentered the gambling arena. Yet the only possible chance of repaying the quarter million was by winning. How long would it take, he mused, to repay $200,050 on a salary of $1,000 a month? It didn't bear thinking about.

He sped through Dallas, Arlington, Irving, and Fort Worth, banking, betting, paying off, collecting from bookies, a man possessed, juggling incoming and outgoing cash, keeping track of fourteen bank accounts so that his checks passed from one to another without the screeching brake of overdraft. And he picked up forty-two traffic violation tickets for speeding and illegal parking, usually in front of a bank. Yet his reputation was that of a bright, young attorney caught up in his work and in the life of the community. He was head of the local Red Cross, Boy Scouts, and Duplicate Bridge Club; he was Sunday school teacher, golf partner, bowling team member, and devoted husband. Pledging each lender to secrecy, he always borrowed $7,800. The fact that his borrowing was multiple never surfaced.

On his way to the Dallas courthouse one afternoon, he passed the building which housed the Dallas offices of financier W. O. Bankston, a prominent Methodist layman and owner of a GM automobile agency. Joe needed a sizable bankroll for Arlington, where he hoped to play hard at craps that evening. Winning, now, was imperative.

He handed his business card to Bankston's secretary. It was one o'clock and Bankston had just gone out to lunch. Joe had learned that if you need to see someone, you wait. For two hours he sat patiently, reading old copies of the Methodist Church's pamphlets, impressed by signed photographs of Mickey Mantle and other baseball greats that lined the walls of the reception room. At three, Bankston returned and took Joe into his private office.

He and Joe had never met, so Bankston came straight to the point. "What can I do for you, Mr. Hodges?"

Joe was equally direct. "Mr. Bankston, I'm in a lot of trouble. I've been gambling and I need twelve thousand dollars right now or I'm going to jail." Joe always carried a copy of his résumé, which included the information that he was an active member of the Methodist Church.

Bankston studied it carefully. A man of about sixty-five, his weathered face showed neither surprise, distaste, nor understanding. The heavy brows moved upward slightly, Joe thought, when he scanned Joe's academic record. Phi Beta Kappa keys were not the ordinary gambler's credentials, much less a law degree and a job as city attorney.

The older man looked up at Joe over steel-rimmed spectacles. "You know Bill Decker?"

"No, sir, I don't know Sheriff Decker, but of course I know who he is." He knew quite a lot about the high sheriff of Dallas County as a matter of fact. He ran his office honestly and well. Everybody looked up to him, even when they were on the wrong end of the law. There was no tampering or messing around with Sheriff Decker, or with his county of Dallas either.

"Well," said Bankston, "you go over there and see him. Tell him what you've told me, and if he calls me and says to give you the money, I'll do it."

Joe drove to the Dallas courthouse at top speed and got to Decker's office at four forty-five. Again he waited. Decker was out, but expected back soon. When he came in, Joe was summoned.

"Sheriff Decker, I'm Joe Hodges, city attorney out in Irving—"

"Oh, you are, huh? What you want?"

Again, Joe told him the story just as he had told it earlier to civic leader Bankston. "And he said if you phoned him and told him okay, he would loan me the money." Joe was sweating, his breath coming in uneven pulls, but he managed to stay in control. Telling this tale to two tough old birds in one afternoon was almost more than he could manage. He felt the cold eyes of the sheriff boring in on him.

"Yeah." Decker turned to his desk phone which was blinking angrily with incoming calls. "Why don't you sit outside there for a few minutes? I'll get back to you."

Deputies were buzzing in and out, ushering culprits to and fro, with harrassed attorneys trailing. Joe sat quietly, sweating out the time—nearly five-fifteen. The banks were closed, but drive-in branches were open until six.

Decker reappeared in the door of his office. "Go on back to see Mr. Bankston. I talked to him and told him to go ahead and let you have the money. I'll see you later."

By five-thirty Joe was in Bankston's office. The weathered face looked more relaxed now. "Well, Bill Decker said it was okay. Now, I own that finance company down the street"—he mentioned the name—"and they'll have a check ready for you. Thirty days now, remember!"

At five forty-seven Joe rushed into the finance company's office, got his name on the loan agreement, picked up a check for $12,500 and dashed to his car. It was $500 more than he had asked for. Five minutes later he drove into the lane of the drive-in window of the Republic Bank, cashing the check and speeding off for the Arlington gambling house with one hundred and twenty-five $100 bills.

Joe felt a surge of well-being. It had been a difficult afternoon, but his nervous exhaustion dissipated in the balm of having met two tough opponents on a field of battle—and won. Surely God's goodness and mercy would follow him right out to Arlington, where his winning would continue. It had to, Joe thought. Had to.

By seven-thirty he had lost the $12,500 to the last dime.

But Joe was in the arena to win. He simply could not quit

now, for there was nothing outside for him except whirling mirrors—and the most unimaginable pain.

He glared at the dealer. "Who's running this place? I've lost a little money here—I need some credit! Who do I see?"

The sallow-faced dealer jerked his head in the direction of the phone booth in the corner of the room. "That guy there, the one on the phone," he muttered, removing the nonexistent ash from his cold cigar. His eyes followed Joe as he hurried toward the phone booth, then he nodded slightly to the manager as Joe approached.

"Sure, Mr. Hodges. Your credit's good. How much do you need?" he said, his thin lips drawing back into a smile.

How much? Joe wanted to say $50,000. "Oh, I'll take five grand."

"Fine. Have a drink and I'll get it for you."

The $5,000 lasted for almost an hour and then it was gone.

Joe wouldn't believe it. He couldn't go home without a quarter. Back to the manager again. "Listen," he said, "I need some going-home money . . ."

This time the manager's smile was less affable. But he said, "You've got it! How much you want?"

Joe grinned. How much? What he wanted was enough to win big. So the question was rhetorical, senseless. "Fifteen hundred?"

Signing the marker for a total of $6,500, Joe left the arena and went home. He couldn't understand his run of horrible luck. The dice seemed possessed of the devil, turning to sevens almost as if controlled by a genie who was intent on Joe's destruction.

As he left, the manager called after him. "This is cash, now. Remember, I got to have it back Monday."

"Yeah, I'll see you Monday. What time you all open up?" The question was reassuring, he had found. But this was one time when Joe knew he would never be back there. Something was wrong. A man just couldn't lose that much that fast. Not lose every bet.

The next day, Saturday, Joe went to Buddy Bramlet's fish market, the $1,500 in his wallet. He found Buddy alone. "I want you to place some bets for me," Joe said. "It's almost time for the games to start and I haven't got time to get over to Hill's much less to Boston Smith. Can you do that for me?" Hill was a Dallas bookie, but Joe had no more credit with him and would have had to go in person, money in hand, if he wanted to bet.

"Sure thing. How much you want to put down?"

"Fifteen hundred dollars," Joe replied decisively. Buddy's eyebrows lifted a fraction. That was just domino hall betting, nothing like Joe's normal bets of five or ten thousand. "Okay," he said. "You got the line?"

He didn't have it, so Buddy phoned his own bookie. Joe carefully selected his four baseball teams and Buddy wrote down the bets to be called in.

"You got them all? Got them right? You won't forget?" Joe asked anxiously.

Buddy smiled tolerantly. "Yep, got 'em, and no, I won't forget."

Joe drove back to the apartment, content. Nancy was waiting for him, getting the last-minute preparations made for a noon cookout. He hugged her and began making his special barbecue sauce for the hamburgers. Somehow he felt that today would be a turning point.

Joe carried his portable radio down to the secluded corner of the yard shared by tenants of the building, making sure its batteries were working. This was one afternoon of baseball he didn't intend to miss, guests or no guests. The other two men listened with interest, but not with the same concentration as Joe. Nancy and the other wives chatted listlessly, then wandered back upstairs where they could escape the sun and the unutterable boredom of the baseball broadcasts.

One by wonderful one, each game came in just as Joe had bet, and by the end of the day he knew he had $13,000 in winnings. The guests left, and Joe dashed to the phone to urge Buddy to get his money. Finally, *finally* it was happening. Something substantial, something he had known was there if only he could pin the right tail on the right donkey. It felt good!

A strange voice answered at the fish market. "Buddy? He ain't here."

Joe gulped. "Well, where is he? When'll he be back?"

"Dunno. He's gone to Minnesota for some minnows."

"What?" Buddy hadn't mentioned such a trip. "Listen, he can't be on his way to Minnesota—I just talked to him this morning—"

"Well, that's where he's gone all right. Minnesota. Said he'd be back the middle of the week."

Joe banged the phone into its cradle, blind with rage, not at Buddy so much as at his own failure to stay on top of his deal. He *knew* Buddy's haphazard schedule of doing business. He *knew* that Buddy never volunteered information of any kind, and was apt to be headed for Minnesota or Tasmania or Timbuktu, without notice. But like a fool, Joe had assumed everything would fall into place—his way.

He drove fast, not bothering to phone Dorothy Bramlet. She was always at home anyway, putting up curtains, taking down curtains, washing curtains. The Bramlets had moved into the expensive new house on Cedar Street, not a characteristic thing for Buddy to do. He didn't like to flaunt his money. Smart gamblers never did.

The new house was in an elegant development, resting comfortably among its peers in the $60,000 to $80,000 price range. All brick, its Tudor beams and diamond-paned windows bespoke its class. Buddy's old pickup truck was parked in the driveway and Joe sighed with relief. The fish market man was mistaken, or at least Buddy had not yet left for Minnesota.

Dorothy chirped a welcome. She always liked to see Joe, and Joe enjoyed visiting with her and Cindy. Frequently he stopped off, giving her an envelope with $10,000 or $12,000 inside for Buddy to book for him. No problems. They were both completely trustworthy.

"Hey there, fella, where you been lately? Get in this house and have a cup of coffee with me. I'm lonesome as hell with Buddy gone—"

Joe froze on the doorstep. "Buddy's gone?"

"Yeah. One of those minnow trips up north. Why he wants to bother with that smelly load of stuff is more'n I can tell you. He's driving his minnow truck up there."

Joe stepped inside, blinking at the darkened room. Drapery and underdrapery guarded the splendor of cut velvet from the late afternoon sun still high in the heavens.

"How long has he been gone?"

"Oh, let's see. 'Bout a hour or two. I didn't pay that much attention—" She looked at Joe, her smile fading. "What's wrong, Joe?"

"Well—" he began, then paused. He could level with Dorothy. She knew everything about Buddy's many irons in the fire, accepting him as he was without judging the moral aspects of how he earned his money.

He stared at the coffee Dorothy placed before him on the doily-clad side table. "Buddy put down some bets for me today —and I won! Thirteen thousand! I've got to get that money fast. How long will he be gone?"

She was serious now, thinking. "Till Wednesday, he said. Listen, I know the guys down at the state troopers station. What if I call them and say to pick Buddy up—that it's an emergency?"

Joe grinned, slapping the table. "Great! Tell them to have Buddy call home as soon as possible, that it's an emergency." Which it sure is, Joe thought. For me, not him.

Cindy came up to Joe and took his hand. "Do you want to hear me play, Joe?"

With the call in to Buddy, everything was done that could be done. Joe relaxed and sat at the piano beside Cindy.

Twenty minutes later, Buddy Bramlet called home collect from a highway phone booth on the Oklahoma Turnpike. His voice was anxious. Dorothy put Joe on the line, quickly assuring him that nobody was sick and that the house wasn't on fire.

Buddy laughed, hearing Joe's voice. "You sonofabitch, what you mean, having me dragged off the road like that?"

Joe wasted no time. "Buddy, those bets—you placed them didn't you?"

"Why, uh—"

"I won. All of them. Every game! It comes to thirteen thousand dollars! How about that!"

Buddy was silent for a minute. "Well, that's good, boy. You got the money, so don't worry about it. The honest truth is, I forgot to make the call. I got your bets right here in my pocket. But don't worry about it. I owe you thirteen grand. You'll have it when I get back Wednesday."

Joe knew Buddy was as good as his word. And he had won close to $60,000 of Joe's money since that first crap game so paying off $13,000 wouldn't be any sweat for him. Joe would get the money on Wednesday, but until then he would have to find another source to raise a bankroll.

Buddy Bramlet paid Joe in full on the appointed day although Joe's skill at pumping money was so keenly honed that he had made two $7,800 loans by then and taken the money to Hill's, Boston Smith, and Arlington, losing it all and nudging his indebtedness above the $300,000 figure. With Buddy's payoff Joe could have extinguished at least one loan, but what good would that have done? It wouldn't have made a noticeable reduction in his debt structure. So the money from the parlay went into new efforts to rack up the kind of heavy dollars he so badly needed. By the time he had hit his nineteenth benefactor with the $7,800 story, he had created a debt structure of $350,000 and he was broke, with no more spots he could go to for a loan.

In desperation he tried Buddy Bramlet, into whose coffers he had poured so much hard-pumped cash. Buddy was sympathetic. However, he was no mooch and not only refused to make Joe a loan, but also to take any bets on credit. Buddy took him to the back room of the fish market.

"So you're really busted, are you?" he asked. "Well, it had to come. Giving you more isn't going to help. But I'm going to do you a big favor. You're probably the only respectable family friend Dorothy, Cindy, and I have. I've watched you lose, saw it coming. First time I got into that crap game with you I knew I had a sucker. You thought I was drunk, didn't you?" Joe nodded and Buddy laughed. "I'm practically a teetotaler. You ought to been smart enough to see it was an act. And the dice? I was rolling in missouts, tops, shaved, the works. You didn't stand a chance. Old Hank brought me in to get his money back."

Joe listened, not surprised so much as shocked at his own naïveté. "And all that gin we've been playing. I suckered you, boy, but that's the way I make a living, buy the family a new home. You needed a card to gin. I saw it wasn't in the deck that hand. You really think I'm sloppy as I look? Look, Joe, you got it all going for you. Give up gambling, leave it to us hustlers. You're a lawyer, you could be a big shot if you'd work at it. Me, I never had a chance to finish high school but I made it as best I could. Now come on over home, have some coffee with Dorothy and me, let Cindy play the new piano piece she learned for you and wish her happy birthday. She's going to be thirteen tomorrow. I got a teenage daughter, whadda ya know?"

Joe, upset and preoccupied though he was, went over to Buddy's for a family hour before driving home to figure out what he would do the next day. There were only another five or six weeks left of the baseball season, and despite his losses he knew he could win on the baseball parlays with just a little luck for a change.

Totally broke, he cast around trying to raise some money, anything, to get down on a baseball parlay. Then he thought of Idus Ash and Sid Wright. They weren't big gamblers but they liked to bet and win. Joe called them and they met in the coffee shop near Joe's office at the Irving Town Hall. He explained his idea.

"I want both of you to give me a thousand dollars, that'll give us a bankroll of two thousand. I'll bet it with Hill's and Boston Smith, run it up and when we get enough we'll stop and split three ways."

"I don't have no extra grand hanging around," Idus replied. Sid was in the same shape. But Joe's powers of persuasion prevailed, albeit eliciting a lower level of contribution. Sid and Idus each turned over $250 to Joe.

"You know that to do any good I'm gonna have to bet it all tomorrow," Joe said.

"Go ahead," Idus and Sid agreed.

The next day Joe studied the sports pages and drove to Fort Worth where Boston Smith's man gave him the line and Joe, nursing the tiny bankroll, picked only two teams to win. Back in Irving he, Sid, and Idus sweated each of them into a winner. "Now we have a thousand dollars up with Boston. Instead of betting single games we'll get into some parlays."

Idus and Sid nodded and the next morning Joe was able to indulge in the luxury of telephoning in his bet instead of having to rush to Fort Worth with cash.

The second day's betting netted the cartel another $1,000 and the third day Joe began placing bets on the riskier but higher-paying parlays.

To the delight of his partners Joe hit the parlay and suddenly they had $5,000 to work with. Each day Joe placed his bets with either Boston Smith or Hill's or both, combining caution with one or two wilder bets, all of which paid off. He could feel the winning streak accelerate and, taking luck at the flood, increased his bets. He expanded his business to include another Dallas bookie, Johnny Stone, and rode the streak hard. When they reached $20,000 Idus and Sid were satisfied and wanted a division of the spoils, so Joe cashed in and Sid and Idus both made extraordinary profits on their $250 investments. Naturally Joe kept plunging. Day after day he couldn't lose. The parlays became more daring and the payoffs sometimes five and even ten to one.

Soon Joe had won $100,000 and was still going strong. He had never known such a high, and it gave him a feeling of power as he paid off his debts.

After his Sunday school class he presented Tiny Meeler with a new Bible at the Methodist Church. "Go on, take a look inside, Tiny," Joe urged. "This is a very special edition."

Tiny opened the Bible and found $100 bills inserted between the covers and all the pages. He stared a moment, gulped, and snapped the holy book shut, a slow grin spreading across his face. Then he began to laugh. "Yes, this sure is a very special Bible. Wait'll I tell cousin Charlie Wyche about this one. And we thought *he* did things funny!"

For thirty-one days in a row Joe hit every bet with the bookies, even making two winning trips to Las Vegas where he was beginning to get the feel of that neon-lit strip of casinos in the desert. He was reducing his debt structure as he won. Of the $350,000 he owed he first paid off the First Federal Savings and Loan, greatly pleasing its president, Bob Nelson. As the winning streak continued, he worked the debt structure down after that from $280,000 to $200,000. When, after the twentieth day of hitting the bookies with wins, Joe had his debts at an even $100,000, he was overjoyed. The figure was manageable. But the wins continued and he worked his way down to $53,000 and then to $19,000. Finally in a blaze of glory, the like of which he had never known, he liquidated it entirely.

It was a sensation so exquisite he couldn't describe it. He now felt truly authenticated as a person. Everybody loved him and admired him. He had paid back every cent he owed and he was thought to be an unusually astute businessman by most of Irving's leading citizens, who had no idea he was gambling.

With the winnings left over from paying his debts Joe triumphantly bought a handsome new house in Walnut Hill, one of the more affluent developments between Dallas and Irving, and a brand-new car in which to transport Nancy to the new house. But Nancy sharply surprised him. She knew he was gambling and she hated it, whether he was on a winning or losing streak. The money itself wasn't important to her.

When Joe drove up to their apartment in the shiny new car, Nancy took one look and refused to get into it. "It's all part of the gambling, Joe. I don't want anything to do with it," she declared.

"But the new house," Joe protested.

"It's all the same—from gambling. I'm staying right here at the apartment. I'm not moving to Walnut Hill if the money comes from gambling." Then she moved close to her husband. "Oh, Joe, can't you stop it once and for all now?"

Disappointed but far from contrite, Joe gave up trying to press the fruits of his winnings onto his wife. He was a happy man these days and square with the world. For a short period, which coincided with the end of the baseball season, he did stop gambling; but then, acknowledging his singular gifts in the field of gaming, he decided it would almost be like spurning a God-given talent not to make full use of them.

Also, after he had made the last repayment on his myriad loans, the fantastic feeling of importance and authentication that came with being loved and admired by his associates and their families began to subside. He was the city attorney again, discharging his duties in the first hour of the day, and time hung heavy on his hand.

He had done it once, and in grand style, why not have another go at the bookmakers? It was the start of the football season and, since Joe had to sell the equity he put up in the Walnut Hill house anyway, he might as well double that money by betting with Johnny Stone and Boston Smith on the football games.

But that spirit of luck that flits to the shoulder of the habitual gambler can as abruptly flit away. Soon Joe and Nancy were living on his salary as the city attorney and then even that was fed out to the bookmakers who two short months before were paying off regularly and well.

Joe went back to Buddy Bramlet to place some bets but more for the pleasure of Buddy's company, and of course he enjoyed being with Dorothy and watching Cindy grow up.

"You're broke again, eh, Joe?" Buddy shrewdly observed.

"Guess I am. I'll probably be out borrowing again."

"Maybe I can help you. Now that you know how I operate, we can work together."

"What do you have in mind, Buddy?"

"There's a couple of old guys, the Taylor brothers. E.C. and his brother H.C. They own Taylor Publishing Company, one of the biggest printing companies in Dallas. The company is worth a fortune but the brothers won't sell. Damn, they love to gamble, can't stop neither of them. Too old to be family men, I guess."

A few days later Joe and Buddy were in a card game with the Taylor brothers. As Buddy dealt a hand he ruefully complained about "that doggone lawyer beating all of us" as Joe won again. At the end of each session Buddy paid Joe 10 percent of his winnings. Buddy took the winnings in the form of stock in the Taylor Publishing Company and as the games progressed he became a major stockholder in the company. Joe was not entirely happy about being a party to Buddy's less than four-square moneymaking, but it gave him something to do in his spare time and watching Buddy operate could be amusing. Each time Buddy paid him $500 he took it to Johnny Stone or Boston or even laid it off with Buddy on the football parlays, supplementing this income by getting back into a borrowing cycle.

CHAPTER 18

As Christmas of 1960 drew near, Joe was beginning to worry. His winning streak was over. He had blown the last of his bankroll, but he was the only one who knew it. His friends were still elated by the big wins he had notched up over the summer at Las Vegas or betting baseball with the bookies. Who on earth could have been $350,000 in debt and paid it all off in less than six months?

Now Joe wanted to bet some of the last football games of the season, but he was broke and the bookmakers weren't taking his action on credit. He would have liked to go over to the First Federal Savings and Loan and get some money from Bob Nelson, but Bob wouldn't let him have any more. He certainly didn't want it to get back to Mayor Paul Laird or any members of the city council that he needed money. He felt almost faint at times when he contemplated the terrible mess from which he had extricated himself. It was no secret that he had gambled in the past, but as far as the city of Irving knew collectively, he was a model of decorum and had long since given up that vicious habit.

The thought of Bob Nelson brought a name to mind, Father Joe O'Bannion, the bursar of the University of Dallas, a Catholic college located in Irving. Bob had happened to mention that Father O'Bannion kept a large savings account on behalf of the college at his bank. Well, Joe thought, he had borrowed from many prominent Methodist churchmen, why not try a Catholic?

It was Friday afternoon. The college games were over, and

the pros were playing on Saturday now. Joe had studied the records of all the teams and the injury lists of the pro clubs around the country. He wondered how much he could ask Father O'Bannion to lend him and decided on four thousand dollars as he drove over to the college campus.

Joe had no trouble locating the Father in the business office and the priest was certainly cordial in greeting the young city attorney about whom he had heard so many positive things.

After the amenities Father O'Bannion leaned forward. "What can Dallas University do for the city attorney?" he asked pleasantly.

"Well, the reason I came to see you is that Bob Nelson at First Federal had so many good words to say about you." Father O'Bannion nodded but did not interrupt. "You see, Father, I'm in some trouble and I hoped you might help me out. A man I thought was a good friend gave me a check for five thousand dollars on an old debt he owed me and I took it down to the Irving Bank and cashed it, using the money to pay back some of my own debts. Well, my friend's check was returned because his account had been closed. The bank was pretty mad as you can understand. Here's the city attorney cashing a bad check. They gave me five days to pay before turning the matter over to the district attorney, and what did I do?"

Joe smiled sadly. "Stupidly, I cashed hot checks of my own all over town to make the check good at the bank. Sure, I got that one behind me, but now the other checks are coming back and here it is coming up to Christmas and I'm going to be in jail if I can't cover those hot checks around town."

"How much is involved?" the priest asked.

"I've used up all my own resources," Joe answered, "but I still need four thousand to keep from being jailed."

"Well, my son, you do have a problem. It is not for me to tell you to be careful who you trust and who you help. Our Lord teaches love of mankind, love thy neighbor, extend the hand of friendship. But it seems this time you reached out to the wrong person."

"I know, Father. And it was my own stupidity that compounded the problem. But if you can loan me that money I'll be able to pay it back in a month or less."

Joe's delivery of the plea, the wording, the facial expressions, had been practiced so often that the performance was impeccable. Father O'Bannion was reaching for the checkbook before Joe's pitch was completed and, to the accompaniment of gentle admonitions, he handed Joe the check.

"Thank you, Father. I'll be back to repay you in just a couple of weeks. Maybe even sooner," he added, thinking of the five-to-one payoff Boston Smith would make when Joe won the parlay.

Saturday morning Joe drove to Fort Worth and found Boston at his usual post at the stockyards. He placed his bets and handed over the $4,000 he had borrowed from Father O'Bannion. Then he drove back to Irving to sweat out the results.

The winning streak was behind him for sure—or perhaps he should stick to baseball and not bet any other games. He blew the Father's loan all in one Saturday afternoon. There was now nothing for him but to try to open up some new spots.

In the back of his mind Joe was storing data on possible spots for loans, but instead of going through the agony of hitting one friend or stranger at a time for relatively small amounts he really needed a single source who could provide all his financial needs.

The week after getting the loan from Father O'Bannion, Joe was in the lobby of Bob Nelson's First Federal Savings and Loan, not far from the Irving Town Hall. At the bank he encountered Tiny Meeler's cousin Charlie Wyche. Charlie had done some business with the city attorney on one of his land deals and in the data processing corner of Joe's brain it clicked that Charlie might be able to be developed into the sort of full-service loan spot he was searching for.

Charlie came up to Joe laughing. "I heard your business is going good. Tiny told me about that Bible you gave him. Now if that ain't the slickest way to repay a loan I ever heard I sure can't think what is. Be worth making you a loan to see how you was going to pay it back."

Joe chuckled with the old fellow.

Charlie was the sort of man of whom legends were spun. He was old and wrinkled and looked older than the seventy years that he admitted to. He had been in some unreported fire several years back and had bad scars on one of his hands and on his neck where the skin was pulled down in a taut and ugly sort of way. He seemed awkward and disorganized. Nevertheless, people spoke in awe about this incredibly successful businessman who lived outside of town in a rundown sprawling bungalow.

Charlie was supposedly the kind of absentminded man who even forgot to zip his trousers. He was a man, it was said, who left literally hundreds of newspapers and Kleenexes lying about his living room in disarray; who had an estate worth millions but whose wife cleaned his clothing by boiling it in a pot in a backyard crisscrossed by wandering chickens and pigs. How does one explain a flinty, cantankerous, kind genius like Charlie Wyche? His intelligence quotient was up around the two hundred range and his financial acumen had earned him some $20 million in real estate wheeling and dealing.

Charlie was in one of his more ebullient moods, happy and bubbling. "Well, Mr. Wyche," Joe said, "you seem in good spirits today."

The old man pulled out a piece of onionskin paper, a pink sheet that was obviously a carbon copy of some agreement, and held it in front of Joe. With it was a bonded check for $3 million. Charlie was laughing.

"What do you think of that, Irishman?"

Joe did not know why he was being called Irishman. Though he had positive feelings about his Irish ancestors, he thought of himself as a Texan and an American. But he smiled back.

"It's great. Where'd you get it?"

"There was a property outside town where I held a third interest. They paid me three million for my third." Charlie slapped his leg and waved the slip of paper like a war trophy. People had said Charlie was like that, but Charlie, instead of appearing eccentric or weird, seemed rather splendid. He was carrying off a coup that was beyond the capacity of any of the suave and urbane businessmen walking past them.

They stood there talking amid the whirl of busy people passing to and fro. Charlie disliked the unctuous Texas businessmen who seemed like transplanted New Yorkers but had liked Joe when he first met the young city attorney.

That same day Joe drove out to the ragtag acreage where Charlie lived. When he arrived there he was surprised even though he'd heard all the rumors. Yes, there really was a huge iron pot in the backyard and clothing was being boiled and stirred within it by a weatherbeaten corpulent woman. There really were masses of dogs and chickens and horses prowling about free and unhindered. And there were motley members of Charlie's family assembled and sprawled across the front porch. It was like the set for a movie whose director had not yet decided whether he was making a comedy or tragedy.

For a moment Joe wondered why Charlie with his millions did not buy something of real value. The man had enough money to live like the governor or any of the other new nabobs of the Lone Star State. But he was satisfied with this. Was it weird? Was it admirable? He only knew he was intrigued and somehow impressed.

Joe approached Charlie directly. Charlie's subservient wife, Juanita, left him alone and they were able to talk about Irving and Dallas, about real estate investment, about the future. What was interesting about Charlie was his instinct. He did not analyze properties or people with tables of data or personal references. He just sized something up and if he liked it, he wanted his share of the action. If it went counter to his impeccable business sense, he would say, "Deal me out."

As they talked over their ideas about business, Joe swiftly came to realize that this leathery old man, this codger with the wrinkled skin and gnarled hand and the gleam in the eye, was sizing him up and approving him.

As was his habit whenever anyone trusted him or approved his character, Joe immediately moved in to test the trust.

"Mr. Wyche, I need twenty-five thousand dollars real bad. I'd like to explain it to you."

The old man smiled and said, "Sure, why not? I can tell you now though. You got it."

They both burst into laughter at that. Joe began to explain the need for the $25,000 but Charlie cut him off with a few words. "Irishman, *you got the money.*"

Between football and the baskets Joe made short work of the $25,000 but Charlie Wyche never even mentioned repayment of the loan.

One Saturday afternoon shortly before Christmas, having just paid off a couple of pressing personal debts, Joe found himself almost completely broke. He needed a $20,000 bankroll, and he needed it in a hurry. He also thought he knew where he could get it.

The manager down at the supermarket on the corner of Ames and Brazos had cashed checks for $1,000 for Joe on other Saturday afternoons after the banks had closed. Never any problem. Joe always managed to cover them by Monday morning, one way or another. Either he won the baseball parlay or the poker game or craps—and always he *knew* he would win this time—or he would think of a new spot where he could borrow in time to get to the bank. Spots were Joe's lifeline. Friends, finance companies, banks. Still, it was no easy job getting himself psyched up to look sincere and businesslike as he explained how he just happened to be caught in an awkward situation on a Saturday afternoon with a big deal in the offing.

The supermarket manager, harried by a late-arriving shipment of tomatoes and an irate matron returning a carton of cream gone sour, looked at Joe with relief. City attorneys didn't pester him with wilting cabbages and such. They had important affairs on their mind, worthy of the manager's talents. Besides, the grocery chain would be requesting a zoning change fairly soon from the city of Irving, which Joe Hodges would allow or disallow. Bright young fellow, steward in the First Methodist Church, had a fine baritone voice and sang in the choir, chairman of the Boy Scouts, speaker at Rotary and Kiwanis Clubs all over Texas. A man like that would have plenty of legitimate deals going for him. Real estate, oil, and stuff like that.

"Twenty thousand?" He conquered his momentary panic, mentally counting the packets of bills in his safe. "I guess—well, sure we can accommodate you, Mr. Hodges. Glad to be of help."

Joe got the money just in time to catch the afternoon flight to Las Vegas from Love Field if he hurried.

In one night of furious crap shooting at the Riviera he blew the entire bankroll.

That Christmas was not a season for jollity in the Hodges apartment. There was no badly wanted child to stare wide-eyed at a loaded tree, no way to give Nancy some munificent gift—or take her on a trip. But one evening in January, Nancy met Joe at the door, ecstatic. "Joe—Joe! We're getting a baby! Hope Cottage just called. They've approved us—"

He held her close. Nancy was normally the calm, unflappable one, hardly registering more than five on a scale of ten, no matter what bonanza came her way. But now! She'd gone past the top of the scale and was almost incoherent with joy.

He grinned, knowing what this meant to her.

A baby! They had been married eight years, tried everything, and now, someone else's child was going to bless their lives. Thank God, thank God.

"When?" he asked.

"Next summer!" She was sobbing now as she laughed. "Think of it—next summer. They said the baby would be born about the third week in June, and then, when it's a week old—"

Adoption was difficult, especially through Hope Cottage, an agency priding itself on the most meticulous investigation procedures involving the matching of parental background, religion, and race and a careful weighing of the likely outcome for both child and adoptive parents. Joe and Nancy Hodges had been given a screening that would have qualified them for admission to Heaven.

Not a tinge of gambling sullied their formal records. Beaumont? Only the highest recommendations from old family friends, bankers, and educators. Joe Hodges had a brilliant record as a student. Phi Beta Kappa, law degree from the University of Texas. Mother and father the salt of the earth.

Zanesville? No mention.

Roswell? No mention.

Irving? A churchgoing, personable, loving young couple who just wanted to raise a family, and couldn't produce offspring of their own. Hope Cottage had checked carefully into the medical records, their findings authenticated by their physician, and found them commendable. Joe's credentials as a civic-minded Irving citizen were impeccable. What more could Hope Cottage ask? Or, for that matter, what finer father could a child have? And young Mrs. Hodges: a model of rectitude, member of Delta Delta Delta and the church, her praises sung loudly and sincerely by countless friends, a dutiful daughter, a faithful wife, a fine teacher . . . . What better mother could a baby want?

Mark was born on June 18, 1961, and was handed to his new mother, Nancy Hodges, three weeks later. Joe had never seen her so glowing, so exalted. She seemed the acme of motherhood. With her son in her arms, Nancy was fulfilled.

Joe had bought his son a little yellow suit to wear home from Hope Cottage. Together, they walked to the car in bliss, carefully holding the awkward soft bundle of precious cargo. Markham Garver Hodges was finally home with his parents.

At least the first step in the adoption process was complete. There remained only a six-month probation period, after which he would be forever their son.

That first night, Joe and Nancy put Mark at the foot of their bed in his crib, watching over him all night without sleep. This miracle of life was theirs and they looked into each other's eyes in wordless humble thanks.

It wasn't long before they took their baby son to show him off to Charlie Wyche. The old man treated Joe as a son now, confiding in him about the many real estate deals he was involved in. Ten thousand acres in West Texas; picking up a parcel of barren ground between Dallas and Fort Worth, "stealing it," as he described what was really acumen. Charlie "stole" only from people who were blinded by momentary greed and unable to see around the next corner and the one after that. He astutely guessed at land's future value when it had little present attraction.

Charlie delighted in outsmarting his bankers or anybody else who saw only what was obvious. Hell, he said, anybody could figure out why a piece of property was valuable after its worth was plain to see. But it was something else to figure it out ahead of time.

Wyche asked Joe to help him make up a financial statement. "Them jokers down to the bank," he complained, "want something on paper to justify a loan of three hundred thousand dollars. Idiots! Anyways," he told Joe, "me and you got to work up a reasonably accurate statement. Make 'em happy, huh?"

Joe got it all down without difficulty. He could figure straight arithmetic better than most. When he went over his bets, calculating the baseball line against his winnings for the day, he never made an error. Occasionally a bookie would miss it by $50 or $100, sometimes in Joe's favor, sometimes not. But he made them get it right. One of Boston Smith's men misfigured in Joe's favor once, and then insisted on paying the larger amount just out of embarrassment.

The Wyche statement came to $20 million—all in land. He never had cash money lying around. And half the time he was being sued for nonpayment of his honest debts. He had various judgments against him, and this minor irritation stalled a sale now and then when the court clerks adamantly forced him to divvy up before the lien could be vacated.

Charlie took Joe aside while the women admired the baby Mark. "Listen, Irishman, I got me a deal coming up down in Mexico. You can help me on it if you want to." He went on to tell Joe that he was putting $200,000 in an account in Joe's name to be used for developing a silver mine in Mexico, and to back a foundry producing parts for Otis elevators.

Joe was touched, more grateful for this trust and confidence than Wyche could know—or would have wanted to know. The Hodges fortunes were at a very low ebb just then, and Joe was pumping money anywhere and everywhere to keep his debt structure from strangling him. He shook his head in amazement. "Charlie, you know I'll do everything I can. Count on me."

As the months passed Wyche never asked for an audit of the bank account, never looked at the books, assuming that Joe was using the bank account exactly as he had intended. And certainly it would never have occurred to Joe to embezzle any part of that money. What did occur to him was a bit of "conversion," meaning that when he desperately needed to cover a bad check or pay off a bookie on a fearful loss, it made only good sense to write a check on the Wyche fund in expectation of replacing it in a matter of days.

But the days turned into months, and soon Joe was short $50,000. Then the amount he had converted reached over $100,000. The situation hurt him like a knife in his heart. Somehow it was much worse, using Charlie Wyche's money for his own purposes, than if it had been his own father's assets. He hadn't repaid his father for the Zanesville and Roswell fiascos, even when just a few months ago he could have cleared them totally. His repaying of his father was such a certainty that for some illogical reason he didn't feel pressured about it.

When Joe had flown home from Las Vegas six months ago carrying $180,000 in cash, he didn't know where to keep the money. He couldn't go into a commercial bank and lay out banded stacks of $100 bills without causing the wrong kind of attentiveness. So he had driven to Beaumont, hidden $50,000 in his father's closet on a high shelf where it would not be discovered, without letting his parents know of the cache. He had long since retrieved and blown the money.

Guilt over misusing Charlie Wyche's funds preyed on Joe to the point where it became intolerable. He needed to confess his deed and the only possible confessor was Charlie himself.

In Joe's mind there were but two different ways the confrontation would turn out. In his preferred mental scenario he could see himself telling Charlie what he had done and imagine Charlie getting annoyed and telling him what a darned fool thing it was to waste good money on a dumb sport like gambling. ("Don't do it again and I don't want to hear about this one more time, you hear?")

He had to admit there might be another, one where Charlie began screaming that Joe was a thief and that he should never have trusted him with a nickel. ("My wife told me you were no good and I should have listened to her instead of trusting you like a son. Now you get your ass out of here and if I ever see your face within a hundred yards of my land I'll blast it from here to doomsday!") But while Joe conceded that this kind of reaction could destroy their friendship, he thought the odds against its happening were considerable. So he went directly to Charlie and told him all.

The old man did not say anything at all. He just got up and cleared his throat and spat over the front porch. Then he turned to Joe.

"You'd better go now," he said. The dismissal came out so simply and starkly that Joe did not recognize it as such the

moment he heard it. It was too short, too incontestable, too final.

In some ways it was the worst it could have been. Joe could have addressed himself to fury or rage, but this— All he could do was limp away, go back home to Nancy and Mark, and brood.

The old millionaire wasted no time demonstrating just how unpromotable he really was. Joe was indicted, arrested, forced to make bail and then released. Henry Wade, the district attorney, knew Joe as city attorney of Irving and sympathized to a degree but could do nothing about the indictment. There was no mention of it in the Dallas newspapers but this unsavory occurrence did not escape the attention of Irving's mayor and council.

There were some strong councilmen and a few pantywaists. None of them relished the job of asking Joe to resign his post. They liked him personally, admitted that he had done a competent job—but they wanted no part of scandal within their ranks. The decision was resignation, then a token appointment as a legal consultant whereby Hodges could retain a semblance of respect without direct affiliation with the city's management. His salary was reduced to $8,500 in the form of a retainer, and Joe was then able to practice privately as well as do small services for the city. He breathed a bit more freely, even though each time the telephone rang, each time an official logo appeared on a piece of mail, his heart flipped over. What next, what next?

Once again Christmas wreaths appeared on Dallas doorways and tinsel garlands crisscrossed downtown streets. One Wednesday night, a week before the big day, Miss Selby Fly, a maiden lady of indeterminate years and the director of Hope Cottage adoption agency, was hostess at her annual pre-Christmas party for close friends and relatives. She liked to do things properly and had decorated her small neat house with plastic holly and an artificial tree at just the right height to fit into the guest room closet from one year to the next. Miss Fly had bought bourbon, Scotch, and rum for this evening's celebration. Not that she or the other women really drank. But eggnogs were appropriate during the holidays, and there was certainly no harm in serving a single drink to her closest friends.

Miss Selby Fly's sister Hazel and her husband, the Reverend Mr. Osgood, arrived at her home for the traditional party. As the drinks were poured and good-natured talk filled the house, Mrs. Osgood was gaily bringing her sister up to date on Beaumont gossip.

Lowering her voice, Hazel exclaimed, "And wasn't it a crying shame about young Joe Hodges! That boy had everything going for him, I hear, and this must have just about killed old Joe and Florence."

Miss Fly paused, her drink halfway to her lips. "What are you talking about? What about Joe Hodges?"

"Oh, didn't you hear? He was indicted for embezzlement. Took a bunch of money that old Charlie Wyche gave him in some kind of partnership—"

Selby felt her fingers slipping from the glass and hastily set it on the table. "What?"

Hazel beamed at her sister. As a minister's wife, she wasn't accustomed to undivided attention. Her head bent toward her sister. "Yes. Wyche was fit to be tied, I hear. Wanted to put him in jail and throw away the key. But he was allowed to make bail . . ."

Selby Fly said not a word. Indicted, was he? With Mark's final adoption coming up for review in two weeks. Her bile seethed up in her throat, almost suffocating her, and she gasped for breath. She *knew* it. She'd felt something didn't quite jell with that Hodges. All along her sixth sense had whispered and repeated a warning. Watch out for that couple! Watch out for the marvelous, gregarious, smart, psalm-singing lawyer man. And now—well, she should have listened to her own intuition.

The board of Hope Cottage was called to an emergency closed-door meeting Friday morning at nine. At ten-fifteen Joe received a phone call at his office from a sweet-voiced social worker representing the adoption agency. "Mr. Hodges, would you and your wife bring Mark in tomorrow for his final visit, please? Yes, right after lunch will be fine. Thanks so much."

Joe took the afternoon off for this great and solemn occasion.

It wouldn't amount to much . . . then what a marvelous Christmas they'd have, with Mark officially a Hodges. Already the baby's presents were under the tree. Joe wanted Nancy to dress him in the same little yellow suit he had worn when they got him, but she laughed and said he'd long since outgrown it.

It was a brilliant sunny day, one he would never forget. Mark looked like a cherub, though of a distinctly masculine variety, with his dark eyes like Nancy's and his fighter's face like Joe's. Remarkable job of matching a kid to his adoptive parents, Joe mused. Nobody would ever mistake this baby for a girl, that was for sure.

Just inside the door of Hope Cottage, Joe's antennae, honed with his bank experience paranoia, picked up on a security guard standing off to the right. Nancy in the full joy of motherhood noticed nothing of the big con about to be perpetrated upon her. A case worker suggested Mark be left in the nursery and, although Joe was apprehensive, Nancy gladly acquiesced. The case worker took Mark, and Joe and Nancy were ushered into the sanctuary of Selby Fly.

She was succinct, firm, mouthing the words as though rehearsed. Mark was being removed from their care. Permanently. It had been done, in fact. The baby had already been taken from the premises of Hope Cottage and Joe and Nancy Hodges were henceforth restrained from seeking to learn his whereabouts, or from resorting to appeal of any kind.

Miss Selby Fly warmed to her attack. "You've been *indicted* —for *fraud*, sir. You're not a fit father, and if you think Hope Cottage is going to permit a man like you to—"

Nancy swayed, grasping for Joe's arm. She seemed to be swallowing, almost choking. But no sound came out.

Miss Fly ignored the interruption. "—to assume the parental duties of one of our babies, you're vastly mistaken! You're under *indictment*, remember!" She made it sound like conviction.

Joe felt as though he'd been bit by a rock slide. Stunned, in shock, he could only stare at the shrieking woman, her eyes blazing, on the verge of hysteria. Nancy was close to collapse, silent, her fingers opening and closing on the sleeve of Joe's jacket. He wished she would scream, do anything except shrink into apparent deep withdrawal under Miss Fly's blast.

But Nancy could not speak. She was far gone into an agony of spirit that made her deaf to any word, any comfort. Joe put his arms around her, wanting to follow her into whatever place she had gone. But it was useless. Nancy was no longer a mother—or rather, God in Heaven, she was a mother who had lost her baby.

Somehow they stumbled out to the car, somehow Joe drove home, and somehow they found their way into the apartment. The sun's brilliance now accentuated the awful vacancy of Nancy's eyes as she looked at Joe, then beyond him, incapable of seeing the gaily decorated Christmas tree, the gifts arranged below it.

It's all my fault. There was no way to keep that spectral knowledge from his mind. My fault . . . my fault. He couldn't find anything in the bathroom medicine cabinet to ease Nancy's grief except a bottle of aspirin. He took two tablets in his trembling fingers and offered them to her with a glass of water.

"What are we going to do, Joe?" she whispered. He strained to hear the words. Would she say it? *It's all your fault.* She reached up and drew him to her, cradling his head in her arms. Joe's sobs tore from his chest in an aching expulsion of fear, sorrow, loneliness, remorse. He looked toward Mark's little crib, still rumpled from his morning nap, and struggled from Nancy's embrace. Burying his face in the baby's pillow, he snatched the sheets and thin yellow blanket from the crib, clutching them wildly.

"What right has she got to take our son? I won't have it, I tell you. It's wrong. God knows it's my fault—but I'm going to find him, get him back—"

"Yes," she said quietly, almost languorous in her state of shock. "Yes, Joe. You can get him back—home—" Her eyes seemed enormous, circled now with a gauntness that aged her girlish features. Her dark hair hung lank and wet around her face and she brushed it impatiently aside.

CHAPTER 19

The final hours of Saturday moved like a cortege. Like an unseen alarm clock, Mark's bathtime, suppertime, bedtime rang in both their heads. Nancy was unable to cope with the emptiness of her new reality. The visions of her son haunted every nook of their tiny apartment, now turned into a prison and a tomb.

Joe's mind was spinning wildly. Simultaneously it was groping for a focus he knew he must find. By five o'clock Sunday morning he knew what the first step must be. He then felt hopeful, not because there was reason to hope, but because he was about to do something. He was getting his adrenaline going again.

Simply, Joe told Nancy his plan. Nancy demurred. "But does he know we're coming? Will he be there? Will he—?" Joe cut her off. "By the time we dress, locate his home and get there, it will be after eight. We'll see him!"

Joe was gambling that at eight o'clock on a Sunday morning Henry Strasberger would be at home, and that he would listen to his plea and help them start the wheels turning that would bring Mark back.

Henry Strasberger was senior partner in the most prestigious law firm in Dallas, the kind of elder statesman of the legal fraternity whose opinions, authority, and presence on a case added immediate weight to his client's position. Joe knew him by reputation, just as a fledgling diplomat in Washington knows the Secretary of State. He knew too that going through channels to try and set up such a Sunday meeting would never succeed.

The door was opened by Henry Strasberger himself. He was a

slight man, nearing sixty-five, Joe guessed, looking smaller in pajamas and robe than he did in the courtroom where he wore tailored suits that widened his shoulders and gave him dignity and bearing. He obviously had no idea who this young couple was but his expression was neither hostile nor inviting.

Joe didn't wait for ceremony. "Mr. Strasberger, my name is Joe Hodges and this is my wife Nancy. I am city attorney at Irving, and we are in desperate trouble. Could we see you for a few minutes?"

The elder man's eyes flickered with interest. He had seen more real trouble than most men, having practiced law for forty years. This was the first time a troubled young couple had knocked on his own front door, though. People didn't barge in on the most prominent attorney in Dallas on a Sunday morning without either appointment or preliminary notice from friend, foe, or advocate. However, one look at the faces of Joe and Nancy was enough for Henry Strasberger to gauge the degree of their trouble. He led them into a paneled study off the enormous living room, now dominated by a lighted Christmas tree that reached the ceiling.

The attorney's eyes never left their faces as they blurted out the story. Joe did most of the talking, looking to Nancy for corroboration now and then. Strasberger noted the warm relationship between the two as he listened to Joe's tortured recitation: gambling, Charlie Wyche, the agony of Saturday, their determination to get their baby back.

He probed shrewdly. Well, that old dame at Hope Cottage was within her rights, but . . . "Was this an action of the board, or did Miss Selby Fly make the decision on her own?"

Joe's heart dropped a beat. "The board made the decision, she told us."

Strasberger grimaced. That wasn't good news. "You kids go on home now, and tomorrow I'll have a talk with Judge Russell. Frankly, I don't think we'll get anywhere—I think you're going to have to accept the fact that this boy is never going to be given back to you. But there's a chance for us."

Nancy shuddered and a little moan escaped her. The attorney looked at her impassively. "It's a hard world, Mrs. Hodges, I know. I'll do my best, though, and we'll just have to hope."

The word rang hollowly. Hope Cottage—where no hope lay.

Joe now said what had to be said. "Mr. Strasberger, we haven't much money, but whatever your fee is—"

Strasberger cut him short. "Don't worry about it."

The next day Strasberger had lunch with Judge Lewis Russell. As every judge and lawyer in Texas would have done, Russell listened to the eminent attorney with respect. He would not, however, try to impose his judgment upon the board of Hope Cottage by reversing their action. No, the answer is no. This board, after all, was composed of leading clergy, bankers, and industrialists. Judge Russell had no taste for overruling them even at the behest of Henry Strasberger.

Later Strasberger called Joe into his Dallas office. "Joe," he began, "I must advise you not to attempt to set the decision aside. You'd be a fool to sue that bunch—you couldn't win the case."

Joe Hodges would not accept this judgment. "Mr. Strasberger, I don't think you understand. This is my son we're talking about —and nothing and nobody is going to keep me from fighting." He bent his head, then continued gruffly, "Your friend Judge Russell has just made the biggest mistake of his career. I'll use his statement to have him disqualified when the case comes up, and—"

"For God's sake, man, you can't do that! You're putting me on the spot. I'd have to swear to what he said, and I—I don't want to do that."

Joe stood up. "Well, sir, I'm sorry. But my life is on the line. If I blow this, I've lost everything in the world. There's nothing left for us. Nancy can't survive; I can't either. So I've got no other choice."

The elderly jurist gazed sadly at the desolate young man. "I see. Well, let's try something else." And he outlined a presentation he would personally prepare for a special meeting of Hope's board which he himself would request.

Joe brightened. This was more like it! He phoned friends and family, former employers, ministers, brother Phi Gamma Deltas, inviting them to attend the formidable affair. The Hippards came from Houston, Joe's parents from Beaumont, eyes glistening, hearts hopeful, ready to pledge their all in behalf of the heartbroken young parents.

The board was adamant. With regret and a good deal of coldness the chairman declined to consider the matter further. Mark would not be returned to Joe and Nancy Hodges.

That night, the Hippards' hostility toward Joe, never exactly concealed, became blatant.

Shouts resounded through the tiny apartment, Hippard blaming his son-in-law for this new atrocity and every other disaster Joe had brought upon all their heads. "You no-good scoundrel," he yelled. "I knew right along something like this would happen. My poor little girl—"

Florence Hodges flamed with anger. "Be quiet. Joe couldn't help what happened. Can't you see he's suffering?"

Hippard turned on her. "Suffering, my foot! Everybody in this whole family has done nothing but suffer ever since your rotten crook of a son married Nancy . . ."

Joe Hodges, Sr., quietly stood in front of his wife. "Joe is a good boy, and I don't—"

Joe interrupted, pleading with them all to be quiet and help make plans for getting Mark back.

Hippard's voice grew louder as he adjusted his hearing aid. "Get Mark back? Man, are you crazy? They'll never give him back to you—why should they? Goddamn embezzler, gambler, cheat, con man—"

Nancy touched her father's arm. She spoke with a new calm and there was a steely note in her voice. "I won't have this any longer. Joe and I will work our future out—alone. Now, all of you, go back home. You can't help us at this point. Joe and I stand together. We're going to get our son back some way . . ."

The Hippards and Joe's parents left the bereaved couple alone at last, returning to their hotel rooms. Then Joe took Nancy's hand. "Come on, we're going to get things moving. Let's go over to Adrian's house and talk to him—tonight."

Adrian Carter was certainly one of the most vigorous and aggressive young attorneys in Irving and he and his wife Sara were by now longtime friends of Joe and Nancy. Together they analyzed the situation and finally Adrian shook his head. "You've got one tough problem on your hands, Joe."

"*We've* got one big problem, Adrian," Joe corrected him, wishing he still had the money he had embezzled from Charlie Wyche. But it had all gone to the bookies and the crap tables at Las Vegas.

He could have used some of it right now, he thought ruefully. Adrian Carter, good friend though he was, loved the sight of the long green. "Adrian," Joe pleaded, "I don't care what it costs—"

Carter then arranged his expression to one of keen concern. Joe and Nancy had discussed Adrian's fee before dropping in on him. There was $4,800 in her own savings account. Joe endorsed the check Nancy had given him. The temptation to cash it the next day and run it up to a big win with Boston or Hill's had been strong. He could have had Adrian working for him without immediate payment. Yet, it was true, he didn't care what it cost to get Mark back. He'd find the money. If he'd been able to raise thumping big sums for the crap tables, he could certainly come through for something far more important than gambling money.

Carter pocketed the check. "Now, about your case—" he began solemnly.

Joe broke in. "Don't worry about it. I'm going to handle it for you. Everybody I know is going to be in on this. Every single soul who can walk or be carried into court on a stretcher is going to be asked to help us. And I know they will."

The next few weeks were composed of eighteen-hour days for Joe. He worked on nothing but the coming trial. Now that he was separated from the city's legal affairs, practicing on his own, he threw everything else aside—for Mark, for Nancy. He organized his lawsuit against Hope Cottage, knowing who their counsel would be, went through back doors to get lists of witnesses being called to testify against him, took any means—fair or questionable—to prepare his attack.

With painstaking care he set down facts Adrian would need to know about every witness, for and against. Ask this man these questions; ask this woman those questions. The answers, he hoped, would roundly confirm the estimable characters of Joe and Nancy Hodges. He gambled on his own testimony, in which he would include the wretchedness of his actions in Zanesville but omit the sentence almost imposed in Roswell. What if the opposing counsel found out? Well, Joe took the chance. The debts he owed his father had already come into the open, but he coached the elder Hodges to say all this money had been repaid. It would be, eventually, Joe knew—but he could live with his failure to repay it in the cause of getting his son back.

Last and most important, he had to square himself with Charlie Wyche. Months had gone by since Joe had taken him $8,000 to apply on the discrepancy. The old man had squinted at him, accepted the money, dismissed him. But now, with so much at stake, Joe went out to the acreage where Wyche held court.

"Charlie, you've got to help me," Joe begged after baring his soul and the pain he and Nancy were suffering. "Whatever you want me to do in return, I'll do—if it takes the rest of my life. But we've got to get our boy back."

Wyche said nothing for a minute, his faded old eyes watering. Then he put out his hand. "Irishman, you got it."

Not even Strasberger would have been daring enough to have every judge in Dallas County disqualified from hearing the case. But Joe went right down the line, knocking Lewis Russell out of the box first. By forcing Judge Russell to acknowledge his serious breach of ethics in telling Henry Strasberger he would not listen to evidence that might change the ruling on the Hope Cottage board's initial decision, Joe embarrassed the most renowned attorney in Dallas. Though this made him the object of Strasberger's ire, it perhaps also earned his grudging respect.

Next Joe entered petitions, or had Adrian Carter enter them, to disqualify every judge in the Dallas area who perforce would have been prejudiced in the case in favor of Hope Cottage, a United Fund Agency, and therefore unable to render an unbiased verdict.

Totally at a loss, the Dallas courts had recourse to a little plains town seventy miles to the southwest, Cleburne, Texas. The judge out there who was chosen to preside was a venerable and able man, Penn Jackson. This was hanging judge territory, where men were men and God help anybody who came poking around to do evil against the upright hardworking citizen. Judge Jackson was not one to be rattled by the fancy law firms in Big D, nor was he one to feel that an old maid like Miss Selby Fly had any call to snatch an innocent baby from the arms of a loving young couple like the Hodgeses. So the daddy had gambled some. So he'd used some money that didn't belong to him. Judge Penn Jackson couldn't have been a better choice so far as Joe Hodges was concerned.

Charlie Wyche was again closely following Joe's fortunes. "Irishman," he suggested, "me and you might take a little drive out Cleburne way. I got business out there, sort of, and it wouldn't hurt none to stop in and pay my respects to my old friend Penn."

The judge wasn't in court when they arrived, wasn't at home, wasn't to be found. But a gas attendant knew exactly where he was. "You know the pond down by Barrett's place? He's fishin' down there. Saw him headin' out there 'bout a hour ago."

Charlie played it cautiously when he and Joe found the judge sitting beside the pond with a line out. There must be no question of tampering with the legal process. They talked about weather, crops, the damfool in the White House and the damfools in the Congress. Charlie said, "I caused my young friend here a lot of trouble, Penn, and I'm trying to get it straightened out. Just wanted you to have my word on it. This Irishman is true blue, and when the trial comes up I intend to stand there and say so."

The courtroom in Dallas was crowded, and it seemed to tall, curly-haired, ruddy-faced attorney Charlie Shields that the room bulged mainly with witnesses called by the plaintiff, Hodges. Charles Shields represented Hope Cottage, and his air of assurance was no accident. He was certain of victory, so much so that he had made a date for lunch, expecting the case to be over within two hours. Now he doubted it, though his confidence was no whit abated. What could this embezzler present to any sane court that would overthrow the mighty board of governors of Hope Cottage! The adoption agency was held as sacred by civic leaders in Dallas, backed by its wealthiest and most powerful citizenry. And anyway, he had not been idle. Shields's investigators had combed Joe's background, dredging up names of bookies and amounts of debts owed to a handful of banks right there in Dallas, not to mention another fistful of finance companies.

Joe had heard about the investigators. He had followed every inquiry they made, making very sure of what they could learn, and what they could not. The Midland-Roswell near conviction hadn't been discovered, he felt sure. And when he got on the stand he was going to bring up and defend his other transgressions himself, before Charles Shields had a crack at them. More important still, Shields did not know that Joe and Charlie Wyche were back together, this time as firm friends. Who would have guessed *that,* when it was the Wyche indictment that had brought on the whole adoption reversal? Shields hadn't an inkling of it.

Adrian Carter was enjoying himself thoroughly. Lawyers actually were more in the limelight of a widely publicized trial than were the principals, and he was aware of how success on this one would enhance his legal reputation. He had done little work in preparation; it hadn't been necessary. Joe was a veritable tiger and had gone into intricacies that Carter would not have bothered with, yet was delighted to have handed to him. He sure as hell knew what to do with a case so well prepared. Smiling, he bowed in mock courtesy to his opposing counsel. Shields returned the salute with an even broader smile.

As the witnesses testified to the fitness and character of Joe and Nancy as potential parents, noon came and Judge Jackson recessed. The afternoon droned along, with Joe's father bringing half the women in the courtroom to tears. A fine son, a noble boy who had inadvertently got into trouble, but was honest enough to make restitution for his deeds. It was a moving testament, indeed almost irresistible.

Nancy spoke briefly, her sweet gentle demeanor saying all that needed to be said. The Reverend Henry Kincaid, minister of the Baptist Church in Irving, which had a huge congregation, made an eloquent and forceful statement describing how Joe had represented him when he was badly injured in an automobile accident—foregoing any fee. Others came forward like stalwarts, helping Joe enormously. But his own minister, envisioning himself as an arbiter of divine justice, began hedging, doubtless remembering a number of times when Joe disappeared from the choir loft to place bets over the minister's own telephone.

Alarmed, Joe quickly jotted down a message to Adrian sitting beside him. Adrian nodded and began direct cross-examination.

"Would you say, then, Reverend, that every sinner should have his children taken from him? That Jesus Christ would deny forgiveness to a man like Joe Hodges? That even though he has repaid every cent of money, he still must go through life without this baby boy—because Joe Hodges is guilty of having sinned?"

The man of God canceled any unsavory impressions he might have left and scuttled down from the witness stand on the double.

Then Charlie Wyche was called. Charlie was no stranger to courtrooms, having testified for many a culprit and aggrieved plaintiff in his time. Usually looking like a candidate for a Salvation Army clothing donation, today Charlie was wearing a clean shirt, unmatched but presentable coat and trousers, and boots with no sign of manure clinging to them.

Shields was furious with him. "Perhaps, Mr. Wyche, you would tell the court how you happened to quash the indictment against Mr. Hodges at the last moment, when you were so intent only recently on its coming to trial at the earliest possible time?" The sarcasm was intended to wither a bronze statue, but Wyche grinned innocently up at the fuming barrister.

"How's that, young feller? Didn't hear you rightly."

Shields repeated the question, underlining the key words with deafening emphasis.

"Oh yeah, I'm dee-lighted to oblige you, sir. Fact is, *if* I hadn't had this opportunity to put matters right for my friend Joe, I'd have took me out a full-page advertisement in the Dallas papers to speak out about it. See, I found that my accountants had made a turrible mistake—" Charlie allowed his ancient face to mirror the dreadful confession to come. "Joe hadn't taken none of my money. No, not a dime. We just got our wires crossed and I misunderstood what had happened. And here I'm the cause of these fine folks losing that little baby—" Charlie worked the muscles in his cheeks to indicate atonement for his own sin and hope of salvation.

Joe's jaw dropped. The old man was perjuring himself. In his wildest fantasies Joe had never imagined anything like this. He watched, mesmerized, as Shields tried to regain ground. Finding himself boxed in, the attorney dismissed Mr. Wyche, who humbly looked out at the crowded courtroom as though pleading for their forgiveness. What a consummate actor this eccentric old millionaire truly was! Joe wanted to laugh and cry at once.

Attorney Shields was now smiling once again. "Will Father O'Bannion please come to the stand and be sworn?" He grinned briefly at Adrian Carter as he produced his trump.

Joe well understood Shields's look of triumph. The Catholic priest could have been a damaging witness, except for fortuitous circumstance. A secretary in Shields's office was accommodating enough to look at the file of subpoenaed witnesses and pass the list along to Adrian. Father Joe O'Bannion's name was there.

Father O'Bannion. Joe had almost forgotten about the priest. The bursar at Dallas University, like others before him, knew only that Joe was the "victim of a friend's bad faith." But it wouldn't do for the priest to take the stand and recite this now familiar tale. So, after two days of exhausting drama in the courtroom, Joe and Nancy's task was unfinished.

At nine that night after the long exhausting second day of the hearing, they drove to the University of Dallas rectory. It was dark inside but the lighted doorway was a sign that the priest was returning later. They waited patiently but it was two in the morning before they heard him sauntering up the walk singing under his breath.

Unflappable, Father O'Bannion swiftly recovered from his momentary fright when the two figures had emerged from the shadows. He listened carefully to Joe's plight, and thanked him for his candor. "I'm so glad you came. I didn't know why I was subpoenaed, but now I'll know what to do."

On the stand Father O'Bannion returned the intent gaze of

Attorney Shields with a look of astonishment. "But Counselor, Mr. Hodges has repaid me. In full . . ."

Shields was sweating now, irritably issuing curt requests to his two assistants and pulling at his collar which had suddenly begun to feel like a noose. His discomfiture was infectious, and Selby Fly glanced uneasily at her coterie of board members. Their case had begun to come apart at the seams, no question about it. But surely the old judge from Cleburne would respect the incontrovertible Truth and Rightness of their position. Still . . .

Judge Jackson peered at the two attorneys. "Any further witnesses?" he asked, obviously assuming there were none.

Adrian Carter rose dramatically to his feet and just then there was a flurry in the rear of the courtroom. Whispered comments fluttered through the crowd as the slight, gray-haired man diffidently picked his way through the guards and approached the bench. For a moment Joe thought old Penn Jackson himself was going to stand up and bow, but he only nodded deferentially to Henry Strasberger.

Charlie Shields couldn't believe his eyes. "My God," he muttered, "they aren't going to put Strasberger on, are they?"

Adrian relished the confusion, calmly observing Strasberger's progress toward the august bar of justice.

"If it pleases the court," he began, "we are honored that a special witness has requested to be heard." He adjusted his neat polka-dot tie, drawing all eyes to himself. Adrian was not a man to pass up an opportunity for theater, not one of this illustrious caliber. "May I present to the court the Honorable Henry Strasberger, who in truth needs no introduction to this assembly."

Strasberger could have taught a lesson in acting technique for courtroom demeanor himself. He bowed slightly to the bench and took his seat in the witness box. "Your Honor, I wonder if I may beg your indulgence—" Mr. Strasberger settled himself comfortably in the chair, turning to Judge Jackson courteously, his crisp black eyebrows raised. "If I may, I would like to testify here with my eyes closed. You see, I have great difficulty with cataracts, and my eyes are bothering me today."

Judge Jackson was agreeing before Strasberger finished his request.

Adrian Carter then interjected a request of his own. "If it please the court, may we have permission for Mr. Strasberger to offer his comments in narrative style rather than the customary question and answer form. After all"—he paused, smiling broadly —"I believe we can assume this witness is perfectly conversant with what information is admissible and what is not." A titter of approval went up from the crowd.

The judge rapped his gavel. "Please proceed, sir," he respectfully directed the witness.

By this time, the presence of the famous attorney in the courtroom as a witness for an indicted fellow lawyer had electrified the courthouse, and several attorneys had slipped into the rear of the room to see what he was up to.

With a wrenching eloquence Strasberger told the spellbound room of his own first encounter with Joe and Nancy. How he had been awed by the courage and determination of the stricken young father in the face of insuperable odds. How he, Strasberger, had been humbled by the singleness of purpose he observed in Joe as he fought on, certain to be defeated yet refusing to give up the battle for his son. Then he opened his eyes to a slit, darting a quick look at the faces before him. He smiled, and nodded slightly, as though to himself. Henry Strasberger was the first man in the room to know how the case would be decided.

He was excused from the witness stand, and as he groped his way toward the counsel table, a ripple of applause raced through the courtroom like autumn leaves in a gust of wind.

Judge Jackson straightened, removed his glasses, and prepared to close the arguments. "I am not asking these attorneys to make closing statements. We've heard the arguments. We know the grounds. I shall need no further time to come to my decision. I've known many men in my time—good fathers, bad fathers. Some of the good ones were not without sin themselves, some of the bad parents were free from apparent transgressions in the eyes of the world. I believe that sin or lack of sin is not what determines how good or bad a daddy a man will be. No, it's how a man feels about his child that matters. To be wanted, loved, needed—that's what every child needs most. And I believe that no child could be wanted more than this little baby, by these young people. I now award Mark to Joe and Nancy Hodges. The adoption is final and for all time."

The sharp rap of the gavel sent shock waves through the stern-faced director of Hope Cottage, Miss Selby Fly, and the once complacent attorney Charlie Shields. "Court is dismissed."

CHAPTER 20

"I.D. please, sir," the cashier at the El Cortez requested as Jonathan Alan Roberts pushed the Western Union check underneath the bars.

"If you call over there they'll confirm this is my check, that I had the right code word."

Without replying the cashier picked up the phone, dialed the number, and apparently recognized the voice of the Western Union clerk. "Jonathan Alan Roberts?" the El Cortez cashier inquired.

She listened a moment and then hung up the phone and began counting cash.

"I'll take it in hundreds," Jon said.

Methodically the money was counted out and the stacks of $100 bills handed to him. Jon took the money and, after folding the fifty $100 bills, jammed the bankroll into his right pants pocket. As long as he was already at the El Cortez he thought he might as well start out right here. He picked a different crap table than the one which had absorbed his last thin bankroll and threw down $1,000 cash.

"Give me twenty-five-dollar chips." Racking his chips in front of him Jon began the play. He bet conservatively now, planning to build his $5,000 up to the sort of money he wanted to have when he returned to the Strip and the class casinos.

As he put a $25 chip on the pass line and took double odds, Jon Roberts' luck took a turn for the better. In seven hours of conservative, attentive play, occasionally buying the numbers but usually only backing up his front-line bet with double odds, he won $17,000. He stepped back from the crap table, cashing in and putting $22,000 in his pocket. He was ecstatic as Kenny Epstein, owner of the El Cortez, walked up to him. "Looks like you done great," the owner said, sounding pleased with Jon's win. "We'd like you to stay with us, Mr. R. We've got a nice suite upstairs for you. Would you care to have dinner with us?"

Jonathan Roberts suddenly was conscious of his dirty shirt, his loose tie, the smell of tobacco smoke and liquor about him. But his thoughts turned to the bigger game ahead of him. He didn't want to stay at the El Cortez tonight.

"Thank you, Kenny. I'll be back."

He walked the two blocks to the Golden Nugget where he got a luxury room and then in the men's shop bought a clean shirt, clean underwear and socks as well as toilet articles. Then he went upstairs to his room to take a shower and get ready for the big play ahead. He called down to the valet to come up and take his suit and press it.

As he sat in the living room of his suite, shaved, clean-shirted, and waiting for his freshly pressed suit to be delivered, his voice and color came back. All he could think of was he had $22,000 now. He had recaptured his aplomb and cool demeanor. He was ready to go out and make the big move. The fact that he was actually thirty thousand short of the money he'd had twenty-four hours ago meant nothing. All that was important was that he had the big bankroll now to go ahead and win.

As he sat reveling in anticipation of the big win, Jon remembered the gorgeous young Chinese girl he'd met two months before. Addie Wong was a shill at the Tropicana. She was paid to sit at the baccarat table and attract attention and gamblers. She sure had attracted them, Jon thought, chuckling to himself.

He decided to call Addie at home. Pulling out his wallet he found her number and dialed nine for a local call and then Addie's phone number. Her exciting, somewhat reedy voice came on the line.

"Addie, Jonathan Roberts here."

"Jon!" Addie exclaimed. "Where have you been?"

"I've been meaning to call you since I got here, Addie. Are you free for dinner tonight?"

"Of course, Jon. Where are you?"

"Come on down to the Golden Nugget. I'm in room 1727."

"Just as soon as I get dressed I'll be there, Jon," she cooed.

The suit arrived and he hung it up, after tipping the valet, deciding not to dress completely before Addie arrived. In a few minutes there was a rap on the door and Jon, dressed in his shirt and underwear, walked over and opened it.

The beautiful Chinese girl, her long black hair parted slightly above the middle of her forehead and hanging down to her shoulders, slid into the room and pushed the door closed behind her. She slipped into Jon's arms and returned his ardent kiss. He led her to the bedroom where he had already pulled the red satin cover back from the round bed. There was no need for conversation. Addie slid out of her Chinese-style sheath dress with its long slit up the side, and they were in bed immediately. The lovemaking was passionate, Addie, as always, superb.

Later, languorously, she slipped out of the bed and walked into the bathroom, Jon behind her. "You have been very cruel to me, Jon," she chastised him. "Why do you not call me for so long?"

"I'll never let it happen again," he bantered.

"I have the night off tonight. Why don't you come over and stay with me?"

"Sounds good," he replied noncommittally. "How about some Chinese food down at Lillie Langtry's?"

She turned to him and nodded.

At the famed Chinese restaurant in the Golden Nugget Hotel, they enjoyed a fine dinner. "Now, Jon, take me to a show, then we'll go back home. I want you to see my house. You will love it. Maybe you'll never leave Las Vegas, just stay here with me."

But it was time Jon tended to business. "Addie, I'd love to do that but I've got these men coming in from New York. I've got to entertain them tonight. We're putting together a really big real estate deal."

She gave him a disappointed look. "I'll help you entertain them, Jon. As long as you come back home with me afterwards."

More pressing and far more important activities were on his mind now. With his physical appetite temporarily sated, his suit freshly pressed, and $22,000 in his back pocket, he was ready for the real action, ready for what life was truly all about. All he could think of was the no-limit game at Binion's. That was where he would really score.

"Look, let me go on to the airport and pick these guys up and then I'll call you," he lied. He well knew there was only one activity that would totally hold his interest tonight. He took a disappointed Addie out to the entrance of the hotel. The doorman ordered her car to be brought around and Jon kissed her as he helped her behind the wheel and closed the door.

She looked at him sadly, waved, then drove off. Her car had not even disappeared down the street before Jon was briskly striding toward Binion's. He walked into the casino and picked up the house phone beside the bank of cashier cages.

"Jack Binion, please."

"Who's calling?" the operator asked.

"Tell him it's Jonathan Alan Roberts," Jon instructed. Moments later he heard the cheerful voice of Jack Binion. "Jon, is that you? I'll be right down."

"I'm here at the cashier's booth, Jack."

CHAPTER 21

After the judge's decision had rung out in the courtroom, the excitement died down. Hope Cottage's lawyer, Charlie Shields, turned to Adrian Carter and said caustically, "I'm certain we're appealing this case."

"Be my guest, Charlie," Adrian replied cheerfully. He knew how difficult it was to overturn a decision like the one Judge Jackson had just handed down. It would be as difficult as Joe Hodges' successful quest, and that had come in the category of miracle. It was a miracle of hard work and astute thinking and perjury and love.

Hope Cottage did indeed appeal the judge's decision, and while it was no miracle that the Hodgeses won the appeal, the foundation kept Mark during the time the appeal was under consideration.

Joe was more than grateful to his good friend Adrian Carter. Sure, Adrian regularly beat him out of money, whether in the form of legal fees or profits from business deals they went into together. From the latter Adrian always emerged the richer, the recipient of Joe's largesse, which was a token of devotion and respect. While waiting for their son, Joe and Nancy bought a silver coffee urn to present to Adrian and had it inscribed, "In Remembrance of You—Mark."

Joe filed numerous petitions to have the child returned during the appeal, but to no avail. Finally, forty-one days after Judge Jackson handed down his decision, the Texas Appellate Court affirmed it.

The day after the decision was announced, a thoroughly disgruntled Miss Selby Fly called Joe and said Mark would be at Hope Cottage at three in the afternoon. Trembling with excitement, Joe and Nancy returned to Hope Cottage for the first time since their shattering experience with Miss Fly so many months before.

Would baby Mark remember them? Anxiously they waited in the nursery for their baby. Finally the moment arrived. The door opened. Mark, by now ten and a half months old, was delivered to them.

An attendant sent him forward in a walker toward his parents, toddling precariously. Nancy and Joe looked down at their son, their eyes wet with tears of joy. Nancy reached out a tentative hand and was rewarded with a wide smile as Mark stretched out both his arms toward her. At last the victory was won, the long ordeal over. Joe and Nancy took their baby in their arms and then Joe carried him out of Hope Cottage and back to their modest home.

Even before Mark's return, Joe had come to a hard decision. His debt structure had now risen to between $30,000 and $40,000, much of it as a result of the expensive trial and its painstaking preparations. Then the trial itself, despite its victorious outcome, had put him on notice that he was no longer a valued citizen of Irving and Dallas.

Yes, he and Charlie Wyche were friends again, of sorts. It was not the way it used to be but at least they had reestablished a warm relationship. Nevertheless, Joe knew he and Nancy had to leave this scene of bitter memories, all of them the fruits of his compulsive gambling.

Joe's fortunes in Irving had begun to deteriorate markedly before the town fathers felt compelled to relieve him of his duties as city attorney. However, it was after he had begun private practice, though retaining some of the city's law business, that another job unexpectedly became available. In the summer of 1961 the disastrous hurricane Carla hit the Gulf Coast of Texas, wiping out homes and businesses from Louisiana to Brownsville valued at millions of dollars.

A new agency within the federal government, the Small Business Administration, was assigned the job of handling loans to help people rebuild. Joe applied for and was given the job of SBA administrator in charge of placing $30 million in federally guaranteed loans. Out of the regional office of the SBA in Dallas, he worked with the banks all along the Gulf Coast to guarantee the loans approved by him and his assistants.

As legal adviser to the SBA with a rating of GS-8, Joe, who had been pumping money to support his gambling, felt somewhat like the proverbial fox in the chicken coop. Here he was dealing daily with bank presidents and loan officers all over Texas, coming to them in the exalted position of the attorney administrator empowered to give them a federal guarantee on loans to the needy.

Joe had received FBI clearance to handle this job with no problem. He was fingerprinted and a full-scale investigation was supposed to have been conducted. Nothing of his shadowy background, not even the local indictment for defrauding Charlie Wyche, came to the bureau's attention.

Shortly after three-week-old Mark's arrival, he had found himself plunged into this exciting new area of endeavor, and his work with the SBA continued even after Mark was taken away. But by the time the trial was concluded and Mark restored to his adoptive parents, the SBA job had been completed. During the time Joe was working for the SBA, he dealt with large sums of money at the National Bank of Commerce in Dallas, among other banks, and was depositing checks there, including his paychecks from the city of Irving and the SBA. He became friendly with the tellers at the bank, particularly with young Bob Jones who was understandably impressed by his important post.

Between the challenging job with the SBA and the tormenting struggle to get his son back, Joe had lost all interest in gambling, and indeed didn't have the time or energy for it. But now, with Mark safely returned and the SBA job completed, he could turn his mind to other thoughts. The first order of business was to move himself, Nancy, and Mark out of Dallas. Houston was the first choice for relocation. He would be closer to his parents in Beaumont and to the many friends he and Nancy had in the Houston area. Houston had just secured a franchise for a National League baseball team and the Houston Astros were coming into being. Once again Joe's old dream of a job in the administrative end of baseball seemed a possibility. He made a one-day trip to see the officials of the Houston Astros and Judge Hoffines, the administrator of the new Houston Astrodome.

Joe's exploratory mission to Houston did not net him a job in baseball. However, he sensed the new excitement that the NASA space-control installations had brought to the already booming city. Though Houston is situated inland, it has dug itself a broad channel to the Gulf and ships out enough oil, grain, and cattle to make it one of the world's largest ports in terms of tonnage.

Joe heard about the big deal made by Exxon with the Del Webb Development Corporation to build a town of thirty thousand homes around the NASA-manned spacecraft center which was to be called Clear Lake City. Big things were obviously happening in Houston and this was Joe's chance to become part of a brave new world of business and industry.

While exploring his opportunities in Houston, he looked up his old friend Jay Crager who had once worked at the American National Bank in Beaumont. He had been hired by a young and enterprising businessman, Walter Mischer, to come to Houston and take over a top position with the Continental Bank of Houston which Mischer had recently purchased. Jay was now a successful young banker and had inherited from his grandparents in Ohio, who owned a sporting goods company, a considerable personal fortune. Despite Joe's compulsive gambling, which had caused a rift in his business relationship with Jay, their personal friendship had never diminished.

Jay gave Joe much useful information on Mischer and his enterprises, but it was not Jay who introduced the two men. Joe himself called Walter Mischer, made an appointment to see him and explained that he had been the city attorney of Irving and had worked for the federal government in the Small Business Administration. Joe had always been a great salesman, and the product he sold best was himself. He presented only the positive side of his personality to Mischer, and the result was that Mischer gave him a job promoting two motels he had bought.

Joe moved Nancy and Mark from Dallas down to Houston where he took over the Carousel Motel out on the Gulf Freeway and the Coronado Motel. One valuable benefit of the job was that it came with a complimentary apartment.

Joe was happy in his association with Walter Mischer whom he saw as something of a younger Charlie Wyche. He discerned on first meeting him that he was a man going to the top, and fast. He was a gambler, too, though not of Joe's type—he only gambled in business, where he was extremely successful.

Nancy was delighted at the move to Houston, and now that Mark was back with her again, the Hippards once more accepted Joe as their son-in-law. Joe left behind in Irving a debt structure of almost $40,000 which, though considerably less than the amount he had owed at one time, was still a worry to him. As always, he carried his list of creditors with him everywhere and kept them informed of where he was and assured them he would pay them back. He was not entirely happy about the move to Houston but for Nancy and Mark's sake he knew he had done the right thing.

By the fall of 1962, when the little family were settled into the Carousel apartment and Joe had started his job with the two motels, he began looking for a local bookie. He was not successful, and so started calling his bets in to one of his old Dallas bookmakers, Johnny Stone. He owed Boston Smith in Fort Worth $5,000 on an unpaid loan and couldn't bet with him. Stone's runner-cum-money collector was known simply as Red and through him Joe quickly evolved a system for betting on the sports.

By telephone he reintroduced himself to the young teller he had known at the National Bank of Commerce in Dallas, Bob Jones.

"Bob, remember me, Joe Hodges, city attorney in Irving, SBA administrator?"

"Of course, Joe. It's been a long time since we've seen you. Where are you?"

"I'm down here in Houston. Running a couple of hotels for an old friend. You might have heard of him—Walter Mischer." Mischer had been featured in the business pages of the Texas newspapers for a year and anybody up and coming in banking would have known his name. Bob Jones was suitably impressed.

"Bob, I've got a little problem I think you can help me with," Joe began his pitch.

"Sure, Joe. Anything. What can I do for you?"

"I have a business associate up there in Dallas, Johnny Stone. I need to get him some money right away. If you could scrounge up a thousand dollars he'll be in to see you in an hour and tomorrow he'll bring you back twelve hundred or I'll wire it to you from here. Okay?"

There was a pause on the other end of the line. "You mean make you an overnight loan of a thousand dollars and you'll pay 20 percent interest?"

"That's right, Bob. Six to five. I guess you know me well enough to know that come tomorrow you'll be paid."

"Oh sure, Joe. It's a little unusual, of course, but I guess I can cover the deal. When's he coming in?"

"He'll be in before lunch, Bob."

"Okay, Joe. Of course I want to be of help." There was a dubious sound to the young teller's voice.

"You won't regret it, Bob."

"Okay, Joe. Send your man in. And be sure to call me tomorrow morning."

The next call Joe placed was to Stone in Dallas. It was December, the end of the football season and the beginning of basketball. Joe picked three teams, betting a total of $1,000, and told Stone to send Red to the bank and see the teller Bob Jones.

The next morning Joe was waiting for the newspapers to come in to the motel lobby at six o'clock. He grabbed a paper off the top of the pile, went back to his apartment, closeted himself in the bathroom and opened to the sports pages. He slapped his hand across the results of the basketball games and one by one allowed himself to see how his teams made out.

"Wow!" he exclaimed aloud. "You won them all. Who says you don't know how to bet basketball?" He could hardly contain himself until he could call Johnny in Dallas at ten o'clock and direct that $1,200 be delivered to Bob Jones at the bank and the rest of the $3,000 he had won be put into his credit account with the bookie. And so Joe's betting system long distance from Houston to Dallas, which would eventually lead to other places, other towns, had been formed.

He began reading the financial pages of the Houston newspapers as well as the sports pages. He became more and more fascinated by the huge development deal between Exxon, Del Webb, and NASA which would result in that instant city out at Clear Lake.

The father of Margene West, one of the girls Joe had known at the University of Texas, had given a large portion of his huge ranch between Houston and Galveston to Rice University which in turn donated it to the federal government for the NASA center. Exxon Corporation had acquired the rest of big Jim West's ranch for drilling purposes and then decided to develop the forty thousand acres adjacent to the NASA center into Clear Lake City.

Exxon, though successful in the oil business, knew nothing about development and had hired the Del Webb company to handle it. Del Webb, himself a shrewd old operator, made a razor-sharp deal with Exxon. His company and Exxon would together develop the city. Exxon would get 70 percent of profits, Webb 30 percent. However, there was one other aspect of the deal which was not publicized but indicated how brilliant a transaction Del Webb had negotiated.

The entire operation would be financed by Exxon and for every $100 million of Exxon money Webb spent, $5 million in cash came to Webb's coffers. In short, the more Webb spent the more it made.

When Joe became aware of the unpublished aspect of the Del Webb–Exxon deal, he made up his mind he'd like to work for Del Webb Development Corporation. This was the sort of deal he could understand and admire, and one of its interesting elements was that the First National City Bank of New York was behind it. Exxon could obviously get all the bank loans it wanted from First National—and bank loans were Joe's forte.

Once again he picked the company he wanted to work for and walked in cold to get the job. After some preliminary conversations, he found himself talking to a vice-president of the Del Webb corporation, Wesley Mohr. Mohr headed up the division of Del Webb that had formed the partnership with Exxon. As always seemed to happen when he pursued a job, luck was with him. Webb needed a man with Joe's credentials: he was a Houston lawyer and he had worked for the city of Irving where he had gained impressive development experiences.

Webb was growing faster than it could staff up and after reading Joe's résumé, Mohr realized how fortunate he was that Joe Hodges had chanced through the door. The company never looked beyond this applicant's obvious credentials and the same day he was given a job at one thousand dollars a month with a substantial expense account. Joe went back to Walter Mischer, thanked him for giving him the motel management position, and quit. At Del Webb he would start in the property management department as assistant manager. Walter Mischer was truly happy for Joe, knowing that the motel job was really far below his abilities.

In less than a week from the time of his interview with the Del Webb vice-president, Joe was sitting in a pleasant office with his name, J. H. Hodges, on the door. Soon he was doing business with some prestigious law firms, with Leon Jaworski's firm in Houston, Fulbright, Crooker; with Andrews, Kurth; and with Butler, Binion, Rice and Cook. Now he was dealing with the First National City Bank in New York, the First City National in Houston, the National Bank of Commerce in Houston, and the Chase Manhattan in New York. He enjoyed his work and was appreciated and respected by his colleagues.

Joe's star rose at Webb. Mr. Webb, meeting him in the corridor, would sing out, "Hi, Joe" or "If you've got a moment, would you drop in to my office?" He found himself promoted above men who had been with the organization for years and became an integral part of the hotels and motels it was building. At Clear Lake the utilities were all being built underground and a $1 million recreation center was in the works. Joe's natural powers of persuasion enabled him to secure for himself a strong management position overseeing Webb's field departments even though, as he confessed, he didn't know how to unplug a radio.

Rapidly as Joe climbed in Del Webb, the evil shadow that lurked within his psyche was never dormant. While Joe worked, the gambler was always there, waiting to absorb the profits. Joe was constantly calling Bob Jones at the bank in Dallas. It was the deal of a lifetime for the young teller who had long since forgotten any misapprehensions he might have had about the legality of what he was doing. Three and four days a week Johnny Stone or his runner, Red, would come by the bank and pick up anywhere from $1,000 to $5,000 from the teller Bob Jones. The following day, or perhaps two days later, if Joe won, Red would return the money plus 20 percent to Jones or, if Joe lost, Joe would wire the money from Houston.

Joe's salary was raised to $2,000 a month and he was given a new office right next to Wesley Mohr's. His new title was Assistant to the Project Manager. It was Joe now who was calling the First National City Bank of New York when the consortium needed $5 or $10 million. First National transferred the funds to the Bank of Commerce in Houston or one of the other large local banks and Joe would arrange the transfer to Webb.

Never had Joe created such lush pickings for the gambler as when he achieved his preeminent position in Houston at Del Webb. As a respectable lawyer he was creating his "spots"; then the compulsive gambler was making use of them. Three and four days a week the gambler was instructing Bob Jones in Dallas to give Red the money he wagered on sports events. When he won, Red brought the money back to the bank. But when he lost, which was becoming more frequent, Joe went down to the National Bank of Commerce or one of the other banks with whom he was doing business and borrowed what was needed.

The 20 percent vigorish which Jones put in his own pocket meant nothing to Joe. All he wanted was to be sure that the money was delivered to the bookie. While he was actually gambling, nothing else mattered. Of course with winter came the basketball season—Joe's downfall in Beaumont and in Zanesville. "The baskets" also drained him in Irving but he had to have his fix of action which insisted on his betting basketball.

Despite his gambling losses, he was an important executive now with the Del Webb–Exxon combine known as Friendswood Development Corporation. When advertising and promotion for the project were needed, he was working with a Houston advertising man named Jack Valenti, today the president of the Motion Picture Association. Jack Valenti was a struggling advertising and publicity man but, with Joe, he was rising fast in the Del Webb operation and sitting in on board meetings with the top executives of Exxon.

Joe was making $2,000 a month, had a generous expense account and membership cards to all the posh clubs in Houston. When business executives came in from New York and from Phoenix, where the Del Webb home office was located, it was his job to entertain them. And he was flying to Phoenix now to sit in on the corporation's board meetings.

Meantime, Del Webb was acquiring casinos in Las Vegas. Joe was asked to fly out and attend the meeting. Of course he had been visiting Las Vegas whenever he could, supplementing his gambling in Dallas through Bob Jones at the bank and Johnny Stone.

At a Del Webb board meeting held in the rooftop function room of its own Sahara Hotel in Las Vegas, Joe suddenly felt confident enough of his standing with the corporation to excuse himself in the middle of the discussion on the pretext of having to go to the bathroom. Once outside the room, he made for the elevators to the casino.

Nobody knew him. The pit boss had no idea that the young man was an executive of the Del Webb corporation.

Joe wasted no time getting his hands on the dice and throwing them down the table. He felt that old winning streak hovering over him. He bet heavily, buying the numbers, in effect betting that he would not throw a seven before each of the numbers he was betting on came out. He was hot. Each time he threw a five, a six, an eight, a nine, or a ten his mound of chips shot up dramatically. Somehow he anticipated the seven and pulled his bets back. When the seven came out, he was standing at the crap table $10,000 ahead in a matter of ten minutes. With the black chips bulging in his pockets, he made his way through a tense crowd of gamblers who had watched his play and at the cashier's cage began shoveling his chips under the bars. When the chips had been counted and a sheath of $100 bills pushed out to him, he counted himself a $11,000 winner. The stack of bills fitted neatly into the left breast pocket of the conservative banker's suit he had worn to the board meeting. They made only a slightly perceptible bulge. He wished he had the time to ride out his winning streak and perhaps run his bankroll up to $25,000 or $30,000. But how long can a man stay away from an important directors' meeting on the pretext of going to the bathroom?

Joe breezed back in to the meeting. Now that he had experienced his gloriously successful win, he could look out over the casinos stretched up and down the Strip without that mind-devouring compulsion to get some action. With his crap table high behind him he turned his mind to the meeting where the purchase of two more casinos, the Thunderbird on the Strip and the Mint downtown, were under consideration. The others at the meeting hardly seemed to notice Joe's absence and return.

CHAPTER 22

Joe managed to get his $11,000 back to Houston intact, but only because the Friendswood meetings that were taking place in Houston required his attention and presence. However, back in Houston it didn't take him long to lose the whole sum, which amounted to about 10 percent of his total debt structure. He reasoned there wasn't any point in paying off his debts with his bankroll which he fully believed he would soon run up into the $100,000 he needed to pay off his back obligations in Irving and Dallas as well as the new bank loans he had run up in Houston.

Typically he would go to Houston's National Bank of Commerce and see the loan officer to make a $7.5 million loan on behalf of the Del Webb–Exxon project. The bank was only too happy to take care of this profitable business.

"Oh, by the way," Joe would say to the vice-president, "as long as I'm here anyway, I need ten thousand to close a deal I'm working on."

"Why sure, Joe. You bet." The vice-president would hand a note across the desk to Joe who signed it for $10,000 and picked up a bank check made out to him personally. There were five trips to Vegas during the time Joe worked for Del Webb, in addition to the almost daily sports betting via Johnny Stone in Dallas who would go to pick up the amount of the bet from Bob Jones, the teller.

As Joe's losses increased, so his ability to pump money decreased. He owed the banks that Webb did business with a total of $60,000 personally as his losing streak continued. However, the occasional win kept him going all through 1963 as he became an increasingly respected executive with Webb. Although by now he was making contact with some of the Houston bookies, he continued wagering in Dallas and had to keep pumping money to cover his twenty-four-hour 20 percent loans with Bob Jones at the National Bank of Commerce in Dallas.

Despite Joe's burgeoning potential at Del Webb, by the end of 1963 and into 1964 the banks and lending institutions to which he owed considerable sums of money were becoming concerned at the fiscal behavior of this rising young executive whose personal needs constantly drove him to increase his loans. Dr. Jekyll was doing very well by Mr. Hyde.

With the banks showing signs of drying up, Joe began tapping his fellow executives at Webb. Being both personable and successful, he had little trouble getting personal loans from other company men and they did not question the sometimes unlikely stories he told them. Although largely unnoticed by his superiors at Del Webb, Joe's compulsive predilection for sweating the games on which he wagered became dangerously time-consuming. The gambler, whose very life depends on the outcome of the games, is not the routine bettor who calls in his wager and in due course receives the results. Also interfering with his work was the study and preparation for the first phone call of the day to his bookie. Then, after the early results from daylight East Coast games, there were the calculations to be made of wins and losses and the call back to the bookie wagering the day's profits on the West Coast games to come. If he lost, he would go out and pump the green to try and break even betting on the later games.

Between the first phone call and the call back, the various games on which Joe had bet the money he had been able to pump that day were under way, and with everything at stake—criminally, financially, maritally—he did sweat out the results. Getting near a radio, even if it meant jumping in the car and driving up to a vantage point where he could bring in a distant station, and fuming at the news reports as he waited for the sports results to come in, took their toll of his time and energy.

In the middle of the afternoon, with New York an hour ahead of Houston, Joe would make some excuse to get out of his office and go over to the radio station where he would hang around and, sweating profusely, close to nervous prostration, try to find out how the Yankees were doing. Even if the team he bet on was 5–0 ahead, he couldn't just shrug and say, "Well, I won that one." You never knew what might happen in the last inning.

His ever-present transistor did not work well in the large steel and glass building that housed that Houston offices of the Del Webb Development Corporation. So with the little radio in his pocket, he would go outdoors and walk around the building catching the results. When the results didn't come in on his transistor, he went down to KPRC or the television station KTRK-TV and stood around at the reception desk where the wire service telex machines are in a glass case and the newsmen come out from the studios to check the news.

He had to maintain the ruse that he was having an extra cup of coffee which happened to be near the ticker machine. He was always conscious of not wanting to look to the police like a big-time bookie or perhaps appear to be disseminating information to other bookies.

Thus every day Joe was inordinately busy. He had to know the results—immediately. He couldn't stand not knowing how his games were progressing from inning to inning or, in the football season, from quarter to quarter. Every day it seemed as though his very existence was bet on those games. It was! Time went sometimes fast, sometimes slowly, and there was no stability to his life. He was on a roller coaster. Perhaps he had $20,000 at nine in the morning, but it didn't mean anything. By nightfall he owed it. His constant need for information on the games was like an addict's need for a fix.

When he learned that he was a loser, at least the sweating-out period was over and he had the feeling, "Well, I blew that game but wait till tomorrow." When he learned that he had won there was still nothing he could do beyond experiencing the wild thrill a win gave him. Until the next day anyway.

There was no way the office could have located him even had they wanted to. Some of the Houston law firms maintained four or five floors in the major office buildings. Joe had always been in a position where he was his own man, whether he was city attorney of Irving, acquiring oil leases in New Mexico, the only lawyer in the Zanesville office of Tennessee Gas, or running his own show in Beaumont. He had never had to worry about a superior coming up and asking him where he was going or where he had been.

Perhaps the greatest waste of time in Joe's daily life was trying to dial busy bookie numbers. He wore his finger to a glaring red sore spot trying to get his bets down with busy bookies who had only two or three lines. Frequently he sat in a phone booth for an hour, dialing and dialing, trying to devise schemes such as dialing all but the last digit, hoping that this ploy would block the numbers off and get him through.

Eventually he *would* get through. On Sundays in particular he was often so frustrated that he placed his bets without regard to the "line," the odds prevailing that the bookie gave over the phone if you could reach him.

Joe and Nancy had joined the First Methodist Church of Houston as soon as they arrived. With fourteen to fifteen thousand members it is the world's largest Methodist church. In Irving they had formed a Sunday school class whereas here in Houston the church already had its classes. But once again, following the old pattern during church activities, Joe had to excuse himself to get to a phone to get his bets down.

Frequently Joe missed the church services altogether as he fought for a line through to his bookmaker on the telephone in the vestry. Nancy sat erect and alone in the pew, concentrating on the service as though it were perfectly natural for her husband to arrive at church with her, seat her, and then have to leave on some emergency matter.

Back at home she had to struggle with herself to keep from chastising Joe for such erratic behavior in church. If she said anything, the rest of the day would be ruined by a sullen husband nursing his guilt feelings and ignoring her. She wanted so much to help yet she didn't know how.

Late in the summer of 1963, Joe began to make gambling contacts in Houston. The lessons he'd learned from his old friend Buddy Bramlet stood him in good stead when the gamblers tried to take him off in games of gin rummy. The gamblers gave up trying to cheat Joe and although he never gave up betting through his Dallas connections, he did begin to use the Houston bookies as well.

Meantime, he kept up his relationship with Adrian Carter in Irving. Joe and Nancy always felt grateful to Adrian for standing by them in the dark hour when Mark was taken away. There was no more appealing man in Joe's life than the Irving lawyer who, at the same time, continued to beat him over and over again when it came to money. Yet Adrian Carter was the only man with whom Joe's relations were virtually sycophantic.

In Houston Joe was finding it costly, or at least frustrating, to find a bookie with whom he could bet, one that he could trust. At the Montrose Club, where he played cards, a bookmaker named Joe Grimes contacted him. On his first bet Joe won $8,000 from the new contact and then couldn't find him to collect. At least he hadn't lost any money. Sometimes when he was stiffed this way he had lost up to $8,000 or $10,000 with the bookie before the big win which was never paid off. So his Dallas contact was still the safest.

One thing the dope addict and the compulsive gambler have in common is the need for the connection. With the gambler the connection is the bookie. With the addict it's the peddler. Action and heroin. The compulsive gambler must have action. The addict must have heroin. Finally Joe made the connection with Fred Harrison. He didn't have the class of Boston Smith in Fort Worth but he was reliable. Now Joe had the action that was his life support system. He made a deal: he would run a credit or debit tab with Freddy and, come Monday, which was payday, pay either the bookie or be paid by him.

He became a solid customer.

Beginning on the Tuesday after making the contact, Joe started betting with Harrison knowing he had until the following Monday to pay off any losses. In the first day he lost $2,500 and each day thereafter went deeper into the loss column. By Saturday he owed his new bookie $9,700. Going into Sunday morning of his first week he was in the red $9,708.

He got up early in order to read the newspapers before going to church. By this time he knew the newspaper delivery boy well and every morning was always out on the sidewalk waiting for him. Turning to the sports section he skinned it back a little at a time so that he wouldn't get all the scores at once. He found another game on the West Coast the night before that he had lost. Now he was in trouble for the Monday payday. He studied the upcoming baseball games for the day and the probable pitchers. Before going to church he picked six games to bet on, five underdogs and one slight favorite, betting them in various combinations and on a parlay and wrote out his bets which for Sunday totaled $6,000.

Joe and Nancy arrived at church just before Joe's Sunday school class began. He had to keep his class waiting while he went to the bathroom, where there was a pay station, and call in his bets to Freddy. Then, with his wagers made, long shots, he returned to the class. After Sunday school came the church services and after these he shook hands with all their church friends and talked with Dr. Allen and Dick Murray, the associate pastor. Then the ardent churchgoer left for home and a monstrous sweat on the six games.

By nightfall, his nerves raw, Joe had won $20,000. Now, instead of owing the bookies $9,708, the bookie owed him $10,292. On Monday morning he exuberantly called his bookie and they checked the figure—yes, $10,292 Joe's way. At twelve noon Freddy pulled up in front of Joe's office building. Their acquaintanceship had been entirely over the phone and Freddy did not know what Joe looked like. Joe told him he'd be standing out in front of his building and sure enough the bookie drove up, leaned out the window of his car, handed Joe the package and then drove off.

Joe needed the money desperately. He had accumulated debts from individuals which worried him even more than his debts to the banks. Also the rent was due and Nancy was not working because she was busy with Mark.

Going over his loans he realized he owed about $30,000 which must be handled immediately. It did not take him long to determine what to do. He called his office at Webb and said he required an all-afternoon session with the legal firms handling the Clear Lake development. Then he drove to the airport, his bankroll firmly in his pocket, and flew out to Las Vegas. He took a cab to the nearest casino, the Tropicana, and in three hours had lost his $10,000. In a black mood he caught the last nonstop flight to Houston that night.

Before arriving in Houston at 6 A.M., he went through a thorough self-castigation session. Remorse at losing the money that could have helped retire some small part of his debts and made life easier for Nancy ate at his soul. He was almost unbearably aware of his deficiencies as head of his small household. Sitting in the darkened interior of the airliner as it sped him back to the time and place of reckoning up his accounts, both financial and spiritual, he prayed silently.

And then the new plan began to materialize in his mind, and with it came relief. Once he knew what he was going to do next, how he would cope, life seemed manageable, even exciting again.

Somehow he managed to show up at his office with a bright businesslike air at eight the next morning. He immediately called Freddy and started betting again. By the following Monday he owed the bookmaker over $5,500. Meeting him at a coffee shop on the appointed "settling up day," he gave him a story about not having the money. Freddy could hardly believe that he didn't have some of the $10,000 he won the previous Monday.

For the next week Joe began pumping everywhere. He had to get money to send to Bob Jones in Dallas and he knew he must pay Freddy so he could continue getting his Houston "fix."

From within the Del Webb organization Joe borrowed $3,500 from his friend Earl Thompson and then went around to other executives making loans. Finally he called on Jack Valenti and borrowed $3,000 from him. A trip that week to the Houston National Bank of Commerce, through which the big loans from the First National City Bank of New York were funneled into the Del Webb–Exxon oil partnership, produced a $5,000 loan. He went to two finance corporations in Houston, making $2,000 loans at each of them, and continued betting through Dallas again. His Houston action was cut off, at least until he paid Freddy Harrison the $5,500 he owed him.

A friend of Joe's, Tommy Glispen, with whom he played gin rummy, introduced Joe to another bookie named Dave York.

Over the next two weeks Joe lost $10,000 to York, money that he had pumped little by little, the most painful way to do it. Then he took another $1,500 to him and bet a five-team baseball parlay. Again the sweating process. The next morning, slowly skinning back the sports page, getting the scores one by one, he absorbed the impact of first one win, then a second, a third, a fourth. Skinning the page back millimeter by millimeter now, he uncovered the fifth score. He had won the parlay, a $10,000 win! He could hardly wait to get out of his office and call Dave York. But York was nowhere to be found. Joe had been stiffed. He remembered York dialing the number to turn in the $1,500 bet. He had watched carefully and memorized it, thinking that perhaps someday he could make the bets directly without going through this sub-bookmaker. In hopes of getting his money back, he dialed the number and found it was the Atlas Fence Company, which built all types of fences around apartments, houses, swimming pools, and industrial complexes.

Joe went over to the Atlas Fence Company and asked for a name he'd heard Dave York mention, "Turk." Turk turned out to be George Jamail, a man of about Joe's age, a black-haired Lebanese. The Turk was frightened of what Joe might have to say when, after introducing himself, he mentioned Dave York. As it turned out, the Turk was a player who dealt with Freddy, to whom Joe still owed money.

Joe and the Turk liked each other on sight. Saying he could lay off Joe's action for him, the Turk immediately called Dave York and tried to get him to pay up, but to no avail. As it turned out, York had been merely using the Turk to listen on the other end of the phone when he pretended to turn in Joe's bet. It wasn't the Turk's fault that Joe had lost his money. He had merely figured that York had some easy mark and it didn't mean anything for him to be listening on the other end of the phone as though he were taking the bet.

The Turk now became Joe's chief source of action in Houston. He was taking Joe's bets in to Freddy Harrison and got his money for him right away when he won. But it was all cash betting. Although the Turk did not identify his big new customer to Freddy, it didn't take the latter long to figure out he was none other than Joe Hodges, or "the lawyer," as they called him. Joe had a peculiar pattern of betting, almost as individual as a signature, a wild sort of wagering on parlays in combinations. Even though Joe owed him $5,500, Freddy continued to let him bet since he was a good solid customer, turning in cash every day, losing more than he won. As Turk became increasingly friendly with Joe, he marveled at the way the lawyer pumped cash to place through him with the bookies.

One day, after the Turk had been dealing with Joe for a few months, he found out how good a pumper Joe really was. Through a friend he had cultivated, Lovett Baker, president of the Texas National Bank, which was on the ground floor of the office building that housed the Del Webb Houston executive offices, Joe borrowed $5,000 to give Turk for that day's action. Despite his preparation on all relevant facts concerning the baseball games that day, Joe lost the entire amount. The next morning he called Turk and asked him to come by once again. Turk showed up in his car as requested and Joe walked out and leaned through the window.

"Turkeytrot," Joe greeted him genially, "you know what I did? I gave you too much money."

"No you didn't, Joe," Turk protested. "I counted it."

"I counted it too, Turk," Joe insisted. "I think there's fifty-two hundred in the stack I gave you."

"You're wrong, Joe. I never make a mistake like that. But hell, I've got the stash in my trunk now."

Eagerly Joe watched Turk get out of the car, walk around to the trunk and unlock it. He had called Turk early knowing that he would have the money until he delivered it to Harrison about noon. Turk unlocked the trunk and opened it, burrowing inside for the stack of $100 bills Joe had given him the day before.

"Here, Joe. Count it yourself. You'll see I'm right."

Joe took the stack of bills and slowly counted it. Exactly $5,000. He folded the stack over and plunged the roll into his right trouser pocket. "I've got to have this money, Turk. I can't give it to you now."

"What are you saying, Joe? I've got to have it. You know I can't go back to Harrison without it. He'll think I took it for myself."

"Look, Turk, I've got a hot check out. If I don't cover it by noon at the bank, they'll have me indicted and in jail. I won't be working. I won't be able to pump and Freddy won't have me for a customer anymore. He should understand that. Oh come on, give me a break."

"Jesus Christ, Joe! You can't do this to me. What am I going to say? My God, you're going to have me in deep trouble. I've got to get that money to him by noon. You know that. Goddamn, Joe, give me that money."

"If I give you the money back, I go to jail. It's as simple as that."

"Jesus, Joe. I'm sorry. I didn't know you were in that kind of trouble. Nobody wants to see you in jail."

"Then go back and explain to Freddy that I just had to have this money. Tell him whatever you want."

Shaking his head and wailing, "Oh my God! Oh my God! You're going to get me in a lot of trouble," Turk exclaimed as he drove away.

"I'll be in touch with you tomorrow, Turk. I'll pay you just as quick as I can, you know I will," Joe hollered after him.

After George Jamail had gone, Joe drove over to the home of another bookmaker he knew but had not done much business with. He had the improbable name of O. C. Bible. Joe handed him the $5,000 and bet what he considered to be a surefire baseball parlay for that day. The next morning, skinning back the sports page, he found he had lost again. Nevertheless he continued pumping, giving much of his action now to Bible, though of course still keeping up the Dallas connection, sending the Dallas runner, Red, over to pick up cash from Bob Jones at the bank.

Working for Webb made it easier for Joe to go to Las Vegas. He had an excuse for being there, thanks to his employer's business interest in the Strip hotels. Whenever he could get hold of between $8,000 and $10,000 Las Vegas was his destination.

It was in Houston that he discovered the commodity market and started dealing in pork bellies and other such gambles. Instead of bookies and casinos he was going to respectable brokerage firms like E. F. Hutton and Paine Webber. But the results were similar. It was small action compared to the money he sent by Turk back to Harrison and to his bookies in Dallas via Bob Jones. Still, he managed to lose $15,000 with the old-line investment concerns in 1963.

Just as he sweated all games, so he sweated pork bellies, going over to the brokerage firm and watching the commodity tickers. At least this was a totally legitimate pastime, though it robbed the Del Webb company of some of Joe's efforts. From his point of view, he was compelled to sit and watch the pork bellies going up and down before his eyes, waiting for them to hit a price that would allow him to sell at a profit.

Due to his caper with the Turk, it was doubly difficult for him to get bets down until he paid back the $5,000 he had so deftly lifted.

He heard about a new, small-time bookmaker in Pasadena, a suburb of Houston. His friend Tommy Glispen took him out there and on the way they stopped at a small bank where with Tommy's help Joe managed to borrow $4,000. He walked out with a cashier's check and immediately went to the bookie planning to bet about $800 with him. It was too late in the day to cash the check the bank had given him so he still had the cashier's check with him when he met the new bookie. He bet $800 on a baseball parlay and to secure the amount of his bet gave the bookie the entire check for $4,000, saying he'd come back the next day.

Early the following morning, skinning back the sports page of his newspaper, he found he had lost. He drove over to Pasadena to get the $3,200 left to him out of the check. When he got there the bookie told him that the $4,000 check had already been turned in to the big-time bookmaker with whom he had laid off Joe's bet. He said Joe would have to wait just one more day to get the change from the cashier's check. By now Joe had accumulated a great deal of experience both with being stiffed and taking a swing at a bookmaker himself, that is, making a bet knowing that if he lost he wouldn't pay off. Something was obviously wrong. He only owed the bookie $800; the bookie had his $4,000 cashier's check and wasn't paying him immediately.

Joe raced to the bank at which he had made the loan just the afternoon before and tried to stop payment on the cashier's check. In order to stop payment on a cashier's check it was necessary to put up a bond in twice the amount of the check. Fortunately, Joe remembered that a friend from the Montrose gaming room with whom he played gin rummy was in the bonding business.

It cost him $200 to get his friend Sam to make out the $8,000 bond. As it happened, the Pasadena bookie had deposited Joe's check in full at his own bank in Deer Park, Texas. The check arrived at the bank just hours after the bond had been put up, and Joe saved not only the $3,200 coming to him but the $800 bet he had lost. The quest for action was always fraught with risk. How could a young well-brought-up Texas University Phi Beta Kappa lawyer, married and with a young son, be constantly at war with bookmakers, crap dealers, and the other sleazy types with whom he spent so much of his time? Why? he asked himself, when he had the capacity to work for the Del Webb–Exxon consortium. As if to underscore the question, the Pasadena bookie hired a lawyer named Sam Hoover who also happened to be the mayor of the town. He called Joe up frequently, threatening him with prosecution and bodily harm. However, less than a year later Sam Hoover was convicted in a sensational torture extortion case and received a sixty-year jail sentence. A far cry from the $4,000 he tried to extort from Joe.

By the spring of 1964, Nancy had gone back to teaching, knowing from bitter experience what was inevitably going to happen in their life. They had an upstairs apartment at a modest rent of $200 a month and Mark, no longer an infant, could be taken to a day-care center when Nancy went to school.

Joe's pumping operations, while never ceasing, became increasingly difficult as his debt structure grew. Bob Jones was always there in Dallas needing money to cover the money he gave to Red on Joe's instructions. Joe had opened accounts at banks throughout Texas, many of which were either inactive or sitting there with $2 in them. But he still had the checks from the banks. Once again the house of cards started to fall in on him.

A call from Dallas spurred him on to new heights of pumping. At the Bank of the Southwest he convinced a senior vice-president to okay a $6,800 check. Before it bounced, he went out to the Fannin Bank just outside the Medical Center in Houston and started a personal account there with a young officer and then began the ingratiating blandishments that were the first step in pumping a new spot.

"Our combine, Del Webb–Exxon, is starting a new enterprise which we call the Friendswood Development Corporation. It should bring a lot of business to your bank." The young officer nodded in agreement.

"I'll tell our president about it, Mr. Hodges."

"As a matter of fact, as the senior development officer here in Houston, I am going to suggest that we open a new account for this development with your bank."

"It goes without saying, of course, that we'd be delighted to be of service." The young officer was now falling into the trap.

"Well, this certainly would be convenient for me. And I'd enjoy doing business with you. Why don't you give me the forms that have to be filled out and I'll take them back and get them approved by the company's comptroller."

Enthusiastic about the new business he was promoting for his bank, the young officer reached in his desk drawer and pulled out all the necessary corporate forms. "You can bring them in any time, Mr. Hodges."

"Fine. It will be a pleasure doing business with you. I'll see to it that the directors of your bank know you brought the Friendswood business into this bank," Joe said in his melodious baritone. "We'll be bringing a lot of money in from New York, funneling it through here for use as we start construction. I'll tell our comptroller that you will personally be handling our business."

"You can be sure, Mr. Hodges, that I will take great personal pride and interest in administering your account."

"Well, I never expected to do business this quickly," Joe said, pleased. He started to get up and the young banker shot to his feet ahead of him, his hand out. "Just call on me any time, Mr. Hodges."

Joe paused halfway between his chair and an upright position, a look on his face as though a sudden inspiration had struck him. "Oh by the way, as long as I am here maybe we can do business even sooner. Our organization encourages its executives to work on personal business deals, particularly real estate transactions. I'm just about to close a deal on a motel site. I plan to make a loan at the National Bank of Commerce downtown. It's only seventy-five hundred I need, but since I'm here perhaps you could handle it for me."

The bank officer sat down and once again reached in his desk and pulled out forms which he handed to Joe. "I'm sure we would be delighted to oblige you, Mr. Hodges. No need going back downtown. We can handle seventy-five hundred. In fact I'm authorized to make a loan of up to twenty thousand on my own initiative."

"Good!" Joe beamed at the banker. "As a matter of fact, before I finish this deal I may need up to twenty thousand."

Twenty minutes later Joe walked out of Fannin Bank with a cashier's check for $7,500. This was Las Vegas-type money. He cashed the check at the First City National Bank, another Del Webb–Exxon banking connection, and dashed out to the airport where he caught the next flight for Las Vegas. At McCarran Airport he cut around the terminal directly to the street where he flagged down a taxi and made for the Sahara. In four hours he had run the bankroll he brought with him up to $25,000—only to watch it dissipate until he was broke.

Dressed in his three-piece banker's suit, he boarded the flight to Houston, depressed and emotional. He looked at the other businessmen knowing he was the psychological deviant aboard. After an hour of self-recrimination his thoughts brightened. He could go back to the Fannin Bank. It was still a spot.

Arriving in Houston early in the morning, he followed his now standard routine. Although smarting at the loss in Las Vegas, he still knew a curious satisfaction at having at least tried to win big. If his bankroll had been larger he could have won and the next time he went to Vegas he surely would win big. The bad checks against which he had "borrowed" money from the banks would be hitting in a storm of first perplexed and then angry bankers. All he really had to do was raise another bankroll. A little more pumping and he would make the big win that would save the day. Also, there was Red in Dallas to whom he could call in his bets.

He visited the barber near his office for a shave and then, having bought the morning paper and feeling considerably improved, he had breakfast and arrived before eight at his desk, well ahead of the other Del Webb executives. He studied the sports pages, deciding how he would place his action that day.

By nine o'clock his colleagues arrived and duly noted that Joe was, as frequently happened, the first man in the office. He was ready to call Turk and have him drive downtown for a meeting at which Joe would hand him cash and write up his wagers. At ten o'clock he left the office with his usual excuse: he had to go to one of the big law firms.

At twelve noon he had a date to meet the Turk on a Houston street corner. He had already picked his baseball parlay, a combination he knew would win this time. He had spent an hour studying the sports section before making his choice. But he needed the cash now to give the Turk. There was only one thing to do. He drove out to the Fannin Bank again where the young loan officer greeted him cheerfully. Joe said that the company comptroller was away at the home office in Phoenix but would be back the next day and he knew that opening the account would be just a formality.

"I just happened to be out this way so I thought I'd drop in," Joe went on.

"I'm sure glad you did, Mr. Hodges. I've already talked to our senior vice-president and he has talked to the president. We certainly will be most happy to work with you. Anything more I can do for you now?"

"No, I'll be around tomorrow with the papers signed."

"I'll be looking forward to seeing you, sir," the banker said happily.

As was the case the day before, the banker was halfway to his feet when Joe said, "Oh by the way, maybe there *is* something you can do for me today. You know that real estate deal I was telling you about. It looks like I'll need another seventy-five hundred to close this afternoon. If you could add that to my outstanding loan I'd greatly appreciate it."

"I believe I can do that for you, Mr. Hodges." The banker reached into his drawer, pulled out the necessary forms and passed them across the desk to Joe who quickly filled them out and handed them back. Twenty minutes later he once again walked out of the Fannin Bank with a check for $7,500. He drove back to downtown Houston, cashed the check at the First

City National Bank, and just made it to the street corner in time to meet Turk.

Joe handed Turk the $5,000 to place his bets and then went back to his office to consider the problem of several checks that would be coming back in the next two or three days. He wished he'd gone to the Fannin Bank before he'd given a hot check to a vice-president at the First City National Bank on an inactive account at his bank in Dallas. And there were, of course, other hot checks in the air.

A phone call from William Manasco, senior vice-president of the First City National Bank of Houston, was not totally unexpected. Manasco was one of the most powerful bankers in Houston.

"Mr. Hodges, can you come into my office today? And have your wife come with you."

Joe felt a tightening in his gut. It had finally caught up with him. "My wife finishes teaching school at three o'clock. Can we come in then?"

"That will be fine, Mr. Hodges. I'll expect you at three-thirty then."

"I'll be there, sir."

The meeting was not a long one. After Joe and Nancy had seated themselves across the desk from the banker, Manasco slid the bounced check across the desk to Joe. There were no appropriate excuses. Joe glanced down at the check and then looked up at Manasco. Until now Joe had always managed somehow to cover the checks he cashed before they actually bounced. But now he was virtually without funds. "Yes, I did cash that check, Mr. Manasco. I took the money to Las Vegas and gambled with it and lost. I've got myself in so deep the only way I can get out is by winning big either at Las Vegas or on the ball games."

"Joe can't stop gambling," Nancy said sadly. "It's been the curse of our lives."

Manasco gave Joe a hard, unsympathetic stare. "What do you intend to do about this check you wrote on a bank in which your account was inactive?"

"I'll repay, of course. There was never any intent to defraud. I was certain I would be able to cover it before it came back."

"Considering your position with Webb, this sort of fiscal behavior is highly irresponsible."

"We'll pay it back, Mr. Manasco," Nancy said with an assurance she hardly felt.

"Today?" the banker asked.

"I'll repay it as soon as I can, sir," Joe said.

"I'm not going to mention this to anyone at Del Webb," the bank executive went on. "That's your responsibility. This bank is not going to take action against you itself. I'm going to turn the matter over to our bonding company tomorrow and let them worry about it. You can work it out with them. For your sake I hope you can come to a solution to this situation, and in the future I must ask you to stay out of this bank."

He stood up and Joe and Nancy left his office. Outside, Joe could feel the inevitable results of his financial depredations closing in on him. There wasn't even enough money for him to try to make the big win in Las Vegas.

Fortunately for him, the bonding company decided not to prosecute him immediately, as was frequently the case in such circumstances. The last shreds of the financial respectability associated with his important job at Del Webb made it possible for him to convince the bonding company to allow him to sign a note.

At the same time the Bank of the Southwest was hit with three bad checks. Joe went through the same procedure with its bonding company, signing promissory notes payable at $200 a month. Then, when his first thirty-day note became overdue at the Fannin Bank, the president began making inquiries and learned of Joe's bad checks at the First City National and the Bank of the Southwest. Once again the matter was turned over to the bonding company and again Joe signed a note and escaped criminal prosecution. By now his debt structure was close to $150,000 though, incredibly, the top executives at Webb, including Mr. Webb himself, were unaware of his extensive "borrowings" on hot checks. This is exactly the term that comes to the mind of a compulsive gambler when he cashes a hot check. Joe signed his own name on existing though inactive accounts, totally convinced he would be repaying the money before the check bounced back to the bank which cashed it.

In one week he had amassed $33,000 in bad checks which had been turned over to the bonding company.

The only way Joe could ever get out of his difficulties was the big win, but he had used up his spots. It was getting tougher every day to raise a bankroll. All he had left was the Dallas connection and he couldn't afford to lose that source of action. Whenever he looked depressed or distracted, Nancy, his parents, and even the Hippards could guess what was wrong and would invariably ask, "Do you have checks out?" That would be their first question.

Joe was constantly working on his list of creditors, juggling it, trying to keep up with payments when due. In order to cover Bob Jones in Dallas, he found another bank, the Liberty Bank in Houston, and managed to cash a hot $10,000 check there. The money, of course, was sent to Dallas to cover the most recent cash payment made by Bob Jones to the Dallas runner, Red.

Indeed he did have a hot check floating when Nancy asked him the inevitable question and this after having straightened out his problems with the bonding company. The day before the check would be sure to light back at the Liberty Bank, he went down to Beaumont to see his father again. He confessed all his problems, and the fact that the bonding company would never sit still for another bank coming to it with a complaint against Joe H. Hodges. This would surely result in criminal prosecution.

Once again Joe's father found an answer—C. W. Conn, Sr., who co-signed with him a note at the Beaumont bank. He handed his son the cash he needed to run to the Liberty Bank and make the check good just hours before it was returned.

Joe did not always lose when he bet with his bookies or took his one-day trips to Las Vegas. He won often enough to continue covering his hot checks, with the help his father had given him on that occasion.

Besides the banks, when Joe needed a bankroll he found that he could cash hot checks at grocery stores for as much as $3,000. At one point, with five hot checks out, mostly at the various Weingarten's supermarkets, he went to see Frank Briscoe, the district attorney of Harris County, Texas. Briscoe was married to a woman Joe knew from Beaumont and he was just announcing his plans to run for mayor of Houston. Although Joe did not know Briscoe well, the latter greeted him in a friendly manner and asked him what was on his mind.

"Frank, I've cashed a bunch of hot checks at Weingarten's and every place all over town," Joe confessed. "They add up to five or six thousand dollars. I'm trying to pump the money to cover them but I'm just afraid somebody is going to file on me before I can do so."

Briscoe looked at his acquaintance in surprise. "That's pretty dangerous, Joe," he said.

"I know, Frank. I got into trouble. I'm getting the money to pay the checks off. I just need a little time."

Frank pressed a button on his phone and soon was talking to the hot check division of the district attorney's office. "This is Frank," he said into the phone. "Do you have anything down there on Joe H. Hodges?"

For two or three minutes the district attorney held the phone to his ear, staring across his desk at an anxiety-ridden Joe. Finally the answer came back. "Nothing now, right?" Frank asked into the phone. A pause and then, "If you get anything at all, don't process it until he's contacted. Here's Hodges' number." He hung up the phone and turned a tight smile on Joe. "Nothing yet, Joe. If anything comes in, you'll be notified. You must see the people where the checks were cashed and pay them all now."

"I will, Frank. I'll have all those checks under control in a few days."

Joe, like the circus juggler, had to keep the plates spinning once again. He pumped the money for the grocery store hot checks from his dentist, his landlord, and the manager of the Texaco station where he bought gas. More spinning plates had been placed on top of trembling sticks.

The list of creditors grew so quickly, Joe required maniacal energy to keep everything going. Yet he maintained his family life throughout it all, desperately obscuring the real truth from Nancy, from his mother and father, and from his and Nancy's closest friends. It was an amazing balancing act which demanded eighteen hours of "work" per day, seven days a week. One minute he was rushing frantically across Houston to cover a hot check; the next he was speeding home to greet three couples

Nancy had invited for supper. One minute—though it might expand to an hour—he was dialing long distance trying to get the "line" on the day's games; the next he was rushing to a Friendswood meeting at the Butler, Binion, Rice and Cook law firm offices. One minute he was standing in line to wire money to a newfound bookie in New Orleans; the next he was picking Mark up from nursery school to get him a haircut. There was no time to breathe.

CHAPTER 23

Despite Frank Briscoe, despite Joe's father, despite all his friends, the day of reckoning had to come. And it came from a source he least expected. Bob Jones had put away about $20,000 over the period he was handing cash to Joe's Dallas bookie and getting repaid two or three days later, making 20 percent profit each time Joe or Red covered the loan. Joe felt confident when he called up Bob one Monday and said, "Bob, that forty-six hundred I should be sending you today, I can't send it right now. I'll get it to you as soon as possible."

"Oh, there's no problem, Joe. Don't worry about it." Bob sounded confident too. After all, he'd been doing this now for a year with no problems.

On Wednesday Bob called Joe back. "How long do you think it will be before you can pay me?" he asked.

"A couple of weeks at the most. I'll try to get it sooner."

The next day Bob called again. "Joe, I'm going to need that money." Joe sensed the fear, the despair in his voice.

"Bob, I just don't have it. Damn it all, can't you just pay it? All the money you've made this last year, you ought to have that much available? You won't have it out long."

"Joe"—there was real panic in his tone—"I bought a house. I don't have the money. The bank examiners are coming in and the comptroller here noticed the money missing. I've just got to replace it right now, this minute."

"Bob, let me talk to the president of the bank. I'll explain it to him." Perhaps Joe had forgotten about his experiences with a banker in Zanesville. Had he been able to foresee the results of his conversation with the president, he would have managed to pump the needed money in Houston where he still had some protection and get the funds to Dallas within the hour. But in his naïve optimism he felt he could persuade the National Bank of Commerce of Dallas that there was nothing to worry about as he, Joe Hodges, would see that everything was taken care of.

Bob switched Joe over to the president of the bank. Joe explained who he was, that he'd been the city attorney for Irving, and went on to give the president a summary of how he and Bob Jones had been working for the last year. He explained that he had always sent the money back within twenty-four hours and that now he owed Bob Jones $5,520 for the $4,600 that the teller had loaned him. "I'll have the money shortly. Whatever you want me to do, I'll be glad to comply."

"I appreciate you calling me like this, Mr. Hodges. The situation is, to say the least, unorthodox."

"I know that, sir. I realize that now, although I didn't at the time since it was not hurting the bank. And you may recall," he added disingenuously, "I did a lot of business with your bank when I was the Small Business Administration attorney making government guaranteed loans. It didn't really seem out of order for me then."

"Mr. Hodges, would you be willing to sign a note?"

"Certainly, sir. I'd be more than happy to. Just make it a thirty-day note for the forty-six hundred or whatever it is the bank has involved in this and I'll be glad to sign it. Mail it today. I'll have it tomorrow and put it in the return mail to you." Joe gave the bank president his office address and his title with the Del Webb corporation and hung up, breathing a sigh of relief.

Badly as he wanted some betting action, he decided he'd better give up on that until after his messy financial affairs were straightened out. He was like a thirsty man doing without a drink, or, more aptly, like a heroin addict suddenly going cold turkey.

The next morning, a Friday, at eleven o'clock, two men presented themselves to Joe's secretary, announcing they were with the FBI. They identified themselves and Joe invited them into his inner office to sit down. They were dressed just as he was in conservative business suits and told him the reason for their call was a communication from the president of the National Bank of Commerce in Dallas. Although Joe was understandably very nervous at the FBI being right there in his office at Del Webb, he couldn't believe the situation was so serious that it would eventually develop into an indictment against him for bank fraud.

It was February of 1964. In great detail Joe explained the entire method of operating between himself and Bob Jones. Exhaustively he revealed all the Dallas transactions, even supplying the dates and the amounts of money he had sent back at six to five or a 20 percent commission to the teller.

Of course he did not deem it necessary to tell the FBI about his more recent banking problems in Houston and the notes he had signed with the bonding company. Forthrightly he admitted that the money he got from Bob Jones was used for gambling. Politely the FBI agents thanked him for his cooperation. They did not go to any of the other executives at Del Webb and nobody but Joe and his secretary knew that the FBI had sent special agents in to question him.

The middle of the following week the agents returned to Joe's office and asked some more questions which he answered. "Well, Mr. Hodges," one of the agents said, "it looks as though this probably will be presented to the grand jury up in Dallas."

"Oh my goodness," Joe said. "I'm going to pay this money. It was not a case of fraud or theft."

"Well, paying the money won't do you any good now," the other agent put in. "The U. S. Attorney in Dallas will be taking it to the grand jury."

Stunned, Joe watched the two agents leave his office. He knew the U. S. Attorney in Dallas, Harold B. Sanders, better known as Barefoot Sanders. In fact, he had even borrowed money in Dallas from an associate lawyer in Barefoot's law firm before he became U. S. Attorney.

Barefoot Sanders had been the head football cheerleader at the University of Texas when Joe was there and they had struck up a nodding acquaintance. Hardly had the two FBI agents left his office when Joe picked up the phone and got Sanders on the line. The amenities were brief and somewhat chilly on Barefoot's side. "I know all about it, Joe, and there's nothing I can do. It will be presented to the grand jury. You'd better call a lawyer up here and get him representing you right away."

Joe immediately called Adrian Carter and told him the whole problem. "I want to appear, I want to go before the grand jury myself and talk to them. I know, Adrian," he said, putting off the protest, "you don't usually do that. But I want to appear and tell my side of the story."

Joe, of course, had to tell Nancy about the possible indictment and the circumstances surrounding it. Two weeks later he was informed that the federal grand jury was convening in Amarillo and he asked Adrian to meet him there. Joe flew up to Amarillo from Houston and Adrian flew in from Irving.

In front of the grand jury Joe told the entire truth about his arrangement with Bob Jones and admitted that he used the money for gambling. He expounded his arrangement with Bob Jones and said that he had done this thirty or forty times, that he was a gambler, but that he was also a practicing lawyer and stood ready to pay the $4,600 as he had always paid every loan he had received from the teller at the bank. He had been ready to pay it the day he talked to the president of the bank but was not directed to do so.

He did not feel he should be indicted. He regarded the borrowed sums merely as extensions of credit, and they had always been promptly taken care of. There was no conspiracy to defraud the bank. There had been a personal arrangement between him and a man who worked in the bank. Joe was as persuasive as always and felt that he had made a positive impression on the grand jury. As he said, he had never asked Bob Jones to go into the vault and take money or in any way embezzle it. As far as he knew Bob Jones might even have been taking the money out of his own pocket. This teller was merely a personal contact in Dallas.

When Joe walked out of the grand jury with Adrian Carter, he was confident that he had acquitted himself well and that he would not be indicted.

The truth was Joe could not help but think in the manner of

the compulsive gambler he was, operating under all sorts of seemingly airtight rationalizations, and the banks had been so permissive heretofore, he really did think of his "loans" from Bob Jones as normal extensions of credit. The essential element in any crime is intent to defraud. Joe never intended to defraud the bank in Dallas or any other bank. As he looked at it, he was not cashing checks fraudulently, knowing they were going to bounce, and then moving on to Albuquerque, writing more checks, getting the money and moving on to Seattle. He was shocked at the attempt to get an indictment against him. He was not Al Capone. He lived on Oakdale right there in Houston where anybody could find him. He'd have the $4,600 in a few days. He was a gambler; the big win was always out there in front. After all, he had solved his $350,000 problem in Dallas and Irving in one fabulous gambling month, betting on baseball games and visiting Las Vegas.

Adrian Carter did not think that Joe would be indicted either as the two of them flew back from Amarillo to Dallas where Joe spent the night at Adrian's home. Nevertheless, two weeks later Adrian called Joe in Houston to tell him that the indictment against him for aiding and abetting an embezzlement had been handed down. Bob Jones was indicted for embezzlement. The case would be heard in Judge Sarah Hughes's court, Adrian added.

Joe heard the news with a sickening sensation. Of all the judges to get, Sarah Hughes was the toughest. She was a liberal in conservative Dallas and as a federal judge had more power over the life of an individual in her area of jurisdiction than the President of the United States. It was Judge Hughes who, in November of 1963, had sworn in Lyndon Johnson as President of the United States after President Kennedy was assassinated. And it was Sarah Hughes who had left the dais when young Joe Hodges gave a speech in Dallas against the extreme liberal policies of the U. S. Supreme Court. Now she would have complete control over his life. He had made the rock-ribbed conservative speech not only in Irving and Dallas, but at one hundred forty other forums in Texas when he had been city attorney of Irving.

When Joe, with Adrian Carter standing beside him, appeared

before Judge Sarah Hughes in late March of 1964, three counts of aiding and abetting an embezzlement from the Dallas bank had been picked at random from the many transactions between himself and Bob Jones. Each count carried a maximum of five years with a $10,000 fine. Joe realized that at last he was in the kind of deep trouble from which not his father, not anybody could save him.

When he first heard from Adrian that he had been indicted, the news had not reached the newspapers. Adrian had learned ahead of time which gave Joe a chance to consider his alternatives. Nobody at the Del Webb corporation, nor for that matter anywhere in Dallas or Houston, knew of the grand jury appearance yet.

Adrian asked Joe to come back to Dallas and discuss the case with him. Joe had sufficient latitude in his job that he could go away for two or three days without the company missing him. At the time Joe came back to Dallas to discuss his case with Adrian, Adrian was trying an attempted murder case in Montague, just north of Dallas, which involved a lower middle-class white couple called the Gentrys, and had recently asked Joe to come up to Montague with him and help him try the case. The defendant, William Adams Gentry, was charged with attempted murder, having hit his wife with a lead pipe as she was coming home from church.

Joe made the closing speech before the jury. The defendant's wife, though alive, was immobile and practically a vegetable. Nevertheless, when Joe had finished giving the summation of the case to the jury, two women jurors were crying and he knew he had been as successful in mitigating the circumstances of the crime as any lawyer in the country could have been.

He knew the truth of the old legal adage that if you don't have the facts or the law on your side, you've got nothing but emotions left and you've got to stress them. Emotions were what Joe was best at manipulating. The defendant got a sentence of only three years and Adrian Carter got Gentry's house as a fee.

Joe went back to Houston where his first step was to go to the bar association in Harris County voluntarily and present himself to the head of the grievance committee. He confessed that he had been indicted on a felony charge in Dallas and had no idea how it was going to turn out. He didn't even know how he would plead. He explained to the head of the grievance committee, a total stranger to him, all the facts surrounding the case and voluntarily surrendered his right to practice law. The head of the committee commiserated with him and said he hoped the case would work out in his favor and to let him know what happened.

It was characteristic of Joe that when he found himself encumbered with guilt feelings he needed to purge himself of them, and the only way to do that in the present situation was to proclaim himself guilty to all interested parties.

Unfortunately, by the time he had decided to plead guilty, he had no money to hire his friend Adrian who, Joe knew, wanted him to plead guilty. He went to the senior vice-president of Del Webb, Jack Keyes, and told him about the whole situation. Thereupon he resigned the best job he had ever had or would have in his law career and went back to Dallas to appear before Judge Hughes.

Another University of Texas friend of Joe's, Ken Mighell, was Assistant U. S. Attorney under Barefoot Sanders. It was Mighell who had been dating Nancy when Joe first met her. But there was nothing that either Barefoot or Mighell could do for Joe now.

Nancy came up to Dallas to be with him when he appeared before Judge Hughes. Mark was not quite three years old and in a way Joe felt it was fortunate that everything was happening in Dallas and not Houston as somehow the publicity might have more of an effect on Mark's future if it took place where he was growing up.

Joe appeared before Judge Hughes with Adrian standing beside him and pleaded guilty. For thirty minutes Judge Hughes interrogated him, asking such questions as, "Are you pleading guilty because you are guilty?" and, "No promises have been made to you?" She was keenly conscious of the new laws put on the books by the Warren court which gave great laxity to the defendant and could even result in his going free at the slightest error on the part of the prosecution or police. So Judge Sarah Hughes, the consummate liberal, was extremely careful of how she accepted Joe Hodges' guilty plea. The very liberalism she so believed in could result in this man's freedom despite his guilty plea if she did not observe every facet of the Supreme Court's new liberal decisions.

Joe never thought he'd be sentenced to a prison term. He was convinced Judge Hughes would give him probation. Perhaps she would have had she not been present that fateful day when Joe gave his speech castigating the sort of liberal Supreme Court decisions that she was so wary of today. She wanted no possibility that he would escape the harsh justice she felt he deserved.

CHAPTER 24

It was three weeks from the time Joe pleaded guilty to the day Judge Hughes set for sentencing. His mother and father drove up from Beaumont the day before sentencing and checked into a Dallas motel. Nancy stayed in Houston with Mark as Joe couldn't bear to have her at the scene of his humiliation. And so at 2 P.M. Joe, with his mother and father and Adrian Carter, went to the court.

Adrian made a short speech of little consequence, asking for mercy in consideration of the fact that this was the first time Joe had ever been convicted on any sort of charge. Joe also made a speech, and then Judge Hughes gave him a stern look and rapped out: "I sentence you to fifteen years in the penitentiary, five years on each count to be served consecutively."

Joe's mother and father gasped at this apparently feral sentence. The despair he himself felt was somewhat mitigated by Judge Hughes telling him that she had to give the maximum sentence under the provisions of a new law which gave her the opportunity to have him brought back before her at some point in the future, 90 or 180 days away, after a period of observation and evaluation in the penal institution to which he would be sent.

This came under Section 4208-B of the code and was known as a "B" sentence when the convict arrived at prison. Thus in actuality the chances were slight that Joe would serve even five years, much less fifteen. After the sentencing, a marshal stalked across the room to Joe, handcuffed him and took him away. As he stood in the hall outside the courtroom, his mother and father came up to him and asked the marshal if they could bring their son anything, cigarettes or food, before he was taken off to jail. The marshal said no.

Florence Hodges could not hold back the tears as Joe, manacled, was led off. Even Adrian Carter could not bring himself to approach him as he was marched away. And Joe was scared to death. All he had heard was "fifteen years" and something about a "B" number which he didn't understand. Up to this point he had been out of jail on a $5,000 bond—but now he was on his way to a federal prison.

Prior to leaving for prison, Joe spent a few days in Sheriff Decker's Dallas County jail. At least he knew Sheriff Decker. It was he who had helped him secure the loan from W. O. Bankston. He arrived at the jail at five o'clock and went through the usual process of surrendering his wallet and watch and all his clothes, which were put in a paper sack. Then he was issued jail garb of dungarees and a coarse shirt. In the nude now, he was given a thorough examination to make sure he was not smuggling anything into jail and then allowed to dress.

Hoping to make his stay in the local jail easier, he pointed out that he had had polio and couldn't walk very well. The guard agreed to put him in the hospital tank. Had he been more experienced he would not have incurred that unpleasantness: it was in the hospital tank that the lunatics and perverts were put. So Joe found himself in a large cage with fifty or sixty of these people. There were a few bunks but mostly the inmates had to sleep on the floor of the cage.

The first night he was attacked by an old man with the DTs on his way to the state hospital for the criminally insane. The only advantage of being in the hospital tank was that Sheriff Decker allowed Joe's mother and father to come in the next morning to see him. They had with them the Dallas *Morning News* and on the bottom of the front page he read the headlines: GAMBLING ATTORNEY GETS 15 YEARS.

Nancy came up a few days later and was able to speak to him through the bars of the cage full of lunatics and deviates. Adrian Carter had looked up the relevant law, talked to the judge, and sent word to Joe that he would soon be taken to a prison somewhere for his evaluation and then brought back for resentencing by Judge Hughes.

Nancy and Joe's parents were as supportive as they could be and tried to cheer him up. Feeling that they were behind him made his stay in the jail less unbearable than it otherwise might have been. A few of Joe's other friends came up to see him. Idus Ash and Sid Wright, who had joined him on the wild gambling spree from which he'd returned a winner, were among them. And Nancy twice flew up from Houston to see him.

A prisoner with the "B" number went through a slower process of classification than the ordinary prisoner. Thus it was a full fifteen days before the Bureau of Prisons in Washington assigned Joe to a prison where he would be under observation and evaluation. His main concern in the Dallas jail was his son Mark whom he thought about constantly. It was largely to give Mark a better break that he and Nancy had left Dallas to go to Houston, but of course the move had only made matters worse. Now he was in jail.

Exacerbating his misery at being separated from his son was the presence in the tank of a man who had smothered his own child to death. The other inmates whipped him frequently, and since he was young and fat he was sexually molested, the rationale being that he was a baby killer. Finally the day came when Marshal Henry White, who had taken Joe from Sarah Hughes's court, came to deliver him to his assigned prison.

"Where are we going, Marshal?" Joe asked. That's the first thing a convict wants to know.

"Leavenworth, Joe," Henry replied. Again the leaden sinking feeling in Joe's stomach. Once Alcatraz had been closed, Leavenworth had become the worst prison in the federal system, inhabited by lifers and the most heinous offenders of all types.

The first stop was Kansas City where Joe spent the night in the local jail, and the next morning he was driven out to Leavenworth.

When Joe saw Leavenworth appearing on the horizon, growing larger as they got closer, his sense of identity was engulfed in dread. It was the biggest and most ominous-looking building he had ever seen. It was a titanic stone growth, over a hundred years old, which spread its gray, sinister tendrils in all directions.

It seemed as if nothing was living there. Yet with four thousand inmates it was a city within walls—walls now waiting to claim *him.* He was handcuffed and shackled along with the other prisoners. The marshals couldn't take a chance that a prisoner, given the opportunity, might try to escape and even kill the marshal.

In front of the imposing gates of Leavenworth, the marshal drew his gun as he jumped from the cab of the prison system vehicle and placed it in a basket which was pulled up to the tower. Nobody was allowed to walk inside Leavenworth with a weapon. It would be too easy for some inmate to nail him and steal his gun.

Joe and the other prisoners were led up a flight of steps. An electronic gate slid aside as they approached and then they were inside. Joe felt he was entering the first ring of Dante's Inferno. Looking up at the gun towers and the electronic doors, a stark and fearful realization seized him: his gambling had finally caught up with him and now he was entombed in a square mile of drab masonry. The guards were everywhere: at the gate, in the watchtowers, behind every door, patrolling every corridor. They stared out of blank, unseeing eyes. They seemed so uncommitted, so uncaring. Yet in their very blankness Joe found a certain relief. He did not want compassion or concern. He felt it was kind of them that they did not care. It made it easier for him.

Everywhere he was ushered by guards. It took the rest of the day to get him processed into prison. The fingerwave to test for contraband concealed in the anus was followed by the delicing, and then, totally naked, he was sprayed. A nervous little doctor with a white smock inspected his body, thumping him as if he were a boiler whose inside was being tested for flaws. The inspection of his orifices stripped him of any remaining sense of dignity and identity with the world. He and the other prisoners were like obedient cattle moving along the butcher line in a slaughterhouse.

Everything was by numbers now and Joe began getting callouts. "Hodges, 81286. Report to the hospital." He went to the hospital and they looked at his teeth. Then he returned to his holding dormitory pending his assignment to a cell block and tried to find something to read.

The most oppressive aspect of prison existence is the dragging passage of time. Life at the penitentiary seemed to Joe like a surrealistic science fiction movie, a *Star Trek* epic where time can be slowed to a snail's pace. The highlight of every day, of course, was mail call. It would be a week or two before Joe started getting letters since there was no way to tell his parents and Nancy how to write him and he hadn't known he was going to Leavenworth until the marshal had him on his way there, a precaution to prevent escapes en route to prison with the aid of a confederate.

Joe's "B" number certainly had its advantages. He knew that at least sometime in the future, maybe 120 days from now, he would have another chance at persuading Judge Sarah Hughes to probate him or at least get him sentenced to a prison other than Leavenworth.

He met his caseworker, who would be supervising the evaluation to be presented to Judge Hughes when he returned to her court. He realized this report was going to be of great importance to him. The authorities wanted him to undergo psychiatric examinations and he was delighted at the opportunity. Perhaps a favorable analysis would increase his chances for probation or of being transferred to another prison closer to Texas and his family. Now he was in with hardened criminals, many of whom were serving up to twenty-five years or life.

So it was that he was brought into the office of a pleasant little man of about fifty, an Italian-American with a half smile built into his face. This was Dr. Passaro and Joe liked him immediately. Dr. Passaro explained that he wanted to talk about things that had happened in Joe's early life and would then try to link those things with his later life. Joe agreed to cooperate in every possible way.

The doctor probed and listened for about two days and then brought up the subject of compulsive gambling. Joe said matter-of-factly that he did not consider himself to be a compulsive gambler. "I gamble because it's what I do best," he asserted. "Once in Galveston I did go to a couple of psychiatrists at my family's urging but they didn't cooperate with me. We got into shouting matches and both of them washed their hands of me."

"Did you do anything to antagonize them, Joe? Did you want them to throw you out?"

"I don't know, to be perfectly frank."

"Are you willing to cooperate with me or would you like to throw me out?"

"I'm willing to cooperate."

"Are you willing to allow me to hypnotize you?"

"If that will help. Why?"

"It's a useful tool, Joe. I haven't treated many gamblers in depth. Few psychiatrists have. Hypnosis will help me to understand you. If you don't object—"

"No, I don't object. But I may not be receptive, I may not be . . . is there a word 'hypnotizable'?"

"Well, maybe and maybe not. Let me worry about that, please. Just get a good night's sleep tonight and tomorrow we'll begin."

Joe did not think he could be hypnotized. Somewhere he had read that only one person in five can be put into a receptive trance and he erroneously assumed that that was true.

When he came in the next day the doctor had him lie upon the examining table while he dangled his pocket watch above Joe's chest, counting backward slowly from ten to one. The doctor did this a few times and nothing seemed to happen. Instead Joe felt himself fall asleep. At least that was what he believed was happening.

When he later opened his eyes he felt peaceful and almost languid. Somewhere in a limbo region on the edge of his mind there were the scattered fragments of a dream. He apologized to the doctor for falling asleep. He was certain that he could not be hypnotized and was chagrined at having wasted part of the doctor's morning.

"Sit down, Joe, let's have a talk. You've been under a long time and told me things we should discuss. I took you back to early infancy and you remembered nursing on a bottle. I gather your mother did not want to nurse you, did she?" Joe began to flush but did not answer the question and the doctor went on.

"And you described the kitchen of the house where you lived and you talked about your mother fretting about the stove. You talked of the refrigerator with the funny-looking coil on the top. You must have been about twenty months old then. You were already talking in sentences. Not complete ones, but sentences all the same." Joe was silent, his eyes glued to the kindly face of the doctor.

"And then there was a most interesting thing. Your mother flew into a rage. You remembered how her eyes looked. You were frightened and began to cry. You repeated her words to me: '*You'll never learn, will you! . . . You can't do anything right, can you?*' She was battering you verbally, tearing you apart with her words. Do you remember any of this now?"

Joe did not remember a single word of it and if he had not implicitly trusted the doctor by now, he would have said the man was making it all up. He felt vaguely uneasy as he listened to the doctor prattle about all the psychic abuse he had undergone at his mother's hands. It was such strange nonsense. His mother had been good to him for as long as he could remember. To his father, yes, she had been bitter, tough, and at times demanding. But Joe didn't think she had abused him psychologically. At least not in any way he could remember now.

Still, he did not want to antagonize or alienate the doctor who was genuinely trying to help him. Already he was rehearsing the stirring speech he would like to make to the parole board and he was determined that he would have a good psychiatric dossier to back up his case. Even though he instinctively felt Dr. Passaro's ideas were rubbish, he did his level best to answer his questions. When every answer brought new questions he answered them too. He talked about his polio attack, about his father, but most of all they discussed his mother.

Joe's sessions with Dr. Passaro extended over several weeks. The doctor found it significant that when Joe had been exposed to polio, instead of following his mother's orders to relax so that the virus would not take, he refused and played baseball and then spent the evening bowling, exerting himself so thoroughly that the polio knocked him unconscious by next morning.

"Joe, is it possible that you were trying to get sick so that you could accomplish her vision of you?" Joe thought that was not so.

"Then let me ask you: were you trying to collapse so that you could deserve her help more? Was it a call for help?" Joe neither understood nor believed this theory.

"Joe, that poem your mother read to you when you were a little boy . . ."

"What poem?" Joe asked defensively.

"I think you remember the one I mean, the poem about Little Boy Blue. It starts off talking about the little boy who says good night to his two new toys, to the toy soldier and the toy dog. The boy goes off to bed and in the night he dies. Forever after, the toy soldier and the toy dog are waiting for him right where he last placed them. And your mother used to read that poem to you all the time, Joe. She—"

"No, I don't think it was like that."

"You did memorize the poem, Joe."

"Well, I have a good memory."

"I want you to recite it for me again, now that you are out of the trance state. This poem seems to have had a profound effect on you emotionally, an effect that is still noticeable."

"I'm not sure I remember it exactly," Joe protested.

"Try."

Joe didn't want to reawaken the flood of memories he knew would overwhelm him but this doctor was his best chance of getting out of Leavenworth.

The poem was written by Eugene Field.

"All right. It began:

'The little toy dog is covered with dust,
But sturdy and stanch he stands;
And the little toy soldier is red with rust,
And his musket moulds in his hands.
Time was when the little toy dog was new,
And the soldier was passing fair;
And that was the time when our Little Boy Blue
Kissed them and put them there.

"Now, don't you go till I come," he said,
"And don't you make any noise!"
So, toddling off to his trundle-bed,
He dreamt of the pretty toys . . .'"

Joe paused in his recitation. He stifled an emotional cough, feeling his eyes sting. What was he doing here, in Leavenworth prison, reciting the poem over which he and his mother used to weep together? He continued with the verse.

"'And, as he was dreaming, an angel song
   Awakened our Little Boy Blue—
Oh! the years are many, the years are long,
   But the little toy friends are true!
Ay, faithful to Little Boy Blue they stand,
   Each in the same old place,
Awaiting the touch of a little hand,
   The smile of a little face;
And they wonder, as waiting the long years through
   In the dust of that little chair,
What has become of our Little Boy Blue,
   Since he kissed them and put them there.'"

Joe resisted the emotional response to the poem which had always shaken him from the time he and his mother had first read it together.

"Did you commit any other childhood poems to memory from those years?" Dr. Passaro asked.

"No sir, I did not. But I don't think this poem is significant."

"How many times did your mother read it to you?"

"Oh, I don't know—not often."

"And you were crying when she read it, weren't you?"

"Yes, but so was she. We were both crying."

"Both of you were crying every time you read it and that was several times?"

"Yes, that's right, I admit, but it doesn't mean anything that I can see."

"All right, Joe, let's go on to something else. Now when did you get polio?"

"It was July of 1943, right in the middle of World War Two. I remember reading that the Soviets had just had their first big win over the Germans in a tank battle at Kursk. I remember that very clearly. It—"

"The polio hit your left muscle in your left side. You had a fever for two months, a high fever. Then it broke. But by the time it broke, you had lost the use of the muscles in the left leg and the *gluteus maximus*. Your parents had to invest huge amounts of money to help you."

"Fifteen thousand dollars," Joe admitted.

"How do you know?"

"Because they told me."

"That's right, Joe, they told you. They let you know that it cost fifteen thousand dollars, and you felt guilty then, and you felt guiltier when they had to sell their comfortable home to pay the bills."

"I regretted it more than I can say. I'm not sure I felt guilty though."

"Let me go further, then. You remember when they spent the fifteen thousand dollars on your health. How did you feel when they sent you to live in that old YMCA in New Orleans to be near the therapy center?"

"I was miserable."

"And lonely?"

"Lonely."

"Did you feel they were punishing you?"

Joe tried to say he did not but the doctor raised his palm, indicating that he should pause first.

"You left the YMCA and came back and finished high school, and then you went off to college where you started gambling."

"Yes."

"Why?"

"It was something that I did well. It brought in money, too. It paid my bills in school and I didn't have to cash my parents' checks. That was the reason."

"You gambled so that you wouldn't have to use the checks your parents sent every month?"

"My mother sent them every month. And I'd tear them up or throw them away. Never used one of them that I can remember. I was proud of that."

"Is it possible that you were trying to make up for the past, that your gambling at school was a way of apologizing for the damage you had done by getting sick and amassing all those bills?"

"I don't think so, I don't know," Joe replied helplessly.

"And is it possible also that you were trying to spite your mother, tell her you didn't need their help, show you could do well enough on your own?"

"I don't know that either. Why don't you tell me?"

"I'm a stranger here myself, Joe," the doctor replied with a sad smile. "Psychiatrists know almost nothing about gambling. Freud didn't understand it when he tried to analyze what made Dostoevski gamble. If you were an alcoholic we could help you. We've been trained for that one and we understand it. But compulsive gambling is not classified as a disease and psychiatrists do not view it as such. Neither do our lawmakers and law-enforcers."

"Then you can't tell me anything."

"I can tell you a little, but only a little. I think you've had a number done on you and quite by accident. I believe you felt inadequate, insecure, maybe even wanted to die. No, don't say anything, please. I'm sure you find this offensive. But I'm only saying that you were so convinced, not that anyone intended it. And I suspect you somehow felt you were bad and even unwanted till you got into gambling. Then perhaps gambling turned the trick, gave you something you could do well, something where your talents were supreme. And it gave you a chance to get back feelings that you belonged."

After that there was a silence while the doctor waited for Joe to say something. Joe only shrugged, however. There wasn't anything he could say because all this psychological information could be neither proved nor rejected. It was like Einstein's theories of relativity. It *sounded* fascinating. Maybe it was true, perhaps it was not. But he knew he loved his mother very much despite her chronic complaining. He did not believe she had ever wished him any harm or mental destruction. The $15,000 that the polio had cost he regretted, but he did not like the idea that his gambling was tied in to that in some way. He would have liked to say all this to the doctor but the doctor was a nice man and Joe did not want to disabuse him of his illusions. Besides, he needed a good psychiatric bill of health.

"What's the bottom line of all this, Doctor?"

"You mean, what is my general analysis of what we've been discussing these past weeks?"

"Yes, exactly."

"Well, there's good news and there's bad news. The good news is that you are not a sociopath and—"

"What's that?" Joe asked.

"Someone with irreversible social patterns, Joe; someone who is irreversibly criminal; someone whom they lock up permanently."

"And that's the good news. Uh-huh."

"The bad news is that you are a victim of deep-seated problems today that stem from your infancy and from your case of polio. Your gambling is merely a result of these problems and not a cause."

"Doctor, I really respect you but I just do not see this your way."

"How do you see it then?"

"I admit that I don't know."

"Then just think it over my way for a while and perhaps you'll come round."

Joe left the consultation room in a divided state. He was unhappy and troubled by the doctor's analysis. It was not easy to dismiss, yet was impossible for him to accept. But he was pleased that his psychological dossier would exonerate him from any suspicion of being a sociopath. There was a chance for probation. Everything depended on the psychiatric evaluation and the force of his appeal.

There was no way for Joe to know how long he would have to wait in Leavenworth before he would be brought back to Dallas to appear before Judge Hughes. There was nothing to do but wait and try to keep out of trouble, and he gave his mind over totally to composing the appeal. Every moment of the day as the bells rang calling prisoners to the showers, to breakfast, to prison jobs, Joe was composing the speech he would give when his day in court finally came.

As he pushed his broom or mop, as he typed at his job in the personnel office, as he ate his meals, he thought of phrases that he would use in that address. At night he wrote them down on small three-by-five cards which he shuffled and arranged and rearranged. Joe knew that it's not merely the content or delivery of a speech that is important, but also the rhythm, the tempo, the pace with which it progresses in developing an argument from one premise to the next. He saw a speech as a symphony requiring time, coordination, speed, and precision. Day and night he worked over what he would say before Judge Hughes, studying and polishing each phrase.

His preoccupation with his appeal helped to soft-pedal some of the horrors that daily occurred. He witnessed several knifings, the murder of a guard, a man thrown off the fifth-floor balcony of his cell block to die on the concrete below, his body shattered.

He counted himself among the fortunate that he was not young enough to be considered attractive to the rapists. The prize victims were in their early twenties and cute. He was thirty-five, rugged, somewhat overweight, and had a bad leg. All this was an advantage. He saw so many inmates being attacked and forced down that the scenes became a continual blur. The only one he remembered clearly was the first. That was when a circle of men had formed around a fair, smooth-skinned boy. They were slapping him on the face with a black leather belt and he was screaming that he did not want to do it. They kept hitting and he kept crying "No!" and they hit him again.

One of the crowd complained that they should not mess up his face because it was too pretty.

"He's a blonde worth two boxes (cartons of cigarettes in prison parlance) so watch out for the face, will you?"

Everyone agreed and began hitting him on the arms and chest and legs. They told him to come back with them and he whimpered that he did not want to do it. But after they had hit him enough he went, walking unsteadily. Joe looked as they hauled him off to a corner where a dozen men surrounded and with groans and grunts began penetrating him.

"Rip him off, rip him off!" someone cried. It was all a mélange of panting and sobbing.

"Why doesn't someone call the guards?" Joe whispered to his neighbor.

"The guards don't care. They think the rapes help control the wolves in here. The wolves and the devils, the ones they worry about, they act better if they get some nookie. So the guards just let it happen."

"Can't we do something?"

"Sure you can but they'd kill you."

"Oh."

"*Oh* is right."

Joe turned again to look and saw the last of the men finish with the blond boy. Then they let him go to bed.

Joe's prime goal now was to keep out of trouble. He tried to avoid all the potential traps for the neophyte convict. One constant source of dangerous commotion was the homosexual liaisons between prisoners and their "girl" friends. A stabbing was frequently the result of a prisoner thinking someone was after his lover. And then there were the Black Muslims with their shaved heads and eyes glowing like coals. Although they tended to stay together, racial tension could broil up at the slightest provocation. Furthermore, the Muslims were being freed from prison by Civil Rights leaders arguing discrimination against their clients, and this caused deep resentment among the prison population.

The great day finally arrived after Joe had been at Leavenworth for 122 days. A United States marshal took him back to Dallas where once again he was deposited in Sheriff Decker's county jail overnight. The next day he was escorted to Judge Sarah Hughes's court.

He had asked his parents and Nancy not to come to the court as he was afraid Judge Hughes would think this was some sort of a manipulation on his part to wring sympathy from her. But Joe was hurt, disappointed, and distressed that Adrian Carter was not there to stand beside him. Not that Adrian could have done anything to ameliorate the sentencing, but Joe felt a deep-seated need for the support of his old friend who had been through so much with him.

He was led into the courtroom and stood at attention waiting for the bailiff to announce the judge. In moments the austere old lady marched up to her seat behind the bench and stared coldly down at this miscreant brought before her for sentencing again.

The preliminaries were rapid and routine. Then Joe was on his feet, the man in the arena, opening with the statement he had rehearsed so many times before. "Help me turn away from

Leavenworth," he began—but as he delivered the words, as he dramatically asked to serve the remainder of his sentence on parole, as he talked about his resolve to live according to the laws of the land, as he did this, he could see that the judge was not impressed or overwhelmed by his oratory. Instead her face was flushed, her brow was furrowed with wrinkles of concentration, and she was perusing Dr. Passaro's report. *Was there something in it that he had not seen?* he wondered. He doubted that because Dr. Passaro had let Joe read it before submitting it. *Then what was bothering her so?* He did not know, but of one thing he was certain: the speech was not having the impact on Judge Hughes he had visualized in his dreams. Somehow he had thought that with his gift of eloquence he could deliver an oration that would stun the court and stagger the judge, forcing her to remove him from Leavenworth.

In his dramatic speech he was not making any reference to gambling. He felt he could not make any promises to quit gambling and had decided it would be a lie to offer any pledge in that direction. He knew inwardly that he would certainly return to it. The only question was whether he could confine it, in particular whether he could confine it within the law. This was his hope and pledge. He would live by the laws of the land if only the law would give him the chance.

When he finished there was no visible reaction from his audience. The deputies looked as bored as when he had begun. The court stenographer continued her work at the same pace and gave no indication that something extraordinary had been heard or delivered. And the forbidding gray eminence of Sarah Hughes continued to scrutinize the psychiatric report of Joe H. Hodges.

Finally she took off her spectacles and laid them upon her table. Then she hit him with the full impact of her discontent, her gray mane flowing.

"Mr. Hodges, you know that I know who you are and"—she said this with added emphasis—"I am well aware of your abilities in public speaking."

She went on to talk of how he had manipulated people in order to get his money for gambling. She spoke of the lives that had been battered by his relentless passion for this vice. She continued with how Joe had dishonored his profession and family and friends. Swiftly she gave the final sentencing: three years under 4208-A to be served in the Federal Correction Institution at Seagoville.

Joe was shocked at not receiving probation, but at least there was some slight hope in that "A", which meant that instead of being eligible for parole only after serving one third of his sentence, he could come up for release at any time during his prison term, even the day after he entered the penitentiary. Though of course this was highly improbable.

He walked out of the courtroom alone and was taken back to jail, this time to await transfer to a penitentiary only a few miles from Dallas. They placed him with a great many younger men in a section with lighter security and he was astonished to find how deranged many of them were. He saw wide-eyed youngsters trying to scale the wire fence and escape even when they were a few weeks from finishing out their terms. He saw riots and breathed tear gas. He saw twenty-two-year-olds fresh from the ghetto fashioning their homemade knives and cutting each other's stomachs open before breakfast. He saw again the gang rapes, which became so frequent as to be boring. He tasted the bland food in the chow lines and heard the eternal ringing of the bells; he noted once more how time strangely became both eternal and fragmented, each moment exactly like the last or the next.

In Seagoville Joe tried to adjust to penitentiary life. He made friends with a young man about his age, Bill Scott. Scott's wife was Billy Sol Estes' secretary until the boy wonder of finance was finally caught in a major scandal and drew a long term in Leavenworth. Joe had casually known Billy Sol at Leavenworth and had not been particularly impressed. However, Bill Scott, who had been sentenced by Judge Hughes for land-sale fraud, appealed to Joe. Scott's wife and three boys came to visit on Sundays, as did Nancy and Mark. Nancy and Bill's wife became friends and Mark enjoyed playing with his sons. Mark was young enough so that seeing his father in prison did not really affect him.

Also in Seagoville was a former vice-president of the Republic Bank of Dallas whom Joe had known. There was a tightly knit little financial community within the prison.

Joe and some of the other inmates who had been part of a more sophisticated life-style when they were in the free world involved themselves in a program called Toastmasters. The Toastmasters within Seagoville were part of an organization called Toastmasters International, a club devoted to public speaking. Both inmates and speakers from outside talked at the Toastmasters' Club dinners at the prison. Joe quickly became the organizer of the speakers' bureau and recruited such guests as Don Meredith, the former quarterback of the Dallas Cowboys, to come and speak. Toastmasters was a popular program and the inmates were allowed to put on a real dinner for the speakers.

Joe's great triumph as the procurer of guest speakers was his successful invitation to Judge Hughes to come out and talk. Bill Scott hated her because she had sentenced him. Indeed, so many of the inmates at Seagoville had been sentenced by Judge Hughes that it surprised Joe when she agreed to come. He himself, however, harbored no bitterness against her.

There were plenty of guards, of course, but still it must have taken some courage on the judge's part to face so many embittered men.

Joe met Judge Hughes at the gate and escorted her to the mess hall which the Toastmasters had decorated. They had planned the menu, too, and even had ice cream for dessert. Joe introduced Judge Hughes to the audience, which was carefully supervised by the guards, and then Judge Hughes gave her talk. The inmates listened attentively—there wasn't a one of them there that Judge Hughes couldn't have freed at the stroke of her pen—and the evening was one of the best attended since the formation of the Toastmasters' Club.

After Joe had served almost ten months in Seagoville, the parole board met for the second time to review his case. His parole plan was approved and a release date was set for April 1965. Two important stipulations in a parole plan are that when a prisoner is released he must have a job awaiting him and an adviser respected in the community. Nancy had gone to see Dr.

Allen, pastor of the First Methodist Church in Houston, who in turn called in one of his assistant preachers, Dick Murray. The Reverend Murray agreed to be listed as Joe's adviser, and then came the problem of getting him a job.

One of the Sunday school teachers, Jim Griffin, knew a real estate man named Ben Kostial. Griffin met with Ben and gave him Joe's résumé. Ben could not fail to be impressed with Joe's extensive experience in property development and he promised to give him a job upon his release. The two crucial requirements of the parole plan were thus met and Joe, bursting with smiles, walked out of Seagoville on April Fool's Day a free man once again.

It was an indescribable feeling. Better than all the wins he'd ever known at Las Vegas. He was given a new suit and $20 along with a small overnight kit. Joe reveled in putting on the suit, and the shirt and tie the government threw in. He didn't want his old suit since the new outfit was coming to him from the Bureau of Prisons and he relished every facet of the release process.

CHAPTER 25

Adrian Carter met Joe in downtown Dallas where the prison van from Seagoville let him out at eleven o'clock in the morning. Joe's thoughts were all on Nancy and he was eager to board the bus, knowing that she would be at the other end waiting. He had been avidly looking forward to this first night with Nancy for so long. Adrian patted him on the shoulder, put a $100 bill in his pocket, and sent him on his way.

Halfway between Dallas and Houston the bus made a rest stop and Joe was thrilled at the opportunity to go into a fast food shop, order a milk shake and a hamburger and pay for them. Being able to do such simple things without anybody knowing he was a convict was a little corner of heaven to him. He was beginning to reclaim his sense of identification with the free world. He discovered great pleasure in talking to the people on the bus, not saying anything that meant much, just exercising the freedom to chat.

Nancy had been completely on her own the whole time Joe was away, teaching school, making enough to meet the bills, and taking care of Mark whom she took to nursery school every morning at seven-thirty. She was as excited as Joe about their imminent reunion. She was more independent now. A little tougher, Joe thought. A little bit less feminine. Joe, who had most certainly been the dominant partner in their relationship, didn't feel quite so dominant any longer. He knew he wasn't automatically going to get his way on everything anymore.

Nancy was ecstatic to have him back. There were no threats,

no imprecations, no insistence on a changed life-style. It was just that Joe instinctively felt he couldn't reach her as he had before.

Now he had to start planning again. While he was incarcerated the only planning he did was focused on how to get out without escaping. Having emerged, he felt no resentment toward anybody. He was even able to accept that Judge Hughes had merely done her job according to her duties as a federal judge, and he would always appreciate her gesture of coming down to Seagoville to speak. He had served his sentence and the past was behind him. Now there was only the future to think about.

Joe did not come out of prison vowing that next time he wouldn't get caught, or that next time he'd build his bankroll in such a way that it would be impossible for him to get indicted again. He had never gone into banks or lending institutions with the idea of defrauding them. He went in with his driver's license and his own I.D. He went in to transact an ordinary business deal, a loan which he would repay. But he was thirty-six when he walked out of Seagoville, no longer a youth. He was a disbarred lawyer with no trade and no likelihood of getting a job if he refused Ben Kostial's offer. These were sobering thoughts.

Nancy, with Mark beside her, picked him up at the bus station and drove him to the small apartment she had taken on Larch Lane in the Bellaire area of Houston while he was gone. It was more humble than the apartment they had lived in before, but no matter to Joe; it was a glorious day and Joe was full of joy.

Mark was not really aware that his father had been in prison, only that he had been away. The boy's visits to Seagoville, while confusing, had made little impression on him.

The apartment, small though it was, thrilled him. It was spic and span. The beds were made and the pillows fluffed up, and Nancy had cooked dinner. She even had a bottle of wine and, after putting four-year-old Mark to bed, they enjoyed an exciting night together.

April Fool's Day that year fell on a Monday and the prison authorities had made Joe serve that last weekend. On Tuesday his first order of business was to go down to the Federal Building and meet with his federal parole officer, Hugh Mack Johnson. Joe liked him immediately. He filled out the forms and made himself acquainted with this man who was responsible for seeing that he stayed on good behavior until his sentence on parole was completed in three years' time, and to whom he would have to report once a month.

The next visit was to the First Methodist Church to see Dick Murray, his adviser for this period. Hugh Johnson had already talked to Dick and the two of them had pledged to do everything in their power to help Joe successfully rebuild his life. Dick Murray, already a friend from the days of Joe's church activities, welcomed him back and wished him well for the future, offering to include him in whatever church-related projects might interest him. That afternoon, Dick said, Ben Kostial was expecting him to come out and discuss the new job.

Joe drove with Nancy over to Ben's office at the edge of downtown Houston on Montrose Avenue. Ben, who was several years younger than Joe, had an office not far from the Montrose Club where Joe used to gamble. He was a heavyset man, somewhat stout, and he greeted Joe affably. Joe saw at once that he was not the judgmental type and would not hold his past against him. Ben briefly explained that Joe would have a desk in the office and help him put together real estate deals. Joe, for his part, found Ben likable and easy to talk to.

Ben explained his current situation. He had bought a lot of real estate and had it heavily mortgaged. "Spec" property, he called it, a speculative type of investment. All the real estate he had was mortgaged to the hilt and his assets were all on paper. Joe's first disappointment came when Ben told him he would not receive a salary, only a commission on any deal he could pull together. Joe had hoped he would have some sort of salary right at the beginning and that in fact had been implied in the relationship Kostial had outlined to the parole board.

Ben's disclosure disturbed him, even made his thoughts flash to gambling, but this was not the time to argue. He was out of prison and one of the reasons he was out of prison was that Ben Kostial had said he was giving him a job. Nevertheless, Joe realized that this was a bad setup for an ex-con. An ex-convict needed to get paid every Friday or every other Friday, $100 or at least something. The manipulator in Joe was challenged.

Somehow he would see his way to making money with Ben. All he needed was to get a little opening and he'd make his own way—Ben Kostial would be the springboard for his future.

While Joe was in prison it would have been futile for creditors to press their claims. During his first few weeks on the outside he was not besieged by creditors either. Of course the bonding companies for the First City National Bank, the Bank of the Southwest, and the Fannin Bank could be expected to press their claims, but as Joe settled into Kostial's office he enjoyed a period of relative peace, even though his application for a commercial real estate license was turned down on the grounds that he had been convicted of a felony.

It was not long, however, before he renewed his friendship with Turk and Tommy Glispen. A small dark cloud was forming on the horizon.

Ten days after Joe came out of prison, April 10, the major league baseball season opened. "My God, I need money. I've got to get hold of some money, make some money," Joe thought. That wasn't to say he considered robbing a seven-to-eleven convenience store. It wasn't that kind of a need for money. What he really needed was not so much money as some action.

Ben Kostial, although his financial statement showed him worth $1,200,000, was basically broke. His equity was all tied up in real estate. As Joe got to know him better he realized that his new employer had never really made any big money. He wasn't a business gambler and though he was always able to borrow money when he needed it, Joe quickly saw that he and his wife Ann were living beyond their means. Still, Ben loved his wife and was anxious that she should have the things she wanted, and they were an appealing couple with whom Nancy and Joe soon became friends.

Turk and Tommy Glispen had no understanding of what a compulsive gambler really is. As far as they were concerned Joe had landed himself in some trouble with a bad check and they hoped he would never have to go to the pen again. Turk was not saying to himself or to Tommy something like, "Oh well, I'd better not mention the baseball season to Joe, I don't want to get him started again." It was just the opposite. Turk was not trying to hustle Joe, but while talking about selling fencing material he would mention baseball games over lunch or drinks and ask Joe what he thought about certain ones.

As Joe settled into his post-penitentiary life, he began to renew other old acquaintances and to meet new people, too. There was nothing for him to be superior about and he found that people enjoyed being with him even if they knew he had been in the penitentiary and for what reason. As Joe saw it, his previous problem had in fact made him an easier person to be around. One of his new acquaintances was Mills Duncan of the very wealthy coffee company family which had been one of the original investors in Gulf & Western.

Somehow, almost unaware that he was doing it, Joe managed to pump $1,000 and get back into action again.

Mills Duncan told him about a small-time bookie, a bellman at the Shamrock Hotel, and Joe began placing small bets with him. Then Turk introduced him to Bobby Wilks in Sugarland, Texas, just south of Houston. Turk said Wilks had a nice crap game going there, so he and Joe drove down to Sugarland and Joe lost $200.

Wilks's father had also run a crap game south of Houston on Braes Bayou. His father was a famous gambler and Bobby, who started working for his father at age six or seven, knew how to run a crap game better than anyone in Texas. Over the next ten years Joe was to lose almost $500,000.

Joe was meeting people out at Wilks's game. It was an afternoon game and this suited him because he was always eager to be at home with Nancy and Mark by dinnertime. Another Lebanese friend of Turk's, George Bofysil, was a regular at Wilks's game, as was Rudy Flato, whose family, an extremely rich one, Joe had worked for during the summers when he was with his parents in Beaumont.

Wilks moved his crap game around from week to week in counties neighboring Houston's Harris County. Sometimes a game would be in his house, other times in a long trailer underneath the warehouse he had built in which cars could be parked, after passing through electronic doors. Although Joe *felt* Bobby Wilks's game was honest, he was never totally certain. It was the action he needed, and he needed it so badly he was prepared to ignore his suspicion that the dice were not perfectly square.

Wilks was the richest man in Sugarland, having been in the craps business all his life. He had a list of crapshooters and when he had a game going in a new location, he'd call his list and announce he was going to have a barbecue that day, giving them the location. And so Joe would be sitting in Ben Kostial's office trying to figure out a real estate deal, itching for action as always, and the phone calls from Bobby would come through. "There's a barbecue out here today," the voice would say. That's all Joe had to hear. If he didn't have any money he would go to Ben and borrow $500 for some good cause, for instance, day-care payments for Mark or a new stove for Nancy "to replace the one that blew out yesterday."

As time went on, Joe would go to Ben, a lugubrious expression on his face, and say, "Hey, I know you can't pay me but is there any way we can scheme up where I can borrow a grand?" Somehow Ben was usually able to arrange the loan.

While working with Ben, Joe felt compelled to start getting something going so he could rise above small-time crap shooting, and he was in fact able to perfect a technique for obtaining takeout commitments.

He discovered that on the strength of some piece of Ben's real estate it would be possible to go to the Republic National Life Insurance Company in Dallas or some equally prominent financial institution and get a letter from them stating that two years hence they would extend Ben a loan of $300,000, taking the few acres he controlled on Bellfort Avenue as collateral. Of course the Republic National Life Insurance Company had no desire ever to loan Ben $300,000 on his property in two years, or at any other time for that matter. So in the second part of the letter it was indicated that the loan would be for a short period of time and all the interest was due up front. Such a deal is not attractive for any borrower and of course the incentive for him is to get busy over the next two years to develop the land into income-producing property, or to sell it.

However, Joe knew that such a takeout commitment letter could be brought to a bank which would lend Ben two-year money on the understanding that the Republic National Life Insurance Company, say, was committed to lending him the $300,000 when the two years were up, a sum from which the bank could exact immediate repayment. The procedure is called "warehousing." It was Joe's intention to get letters of this kind and then find banks that would warehouse the commitments and lend Ben the money to develop his property to the point where it represented a solid economic base.

In Houston all property was increasing in value as the city grew. It was a well-known fact that no city in the country rewarded its promoters and speculators more handsomely than Houston. Thus the land Ben had purchased for speculative purposes, basically second-rate commercial development property, could be parlayed into cash with an experienced bank negotiator like Joe.

For writing the takeout commitment letter, a financial institution is given 5 percent of the total amount of the pledged loan, even if the chances are minimal that the loan will ever be made.

Thus Joe got himself into the money business and that of course suited the gambler in him perfectly. He had not been able to acquire a salaried position, but the gambler doesn't like salaries. They are never enough for his purposes. But if he can get into the money business, well, that's great.

Joe persuaded Ben to finance a trip to Dallas that would enable Joe to visit the Republic National Life Insurance Company and attempt to secure a takeout commitment on the Bellfort commercial property. Although Joe knew none of the executives of Republic, he had done his homework. It had a net worth of $200 million and was reputed to be a swinging financial institution.

Without appointment he walked into the insurance company's offices and discovered that the two executives he would have to see were A. E. Streitmatter and A. W. Atkinson. In a few hours he had managed to whet their appetite for the deal. He showed them the letter placing a value of $450,000 on the land, and Streitmatter agreed to come to Houston and look at the property himself. The deal was only worth $15,000 to the company, but all that was required from them was a letter.

Back in Houston, Joe persuaded Ben to hire a limousine and chauffeur to meet Streitmatter at the airport and take him to the

Bellfort site, and then to put him up at the Sheraton Hotel and do a bit of lavish entertaining. When Streitmatter arrived he met two apparently wealthy and earnest executives, saw the property, shook hands with some of the real estate people in Houston, and was taken to dinner by the two promoters at the best restaurant in town.

So Joe and Ben managed to take Ben's Bellfort Avenue property and secure the takeout commitment from the Republic National Life Insurance Company for $300,000. A prerequisite, of course, was persuading some real estate "experts" to give certified appraisals on the property's value. Since Ben had paid less than $100,000 cash for it, Joe had to cast about, but finally he came up with the appraisal letters.

Ben watched the complicated maneuvers Joe went through to acquire the takeout in amazement. But this was just the beginning. With the commitment in hand he would next have to find a bank that would do the warehousing.

Joe approached his old employer Walter Mischer who had bought the Continental Bank and was becoming one of the biggest financiers in Houston. Mischer knew all about Joe's conviction and imprisonment but he was interested in the proposition. There was no way the bank could lose, and despite Joe's bad record, warehousing the takeout commitment of the Republic National Life Insurance Company was a good deal.

While Joe was at it, he asked Walter if he could get a personal loan for $2,000 from the Continental Bank.

Mischer shook his head in wonderment, grinning at the paroled ex-convict before him. Finally he said, "Okay, Joe, I'll take a ticket on you." He sent him down to see Jay Crager, Joe's old friend from Beaumont. Jay could hardly believe his eyes when Joe came in with a note from Walter Mischer telling him to go ahead and give Joe H. Hodges a $2,000 loan on a ninety-day note. But Mischer had said that he would "take a ticket" on Joe, so Jay had no choice but to hand him the proper papers. Joe immediately signed them and walked away with a bank check for $2,000.

Next Joe went to the president of Mischer's Continental Bank with the takeout and tried to negotiate the loan that Mischer had said his bank would make. However, the banker created so many problems for Joe, insisting among other things that he get more appraisal letters, that finally Joe went over to the Houston Citizens Bank and opened negotiations there. He succeeded in his quest and Ben received a check for $300,000 from the Houston Citizens Bank minus $6,000 for two points which the bank charged for warehousing the loan.

Now Ben was able to pay off $100,000 that he owed on the property he had purchased, and he gave a real estate man who had worked on the acquisition of the Bellfort property $25,000 as a commission for putting the deal in his hands.

Ben and his wife Ann took off for a vacation in New York City the day after the deal with the Citizens Bank was closed. But when it came to recompensing Joe who had manipulated the loan, Ben merely thanked him and told him to watch the shop while he was away. Joe got nothing for putting the deal together.

Joe was wounded by Ben's glaring lack of consideration for him. He was still receiving no salary, yet he had helped put together a deal that Ben could never have swung alone—and now Ben was waving goodbye as he and his wife left on vacation.

Back at home, Joe could only lie to Nancy and tell her, "Oh yes, when Ben gets back I'll get some money, my share of the deal."

Now all Ben had to do was somehow sell the property or develop it to a point where in two years he'd be able to repay the $300,000 plus the 8 percent interest. But for a real estate promoter in Houston two years was a long time and Ben would come out well ahead, particularly with an enterprising man such as Joe working with him.

After Ben left, Joe took $15,000 from the cash that Ben had received to the Republic National in Dallas—the 5 percent they got for writing the letter that made the deal possible. It was a beautiful transaction which not only got Ben out of his cash bind, but gave him some surplus to work with and live on. His financial savior, ironically enough, was Joe, the ex-convict whom he had agreed to help.

Nancy worried more than Joe about Ben neither giving him a salary nor, as she came to learn, a commission on the deal. Just the same, Joe had to keep her thinking that Kostial was treating him better than he was. When he borrowed the money from Walter Mischer he told Nancy it had come from Ben, whereas what money he had so far got from Ben was always in the form of a personal loan for which Joe signed.

Meanwhile Joe was betting baseball games, sweating the results out as always and continuing his activities in Sugarland.

When word of Ben Kostial's takeout commitment and successful warehousing loan began to get about Houston, Joe found himself with the reputation of being an innovative money manipulator. His phone rang constantly while the Kostials were away on their New York vacation. Financial promoters were interested in having him make similar deals for them. During the negotiations he had established a solid business relationship with important executives of the Republic National Life Insurance Company and they were amenable to going ahead with similar deals.

By the time Ben returned, Joe had been doing a lot of thinking about his successful deal on Ben's behalf, and about its implications. If the takeout commitment and subsequent warehousing would work with Republic National Life Insurance Company with its $200 million net worth, why couldn't it also work with an individual who had a net worth of $10 or $20 million?

CHAPTER 26

Joe had thought of Charlie Wyche often while he was in prison and again frequently as he began maneuvering Ben's real estate into a cash flow situation. The last time he had written up a net worth statement for the old man the figure had been about $20 million.

Joe persuaded Ben to finance a joint trip to Dallas so that Joe could visit with Charlie. Ben was hesitant at first but finally agreed. After flying to Dallas they rented a car and Joe drove his reluctant business associate over to Irving and out to Charlie's.

Charlie was sitting on the rickety front porch when Joe and Ben drove up.

"Wal, hello there, Irishman," he greeted Joe laconically.

Joe introduced Ben to the wizened old man and the three of them sat on the porch making inconsequential conversation for a while. Then Joe asked, "Say, Charlie, how's that financial statement of yours? You got it all in good order?"

"Hey, goddamn, I'm glad you're here," Wyche exclaimed. "That statement sure needs to be updated."

"Well, let's do it."

Inside the house Charlie brought Joe all his latest financial statements and bank accounts, laying them out on the dining room table. In a few hours, as Ben waited, trying to keep from showing his impatience, Joe completed a new financial statement for Charlie. Much of the property Joe had helped him buy was now being developed or had been sold at considerable profit.

When Joe finished adding up Charlie's income and assets, and subtracted the liabilities from them, he came up with a net worth of $23 million.

"Charlie, I think I can run us down some deals. If you'll just sign them we can make us some money."

"I know you, Irishman. I figured you had in mind something like that. Well, see what you can do with my statement. Then come back to me."

Joe glanced at his watch. "Charlie, I've got just time to take this mess into town. I'll go to Adrian Carter's office, get them to type it up all nice and neat and bring it back to you. You sign it and then I'll see what I can do."

"Go ahead, Irishman."

Joe and Ben drove over to Adrian's office and two hours later were back on Charlie's porch where the old man was still sitting in his favorite rocker, his feet up on the rail.

"Here you go, Charlie. I brought you a bunch of copies in case you need them. You're all up-to-date now." He handed Charlie one of the copies of his financial statement and the old man duly signed it. Joe slipped it into his briefcase. "Okay, Charlie, let me see what I can do and I'll get back to you."

On the way to the airport Ben shook his head. "My God, you embezzled his money, you didn't pay him back, he had you indicted . . . Even though he quashed the indictment, he'll never guarantee any loan for you."

"Well, he's Charlie and I'm the Irishman. We'll see," Joe answered jauntily.

Shortly after Joe's return to Houston with a signed copy of the Wyche statement, Jim Nash, a gambling buddy from the past, took Joe to an old part of downtown Houston and introduced him to a young man named Earl Atwood who owned a company he called Inland Waterways, Inc. Nash felt that Earl Atwood could benefit by Joe's sophistication in arranging financing and that Joe could perhaps do something with Earl that would benefit them both.

Earl Atwood was playing the red flag dodge, a deal that can only prosper around booming cities like Houston or Dallas. Most people seem to have a great desire to own a piece of land.

Whether they work at a refinery or a shipyard, a steel mill or a chemical plant, no matter what their income and station in life they yearn for their own plot of ground.

Houston was moving, developing fast along the East Texas Freeway in the area where Lake Houston is located, supplier of much of the town's water, and Earl Atwood was launching his career as a land developer. The east side of Houston is not like the west where the expensive, exclusive homes are located, but it was attractive wooded property near the lake. Atwood had made a deal with a man named May to take over a thousand acres of May's land. He cut the property up into small lots, bulldozing dirt roads and selling them to the people who worked in refineries and factories and wanted a place of their own out in the country for weekends and vacations. The desire of these people to dig their fingers into their own land and say, "This is mine," cannot be underestimated, Earl Atwood shrewdly reasoned. The lots were not on the lake but an easy drive or a long walk from it. Earl sold his lots by putting a "deeder" in the classified section of the newspaper, the advertisement proclaiming two acres for sale on Lake Houston for $2,995. That of course is a very cheap price for lakefront property and a mass of people could not resist dialing the advertised number.

Earl Atwood's office was basically a bucket shop, Joe recognized—a place where girls were trained to answer the phone calls that came in. While he was there a factory worker in pursuit of his dream of owning land called in and one of Earl's girls sitting at a telephone bank picked up. Joe listened as she went into her spiel.

"Oh yes," the girl said into the phone, "that was my daddy that took the ad. He's out there now so if you want to see the property drive to Huffman out by the lake. I'm sure he'll be glad to show it to you." A pause and then, "No, it hasn't been sold yet but Daddy's getting a lot of interest. If you're interested you'd better get you in your car and drive out there." She gave directions as to how to find her "daddy" and then hung up.

Almost immediately the phone rang again and it was another inquiry.

"Now let me take you out to Huffman and show you the deal,"

Atwood offered. On the way there in Atwood's car, Joe reminisced about a time when he was twenty and bought an acre of land in Houston on credit and cut up the acre into some 43,000 square feet. Then he advertised in the San Francisco newspapers under the headline OWN A PIECE OF TEXAS FOR $10.00. Soon his mailbox was flooded with envelopes containing $10 bills from people who wanted to boast about owning a piece of Texas even if it was only a square foot.

Joe duly sent out deeds to each square foot of property. It seemed like a fantastic get-rich-quick scheme until he was stopped. The buyers, after receiving their deeds, wanted to record them at the county clerk's office which drove the personnel there insane. Finally the county clerk got out an injunction against selling a square foot of property in Texas. But Joe, from this experience, could well understand how Atwood could make a success out of selling lots of land to property-hungry workers in Houston. He himself made $8,000 on his "own a piece of Texas" promotion before he was closed down.

Out near Lake Houston, Earl showed Joe the property advertised in the newspaper for $2,995. True enough it was on the lake, but it was down deep in a gulch totally unsuitable as a building site. While Joe was with Earl at his property, several couples arrived from the city and after seeing the gulch were led over to the wooded property which was away from the lake but still attractive land. Earl had cut lots into half, quarter, and even eighth-of-an-acre pieces. His problem, as Joe could see, was that he had very little cash to develop the one thousand acres. Every day he made sales for $100 down and $50 a month to buy these little bowling alleys, as Joe called them, because they were long and thin. Somehow he had to finance this development. Each time Atwood took a down payment on a lot he had to turn over half of it to the owner of the thousand acres, Mr. May, and then as the payments came in continue paying them to May until the individual lot was paid for. Thus, while the overall long-term prospects of Inland Waterways, Inc. were good, the immediate cash problem was a difficult one to solve.

During the thirty-mile drive back to Houston from Lake Houston Joe and Earl discussed the deal at length. At the Inland

Waterways' bucket shop they figured out all the financial aspects of the property development. Basically, if the entire thousand acres was sold at the price Inland was now getting in this red flag bait-and-switch-land sale scheme, it would mean $11 million gross to Atwood. He had to pay May $2 million which would leave him an overall profit of $9 million. The down payment of $100 and the $50 a month until the bowling alley was paid for was a slow way of making money. Just the same, the land that had already been sold would net $156,000 when all payments were made and Earl had paid off May at $2,000 an acre.

"Tell you what I'll do, Earl," Joe said to the cash-starved young developer. "I'll try and get you a loan of a hundred fifty thousand on a takeout commitment. Put together a good package on the deal and give me three hundred dollars to go up to Dallas for a weekend and I'll take a swing."

Earl was not anxious to give up even $300 of badly needed cash, but after he and Joe had discussed the situation for several days and had made up a professional real estate presentation, he finally decided to send Joe on his way.

In Dallas, Joe went to the offices of Republic National Life and found A. W. Aktinson in his office. Atkinson studied the proposal for two days while Joe stayed in Dallas awaiting his decision, craving gambling action but not able to do much with the paltry expense allowance he had received from Earl. Atkinson agreed to take a trip to Houston and see the land at firsthand. This property was nowhere near the quality of the property in the Ben Kostial transaction, Joe realized, but then they were only asking for a takeout commitment of half as much.

Back in Houson, Joe reported to Atwood that the proposition he had made was favorably received. Now he would need $6,000 up front to clinch the deal.

Atwood was shocked. He had no way of coming up with that amount of cash. "Are you sure that if we do get up the money the deal will be made?" he asked.

"I'm not sure of anything," Joe replied. "But it's going to cost the six just to take the swing at them."

"Do we get the six back if the deal falls through?" Atwood asked reasonably.

"Oh certainly," Joe reassured him.

"I'll have to see what I can come up with. That's a lot of cash for me right now."

Joe had made up his mind that this time he wasn't going to have a repeat of the Kostial situation where Ben and his wife had taken off for a vacation and Joe had been left with no piece of the action.

For the several weeks it took Atwood to arrange a $6,000 loan, Joe kept Atkinson interested in the deal on the phone. All Republic would be getting out of the takeout commitment was its 5 percent fee, which was $7,500, so it wasn't of great moment to Atkinson one way or the other. Finally, on a Wednesday, Earl called Joe and asked him to be in front of the First State Bank of Bellaire at 11 A.M.

"Can you make that ten a.m.?" Joe asked, knowing just what he was going to do.

Atwood agreed and Joe was at the bank and talking to its vice-president, Pat Hamilton, and Earl right on time. Hamilton made the loan of $6,000 to Earl who immediately cashed the check and gave the money in $100 bills to Joe.

Joe sped out to the airport with the money and caught the noon plane to Las Vegas. Four hours after he had walked out of the bank he was at the Flamingo casino sopping up the stimulating action at the crap tables. It was like slaking a parched thirst, like a shot of heroin to an addict, to be rolling the cubes again at Las Vegas.

In under four hours Joe had won $12,000 and was taking the next plane home with his $18,000. At first he thought of giving back the $6,000 to Earl but changed his mind. Instead, he telephoned Atkinson and told him to fly on down to Houston. Joe and Earl picked Atkinson up at the airport and drove him out to see the property; then they went back to the Inland Waterways offices. Atkinson was impressed with Earl's development.

"He's a pretty good little promoter, isn't he?" Atkinson commented to Joe. Atkinson checked out the deeds to the property that had been sold and made a few random calls to the people who were making payments on the land to check that the sales were real.

"How much is it you want?" he asked finally.

"A hundred fifty thousand," Joe replied.

Atkinson nodded. "I'm going to shoot from the hip with you. If you give me six points instead of five, I'm going to give you the takeout commitment for a hundred sixty-five. How does that suit you?"

Atwood was speechless for a moment and then said, "That suits us just fine, Mr. Atkinson."

Joe and Earl went back to Dallas with Atkinson the next day and the deal was closed. It took Earl Atwood a week to get the bank loan on the basis of the commitment, but get it he did. After all, there could be no more solid paper than Republic National's. With the loan granted and the money in Inland's bank account Earl gave Joe a $5,000 commission for making the deal. Furthermore, Earl was so impressed with Joe's financial acumen that he made him president of Inland Waterways at a salary of $500 a week.

Of course it didn't take Joe long to lose all the money he had won on the Vegas trip plus the $11,000 he had made on the transaction. But every Friday he was receiving his $500 paycheck and this gave him the sense of stability he needed. Earl was moving land quickly now and building up Inland Waterways with Joe's help. He hired an accountant, Harry Hill, to keep the books straight and write out checks.

That Friday paycheck was the most important thing in Joe's life outside of his family, though nothing stopped him from betting the baseball games and he continued pumping wherever he could to finance his action with the bookies. Then one Friday the company funds hit a low ebb. Earl was sending money to some New York promoter whom Joe considered an outright thief and was spending company funds carelessly in Joe's view. When the Friday check didn't arrive at his office Joe called the accountant's office, and when he asked the secretary for his check he was told that Mr. Hill had not written it that day. "Mr. Hill said you wouldn't be needing it," the girl added.

In a rage Joe stalked down the hall to Hill's office and threw open the door. The accountant looked up startled from his desk on which lay the neatly rolled umbrella that he always carried. It had become a sort of trademark with him.

"Harry, I understand you didn't write my check today," Joe said in barely suppressed fury.

"No, I didn't think we could stand it."

Livid, Joe snatched the umbrella from Harry Hill's desk and put the point of it against the executive's left breast. "I'm going to stick this umbrella in your heart and open it if you don't have that check in my office within five minutes!" The feral intensity in Joe's voice shocked the suddenly terrified Hill. Joe glared at him balefully, then dropped the umbrella onto the desk, turned on his heel and marched out of the office.

In less than five minutes Hill's secretary scurried into Joe's office and placed the check on his desk, retreating in fright.

Between Bobby Wilks's crap games and the Turk, Joe kept up his daily quota of betting action, often ranging from $2,000 to $3,000 a day. Because of his reputation as a financial expert, acquired through the Kostial deal and enhanced by his success at getting the takeout commitment and loan for Inland Waterways, he was constantly being contacted by entrepreneurs wanting him to put his expertise at their disposal too. He almost forgot he was on parole until he hustled some up-front money to provide financing for one of Earl's friends, Jack Dagle. The front money was soon lost and Joe was unable this time to consummate the financing package he had undertaken.

When Dagle found out that Joe was on parole he threatened him with violation of parole and a return to prison if he didn't repay the money he'd taken to try to put the deal together. Joe managed to pump up the $4,000 Dagle had paid him and once again escaped disaster.

Joe continued to go to Wilks's crap game. The afternoon action was irresistible to him, even though he virtually never won and suspected that the dice were crooked. The action seemed more important than the losses.

In his constant search for "spots" he found a small bank in Houston called the Downtown Bank. He cultivated a vice-president there, a young man named Hollis Walters, and started putting Inland Waterways deposits into the Downtown Bank. This gave him some leverage. Hollis Walters was also a friend of Ben Kostial's and Ben still occasionally co-signed notes for Joe, including a $5,000 one with Walters. Joe opened his own account at the Downtown Bank and Hollis joined the ranks of young bankers who protected him when he got involved in financial manipulations.

On one of his increasingly frequent trips to Las Vegas Joe blew his bankroll at the crap table and, rather than return to Houston in defeat, took a flight to Los Angeles. He made his way to Pasadena, walked into a small branch bank and presented a check on his account at the Downtown Bank of Houston for $6,000. Obviously there was no money in his account but he brazenly told the Los Angeles bank vice-president to call the vice-president of his own bank in Houston, taking a chance that Hollis would back him up.

The vice-president of the Pasadena bank indeed did call Hollis Walters who told him that the check was not good at the moment but by the time it got to Houston it would be covered. With that the Los Angeles suburb bank cashed the check.

With the $6,000 Joe returned to the Los Angeles airport and caught the next plane to Las Vegas. Why was he doing this? he asked himself. What exactly was the uncontrollable compulsion that gripped him? He would rather be home with Nancy and Mark spending a tranquil afternoon in the backyard, perhaps cooking steaks with good friends. He didn't really want to expend the large quantities of psychic energy it required to fly to a strange city, pump an unknown banker, and then head back to the casinos for the exhausting, albeit exhilarating, attack on the crap tables.

On the short flight to Las Vegas he thought of that cold, rainy night when he had left Nancy alone in their cozy Beaumont apartment and made the dangerous drive on slippery roads all the way out to the crap game in another county only to lose everything. But at the time he *had* to do it, and the same was true now.

Before the plane landed at Las Vegas he had put away all such thoughts. Only the garish casinos mattered.

This time when he walked up to the crap table, however, he was a little more cautious. He took only $200 of the $6,000 and bought a stack of chips at the Sands, promising himself not to touch any more of the money.

He walked into the casino at 10 A.M. and fourteen hours later walked out—the winner of $17,000!—amazed to see it was pitch dark outside. After flying back to Houston, he immediately covered the check Hollis Walters had said would be good by the time it reached the bank there. Naturally his win did not last very long. Once again he couldn't resist going out to Wilks where he soon dropped most of his Las Vegas winnings.

In his desperation to support his compulsion for daily gambling action, Joe persuaded the Turk to introduce him to a six-and-five man in Houston. That meant that he could borrow $500 or $5,000 and one week later have to pay back $600 or $6,000. Soon he was borrowing money from Chicago six-and-five men. With the Chicago mob the collateral is your body. Joe now had two weeks to pay $12,000 back on the $10,000 he had borrowed; and one day before it was due he received a phone call at Inland Waterways reminding him that the money was to be paid the next day.

Getting the money for his gambling was becoming expensive. He had to fly to Chicago, pick up the money, and then fly back there to repay it. This time he didn't have the money to repay it, and the telephone call had reminded him that his body would never be good for anything again if he didn't find it fast. So he went to his banker friend Hollis Walters and smashed a hot $12,000 check with him. He would worry about making it good later. With $12,000 in his pocket he flew to Chicago, paid the money, and came home only hours before he would have suffered the fate he knew was in store for him. The six-and-five men were a far cry from the relatively permissive bankers and moneylenders he had been doing business with.

Nancy was still teaching school and paying the rent, buying the groceries and keeping their house together. Despite the large amounts of money that flowed through his hands, Joe never had even the cash to do more than occasionally buy some grocery items.

It was, of course, a time of despair and sorrow for Nancy. She could plainly see the old cycle repeating itself. She loved her husband, and her pledge at the altar was sacred to her, but was there no way she could bring a halt to the downward spiraling fortunes of the little family she and Joe and Mark had become? She couldn't find one.

Nancy was no longer naïve or permissive, but she was frustrated, stymied by her husband's compulsion which was tearing the fabric of their life apart. She had nobody in whom she could confide. To tell her mother and father what she was going through would only have invited a tirade and importunings to leave Joe and go back to California with Mark, this time for an indefinite visit with her mother.

When Joe returned from Chicago after buying back his body in good condition, he faced the $12,000 hot check that would be floating back to Hollis Walters. Now what was he going to do? There seemed only one answer. Get a bankroll and go back to Wilks's crap game and hit it for a big win. With a brazenness born of desperation, he visited Walters and added another $2,000 hot check to the original sum and drove out to Sugarland. He hit the crap game at three in the afternoon and rolled hard and high until eight that night.

For one of the few times at the Sugarland crap game Joe walked out a winner; not a big one, but he left with $5,000 more than he came with. Unfortunately, he needed much more; he needed at least $12,000 to take care of the heat and leave himself a bankroll for the next day.

It was like coitus interruptus, pulling out just as he felt the heat of a winning streak upon him. Perhaps taking home $5,000 was better than losing, but he had stopped short of orgasm and felt physically and emotionally cheated, even resentful of Nancy who had made him promise, virtually on the Bible, he would be home for dinner. By the next morning he was sure the first hot check would be back on Hollis Walters' desk. He could pay off $7,000 against it but that really wasn't enough.

He didn't get back by dinner and Nancy was waiting for him. She had told herself that this night she would try to be comforting and supportive no matter what he had done, and merely said, "I'm sorry I couldn't keep dinner warm for you, dear." She couldn't miss the rumpled, grubby look about him and the stale smell of the crap game, but made no comment.

"I'll just go in and take a shower," Joe replied.

Nancy was reading in bed when Joe came out of the bathroom. She put the book away, turned off her light, and got up.

"Feel better?" she asked. "I don't know how you get so dirty at a business meeting."

He felt clean and fresh again after the shower. He didn't say anything as he buttoned up his pajamas.

Nancy came to him. "Let me do that."

Her figure was good. He could see it through the nightgown. He touched the almost transparent material. "Is this new?"

"No, silly," she said. "I bought it just before we got married." She looked at it. "Haven't worn it much. A little too daring, isn't it?"

"Not at all. I like it."

Nancy put her arms around Joe and held him tightly. She kissed him slowly, passionately, expressing her hunger. Joe responded as best he could, holding her closely. But Wilks's had taken too much out of him, and he had Hollis Walters to face in the morning.

"Not tonight, sweetheart. I'm too tired," he whispered in her ear. Nancy slowly let go. "Tomorrow, I promise. I won't be so tired, won't go out. We'll have the whole night to ourselves."

"Promise?" She smiled knowingly.

"Yes."

Nancy didn't say anything as she got into bed. There had been too many promises that had been broken. Joe wanted to tell her, to explain. Maybe he could unburden a little, maybe they could share some of the load.

Joe sat on the edge of the bed, his back toward Nancy. "I have to see Hollis Walters early tomorrow."

"Oh?"

"A loan." Nancy didn't say anything. Joe continued, "I need five thousand dollars."

"Five thousand dollars!" Nancy couldn't believe it. She sat up and repeated the amount of money, shocked.

"I got into some trouble . . . a few bad deals."

"Your Chicago deal?" she asked angrily. She couldn't help herself.

"Yeah, that's falling through . . ."

"Go on."

"Nothing much happening at the office." In practically a whisper he said, "Lost a few bets."

Nancy didn't seem to hear that. "Five thousand is a lot of money. In a year I don't make much more than that as a schoolteacher." She turned toward him, determined to find out what had happened. "What did you need all that money for?" she asked sharply.

Joe still sat with his back to her. "I just needed it. Hollis will help me, don't worry."

"Will you please explain?"

"Not tonight. I'm too tired." Joe fell into bed and shut off the light.

The room was dark. Nancy, furious, sat up. "You're not going to sleep, Joe Henry Hodges, until you tell me what's happening to us. I won't be put off."

"No," Joe said as he turned on his side away from her. "I'm too tired. Go to sleep." He could never explain about the hot check when she was in this kind of mood, or any mood for that matter.

"What did you need the money for? What did you do with it?" Nancy asked.

No response.

"You're not going to sleep! Not until you explain. I have a right to know." All the frustration and bitterness she had hoped to put aside tonight welled up in her.

Joe closed his eyes. He shouldn't have said anything. A lie might quiet her but he couldn't think of any now. Tomorrow he'd give her some story, work it all out.

Nancy lay down, furious. She let Joe fall asleep and then started kneading his back under the covers, her feet pressing hard against his flesh, pushing it up and down, up and down.

Joe woke up. "Stop that!"

"No! You won't sleep, Joe. Tell me what's going on. Please!"

"No."

Nancy stopped. She was confused, puzzled, hurt, and unable to sleep.

A half hour later she started in on Joe's back again. Cold feet moving up and down, squeezing the flesh.

"Stop that!" Joe cried. "I need to sleep!"

In twenty minutes she started again. She stopped, and twenty minutes later repeated the process. She kept repeating it at regular intervals. Joe gave up trying to sleep, but he wouldn't respond. Neither said anything.

About three-thirty in the morning Joe couldn't take it anymore. There was no way he could explain. Picking up the radio beside the bed, he hurled it against the wall. The radio smashed to bits, the noise overwhelmingly loud in the quiet bedroom. The momentary resort to violence had its effect.

Nancy, not saying anything, turned from him and started to get out of bed.

"Leave it!" he yelled.

She got back into bed. She would not allow herself to cry. She was determined he would not hear her cry.

Joe waited until he thought she was asleep. Tomorrow everything would be fine. He'd give Nancy some explanation. Hollis would convert the rest of the money he owed into a loan. He could handle him. Tomorrow he'd have no problems. He turned on his stomach and slept like a baby the rest of the night.

CHAPTER 27

Except for that one win that temporarily saved Joe with Hollis Walters at the Downtown Bank of Houston, Bobby Wilks was beating Joe like a bass drum. Joe just couldn't win for losing. His debt structure was $150,000. He was still paying off the Fannin Bank, First City National Bank, the Bank of the Southwest, and six finance companies.

Nevertheless, his reputation as a money raiser was getting around. From Pensacola, Florida, he heard from a local entrepreneur, Harry Newkirk, who had been told that Joe did takeout commitments and had a moneyman behind him named Charlie Wyche.

Charlie's financial statement was a major part of Joe's pitch kit and somebody who knew Newkirk had evidently mailed a copy of Wyche's financial statement to promoters with whom Newkirk was associated. Newkirk wanted Joe to become involved with him in a land development deal at Lake Charles, a city sixty miles inside Louisiana from the Texas line.

Joe agreed to drive to Lake Charles, meet Harry Newkirk, become acquainted, and examine the deal. He met Harry at the airport and the two of them immediately liked each other. Although Harry was a promoter, there was another, unusual side to him. He had founded a music conservatory in Pensacola and when not involved in drilling oil or gas wells and other promotions he and his wife, also named Nancy, taught at their music school. Harry was formerly a gifted concert pianist and a graduate of Peabody in Baltimore.

Joe quickly came to the conclusion that if Harry, who was loved by everybody in town, would only stick to music and forget the wheeling and dealing, he would be a successful and happy man. However, he had not come to Lake Charles to involve himself in life counseling.

Harry Newkirk had come across two promoters named Charles Mobley and Nathan Samuels who came, respectively, from Mobile and Dallas. He had Mobley with him in Lake Charles. Joe's sensitive antennae gave out a series of high-pitched warning bleeps. Mobley had to be some kind of a hustler. Mobley and Samuels had both seen the Charlie Wyche financial statement and they assumed Joe was influential with the old man.

At Lake Charles, Mobley took Joe and Harry out to a beautiful, large lakeside property owned by Charles Lawrence and his son Burton Lawrence. Mobley professed his and Samuel's desire to develop the Lawrences' highly desirable property. Mobley estimated that a $5 million development loan was required. They had multimillion-dollar investors in New Mexico who would come into the deal with as much as $10 million of equity money once the development was underway.

After studying the property and thinking about Mobley's proposition, Joe came to the conclusion that he and his partner had nothing more in mind than getting a loan and running with the money. However, he did not confide his suspicions to either Harry or the Lawrences. He merely nodded and said, "Yes, this is the sort of deal Charlie goes for. He knows good property. He's made his fortune getting in on the ground floor of fine development land. I can get him to guarantee a loan for this purpose, I feel quite certain."

Mobley, of course, was delighted and Harry, financially beleaguered and on the verge of bankruptcy, felt that deliverance was at hand at last.

Joe went back to Houston and let matters develop. It wasn't long before he got a phone call from Mobley who was in Dallas with Samuels. They were both extremely anxious for Joe to come up to Dallas and arrange for Charlie to sign the $5 million loan agreement.

"I only work on one basis, Mr. Mobley," Joe said on the phone.

"Twenty-five thousand dollars up front which goes to Charlie. Then I'll get his signature on a guaranty."

A few days later Mobley flew to Houston and again extolled the virtues of the Lake Charles land development and stressed the fortune Joe could make out of the deal once they got it started. Harry Newkirk's involvement was already forgotten. All that was needed was the guaranty by Charlie Wyche.

"When you've got the twenty-five thousand I'll get his signature," Joe insisted.

A few days later Mobley called Joe from Mobile saying he was catching a plane to Dallas and wanted Joe to meet him there. Joe did not retreat from his demand. "When you have the twenty-five thousand let me know and I'll be up there." The very next day Mobley called Joe again and told him they had the cash ready. He said Samuels would meet Joe at the Executive Inn close to the Dallas airport. Mobley had an appointment the next day but would join them as soon as he could get away.

"How will Samuels know me?" Joe asked. His acquaintanceship with Samuels had been strictly on the telephone.

"I told him you limp a little. He'll recognize you."

"Send me a prepaid air ticket and I'll be there," Joe replied. He had made up his mind that he was going to try to take off these con men and they weren't going to get him for any more of an investment in the deal than cab fare to the airport.

The next day Joe flew up to Dallas and met Samuels at the Executive Inn. They discussed the deal for some time and then Mobley arrived and they had lunch at the coffee shop of the hotel.

Sitting at the table Samuels let Joe actually see the cashier's check for $25,000 he had brought with him, and then Mobley leered at Joe. "Hey, that broad over there, she's really giving you the eye, Joe."

Joe did not even look up, making some self-deprecatory remark. His only interest now was in extracting the cashier's check from the two men who were trying to con him.

Samuels looked over at the girl and then back to Joe. "She *is* looking at you, Joe. She's really staring at you. What a sweetheart."

Joe finally looked up and saw the girl who was indeed staring at him. She was gorgeous, about twenty, he thought. Interested as he was on plucking the cashier's check from Mobley and Samuels, he was not one to ignore such a lovely young woman with such an obvious interest in him. He excused himself and walked across the dining room to the girl's table. There was something familiar about her and he probed his memory trying to remember what it was.

Suddenly it struck him. He hadn't seen her since she was thirteen years old. My God! he thought, little Cindy Bramlet has grown up. And look what she's turned into. She was a brunette, dark-complexioned, with lovely white teeth and flashing eyes—and what a figure! Old Buddy. How badly Joe had felt when he heard that he had died. What a shame Buddy never lived to see his daughter grown up.

Cindy was the secretary to the manager of the Executive Inn. They talked animatedly for some minutes about her mother and the family. Then Joe asked her if she could get him a room at the inn. Cindy immediately picked up the phone, called the desk and made the reservation for him.

"Cindy, I'll be through with my business about five o'clock. If you're not doing anything give me a call. I'd love to see more of you."

Cindy nodded and gave Joe a wink. "Five o'clock, Joe. I'll call the room."

He went back to the table and enjoyed the envious looks on the faces of the two con men he was about to skin. "Okay, let's go to the telephone and I'll give Charlie a call."

This was the moment Mobley and Samuels had been waiting for. Eagerly they followed him to the pay station and listened as Joe dialed a number. It happened that he called Adrian Carter's office. "Hello, Charlie," Joe said into the phone when Adrian's newest young secretary, Sheri, answered.

"Hi there, turkey. What the hell are you doing?" came back from the other end of the line.

"Charlie, this is the Irishman. On that deal I've been talking to you about? I think I've got the twenty-five thousand worked out but I want to be sure you'll sign it." Joe glanced at Mobley and

Samuels who were virtually twitching in anticipation. They were about to pull off the biggest con of their career, they thought. A $5 million development loan, most of which they would expropriate.

For some minutes Joe put on a show over the line, Sheri listening and occasionally coming back with rude remarks calculated to break him up.

"Well I don't think so, Charlie. I can handle it for you," Joe persevered, fighting not to laugh at Sheri's retorts. "Oh yes, I know it's got to be cash. Okay. Well, it's a cashier's check. I know. Okay, I'll take care of it." He let his voice get hard. "Now I can count on you and it's a deal?" He listened a moment. "All right, I'll draw up a paper for you to sign. I want to get that commitment signed before the end of the day. All right? Okay." Joe hung up the telephone and turned to Mobley and Samuels triumphantly. "All right, boys, you've got your deal. Now look, Charlie doesn't want his wife to know about this. Sure, he's worth twenty million dollars or so but, hell, this is a risk. He doesn't want to worry his wife. He doesn't know you all and he's really got no business doing this."

"Of course we'll protect him, Joe, you can be sure of that," Samuels said suavely.

"There's just one thing I want to tell you now: I'm in for five points out of that five million." Joe knew there was never going to be any such deal but he had to emphasize where his end of the bargain lay since he had told them that the $25,000 was going to Charlie.

He pushed on. "Now let's sit down and draw up a piece of paper. I want my deal signed up before I go out to Charlie and have him sign the loan agreement." They headed back for the table, Joe giving Cindy a wink as they passed her, the two con men staring at her unabashedly.

Sitting down they drew up a five-point agreement right there at the coffee shop and Joe made them sign it. Joe's 5 percent of the $5 million was of course worth nothing since there was never going to be a deal, but the more Mobley and Samuels haggled, the more convinced they were that the loan with Wyche as cosigner was going to go through and they would walk away with most of the \$5 million. Mobley and Samuels had no intention of honoring the piece of paper they were spending so much time laboring over.

"There's one other point here, gentlemen," Joe said. "The money has to be in cash. Charlie doesn't like cashier's checks."

"Oh my God, cash," Samuels groaned. "We'd have to drive all the way out to the Fair Park Bank for this."

"I don't care where you have to drive, we'll just drive." Joe looked at his watch. "It's almost two-thirty. I'll deliver the paper from Charlie this afternoon but I've got to give him the cash. I'll handle my end of the deal, you handle yours."

Already planning on how they were going to abscond with the \$5 million before it ever got close to being put into a development, Mobley and Samuels drove out to the Fair Park Bank with Joe. They went to the manager who knew Samuels, a bank customer, and cashed the check written on the bank. Samuels handed over the \$25,000 which Joe put into his pocket and then they drove him back to the Executive Inn where he rented a car. Now he was in a hurry. He wanted to take an agreement out to Charlie Wyche, get him to sign it, an agreement which wouldn't mean anything, and deliver it to Samuels and Mobley. Most of all now, Joe was anticipating returning to the motel by five o'clock when Cindy would call him.

His first stop was Adrian Carter's office where he sat down at a typewriter and banged out an agreement. It was very short—two lines: "I, C. D. Wyche, do agree to be the endorser of the note to develop the Lawrence property of Lake Charles, Louisiana."

Adrian was curious. "Now what was that call all about that Sheri took from you, Joe?" he asked.

"Never mind what it's about. I'll do my thing, you do yours."

Adrian laughed at the mystery of Joe's operation. Then he asked, "Who are you dealing with here? I might as well know now, since I'll probably be in on it one way or another."

"A couple of guys named Charlie Mobley and Nathan Samuels," Joe said, not looking up from the paper he was rolling out of the typewriter.

"Nathan Samuels!" An angry tone came to Adrian's voice.

Joe looked up. "Yeah. You know him?"

"He's a thief. That sonofabitch took me for eighteen hundred dollars on a deal."

"I don't think he's so bad. He has given me twenty-five thousand today to work on a deal for him," Joe replied blandly.

"You're a liar," Adrian growled.

Joe gave him a beatific smile as he stood up. He patted the left breast of his suit coat, reached inside and drew out the sheaf of cash which he held out for Adrian to see.

"God almighty. I do not believe it. A deal with Charlie?"

"Yeah, he's going to do a deal." Joe refrained from giving Adrian any details.

"Samuels will be behind bars someday and I'd love to put him there myself," Adrian snarled.

"I've got to get out to Charlie now with this agreement. What say we take the late flight to Vegas? I'll bankroll you—"

"Now you're talking," Adrian agreed happily. "Meet you out at Love for the last Delta flight."

With that, Joe left Adrian's office, got into his rented car, drove out to Charlie's place and found the old man sitting in his usual chair on the front porch. Joe mounted the steps to the veranda and handed Charlie the agreement he had just typed out. "It doesn't mean anything, Charlie. All you have to do is sign it. It doesn't really commit you to anything as you can see."

Charlie looked at the paper, read it over, and then cocked an eye at Joe. "Irishman, what are you making on this deal?"

"Twenty-five thousand dollars. All you have to do is sign it."

Charlie laughed and slapped his thigh. "How dumb do they think this old codger is?"

"They don't know you, Charlie. All they know is your statement and that makes you eligible to guarantee a five-million-dollar loan." Joe handed Charlie a pen. "It's not worth toilet paper."

Charlie nodded, took the pen, and signed.

Joe took the paper, thanked Charlie, and hurried back to his car. He drove straight for the Executive Inn at the Dallas airport where Mobley and Samuels were waiting for him. They took the commitment, read it over, and were satisfied. Mobley then left to get a plane to Mobile and Samuels went back to his office to work on putting the deal together.

Joe bought a bottle of whiskey, went up to his room, and had just taken his shoes off and was pouring a drink when at ten minutes after five there was a knock on the door. He walked over and opened it. There was Cindy, looking even more beautiful than she had when he'd seen her earlier. She kicked her shoes off too and, without wasting words . . .

"You know, Joe," she sighed, "even at thirteen I think I loved you. You were a sort of symbol of what I wanted in life. I loved Buddy, of course. He provided well for Mother and me while he was alive but I wanted to know grown-ups who were respectable people in town. Those gamblers that he always had around" —she paused—"well, they were Dad's friends so I was respectful to them . . ."

Joe understood. He had, curiously, represented stability to Cindy and her mother, and Buddy clearly was a West Dallas hustler, no more, no less. To Cindy and her mother Joe was the city attorney, the lawyer, Dad's respectable friend.

"I used to try so hard to learn new piano pieces to play when you came to visit," Cindy went on.

"Are you keeping it up?" Joe asked.

"I just don't have the time. My job here at the Executive Inn keeps me very busy. Dad always *had* plenty of money but when he died there wasn't much of anything left for Mom and me so I went right to work."

Cindy raised herself on one arm. "But tell me about you, Joe. Where you've been and everything. When you stopped coming around to see us I was so sad. Nobody but you talked to me like an adult or seemed to understand me. Dad just didn't have anything but gamblers and even people who had been in jail for friends."

"We've got a lot of catching up to do, Cindy," Joe answered. "Where are you living?"

"I share an apartment with another girl. I wish I had a place of my own."

"Well, I sure hope we can see each other again. I get up to Dallas pretty often on business so give me your home number so I will know how to reach you."

Cindy clapped her hands. "Joe, you mean we can see more of each other?" She grinned impishly. "How great. I'm thrilled."

Joe could hardly believe how quickly he had become involved with this beautiful young woman who had been an entrancing child when he first met her.

"Before you get the wrong idea, I'd better tell you I'm no better than Buddy's other friends. I've served a term in the penitentiary too."

"You did? What for, Joe?" She sounded delighted with the revelation.

"I guess you didn't see the papers. It was a bad deal with a bank here in Dallas."

"I understand, Joe," she replied seriously. "Tell me about it."

It was a relief for Joe to unburden himself with a nonjudgmental companion. He told her of his love for Nancy, all about Mark, and how his gambling habit seemed to be destroying him. He poured out all his troubles, his aspirations, his frustrations. To have her listen and respond made him feel wanted again. This twenty-year-old girl was bringing him back to life.

It was 9 P.M. before they knew it and Joe realized he must break the trance he was in. He took Cindy to dinner and hurriedly took her to her apartment as other voices were calling him now.

He kissed her goodbye and then he was off for the airport on a monumental high. He'd made a $25,000 fee, he'd found a beautiful young woman who had provided the sanctuary and ego boost he so badly needed, and he was going to Las Vegas with the man he most enjoyed being with, Adrian Carter.

Just to make the twenty-four-hour period perfect, Joe won $10,000 at Las Vegas and made $2,000 for Adrian. Then they went back to McCarran Airport, Adrian heading for Dallas, Joe for Houston and home. In his pocket was a $35,000 bankroll!

CHAPTER 28

Jack Binion came down to the floor of his casino and walked up to Jonathan Alan Roberts, a smile on his face. "Good to see you here, Mr. R," he welcomed Jon, shaking his hand. "Let me buy you a drink."

What Jon really wanted was to get right to the tables, but a thought lurking at the back of his mind told him that even though he knew he was going to win, it was always good to be able to get credit. The most important thing was to be able to play again.

After the drink he bellied up to the nearest crap table and spread $5,000 in $100 bills across the table to the boxman. It was important that this show of wealth be well observed.

A tall black man stepped up to the head of the table and made ready to roll. Jon waited for the first roll which came out a six and then made a bold start, buying the numbers four, five, six, eight, nine, and ten for $500 each. He had $3,200 now at risk on the next roll. The dice came up five and Joe pressed the bet with the winnings, the croupier stacking $1,000 to ride on the five.

Jon decided he was betting on a good shooter.

Each time he rolled a number he won again, letting the chips double back as the shooter hit the numbers. Since Binion's was a no-limit casino, the winnings mounted up as the shooter continued to roll Jon's numbers without hitting a seven. Finally he shot a six. A mound of chips was pushed over to his position and he racked them up in front of him. Once again the shooter rolled, this time a ten.

"One thousand dollars across all the numbers," Jon ordered, sliding additional chips onto four, five, six, eight, nine, and ten. Again the shooter had a prolonged series of rolls without coming up with either a seven or a ten. Each roll netted Jon a new stack of chips and he was racking and pressing upward simultaneously.

Finally, once again, the shooter rolled a ten and Jon racked in his winnings. By now he had changed them from $100 chips to $500 chips and was upping his bets with abandon. In twenty minutes he had won over $80,000 and was still going strong. He could feel the streak, he was in it; there was no abandoning it now even as he reached and then passed his $80,000 goal. Why stop? he asked himself. That would be an insult to the luck that had settled on him. He came close to the $100,000 mark and knew he should cash in and go home. But the little voice inside urging him to cash in, go home, pay his debts and live a little was ignored as win after win caused his fever to mount.

He kept his bets in place, winning $3,500 to $5,000 on each roll. It was a breathtaking experience, a high that took over his whole being and made him impervious to any inner voices whatsoever.

He knew he was making the big win when Jack Binion suddenly appeared beside him and stood there watching the play. With false enthusiasm Binion congratulated him as his streak continued.

When Jon accurately estimated his rack contained $140,000 worth of chips, the fleeting voice within became urgent, begging him to take his winnings and run. But by now the crowd was roaring its approval, clapping in unison like Africans at a prayer meeting, and the excitement, the momentum, had him hopelessly caught in its embrace. There was no way he could break free; he was in the grip of voodoo. If he had $140,000, why not $200,000? Somewhere inside him he knew such a dizzying thought had to portend disaster.

Instead of cashing in his chips he called out $10,000 across the numbers. The spectators gasped. Sixty-four thousand dollars he was laying that his numbers would come up before the devil seven appeared. The chip man stacked the $10,000 piles of chips on four, five, six, eight, nine, and ten and the shooter rolled.

A spasm clutched at Jon's heart as he saw the six-ace stumble up toward him. It couldn't be but it was. He had just lost $64,000 at the blink of an eye. Still, there was $80,000 left in front of him—his goal had been achieved. Again that voice nagged at him, the voice of the man inside who paid the bills, promoted the money for Jon to gamble, and explained why debts weren't paid and loans were ignored. But he had seen $140,000 in front of him, he had tasted the heights. He would taste them again in just a few rolls. The winning streak surely had not deserted him.

Jack Binion, still standing beside him, feigned a disappointed grunt. "Don't let it get you down, you'll be right back up there again."

Jon grinned at the casino owner but nevertheless made a more restrained bet on the next shooter whose first roll came out eight.

"A thousand across on all the numbers," he said, pushing his chips forward. "That's twelve hundred on the six and eight."

The shooter rolled again and made his eight and Jon pulled his chips back, picking up the $1,400 profit. That was more like it, he thought. But if he'd had $10,000 across the numbers he would have done better.

Although he appeared to be totally oblivious of the commotion about him, the excitement, the cries of joy each time he won a big bet, he couldn't help but let the atmosphere get to him. Once again the shooter at the head of the table let the dice fly and they dropped, four-four. The number was eight, again.

"Two thousand dollars across the numbers," he bellowed. Binion watched the betting implacably. He well knew it was only a matter of time before the house odds took care of all such temporary runs on the bank. Sure enough, the shooter threw the easiest number to roll, a seven. The chips were raked away.

Jon should have read the signals when Binion, a slight smile of satisfaction on his face, walked away from the table back to his office, the crisis, as far as he was concerned, having ended.

He was, however, acutely aware of the dwindling racks of

chips in front of him. From $140,000 he'd gone down to $80,000 and now he was back to $55,000. He could still walk out ahead but that was impossible. Nevertheless, he knew he had to restrain himself. His tie and collar were loose and sweat was rolling down his cheeks as he struggled to build his chips instead of watching them dissipate. Muttered curses escaped him and he berated himself as now bet after bet was swept away by the croupier's stick.

"Shoot, man, what's the matter with you?" Jon irritably snapped at the shooter who looked at him in surprise. Jon knew he was losing his aplomb and could feel his self-control ebbing away. The $500 bet on the pass line, backed up with a $1,000 odds, won for him when the shooter's six point reappeared. He watched hawk-eyed as the croupier slid the chips to him. "You owe me another hundred dollars," he lashed out.

"No, Mr. R, it's right."

He took another look and saw that he was wrong, the chip man correct. His own irritability was bothering him and he struggled for control. The hand ended with one pass, Jon deciding that it would have continued if he hadn't held the dice up to argue over $100.

It was becoming obvious that it was over. It was as if his very blood was oozing out drop by drop. Within moments, it seemed his chip rack was almost empty. The gawkers faded away.

Shooter after shooter, including Jon, went out on the first or second roll. He felt in his coat pocket to see if his remaining $17,000 in cash was still secure and, as he fondled it, a swift-biting four-trey cleaned him out.

He heard laughter in the background and he was certain it was directed at him. With raging anger he threw two $5,000 bundles of $100 bills onto the table as the weather-beaten old man next to him prepared to receive the dice. "Coming out new, now," the croupier intoned in his singsong chant. "Bet with him, he bet with you."

Jon watched the shooter toss a nine. "Let me have a thousand dollars on all six numbers," he shrieked, not wanting to delay his action long enough to receive the chips for his cash which was meticulously being counted. With the cash safely in his hand, the boxman ordered "put him up" and the chip man obediently placed a total of $6,400 in chips across the board while the boxman placed markers for $6,400 in the middle of the table.

Impudently, on the very next roll, the dice abruptly settled on six-ace right below Jon. Even before the chips for his $10,000 buy-in were disbursed to him, the house deducted $6,400 to cover his lost call bet, setting over only $3,600 to him in return.

Suddenly he was assailed by the realization of how dumb it had been when he was down to so small a bankroll to buy the numbers that way. He had to work his bankroll back up again judiciously before he could sustain such high-stakes betting.

He reached in his pocket and pulled out the last $7,000, tossing the packet of cash on the table. Now, adjusting down to what he considered normal betting, he began the long, cautious task of rebuilding his money supply. Patiently, over three more hours, he kept placing his bets, winning and losing. But eventually the mathematics of the long grind must prevail, and they did. The house edge always wins eventually.

Jon watched appalled as his bankroll steadily decreased and he was down to a few hundred dollars in $25 chips. Gamely he kept putting his chips on the board, trying to turn the corner and come up again. He refused to give up, he refused to give in, he would not retreat from the crap game until literally his last chip had been gobbled up by the table and he had staggered away broke.

Immediately he headed to the house phone beside the bank of cashier cages.

"Jack Binion, please. Jonathan Alan Roberts calling him."

Jon was well aware that Binion would already know that he had gone broke. That eye in the sky above the table would have him tagged, of course.

"Hi, Jon," Binion's voice came over the phone. "What can I do for you?"

"Can I see you for a minute, Jack?"

"Of course. Be right down."

In moments Binion appeared on the casino floor knowing full well what Jon wanted to talk to him about.

"Jack, I need ten thousand credit," Jon began.

Binion put him off with a sympathetic shake of the head. "Sorry, Jon, we can't do that."

"What? I left a lot of money with you here. You know I'm good for ten grand. I'll write you out a check for it."

Friendly though firm, Binion shook his head again. "I'd like to help you, Jon, but I can't."

"Okay, Jack, at least let me have some walking around money until I can get back home. Can you cash a check for fifteen hundred for me?"

Binion's objections finally collapsed. "Okay, Jon, I'll personally give you fifteen hundred so you can have some dinner, check into a hotel, and get home. But no more playing."

Jon followed him to one of the cashier cages and heard him say, "Give Mr. Roberts fifteen hundred and let him sign for it."

"Thank you, Jack, I really appreciate that. I'll be bringing those New York guys over here to play."

Jon put the $1,500 in his pocket beside the $6 which was all he had left. His desolation over losing the $140,000 faded in the glow of having $1,500—$1,506, he corrected himself—in his pocket. Hell, that was enough to move up to the sky!

At 3 A.M., buoyed by optimism, he walked at a lively pace from Binion's to the California Club down the street. He was certain to push his go money from Jack Binion back up to another big bankroll. Besides that, and more importantly, he was back in action.

The California Club limit was low and Jon changed the $1,500 into $25 chips. Starting anew, confident of victory, he began buying the numbers across for $25 and $30 each.

Eighteen minutes later he had lost Binion's $1,500 and was down to six $1 bills in his shirt pocket.

Jon staggered into the men's room of the California Club. Suddenly he contracted all his muscles as if he had received a severe blow to the solar plexus. He felt a tightness in his throat and tears on his cheeks. He sobbed, agonizing over how painful it was to lose so much money, money which he needed so badly. He had thought he was going to win. He should have won. It just didn't seem fair. He had horrendous debts and they needed to be paid. He felt he only wanted to win in order to repay those who had loaned him money, trusted him, liked him. He was startled when he looked into the lavatory mirror. He saw a face harrowed by sickness and remorse, and was shocked. He began a train of gloomy reflections that was interrupted by a spasm of diarrhea. He felt he would vomit but the antacid he gulped gave him some relief. The knowledge that he hadn't won, that he couldn't repay what he owed tormented him. Maybe if someone could understand the kind of thing he was going through, he would not have to go through it in a casino toilet. God, he was lonely. Suddenly, surprisingly, he felt better. He washed his face and took some more antacids. He straightened up, took a deep breath and thought, how I hate weak people. I can take care of myself if I can only get another bankroll. Yes, he felt better. He went to the coffee shop and over black coffee began to plan for another stake. He knew who he could touch. The thought made him relax and the image he had seen in the mirror was forgotten. There remained, nevertheless, a gnawing ache in his stomach. Jon was showing signs of stress. At moments he wanted to succumb and admit defeat—but this meant death. He refused to succumb. He would return—and win!

CHAPTER 29

When Joe first visited Houston as a youth the population was around three hundred thousand, but going into the year 1967 the metropolitan area had grown to almost two million and was burgeoning every day. As a result, all types of speculation and promotion were rampant and usually profitable. Fortunes were being made overnight and Joe was certainly nibbling away his share of the money the promoters were making, though he never kept any.

He was constantly on the move. If he was not with Turk or trying to find a new bookie or flying to Las Vegas, dealing with Earl Atwood and his red flag scheme or seeing people about the takeout commitments or working on Charlie Wyche deals, he would go to E. F. Hutton, Bache & Co., or one of the other brokerage firms and watch the commodity board. Although this was humdrum compared to crap shooting, it was about the fastest-moving legitimate and respectable type of gambling available in Houston.

In a matter of days Joe could lose $10,000, $20,000, or more on pork bellies or wheat or corn futures. Commodities and basketball were his two most destructive forms of gambling—those and of course the irresistible crap games at Wilks's. Buying pork bellies was volatile. The prices moved. Buying blue chips stocks was a very slow type of action. It might go up or down an eighth but fortunes could be made and lost in pork bellies. The fluctuations in the price of pork belly futures was dependent on everything from the weather and how many pigs would hit

Chicago in a day to what the crooks were doing and who might be trying to manipulate the Chicago Board of Trade.

Joe eventually lost $5,200 on the price of May wheat because instead of the bad weather they were expecting, nothing but sunshine hit the wheat belt. As Joe learned, the commodity market was not his game.

The professionals who really know the market and the big commission houses end up swallowing the little players all over the country just as Las Vegas swallows all the little compulsive gamblers who fly into town.

One of Joe's lifelong friends, C. W. Conn of Beaumont, had a pair of twin brothers eight years younger than he. One of the twins, George, had gone to Texas University law school and Joe had helped to get him pledged to Phi Gam as he had C.W. eight years earlier.

George liked to gamble too, and had lived in Virginia for a few years before coming back to Houston.

Like most developers and promoters George Conn was involved in real estate. Joe had found a piece of property for him up in Conroe, north of Houston, and George had bought it inexpensively. When he sold it to a consortium of doctors at the Texas Medical Center, he had made a substantial profit. Therefore, it was not unusual for Joe to be around George's office.

One day as he was sitting across George's desk, and the young promoter was busy on the telephone, Joe noticed a checkbook in front of him. In gold letters it said: Farmers and Merchants Bank of Virginia. Joe realized this must be a book of old checks. By now George would certainly have discontinued his Virginia account.

Surreptitiously, as George was busily talking on the phone, Joe opened the checkbook, tore two pages of checks out of it and slipped them into his pocket for future use.

George, who had been standing facing the wall, finished his phone call, turned around and resumed his conversation with Joe. "So you're playing the bellies now, Joe. Have you met Tim Fowler down at Hutton? He's there most every day."

The name was familiar to Joe. Tim was from Beaumont and a contemporary of George's. "Where Tim really made it was in

Westec," George went on. Although Joe did not play the stock market he was aware of the new glamor stock on the market since Westec was a Houston firm, though now it was run out of New York by New York operators. Even if Joe had been in the market he would not have bet on Westec since he had a fundamental mistrust of the Eastern manipulators.

"Remember how the stock went from three dollars to seventy in the last two years? Tim bought in at twenty-five and has been buying it up on margin ever since. Really done nicely."

"I don't like that margin," Joe commented. "If the stock goes down all of a sudden they're climbing all over you to come up with money to cover. I just like to bet cash and, win or lose, it's all over—next play."

On George Conn's suggestion Joe introduced himself to Tim Fowler at the commodities room of E. F. Hutton where he went when he had nothing else to do.

One day in February 1967, with no baseball to bet, Joe walked into Hutton to sweat the ticker for a few hours. He was carrying his briefcase and happened to see Tim Fowler. As they talked Joe said, "If I had fourteen thousand five hundred I could put a loan deal together and make myself an eighty-thousand-dollar fee."

"Sure enough?" Tim asked.

"Oh it's nothing like the bellies. You wouldn't be interested."

"I might be, you never know. Tell me about it," Tim invited. "Fourteen thousand five hundred? I can get that."

"Well, come on, we'll have a cup of coffee." When the market closed Joe and Tim went over to a nearby coffee shop and Joe explained that he had a package deal that he was working on with the mayor of Houston and two or three of his political friends. "If I can arrange this loan for them, and I'm sure I can, I can make an eighty-thousand brokerage fee. But I can't come up with the fourteen thousand five hundred I need out front. The bellies have wiped me out."

"I might be able to come up with it, Joe," Tim volunteered.

"Well, if you want to, I'll sign a deal with you to the effect that if you'll loan me fourteen and a half grand I'll try to make the loan and if I can't I'll pay you your money back. If I make the loan I'll split the commission with you."

Joe was only four months away from serving out his parole, which would end in June of 1967, when he took Fowler's $14,500 cashier's check out to Las Vegas and cashed it with Artie Newman. This time Newman vetted it, found it was good, and gave Joe the cash. Joe won $15,000 that afternoon and caught a plane back to Houston that night, getting in at 8 P.M. for a party he had promised to go to with Nancy.

The next morning he went to a bank and purchased another cashier's check payable to himself for $14,500. Then he went around to the commodities board at Hutton and found Tim Fowler. Joe was elated. He had made $15,000 in a few hours with Tim's money. He was not quite ready to give him back the money but he flashed the check at him.

"I cashed your check, Tim, but I haven't been able to put that loan deal together so I went and bought another cashier's check." Tim looked at the cashier's check and nodded. "It's going to take me a little more time than I thought to make this deal, but there's your money back if you want it. It's going to take me at least another thirty days to get the loan down. Do you want the money back now or not?"

Joe was a good judge of character, and he wanted to buy time, to keep that extra $14,500 a little longer to finance more action.

His assessment of Tim Fowler was correct.

"Oh hell no, keep the money," Tim urged. "I don't need it, don't worry about it. Just get that deal made."

In two weeks' time, between another trip to Las Vegas and to his bookies plus disastrous visits to Bobby Wilks's crap game, Joe was broke again.

Through most of February, Fowler did not press Joe for a repayment of his loan and when he inquired about it Joe merely said that the deal was coming along fine.

Early in March, Westec, the corporation in which Fowler had most of his money invested and in which he'd made enormous profits on paper, collapsed. It was a major scandal and trading was suspended on the stock exchange. Investors like Tim Fowler lost heavily. It was a chain of circumstances completely out of Joe's control.

Fowler was wiped out, and he owed $100,000 to a bank in

Alvin where he had borrowed the money to buy the Westec stock which in turn he had used to collateralize the loan. Now the call came. The financial reversal panicked him and caused him to go crazy over the $14,500 Joe owed him. He put heavy pressure on Joe to pay him back. Joe made the same error he had with Charlie Wyche. He confessed everything: that he'd taken the money to Las Vegas, that he'd doubled it and then blown it all. There might have been a time when Fowler would have been reasonably understanding, but this was not it. He was furious.

Joe even got calls that his little boy had better be careful when he walked across the street to school. And that did frighten Joe. Had Tim gone insane to threaten a small child? The truth was he was terror-stricken; his very life-style and family relationships were threatened by the Westec collapse. Joe began pumping to the best of his ability to start paying him back. Finally he had him paid down to $8,000, but even that was not sufficient to cool Fowler's anger.

Fowler succeeded in getting Joe indicted by the grand jury for theft and unfortunately Joe, in his confession, had told Fowler that he was on probation and the young investor facing bankruptcy went to Hugh Mack Johnson, Joe's probation officer, with his lawyer. So irrational had he become he tried to get Johnson to put Joe back in jail by declaring that his parole had been violated. Hugh Mack called Joe into his office and, after learning the facts, made his decision that there was no violation of parole and that this was a civil matter. Nevertheless, Fowler's lawyer had been able to get the indictment against Joe by the Harris County grand jury.

The indictment was handed down seventy days before Joe's parole was to have expired, on May 26, exactly three years after Sarah Hughes had sentenced him. Even though Hugh Mack Johnson felt that no criminal charges could legally stand up in court, he felt it necessary to inform the parole board in Washington, D.C., that the indictment had been handed down.

The Washington board issued a warrant for Joe's arrest but stamped on the back of it the order DO NOT EXECUTE. At the same time they stopped crediting time against Joe's parole so that he still owed seventy days on his sentence which was no longer being extinguished. The parole board's position was, "Let's hold Joe H. Hodges in suspended animation. If he goes to trial and is convicted, we have issued our warrant prior to the expiration of his parole and then we will execute the warrant if he's convicted of defrauding Fowler. If he is exonerated, we will release him and his parole will have been served."

Thus Joe was, in effect, in a state of almost permanent parole until there was some resolution to the matter. It was another sword of Damocles hanging over his head. A parole violation makes no provision for an arrested man to get out on bond.

Joe would have continued paying Fowler the entire $14,500 but the calls threatening Mark made him so angry he didn't want to give him another cent.

The indictment was neither quashed nor acted upon and the case never came to court as there was no criminal charge that could be legally substantiated against Joe since Fowler accepted a promissory note when Joe obtained the money from him. Still, he was in the uncomfortable position of being on parole and not working it off. The slightest violation would have had him back in jail serving the entire two years remaining on his Dallas sentence.

CHAPTER 30

As the baseball season of 1967 opened, Joe felt an overwhelming urge to get some action down. It was becoming increasingly difficult for him to promote money at the banks since they all knew him all too well. He had even used up Earl Atwood's friend Pat Hamilton from whom Earl had borrowed the $6,000 to give Joe so he could go up to Dallas and get the takeout commitment. Joe was just plain running out of spots. He had to keep going farther and farther from Houston. His days had a quality of sameness about them, too, except when he could promote a big-enough bankroll for Las Vegas.

On April 28, 1967, Joe was, as always, standing out in front of his apartment at six-thirty in the morning waiting for the newspaper delivery boy to arrive. He was one of the few customers the delivery boy saw every morning. Today he took his paper, walked back into his apartment and sat down in his office, the bathroom. He immediately turned to his financial page, the sports section, and skinned it back, sweating the baseball scores on the games he had bet the afternoon before.

"Oh my!" he exclaimed as he came to the first game and found he'd lost it. The same was true of the second game. Now his round-robin was lost for sure but some of the individual bets might hold up. No, again he had called it wrong. He had won only one out of six games. Not enough to give him a bankroll for the day. Even so he perused the sports stories, checking on who would be pitching that day, and after an hour of preparation he had his four games picked out. Now he needed the bankroll. Turk would be ready to meet him at the drugstore by 4 P.M. and Joe wanted to give him at least $3,000. He was totally confident that he would dope out the winners of today's games. He knew he'd win. But he had to have the money.

Joe started thinking about where he was going to pump the money. Where would he go? He was prepared for a visit to a friendly bank; he still had the blank checks he had purloined from George Conn.

Now, with his bets for the day determined but needing money in time to lay his bets down with Turk at four, a plan of action unfolded in Joe's mind. He had never tapped the bank up at Conroe in Montgomery County.

He took one of the George Conn checks on the Virginia bank and slipped it into his typewriter, making it out to W. F. Rogers and Joe H. Hodges, attorney, for $4,500. Then on the back, in spidery handwriting, he signed W. F. Rogers. Attorneys frequently collected checks made out jointly to them and their client. Illegibly Joe scribbled George Conn's name as the maker of the check and he was ready to go. He was really very uptight. He had no money, no bankroll, just that tremendous debt structure. The only thing that could make him feel relaxed and optimistic was to get his bets down on the baseball games. He just needed to get hold of the $4,500 he had calculated would bring him $25,000 when he hit the parlay on the winning ball clubs today.

With his course plotted he calmly set out to do his thing. He made the hour's drive up to Conroe and parked outside the First National Bank of Conroe. He knew nobody at the bank—he'd never been in it before.

In his freshly pressed vested suit, Joe walked into the bank and up to a desk in the officers' area. He looked at the nameplate on the desk of Mr. J. P. Stimmens, Vice-President.

"Oh hi, Mr. Stimmens. You remember me, don't you? Joe Hodges."

Of course Joe and Stimmens had never met before but the bank vice-president said politely, "Oh yes, Mr. Hodges. Nice to see you again. What can I do for you?"

"Well, I've got one of those darn client checks again like the one you cashed for me before. I need to get this money up here to Mr. Rogers who my law firm is representing. We've got another real estate deal going."

Joe paused, smiled, and went on. "Well, Mr. Rogers and I know that old sonofagun, he wants his money. Now if I can get a cashier's check from you I think he'll take that." He forced a tolerant laugh. "Even Rogers should know that a cashier's check is good as cash."

With that Joe handed the check on the Farmers and Merchants Bank in Norfolk, Virginia, to the Conroe banker. The banker looked down at it and hesitated. Joe immediately proffered his card, proclaiming him to be Joe H. Hodges, Attorney at Law. "I am a Houston lawyer but we do get business out this way too." Joe opened his wallet and showed some of his other identification cards. "As you can see, Mr. Rogers has already endorsed this check. I'll endorse it now so you can see it's my signature." Hastily Joe whipped out his pen and signed the check with the authority which bespeaks a check's authenticity. "I put down my address and phone number," he pointed out.

The banker looked at the check and then up at the well-dressed, open-faced lawyer. He smiled. "I guess this is all right, Mr. Hodges. Glad to be of help." With that he wrote his initials on the top of the check.

Joe thanked the banker and turned from his desk, heading for the teller's cage. In his eagerness to get the money and meet Turk at the appointed hour, he made a mistake. He had told the bank vice-president that he wanted a cashier's check. But when he got to the teller he asked for the check to be cashed. The teller, looking at the vice-president's initials, counted out $4,500 which Joe put in his coat pocket.

Although Joe was unaware of it, Mr. Stimmens had watched him walk to the teller and ask for cash instead of a cashier's check. Had Joe told the bank officer in the first place that he was going to cash it instead of saying he wanted a cashier's check, the chances are he would not have raised the banker's suspicions.

At 11 A.M., with the precious $4,500 which he was convinced would get him $25,000 the next day, Joe stopped for an order of bacon and eggs and then telephoned Turk at his office at Atlas Fence to confirm their 4 P.M. rendezvous.

"Turk, meet me at the drugstore. I'll be there by four o'clock. Can you have the line?"

Turk agreed to meet Joe with the betting line which would give him the odds on all the games that day. The New York Mets, for instance, were in their usual losing streak and a bet of $1 on a Mets game would bring back $1.80. On the other hand the Yankees were winning and $1 bet would return only 50¢ for a win. But it was the parlays which would net the big payoffs that really interested him. He drove back to Houston and spent two more hours studying the proper placement of the precious bankroll before meeting Turk at the drugstore where they exchanged money and bets.

Joe decided to bet only $3,000 of the $4,500 the first night. He gave Turk the cash to take back to the bookmakers and then, exhausted, headed back to his apartment on Larch Lane where he found Nancy's car in the driveway. He was ready for his night of sweating out the baseball games. It would be an all-night sweat, with some of the late results not coming in until the morning paper.

Joe didn't notice it but down the block a car marked Sheriff of Montgomery County was parked.

When its occupants emerged, Joe was stunned. "Oh my God!" he exclaimed aloud. "That's the banker who okayed the check I smashed this morning."

The bank vice-president and the sheriff, who was following him with another officer, made directly for Joe. The sheriff jerked the left-hand door of Joe's car open and pulled him out.

"We want forty-five hundred dollars right now or you go to jail." That was all there was to it. What distressed Joe most was that Nancy and Mark were in the house, and he did not want them to see any of this scene.

There was not much point in arguing. Joe merely said, "What? What did you say?"

In a stern voice the vice-president, Stimmens, said, "I called Mr. Conn's bank, the Farmers and Merchants in Norfolk, Virginia. He no longer has an account there." Stimmens had located George Conn in Houston and of course George vehemently denied giving Joe the check. Joe had made no effort to conceal his identity. His address, 4714 Larch Lane, Bellaire, was legibly written on the back of the check complete with his phone number. He had planned to do his usual thing the next day: go see Stimmens, tell him that he had just learned the check he had given him the day before was no good and pay Stimmens the $4,500 in cash. But because he'd made a mistake, raising the banker's suspicions by taking cash instead of a cashier's check, he had lost that grace period. Now he was faced with immediate arrest and of course, being on parole, his next stop would be prison again, to finish out his term.

Joe knew exactly where he could reach Turk. He also knew that Turk would still have the $3,000 with him, having phoned in the bets. And right in his pocket he had the $1,500. Turk would have given him the $3,000 back and called off the bets. But Joe didn't want the bets called off; he was positive that if they were they would all win, all those parlays which would have brought him in the $25,000 he so desperately needed. He felt his bowels loosening.

"I can go call the man I've been dealing with and get your money," Joe said. "I don't know if he'll be there but I'll try to reach him. I've got fifteen hundred right here in my pocket. But I had this deal I was working on and my partner's got the three thousand. I can have it all for you tomorrow."

Both the bank vice-president and the sheriff were enraged. "We want the money right now or you're going to jail in Conroe, right now!"

"We just want that money, Mr. Hodges," Stimmens said more calmly. "Forty-five hundred if you don't want to go to jail tonight."

"Give me a chance to get the money. Let me drive around the corner and make a call."

"All right, Hodges, we'll follow you," the sheriff agreed. One of his deputies got into Joe's car behind him and the bank officer and the sheriff followed in the police car.

Joe didn't know what to do as he drove away from the front of his house, but at least he had removed the trouble from Nancy's doorstep. At all costs Nancy must be shielded from his depredations.

He drove around the block to Bang's Drive-In, a small

grocery store and beer joint. There were two pay phones there and Joe of course could have called Atlas Fence right then, found Turk, had him come by with the money. But instead he made two fake calls and then turned to the sheriff. "I can't get my man. But I'll have it tomorrow. Take this fifteen hundred and I'll bring you the three thousand first thing in the morning."

Joe knew he would have the money; he knew his bets would win, and that he would collect and drive right out to Conroe and pay the banker.

The sheriff was in no mood for equivocating. "We're taking you out to the Montgomery County jail right now, Hodges," he said menacingly. Still Joe could not bring himself to call Turk and cancel the bets. Suddenly an idea came to him. The First State Bank of Bellaire was close by. Pat Hamilton, the vice-president of the bank from whom Earl Atwood had borrowed his money, might still be in his office even though it was now 5:45 P.M. The bank, of course, would be closed but maybe Joe could get hold of Hamilton anyway.

Joe called the bank knowing Hamilton had the reputation of being the last banker in town to leave his office. Hamilton was well aware of Joe's previous troubles and bad check charges, but just this one time he might be willing to help. It was a long shot. Actually, Joe had borrowed money from him before and paid it back, but recently Hamilton had refused to lend him any more and had closed his account. To Joe's great relief Hamilton answered the phone.

"Pat, this is Joe Hodges," he began. "I got myself into a bad deal here. The sheriff of Montgomery County came down and arrested me. It seems like I had a check returned up there and I owe them three thousand dollars. I want you to lend it to me. Otherwise they're going to put me in jail."

Joe knew that Pat Hamilton was one of the smartest bankers in Houston. He'd been smart enough to close Joe's account rather than take a chance on having more problems with him.

Pat's voice came strong over the phone. "Well I'll be hanged." It was not like him to talk that way. Then he was silent for a minute. "You know what time it is?"

"Yessir," Joe replied.

"Where did you say you are?"

"I'm right up here at Bang's on Bissonett and they're going to take me to jail if I don't give them three thousand."

"You're in the sheriff's car?"

"Yessir, or I will be when I hang up."

There was another silence on the phone. Then a reluctant Pat Hamilton said, "All right, come on down. I'll open up the front of the bank."

Joe instructed the sheriff to take him down to the bank. They got there at five fifty-five. Stimmens, the sheriff, and the deputy were with Joe when they drove up in front of the bank. Joe was thankful he had left his car at Bang's, not in front of the apartment. No matter how bad the trouble he got into, he tried to keep it away from Nancy and Mark, who was beginning more and more to understand what was going on around his dad these days.

The sheriff allowed Joe to get out of the car and walk up to the front door of the bank. Pat Hamilton met him. "I can't even get in my vault, Joe," the banker said. "I'm going to have to get the money out of a drive-in teller's box. Now when can you pay it back?"

"Two weeks, Pat."

"I can't even give you a note at this time of night. I'll just have to handle it myself. You bring the money back in two weeks."

"Yessir, you can count on it." Hamilton went back into the bank and was gone for four or five nerve-wracking minutes as Joe waited in the sheriff's custody. Finally he came out and handed Joe an envelope containing $3,000 in cash. "Two weeks, Joe."

It was straight up six o'clock when Hamilton handed Joe the money. Another minute and even the drive-in teller's cash would have been put in a time vault and there would have been no money accessible. Relief coursed through Joe's body. Then Hamilton gave him a hard look. "Don't call upon me any more, Joe Henry Hodges, to pull your chestnuts out of the fire." So saying he turned on his heel and walked back into the bank, locking the door behind him.

Joe took the $1,500 out of his pocket, put it with the $3,000

Hamilton had given him and handed the sheaf of bills to Stimmens. The sheriff left Joe standing in front of the bank and headed out to Conroe, mission accomplished.

With a light step, Joe walked the fifteen blocks back to Bang's, got into his car and started to drive back to the apartment. The thought crossed his mind that there had to be something wrong with his process of reasoning. Even with the sheriff having him by the nape of the neck and prison gates looming, he would not call Turk to bring back his money and call off the bets.

It was shortly after six when Joe walked into his apartment and cheerfully asked Nancy, "What are we having for dinner tonight, dear?" He hugged Mark and then settled down to sweat out the bets.

The next morning at six-thirty he was waiting for the newspaper delivery boy in front of his apartment. In the bathroom he skinned the sports page back, sweating out his bets one by one. Every one of them lost, the whole $3,000 worth. Crushed, Joe went outside to get some early morning air. Now how was he going to raise the bankroll today to get his bets down, pay back Pat Hamilton, pay back the other debts? Well, he always managed. Some way he'd get the money to Turk today—it was one of those many days when he knew he couldn't lose.

One week later Joe somehow pumped the $3,000 to pay Pat Hamilton. The banker took the money wordlessly and Joe, even though he needed a bankroll, for once didn't have the nerve to ask him for another loan.

CHAPTER 31

Joe had the uneasy feeling that he was on a train moving inexorably toward a destination marked Disaster. All he could do was ride it out and hope for the best.

In 1967 Adrian Carter planned a June vacation and he asked Joe if he'd come up to Irving and sit in his office while he was away. Adrian's faith in Joe's ability to handle unexpected trouble was unbounded. Even though Joe was an ex-con and a disbarred lawyer, Adrian told him that he'd rather have Joe H. Hodges watching out for things while he was away than any of the young lawyers working in his office. To capture Joe's interest Adrian mentioned that he had a promising financial deal working that Joe could handle to their mutual profit. The prospect of filling in for his friend Adrian, perhaps making a fast takeout commitment deal, and talking with Cindy Bramlet made it easy for Joe to make up his mind.

He arrived in Adrian's office the day before the lawyer was due to leave for his vacation on Padre Island, a posh Gulf resort, and met with T. R. Burgess, a whip-lean sharp-faced, sixty-year-old businessman originally trained in the law. Burgess had taken over a house trailer manufacturing company in Arlington just outside Dallas and was badly in need of financing.

"Joe is not only one of my best friends but one of the great financial experts in Texas," Adrian assured Burgess before he left. Within a few days Joe reported to Burgess that he thought it would be possible for him to get the $250,000 loan he needed to refinance his business but it would cost $15,000 in expense money up front. Burgess handed over the $15,000 which Joe immediately put into an inviolate bank account since this involved Adrian as well as himself.

It didn't take Joe long to realize that the deal was tough. He tried to obtain a takeout commitment and when that failed all he had was Charlie Wyche.

He telephoned Adrian at Padre Island to say he was afraid he couldn't make the Burgess deal and that he ought to refund the old gentleman's money.

"Oh, don't do that so quickly," Adrian cried out. "You'll figure it out. We could use the money." Joe hung up, worried. If a loan deal of this sort doesn't go down quickly it never will. He had tried his best with every source and failed.

Cindy Bramlet was becoming an increasing source of sanctuary to Joe. Although he loved Nancy and no other woman could ever supplant her in his affection and respect, he could talk to Cindy more freely about his problems. Cindy was nonjudgmental; she deeply cared for Joe and although only twenty years old was remarkably mature. Having grown up with Buddy's friends she had a better understanding of the dark side of Joe's nature than almost any woman he could have found. She listened solemnly to his stories, dispensing comfort and forgiveness. It was because of Cindy's sincere interest in everything that touched on his life that Joe found overseeing Adrian Carter's office a happy and satisfying experience.

When Adrian came back from vacation he suggested that he and Joe divide the $15,000 equally between them. The money had been put in Joe's account, not that of Adrian's client, so when Joe gave Adrian $7,500 there was no tracing the money to the lawyer.

Joe went back to Houston, only able to prove that he had spent $1,500 of Burgess' money for airplane trips to Chicago and on incidental expenses incurred while talking to other money brokers. He had wanted to earn the money legitimately.

T. R. Burgess was not one to take a loss lying down. After several futile phone calls to Joe in Houston, he hired a private detective to check up on Joe H. Hodges. It wasn't long before Burgess discovered the truth. The detective followed Joe to the E. F. Hutton commodities room, found out he was on parole, and even followed him out of Bobby Wilks's crap game, where Joe had lost as usual, and then tailed him to Las Vegas. There was little about Joe that Burgess didn't know when he finally gave him an ultimatum. He wanted his $15,000 back in one week or he would go to Joe's parole officer and see to it that he was put back into prison.

Joe called Adrian desperately for help. However, none was forthcoming. Adrian merely said, "You'll figure something out."

"I'm broke," Joe pleaded. "I can pump the money to pay off my seven thousand five hundred. Can't you do the same?" Adrian's reply was that Joe was a very resourceful guy and would think of some way to get out of the problem.

By a monumental pumping effort Joe finally got hold of $10,000, borrowing it from every source he could still find open. On a Friday he called Burgess and said that he would pay him the $10,000 now and the other $5,000 when he could. This did not appease Burgess. He set a deadline for the following Monday.

There was only one thing for Joe to do. He told Burgess to meet him at Love Field, the Dallas airport, on Monday at noon. He'd have the money then. This time Joe was really frightened. Burgess had spent a lot of money gathering a damaging file which Joe knew, if presented to his parole officer, would have to be sent on to Washington and would surely mean his return to prison. Even Tim Fowler's threat against Joe's young son Mark hadn't scared him as badly as this. The man had him dead to rights and Adrian was not going to help.

On Sunday Joe flew to Las Vegas with $10,000. He only wanted to win $5,000, and to win $5,000 with $10,000 was not such a tough undertaking if you watched yourself. By early Monday morning he had $15,050, and he flew to Los Angeles to get a flight for Dallas in order to make his twelve noon deadline.

He walked into the airport lobby and found Burgess and a lawyer waiting for him. Before delivering the $15,000 Joe insisted upon, and received, a notarized release of all complaints against him; then, handing over the $15,000, he flew back to Houston without even calling Adrian. Once again Adrian had hurt him badly. But then, he philosophized, that's the way Adrian was.

Later on that summer Earl Atwood was indicted for selling land out at Lake Houston without paying off the owner of the land and getting the lots released. Earl did not deliver clear title to the buyers, allegedly pocketing the money due the owner.

Joe asked Adrian to come down to Houston and try to get Earl out from under an impending jail sentence. Working in the background himself, he turned up technical evidence that worked in the entrepreneur's favor, and Earl Atwood was indeed found not guilty.

Adrian was impressed with Earl's capabilities as a promoter and suggested that he come up to Dallas. He would back him in the land promotion business, red-flagging a subdivision in a new development near Dallas.

After the acquittal, Adrian, Joe, and Earl were in a happy state of mind and decided to go to Las Vegas together. Joe pumped up a bankroll for himself and they checked into the Flamingo Hotel. On the way out Adrian had asked Joe for some gambling money, saying he'd pay him back. Joe had peeled $1,000 off his bankroll and handed over the money. Joe liked the casino at the Dunes Hotel, and in one night of gambling he ran his bankroll of under $10,000 up to $50,000.

While Joe was performing this feat, Adrian was showing himself more interested in the girls he met hanging around the hotel and the bar. Earl, on the other hand, was watching Joe gamble, fascinated by his skill and daring at the crap tables.

At ten o'clock the next morning Adrian gave Joe the sad story of how he'd lost his bankroll and gone broke. Now he wanted $5,000. Joe didn't want to give it to him. He had $50,000, which he needed desperately, and was ready to go home.

Joe tried to tell Adrian about the list of people he owed money to in Houston, but Adrian wouldn't listen. He reminded Adrian of the trouble he'd had getting out of the Burgess deal with no help from him. Finally he gave up. "I don't mind giving you the money but when you get back to Dallas, you've got to wire it to me."

"Oh I swear. I know you need it, Joe. I'll send it to you," Adrian promised.

So Joe gave his old friend $5,000 in cash which left him $45,000. He was going home with a respectable bankroll nonetheless. However, as he walked through the Dunes casino anger rose in him. "Damn, I've got to be crazy," he grumbled to Earl Atwood. "I've got to be the chump of chumps. Why do I keep letting Adrian take me off." He paused at one of the crap tables and then turned abruptly to Earl. "I've got to get that five thousand back."

As Earl watched, Joe threw $500 on the crap table, betting that the shooter wouldn't pass. The shooter won and Joe lost. He continued to bet against the shooters and in a short time lost $3,000. He only wanted to win that $5,000 he had given to Adrian and then he would walk.

For the next four hours he went from one crap table to the next trying to work his bankroll back to the $50,000 he'd had when Adrian took $5,000 from him. In those four hours he lost the entire $45,000. It was a stricken Joe who finally walked out of the Dunes casino broke, muttering to himself that if Adrian Carter hadn't stolen that $5,000 from him he wouldn't have lost the rest.

Adrian had screwed him on the Burgess deal, Joe railed, and now he'd done it again. That afternoon Joe flew home to Houston alone, leaving the others in Las Vegas. A few days later he called Adrian, but he was to never get the $5,000.

Joe was never able to understand the virtual fealty he paid Adrian. For some reason he idolized him, was infatuated by him, enthralled with what to him was a tremendously charming personality. And Adrian told everybody that Joe was his best friend. Joe really thought he meant it. But Adrian was incapable of doing right about money with anyone, particularly Joe. Perhaps it was an inferiority complex in Joe that played to Adrian's arrogance. Maybe Adrian thought he'd given Mark Hodges back to Joe and that therefore no amount of damage he could do him henceforward would ever make up for that priceless boon.

Whatever the reason, Adrian was the only human being on earth who could exploit Joe time after time, year after year, with Joe's knowledge.

CHAPTER 32

Little was known in 1967 about compulsive gambling. Joe himself did not really know what afflicted him. He just knew he had to have action; and without the constant possibility of the big win, he sank into states of black depression. Of course he knew that all the deals he had been involved in since his release from Seagoville were vaguely questionable, and he realized that somehow he had to clean up his life, pull his chestnuts out of the fire, as Pat Hamilton had warned him he should. He had to develop a sane routine of living and try to get off that express train to perdition. Only he could take his life firmly in hand and steer it into a productive course. It was something he must do, and do immediately.

Nancy had the patience of a saint, he realized. Yet did he appreciate it? In fact he did. The trouble was he couldn't live up to it.

Joe became impatient easily, and he still hadn't been able to find a lucrative proposition that would provide him the cash he needed so badly. For several months he had been trying not to gamble in an effort to arrest the habit but was experiencing withdrawal symptoms not unlike those of a drug addict or an alcoholic who stops cold turkey.

One day, Marty Shoemate, an old Houston gambler who dabbled in real estate as a front, approached Joe with a potential land development deal near Sugarland. Joe was well acquainted with Sugarland but had never thought there might be a moneymaking opportunity out there aside from the crap table.

"I made a nice commission on the land deal you steered to me, Joe," Shoemate said. "Maybe I can put you into something. This young fellow Fred Cannon, his father just died and left Fred and his sister seven hundred twenty acres of prime rice-growing land. But the way property is developing around Sugarland, Fred tells me he can't see his share of the land being used to grow rice. I'd handle the deal myself but I'm pretty busy down here in Texas City. Would you like me to call Cannon?"

Since Joe had nothing else going, he agreed, and Marty put through the call, introducing Joe to Fred Cannon over the phone.

Joe conducted a casually searching telephone interview and learned that beside the acreage, Fred had also been left a cash inheritance and was considering putting some of the money into developing his land. Before the conversation was finished, Joe felt the gambler in him taking over.

He made an appointment to come out and see Fred the next day, thanked Marty Shoemate for the introduction, and drove back to Houston.

Out at Fred Cannon's property in Sugarland he quickly sized up the situation.

Fred mentioned that he had $200,000 cash, left by his dad, and again brought up the possibility of developing the land. He at least had the foresight to realize that his acreage was too valuable to use for rice farming.

Joe asked for plot plans of the property and said he would call shortly. He noticed that Fred seemed to be almost in awe of him, as though he could hardly believe that he had come out to see them.

"If you are too busy to handle this yourself, Mr. Hodges," Fred ended their first meeting, "we will be happy to work through whomever you might recommend."

"No, Fred, I promised Mr. Shoemate I would personally try to help you in arranging for the best development program to be carried out," Joe answered magnanimously. "You can be sure I'll contact you soon."

It wasn't until Joe was driving back to Houston from Sugarland, wishing he had the bankroll to stop by Wilks's crap game, that he suddenly realized why Fred Cannon seemed to regard him with such awe. Of course! A new president had just been appointed to the Medical Center Bank and, as he had learned from several joking congratulatory telephone calls from some of his gambling friends, that president happened to be named Joe H. Hodges!

For a few days Joe forgot about Fred Cannon's land; he was more consumed by the action he craved and his need for a bankroll. A week later, on a Saturday morning, he called Fred at his home. Joe had no particular plan in mind but he was sharply conscious of the $200,000 Fred had in his bank account.

Over the phone he asked Fred if he would drive into town and meet him about ten o'clock at the Holiday Inn outside Houston on the way to Sugarland. Fred was pleased to hear from Joe and happy to meet him. He still called him Mr. Hodges, even though he and Joe were about the same age.

Arriving at the coffee shop before Fred, Joe addressed himself to his ever-present problem of raising a bankroll. Las Vegas was beckoning urgently. Looking up, he saw the country boy approaching the table and motioned him to take a seat. Mindful of the illusion in Fred's mind, he had donned his best banker's suit.

"Morning, Mr. Hodges. How's everything at the bank?" Fred greeted him. "Nice of you to spare me some time."

"Bank's quiet this Saturday morning, Fred," Joe replied. "That's why I suggested we meet today."

Fred seated himself opposite Joe in the booth and after ordering a cup of coffee looked across the table eagerly. "You come up with any new ideas on developing my acreage, Mr. Hodges?"

The gambler could see he didn't need any elaborate explanation and moved right to the point. "Fred," Joe said confidentially, "I've got one hellaciously fine deal going and I know I can trust you. That's why I called. I need twelve thousand dollars on a real estate deal. I need it today. You see, I don't want it from the bank. It wouldn't be right to comingle personal and bank business, you understand that."

Fred Cannon nodded earnestly. "Oh sure, Mr. Hodges, I can sure see that."

"So, I thought I'd give you an opportunity to loan me twelve thousand and get in on this real estate deal with me. I'll put you right in there alongside me."

Fred was still nodding enthusiastically. He did not probe for specifics about the deal, or ask what percentage he'd be in for. Nor did he inquire whether there were any papers on it.

"Oh certainly, Mr. Hodges. I'll have to get a check for you on my Sugarland State Bank account."

"Fine," Joe replied. "They're open on Saturdays."

"My checkbook is at home, Mr. Hodges," Fred replied.

"Well, let's you and I drive out there together," Joe suggested pleasantly.

As they drove out to Sugarland, Joe, seeing what an easy mark he had developed, suddenly exclaimed, "Oh my God, I forgot about something. I've also got to send eight thousand to San Antonio. Damn, we'll need to get twenty thousand on this deal."

"Oh yes, Mr. Hodges, no problem," Fred reassured the man he thought was president of the bank at the Medical Center.

Out at his home Fred found his checkbook, and they dashed to the Sugarland State Bank. There Fred drew out $20,000, moving his account down to $180,000. The computer okayed the withdrawal to Fred and he obediently handed the check to Joe.

Joe thanked him, told him it was great to be in business with such a fine partner, and said Fred would be hearing from him next week. Then he went home. Ordinarily he would have been off to Las Vegas on the next plane, but today was Saturday and he tried never to be away over weekends.

Nancy looked forward to the weekends when she and Mark and Joe could be together, and despite the gambling urges that were invading his soul once again, Joe would not deny her this pleasure. Only when there was absolutely no alternative did he make a weekend trip to Vegas. There was the recent episode with Burgess when he had to go and run his $10,000 up to $15,000 for the Monday payoff. But now, with a sure bankroll, he put off his trip until Monday. On Monday he cashed the check at the Sugarland State Bank and rushed to the airport for a morning flight to the mecca of gambling.

By Tuesday the $20,000 was gone. Naturally Joe felt depressed about it, but of course he had told Cannon it was going to take him some time to put the deal together and he hadn't signed anything, not even a note.

The moment he got back on Tuesday he called Fred again

and said he wanted to talk to him further about the deal. "I really want to get you involved in it," he said ingratiatingly.

Once again Fred came in to meet Joe and they sat down at the Holiday Inn coffee table where Joe outlined the overall proposition. He fantasized a beautiful land deal out in Sugarland. He was working on tying up property out there, probably not as good as Fred's, he said, but they could bring people out, show them Fred's land, and then sell them a development in the other property. After that Joe explained the red flag technique which fascinated Fred and awakened his dormant greed. He would get a commission on every piece of land that was sold, land he didn't even own. He would just show the buyers his land and then sell them a lot on the other property. Sugarland was about ready to go into full development due to its strategic location near fast-developing Houston.

Joe went on to spin his tale. "When it comes to developing your land we'll probably go ranchette—cut up the property into two-and-a-half-acre ranchettes—and of course we'll need to put some roads in there." The term ranchette, little ranch, appealed to Fred Cannon. As Joe saw Fred becoming ensnared in the scheme, he chose the right psychological moment to say, "Yes, Fred, we'll do all these things. But first I'm going to need some more money. We'll need to ship twenty-five thousand down to Miami and bring in a couple of men I know who will invest in our plan. They'll take us out, get your cash back, and we'll be operating on their money. It takes money to make money, you know."

"Oh yes, Mr. Hodges, I know that," Fred agreed.

They went down to the Sugarland State Bank and this time Fred drew $25,000 from his account. It was easy, took only a few minutes, and Joe, once he had the money in hand, immediately flew out to Las Vegas where he blew the whole sum overnight.

Joe was frequently out in Las Vegas these days, gambling with large sums. The pit bosses and casino managers had seen him win, but now he was a consistent loser. "That Joe Hodges has got to be a real moneymaker," he imagined them saying. A high roller. The kind of man they wanted out there. Joe was betting with Artie Newman at the Flamingo but also at the Dunes, the Sands, the Stardust, all the major casinos.

He also knew where not to go on the Strip, places such as the Nugget and the Freemont where he'd smashed phony cashier's checks and his name would conjure up less benevolent thoughts. But Las Vegas has scores of casinos, and Caesars Palace was just being built.

In three weeks Joe had drawn $70,000 out of Fred Cannon's bank account. The process got easier each time. He took to just making a call to Fred, not even meeting him, and saying, "By the way, you'd better pick up fifteen thousand so we can ship it on over to Miami. They're going to have the master plan of our area drawn up."

Actually, Joe was truly attempting to make some kind of a land deal on the Sugarland acreage. He hoped to make enough money to pay back the $70,000 he had so far taken out of Fred's account. He had no other way to repay it.

He brought Ben Kostial out to see the property and his erstwhile partner was deeply impressed.

Ben and Joe discussed the possibilities of subdividing Cannon's acreage, but Ben shrewdly decided that it was too early. There was too much undeveloped property around it.

Joe went back to Fred and continued to extol the development potential of the property while stressing that they would need some more development money first. He offered to get Fred a $100,000 loan on the land. This of course was easy. Any banker would make a loan on such valuable property.

When the $100,000 loan was consummated Joe took $80,000 and gave $20,000 to Fred. "We're going to need this money to realize the future potential here," he said sagely. Fred agreed. Three weeks later the gambler had blown the entire $80,000.

The gambling fever was on Joe as never before. No sooner had he left Vegas than he had to get back. With Cannon's funds exhausted, he had to go on to other deals, whatever he could find, to keep pumping the money to fuel his insatiable craving for action. He also felt acutely pressured by the need to get Cannon his money back.

While working with Cannon he had instigated some deals with the Rogers brothers of Beaumont. They had founded the

Texas State Optical Company which examined eyes and made and fitted glasses. It was the cheapest way to get a pair of glasses in Texas and the Rogers brothers had developed hundreds of outlets.

When Joe went over to meet Ben Rogers, he already knew him slightly. Moreover, Nancy had taught some of the Rogers children in school so the Rogers brothers knew who Joe was.

The deal that Joe was trying to promote with the Rogers never did work out, but it gave him the opportunity to renew his acquaintanceship with Ben. Ben, Joe discovered, was a director of the bank in the Meyerland shopping center only eight blocks from Joe's home in Bellaire, and Joe was always interested in establishing credible relationships with banks and lending institutions. His debt structure in the summer of 1967 was between $700,000 and $800,000, the money owed to institutions and individuals in Beaumont, Irving, Houston, and down along the Gulf. He survived by frantically keeping the plates spinning, paying here, withholding there, just managing to keep charges from being filed against him in court.

In the back of his mind he could never forget the great coup he had pulled off in Las Vegas and with the Dallas and Fort Worth bookies on the baseball parlays: $350,000 in just thirty-one days of gambling. He had paid off everything he owed around Irving. If he could do it once, he thought, why couldn't he do it again?

Meanwhile, down in Pensacola Harry Newkirk was never off the long-distance telephone, calling contacts all over the country and touting Joe as the slickest money broker around. The deals were coming in and Joe was taking cash up front to go out and raise money for businessmen and lawyers who came to him. He knew he couldn't make any more takeout commitments, except perhaps with Charlie Wyche. And even Charlie Wyche wasn't too happy about the way Joe's gambling was flaring up again.

Late in the summer of 1967 Joe decided to try his luck at the Meyerland Bank. It was one of the few nearby ones he hadn't hit, perhaps because Ben Rogers was a director. Or perhaps that was the very reason he was now going to it.

It was late on a Saturday morning, Joe's favorite time for smashing checks. He was dressed up in his best clothes and carrying his briefcase when he walked in and noticed that the president's desk was empty. He saw a young man sitting behind a desk featuring the nameplate Victor Vermillion, Vice-President. Joe slipped into his tried and true method of operating. "You remember me, don't you, Mr. Vermillion? I'm Joe Hodges." Victor Vermillion was small, Joe noticed, as he stood up from behind his desk to shake hands. He was a pleasant-looking man with a soft, well-modulated voice, evidently a nice amenable type with a bright personality.

"You helped me about six months ago when I needed to send that money to New Orleans," Joe continued. "You cashed those checks for me."

Vermillion nodded and chuckled. "I tell you one thing, I'd remember you if they had come back."

Joe laughed. "Yes, I guess you would." Joe figured Victor Vermillion must be about thirty years old. "Well, I've got to do it again."

"Okay, what have you got?"

Joe showed him a check for $5,500 he had written to himself. "Do you want to do what you did before," he asked solicitously. "Write my bar association card number down?"

Vermillion studied the check. "Oh no, that's not necessary. It's got your name and address on it. Just endorse it on the back." Joe endorsed the check under the other spurious endorsement of a nonexistent client to whom it was made out jointly with Joe H. Hodges. Vermillion looked at the address, noticing that Joe Hodges lived only eight blocks from the bank. As always Joe's real phone number was on the check as well. This was one of a number of counter checks he had picked up at the airport branch of a Phoenix bank en route from Las Vegas to Houston.

Joe sent the money to Idus Ash in Dallas and called in his bets. But it wasn't his weekend. He lost the whole $5,500.

On Tuesday he went to Ben Kostial and told him about the bad check he had laid on the vice-president of the Meyerland Bank. Ben lent Joe $5,500 which he took to the Meyerland Bank, once again walking up to Victor Vermillion.

"Say, that guy that gave me the check for five and a half grand you cashed for me on Saturday—I just got a call from him. He wired me the money, the check's going to come back. But here's the money to cover it."

Vermillion was pleased. "Okay, Joe. I appreciate that. I wish all our customers were like you. I see you live nearby. Drop in and see me again when you have a chance."

"I sure will, Victor." Joe left the bank and didn't see Victor again until late September.

CHAPTER 33

At the beginning of the football season of 1967 Joe had managed to float $56,000 worth of hot checks, all of which were in the air ready to descend upon the banks which had cashed them. Bill Russell, for whose company, Southwest Tool and Drill, he had secured a loan guaranteed by Charlie Wyche, was going down the drain fast. He had also become a Las Vegas regular and often accompanied Joe there via Dallas. It was obvious that Joe had put Charlie into a really bad deal this time, although the eccentric old millionaire didn't know it yet. But now Joe had a lot of heat to take care of, and the specter of being on permanent parole always hung over him.

He made an attempt to borrow $50,000 from Charlie who had the good sense to say, "No, Irishman, I'm not going to loan it to you." He pointedly reminded Joe that he was already on the $250,000 note for Russell's company.

Despite Joe's agonized remonstrance that he'd go to jail if he didn't get the money, Charlie held fast. Leaving the old man's ramshackle house, Joe contacted his gambling friend Ash who turned in bets for him. He told Ash he was on his way out to Las Vegas and needed the $6,000 the bookie owed him.

In the past Ash had separated Joe from a lot of money in Hot Springs and in domino halls, taking sports bets, and of course it was Ash who prepared the way for Joe's disastrous gambling renaissance after the first years in Irving as a respectable city attorney.

Joe had been betting steadily with Ash and had sent him

$10,000 the week before against the bets Joe constantly called in. Ash met him out at Love Field with the money, and Joe and Bill Russell were off to Las Vegas.

Joe knew he had only a few days before the hot checks would hit with shock waves that would blow him back into prison. He and Bill Russell got to the Stardust Hotel casino at 8 P.M. on Thursday evening. Joe started playing baccarat, a game at which a fortune could be won or lost in a turn of the card. Five hours later he had $60,000 in front of him. He was a $54,000 winner. He turned to Russell, who had been sitting watching him play though not participating, and said urgently, "Go to the phone and get us a plane out of here right now."

While he was waiting for Russell to make the call, Joe put $56,000 to one side and bet $1,000 on the next turn of the cards. The gambler was talking to him now, saying, "Joe, if you go back home with the fifty-six thousand, sure that will cover the hot checks. But, Joe, why did you write those hot checks to begin with? You must have been busted. If you go back there with only fifty-six thousand you've got no bankroll."

He lost the first $1,000 and then struggled with himself. He was expecting Bill to come back at any minute and say there would be a plane leaving in twenty minutes for Los Angeles, from where they could get a flight back to Houston.

He bet another $1,000 and lost it. Then he bet another, glancing at his watch and wondering where Bill was. He looked at his chips. There was $56,000 worth sitting off to the side not to be touched and the $2,000 left that was his. He didn't consider the $56,000 his money now. That had to go back and pay off the hot checks. He bet $500 and blew it on the next turn of the cards. He followed that $500 with another and lost that. Still Bill Russell was not back. All he had to do was go to the phone and get a plane reservation, Joe thought in intense irritation. He quickly lost the last $1,000 and now was sitting with only the $56,000 which really wasn't his.

By the time Bill Russell did return, fifteen minutes later, Joe had dipped into his hot check money and was down to $51,000. "We've got a plane for Denver where we can change for Houston," he informed Joe breathlessly.

"Damn, I can't go back now. I've blown off five grand. I've

got to get it back up to fifty-six thousand before I can leave. Go back and cancel the plane. Forget it."

Bill Russell shrugged and walked back to the telephone. By 2 A.M. Joe was down to $10,000.

Well, that was $4,000 more than he came to Las Vegas with, but he felt drained emotionally and physically. He pushed his chair back and stood up. "Screw this game," he said to Bill. "I'm not going to lose my last ten grand here."

Followed by Russell, Joe walked across the street from the Stardust to the Desert Inn and bellied up to a crap table. By 8 A.M. he had worked his $10,000 back up to $60,000, playing virtually by himself. Russell was sitting, watching him, so tired he could hardly keep his eyes open. But Joe kept struggling.

Having hit the $60,000 Joe was about to cash in his chips. But he heard that voice again: "Well damn, if I go home with this, why did I write the hot checks in the first place? I won't have a bankroll."

He turned to one of the casino girls and asked for a cup of black coffee. He'd been on his feet all night long at the crap table and was physically exhausted even though the trauma of the game gave him a false sense of energy.

"Joe, for chrissake, let's go take a rest," Russell pleaded.

"No, don't mess with me now. I haven't got time to rest. I've got some hot checks out in Houston."

"You've got the money right there. Let's go, Joe."

"Well, all right, but I'll be busted. You want that? If I go back busted, what am I going to do then?"

"Okay, okay, go ahead if you want to," Bill surrendered hopelessly.

All day Joe played the craps, running the $60,000 up, down, up and down again. By 6 P.M. he had lost everything but his air fare home. He and Bill got on the plane for Houston, both broke. Silently he repeated the prayers he recited at the Methodist Church on Sundays. He thought of Nancy and winced. Was there any help for him, any hope of redemption? Where could he turn?

After the first hour of black despondency, his old resiliency bounced back. It was Friday evening, the football season had started. "What the hell, it's Friday and I'm not in jail yet," he consoled himself. "Probably the banks don't know about the hot checks yet."

By the time he had driven himself home from the airport he had his plan thought out and his mood was cheerful. "Hi, dear," he greeted Nancy. "How are you doing?"

"Where have you been?" she asked, worry strongly evident on her face.

"Well, we had a tough trip. Old Charlie really put me through the wringer. Then I had to drive up to Wichita Falls."

"Why didn't you call?" she asked petulantly.

"I told you I'd be gone," Joe replied, annoyed now. "You knew where I was."

Hearing the edge creeping into his voice Nancy did not push the subject. "I'm really tired, Nancy. I want to rest up this weekend." She shrugged and walked out of the room.

The next morning Joe was up, showered, shaved, and in his vested suit, about to walk out with his briefcase, when Nancy said, "I thought you were going to stay home this morning."

"I forgot, I've got to go see Ben." Joe had already met the newspaper boy, and studied the football games.

Once out of the house, he started driving about the environs of Houston looking for a strange bank. Saturday morning was his best time to operate with the smaller suburban branch banks since usually the main office banks were not open. He picked the small First Pasadena State Bank. His customary "You remember me, Joe H. Hodges" worked with the vice-president. He smashed his last Arizona check there for $4,000, then, with another check he had been saving, visited George Holmes, a vice-president at the Gulf Gate State Bank in South Houston. He'd met Holmes once before but Holmes had evidently not heard about his reputation as a smasher of bad checks. Joe picked up another $4,000 and then rushed to Western Union to send the $8,000 to Ash in Dallas so that he could get bets down for the weekend football games.

Once he had taken the money to Western Union and sent it off to Ash, he got his bookie on the phone in Dallas and gave him the football games he was playing that day and Sunday. Now he was feeling better about his Las Vegas loss. He had given his bets to Ash and as soon as Western Union in Dallas called the bookie and said, "Mr. Ash, we have an eight-thousand-dollar money order for you," the bets would be down with the main bookmaker in Dallas, Ralph Shotz.

"Have you got the money yet at Western Union?" Joe asked Ash after he had given him his football action. The money hadn't come through.

"Well, some of the kickoffs are at twelve noon. Call Western Union again and see if the money's come," he begged. Ash checked Western Union on another phone while Joe waited.

"The money hasn't come in, Joe," Ash reported.

"It'll be there. Keep checking, will you?"

"Sure. But the bets don't go down until the money's in."

"I know, I know. I'll go back to the Western Union office here and try to push them."

Frantic, Joe rushed back to Western Union, made sure the money had been transferred, and then called Ash. It was now almost twelve noon, 1 P.M. back East. Ash held Joe on one phone while he called Western Union. Joe waited, furiously feeding quarters into the box until Ash reported back that the money had just come in.

With a sigh of relief he headed home to sweat out the football games.

The college games in the East were well underway when Joe got back and by four o'clock, having used many ruses to slip away from Nancy and get into the bathroom where he had his transistor radio hidden, he found he had won three games out of four, two of them key games which gave him a big start.

Now, instead of having $8,000 bet, he had $19,000 owing him. Meanwhile he had told Nancy to go out and get her shopping done and he'd stay home with Mark. Nancy returned just when he wanted to go out and call Ash again. He had a $19,000 credit and it was time to get some more bets down. Hardly had Nancy come back than Joe was on his way out.

"Where you going, Joe?" she asked.

"I ran out of cigarettes."

"But you had a carton just yesterday."

"I can't find them. I don't think I had a carton yesterday."

Without another word he rushed out, drove around the corner to Bang's and, feeding quarters into the coin box, started dialing

Ash in Dallas. The line was busy. It remained busy. He was using one sore finger after another dialing, dialing, dialing the bookie in order to use his just acquired leverage to increase bets on other games and place new ones. Finally, after an hour of trying, he had Ash on the line and bet his new slate of games.

When he got home Nancy was upset. "Where have you been, Joe? It doesn't take an hour and a half to buy a carton of cigarettes."

"You'd never believe, Nancy, but I ran into Bill Scott, who was in Seagoville with me. Well, there was Bill right there buying a beer. He doesn't live around here but for some reason there he was. So naturally I had to sit down. We had a couple of beers and talked about old times. You can't expect me to just stay home all the time. When I see a friend I want to talk to him."

Nancy let the argument die out.

The West Coast games were underway and Joe had discovered a service, *Dial-a-Score*. Whenever he thought Nancy's attention was diverted he would take the telephone on its long extension line around the corner from the living room and dial.

As winning scores came in and Joe was amassing more credit with the bookie, he had to continue to find excuses for leaving the house so he could go to Bang's grocery and call Dallas.

Nancy suggested that they go to see a movie. Joe protested, saying he had worked hard all week and just didn't feel like going out to a movie that night. There was no way he could go to a movie or do anything other than just sweat out the games.

He went into the bathroom once again and, turning the radio down till it was barely audible, listened to the UCLA game. Joe had the Bruins and they were on the seven-yard line; the Bruins fumbled and lost the ball.

Joe sobbed out curses. He was shattered.

There was a sharp rap on the door. "Joe, are you all right?" Nancy called.

"Of course I'm all right. I'll be right out. Just give me a minute. You know my ulcer's bothering me, you know I've got diarrhea. Can't you give me a little peace?" He heard Nancy's footsteps retreating from the door to the bathroom. Despite the fumble UCLA won and Joe's winnings were going up.

Sunday morning was church time. But when he and Nancy went to church he took with him his case of diarrhea. He was going to have to call Ash before the end of the morning and get the line on the games for Sunday. He had to know how many points he was giving up on each game that he bet. Trying to put bets down while in church was the worst type of ordeal, more debiliating than any activity he had ever known.

Joe and Nancy arrived at the Methodist Church. Joe seated her and said he'd be right back. Then he went into the vestry where the venerable coin telephone was located. His pocket was bulging with quarters as he called Dallas and, after several busy signals, got Ash on the phone.

"What's the line on the pro games?" Joe asked.

"Gee, Joe, I didn't get them yet."

"Damn, Ash, you knew I was going to call you this morning, why didn't you get the line for me? If it's going to be the Packers minus seven I want to know."

"Hang on, Joe, I'll call and get it for you," Ash called back over the phone.

With the minister about ready to start preaching his sermon and Nancy wondering what was really wrong with him, Joe listened to Ash's report. "Okay, Ash, I'm up to thirty-five thousand. Here's how I want to bet it on the games today." He rattled off the teams he was betting on, having spent an hour before he and Nancy left for church doping out the games. With his bets all safely down, he rejoined the congregation, settling himself comfortably in the pew beside Nancy.

Back home with Nancy, he started sweating out the professional games.

He had hidden his carton of cigarettes so that Nancy wouldn't find them and when, at three in the afternoon, he had already won four East Coast games, he made an excuse to go buy cigarettes again. He told Nancy he bought them one pack at a time to help cut down his smoking.

He got Ash on the phone, placed his bets on the West Coast games which were just about to kick off, and then went home again.

By late Sunday night he had won $70,000. On Monday morning he flew to Dallas. It was his biggest football win ever and made up for the exhausting twenty-four-hour session in Las Vegas when he had run his small bankroll up to $60,000 twice and then lost it.

Joe collected $60,000 from Ash, leaving $10,000 to bet with later, and rushed back to Houston. He had to race his car around to the banks, where he went through his routine.

"You remember me, Joe Hodges. You cashed a check for me Saturday morning. That sonofagun check is going to come back. That guy wired me the money. Can I give you this cash to cover and you give me a receipt for it? When the check comes back just mail it to me."

"Oh yes, Mr. Hodges. We wish all of our customers were like you."

By noontime on Tuesday he had cleaned up all his bad checks, including the one he was least worried about, that on the Valley National Bank in Phoenix. He particularly liked writing checks on the Valley National. You could send a check out there and it would rattle over every city in Arizona from Tombstone to Tucson trying to locate a home. One branch would send it to the next and it might even be a month before it was sent back to the bank where it was originally smashed.

Now Joe was ready to start all over again.

CHAPTER 34

In mid-September of 1967, in need, as always, of a bankroll, Joe wrote out one of the checks he had collected in his travels and decided to try the Meyerland Bank again. In July he'd cashed a $5,500 check and three days later paid it off, thus scoring positive points with the vice-president who had okayed it. Victor Vermillion recognized him the moment he walked into the bank and stood up, hand extended, as Joe approached his desk.

"What can I do for you today, Joe?" Victor asked. "It's been a long time since we've seen you."

"Well, I've got to send some money up to Dallas, Victor, and I need to cash this check for twelve thousand."

"You ought to bank with us, Joe. You live nearby. You want to let me open an account for you here?"

"Yeah, Vic, that's just what I'd like you to do," Joe answered. "As soon as I get this deal worked out up in Dallas and get some money in here, I'm going to give it to you. I appreciate the help you've given me."

"You do that, Joe. What have you got there?"

Joe handed the check over to Victor who gave it a cursory examination, initialed the corner, and handed it back to him. Joe cashed the check at the teller's cage, tucked the money into his jacket pocket, walked out, and drove directly to the airport.

Joe was charged. He had a substantial bankroll and was ready to hit the casinos. He heard the vibration of the flaps beginning to lower and knew Las Vegas was only minutes away. He had observed what he considered a competent businessman on the trip from Houston. This companion passenger had been working on business matters since he left Houston. He seemed relaxed, secure, organized, thoroughly in control. Joe felt envious. He admired this man. He could see him arriving in Las Vegas and working in his room all evening in a casino hotel. He would not have an urge to place a bet. He would have a productive business meeting tomorrow and return to his family. The companion said he had a cookout planned at home the next evening and would be glad to be out of Las Vegas early after he completed his business.

Joe closed his eyes and leaned back. He wanted to be like the man beside him. He admired him for his neat appearance and calm demeanor, his clear-cut business objective, his commitment to his family and friends, and his pleasure in a simple cookout. Joe had dreamed of these values. What had happened? He loved this simple life but he was now entwined in a complex world of money, gambling, finagling, and often nauseating tension. Nostalgia for a simple life with Nancy, Mark, and their friends hit him like a wave. He loved them. How he would like to share their uncomplicated life-style. For a moment he imagined himself like this plane companion, stable, clear-headed, cocooned in the normal.

The slight screech of the landing at McCarran Airport shook him into his personal reality. Adrenaline had blunted his nostalgia. He hurried away from the man who had stimulated such uneasy thoughts. Gambling would relieve his uncertainty and confusion. As he rode the cab to the Flamingo, he tried to shake loose the memory of his admiration for his fellow passenger's contentment. Then the dice rolled across his mind, making him forget completely.

The $12,000 lasted just over four hours at the Flamingo crap tables. Once again stripped down to taxi fare, Joe headed out for the airport and home.

For the next few days he pumped everywhere trying to get $12,000 to cover the hot check before it floated back to Victor Vermillion's desk. By now most of his spots had been exhausted. There just wasn't any place he could pump the money he needed to take into Victor with some story about why the bank would be getting that check back again.

Finally, when he knew the hot check had been in the air about as long as it could fly, he went back to the Meyerland Bank around noontime and strode up to Vermillion's desk.

"Hi, Joe," the banker greeted him. "How are you doing?"

"I need to talk to you, Victor." Luckily Victor was alone.

"What's on your mind, Joe?"

Joe chose his words carefully. "We have a heck of a problem, Vic."

"What's that, Joe?"

"You remember that twelve thousand? Well, I'm dealing with some screwy people up there in Dallas and I'm going to need a little time on it. That SOB check is going to come back. Those other checks you cashed for me are all good of course." Victor looked perplexed. He couldn't remember cashing any other checks for Joe other than the one Joe made good before it bounced. But that was Joe's technique—make them think they've done a lot of business with him.

"By the way, so that you'll understand the situation, Ben Rogers is a good friend of mine," Joe went on.

"Oh really? He's on our board, you know."

"Yes, I know he is. Now we've got to figure this problem out."

"How long do you think it will be before the check is good?"

"I really don't know but I've got an idea. As a matter of fact, why don't we have lunch and talk about it?" Joe was feeling better about the situation now. He could see that some way he and Victor Vermillion would solve "their" problem. "Let me buy you lunch tomorrow," he invited.

"I can't tomorrow but how about Thursday?"

Joe left the bank almost whistling.

Two days later, the check still hadn't returned, and Vermillion met Joe at the restaurant. Joe was ready. He placed a file on the table between them. Inside the file envelope was Charlie Wyche's financial statement. "I want you to read this and tell me what you think."

Vermillion looked over the statement for a few moments and then looked up. "My goodness, Mr. Wyche is worth a lot of money. Who is he?"

Joe told him of his relationship with Charlie Wyche, embellishing the old man's reliance on Joe as a close friend who helped him in his financial dealings. Then he pulled out another file and showed Vermillion the details of a land deal in West Texas. "This is a deal Charlie wants me to work on. Big money here but I've got to put *up* some money. And now I've gotten involved with that check for twelve grand that's coming back." Victor Vermillion, with a banker's natural interest, looked through the folder on the real estate deal.

"I'm not asking you to give me a note to sign on that bad check," Joe said. "And you can be sure I'm going to pay it."

"Well, I think I told you my authority stops at ten thousand dollars. Any more than that and I have to go to the board of directors."

"I don't expect you to let me give you a note for it," Joe repeated. "But if there's a way I can figure out to get hold of a few dollars, I can make some money and get this twelve thousand problem liquidated. But I've got to have a bit of money."

"How much are you talking about?" Victor asked.

"Well, let me think about it here." Joe did some ad-libbing on the land deal and then said, "I need about thirteen thousand or something like that. Well, maybe not quite that much. I need about eleven thousand eight hundred." He gave Victor a shrewd look. "I sure want to solve our problem. But I've just got to get some cash money so I can close up this deal in the next two or three weeks. Maybe there's some way you can help me. I've got the note here from old man Wyche."

Joe's stock-in-trade was always to have available promissory notes with no figure written on them. Charlie Wyche's hand being withered from the burns he'd suffered in the accident many years ago, Joe frequently used to sign Charlie's name to checks with the old man's permission. He had become so adept that he could sign Charlie's name better than the eccentric himself could. And he had signed the open promissory note "C. D. Wyche," just as Charlie had signed his financial statement.

"There's one thing we might do, Victor. You could take this current financial statement and put it in your portfolio, then use this note Charlie signed to me to advance me the monies I need. We can write in any amount we need. That way I can get us out of this." Joe looked across the table at the young banker speculatively.

"I think I might be able to do something," Victor said thoughtfully.

"Boy, I'd sure appreciate it. The Bank of Texas loaned a quarter of a million on Charlie's signature. You could call down there and check it. It's current by the way. Southwest Drill and Tool Company."

"What's your office number? I'll call you," Victor said.

"I'll keep in touch with you, Vic." Joe didn't have an office now. "I tell you, I'm so scared about this twelve thousand I don't know what to do."

"Don't worry about that, we'll handle it some way."

"I know it's not back yet, but a hot check is a hot check," Joe went on, utilizing his square John approach. "I'll tell you one thing, Victor, it worries me."

"I understand your worry and I appreciate that but, hell, you had that other check and you brought the money in, didn't you?"

The following day Joe called Victor at the bank and was greeted: "I think I've got it worked out, Joe. Come on over to the bank."

At the Meyerland Bank, Victor announced, "I'm going to open you a twenty-five-thousand-dollar account and when the check comes back we'll just charge that bad one against the account and then you can draw on these funds if you need to make this deal." He gave Joe a friendly smile. "It's a little more money than you needed."

"Victor, I can't tell you how much I appreciate this." Joe watched as Victor filled out the deposit slip and a loan on the note to which Joe had signed Charlie Wyche's name. "Now I'm going to hold these funds on the twelve thousand, but you've got thirteen thousand of spendable money here."

"Boy, I sure thank you. You really saved me this time."

"Well, good luck on your deals. And don't forget the Meyerland Bank."

"I'll never forget you, Victor. As a matter of fact, I'll need about four thousand of it now."

"You don't have a check or anything then, Joe?" Victor asked, a slight crease of concern showing on his forehead.

"Victor, if I had a check it wouldn't be any good. I can get a check."

"Well, get a check and put it in that bank account."

Joe went home, got one of the checks he had collected in his travels around the country, made it out for $27,116.20, wrote out a deposit slip for it and gave it to Victor to put in his account. Then he wrote a check on his Meyerland account for $4,000 which Victor okayed. He took it to the teller and walked out of the bank with the cash; then he jumped in his car and drove out to Bobby Wilks's crap game outside of town.

In less than ten business days after the account had been started, Joe had withdrawn $50,000 from it. He was wiring money to Idus Ash in Dallas and betting with Turk, and he made a trip to Las Vegas. All of his action lost.

Each Monday, after he'd blown his money, he returned to the bank to tell Victor that he was going to need some more money to put his deal across.

"Get out for a while this afternoon, Victor, and let's have a drink," Joe suggested, and the banker agreed. By September 30, Victor Vermillion was becoming worried, although he had not yet lost faith in Joe. It was very much like the deal with Fred Cannon except that the banker surprised Joe with his leniency. Nevertheless, Joe kept up his confident demeanor and assuaged Victor's fears.

"That first check came back, Joe," Victor mentioned over a drink. "I've had to charge your account."

"Yeah I know, Victor, but I deposited that other one."

"Sure you did, but you know and I know it's coming back."

"Yeah, I know you're expecting it back and I've got to put an even bigger one in there. I'll tell you what I'll do. When this deal goes through it will be because of you that I made it. I should draw down about four hundred thousand and I'll split it with you when it comes through."

"Oh, you don't have to do that," Victor protested.

"I know I don't have to but I want to, Victor. I know that Mr. Wyche would not mind at all. And remember, if you need to talk with Mr. Rogers, go ahead." Joe well knew that Victor Vermillion wasn't going to talk to Ben Rogers. A bank vice-president doesn't go to the board of directors when he's protecting a questionable deal involving $50,000 outstanding.

"No-no, I don't have to talk to him," Victor predictably replied.

"How would you like me to handle it?" Joe asked after they had started their second drink at the bar.

"I guess you'll have to put another check in. Bring one around tomorrow morning." They finished their drinks and a concerned Victor Vermillion walked back to his bank.

The next day Joe arrived at the bank, this time with a check made out for $56,122.15 which he deposited in his account.

When the second check came back, Victor was careful not to let any of the tellers see it. He personally went to the bank computer and charged Joe's account for the returned check, the new one having already been deposited with the teller. Now Joe had plenty of money in the account. He was always one check behind, of course, each one bigger than the last, but before everything fell apart and was exposed, he knew he'd have the big win that would take care of all his troubles.

CHAPTER 35

On September 30, 1967, Nancy, Mark, and Joe moved to 4620 Braeburn Street in a pleasant residential area which was actually a few blocks closer to the Meyerland Bank. Their new home was a nice rental house with a room for Mark and a neat fenced backyard. Nancy had made all the arrangements and was paying the rent of $140 a month out of her teacher's salary.

The move was precipitated by a piece of incredible news. After sixteen years of marriage Nancy was going to have a baby. Joe was elated and his mother and father thrilled at the prospect of having another grandchild.

As they were moving over the weekend, Joe had his radio going the entire time, sweating out the football games.

Directly across the street lived Pat and Robert Strobel who dropped by while their new neighbors were settling in and invited them over for a meal. Robert was a handsome man and Pat, of Spanish extraction, was a beautiful girl with long black hair, fair skin, and deep sympathetic eyes. She seemed interested in all her neighbors and spoke feelingly of everyone's problems. Her three sons kept her busy but not so busy that she and Joe and Nancy were not able to have many conversations together—conversations in which, naturally, Joe's gambling compulsion was never mentioned. All the couples in this pleasant housing area for upwardly mobile young families were ten or twelve years younger than Joe and Nancy.

Joe hedged about his business when his neighbors asked. "Oh, I'm in the brokerage and land business," he'd say. When asked if this meant he was in real estate, he answered, "No, I'm not an agent, I don't sell houses. I'm just in what you might call . . . land business." This, of course, always aroused interest since everybody knew how land was skyrocketing in Houston.

Joe and Nancy enjoyed their friendships with all these young folk and spent many a pleasant evening with them. At one neighborhood party the Strobels introduced Nancy and Joe to Nelda and Hugh Fonville who lived two houses down, and the six of them became good friends. Joe took great care never to breathe a word about his gambling mania.

Meanwhile, every week, Joe was sending a Western Union money order up to Idus Ash in Dallas and running his account up with Victor Vermillion who was understandably becoming seriously concerned but was in so deep there was little he could do except keep giving Joe money when he asked for it. Always Joe's big land deal was just about to come off and everything would be taken care of.

In his desk drawer Vermillion kept what he thought was his one piece of security on the Joe Hodges matter, the open note from Charlie Wyche which the banker could, if necessary, fill in for the amount of money Joe owed.

On Joe's thirty-ninth birthday, November 1, 1967, he took another $20,000 from Victor which brought his debt up to $330,000. Victor was trapped. Deep lines of worry came to his face now each time Joe asked for money. Always it was the last loan Joe would be needing until the big deal came through.

Joe left for Las Vegas on his birthday owing $330,000 to the Meyerland Bank. Actually he owed it to Victor Vermillion who hadn't dared let anybody in the bank discover the shocking facts of the Joe H. Hodges account.

It happened that this birthday was a lucky one for Joe. He left Las Vegas a $50,000 winner. The next day he appeared at the bank and gave Victor $40,000, then sent $10,000 to Idus Ash. If his luck had turned in Vegas, he just could not hit the football games after that first big win of the season. He lost every week.

A few days after his birthday Joe came back from Las Vegas with $80,000 and now Victor, though still concerned about getting the account straightened out, thought he was seeing a turnaround.

In the middle of November Joe jubilantly called Victor from Las Vegas after another win. "I'm having a helluva time with this deal, Victor. But I got another fifty thousand for the bank. I'll be bringing it around to you tomorrow."

"That's good news. But, boy, you've got to do something. This just can't go on," Victor answered. "Can't you get the account square in the next few days?"

"I'm sure trying, Vic," Joe replied wearily.

With a big win behind him, money he was holding back, Joe decided to call Ben Rogers in Beaumont. This was the time, if ever, he needed help with the bank. With a pocket full of money he felt he could bring the float at the Meyerland Bank to within what he considered hopeful range, in the neighborhood of $100,000. From a high of $330,000 down to $100,000 would be a considerable step in the right direction.

On his credit card Joe put the call through to Ben Rogers.

"Hi, Ben, this is Joe Hodges," he began. "I'm calling you from Nevada."

"What do you need, Joe?" Ben asked.

"Ben, I've got a helluva problem. I know you're on the board over at the Meyerland Bank. You know Victor Vermillion?"

"Oh sure, he runs the bank for us."

"Well, I owe them a hundred fifty thousand. And Victor is really worried. Now I can pay fifty grand and bring it down to an even hundred if the bank will give me a little breathing room. Like I said, Victor is real worried." He paused, but there was a cold silence on the other end and he went on hurriedly. "I thought maybe you could ask them to give me some time. I'm in a really big deal with a multimillionaire named Charlie Wyche and if there's any way you can help me at the bank I'd sure appreciate it."

"I didn't know you owed all that money, Joe," Ben replied. "But there's nothing I can do to help. Victor is worried, is he?"

"Yes. That's why I called," Joe answered.

"Well, bankers are always worried." Ben sounded more cheerful. "That's what they're paid for. No, you're going to have to get yourself out of this problem on your own, Joe. There's no way I can help you."

That was the end of Joe's seeking help from Ben Rogers on the Meyerland deal. But he had alerted the director that a serious problem was festering at the bank.

Each weekend was a football disaster for Joe but he managed to recover from the losses, thanks to his Las Vegas winning streak.

November was a good month and as the days went by and he brought cash in from his Las Vegas successes, Victor seemed less intense. Joe had reduced his float from $330,000 to $115,000 and the day before Thanksgiving, even though he had been a consistent loser at the football games with Idus Ash, he decided to send the bookie $30,000 to bet on the Thanksgiving Day games. He was certain that he had these games accurately handicapped.

Joe put a call through to Victor telling him he needed $30,000 right away. Assuaged by Joe's recent reductions in his glaring imbalance at the bank, Victor agreed to bring him the money. Nowadays Joe did not go into the bank personally. He was frightened that even though his manipulations had not been discovered, some day they were bound to catch up with him.

"Victor," Joe said cheerfully, "I'll be parked in front of Cokins Restaurant on Main Street in downtown Houston."

"Yes, I know the place," Victor said unenthusiastically.

"I'll be sitting in my car. Just get that money down to me in an hour, will you? I've got to ship it off to Dallas to put together the last of my land deal."

Thirty thousand dollars in an hour was not an unusual order from Joe. But this time, the day before Thanksgiving, Victor made the fatal error that brought the inevitable collapse of Joe's money-pumping at the Meyerland Bank. Instead of going into the vault himself as he usually did, Victor called a teller over to his desk. He asked her to go into the vault and bring him out $30,000 in a bank bag.

It was with misgivings that the young woman packed up the cash in the cloth bag stamped Meyerland Bank and laid it on Victor's desk. Until now Victor had prudently kept all the operations concerning Joe Hodges strictly in his own domain. He personally wrote out all deposit slips and handled the returned checks and the cash Joe brought in from Las Vegas.

He put the bank bag into his attaché case and left for the rendezvous. He was one worried banker again. But he was so stiffed into Joe's operations that there was no turning back now. He drove from the Meyerland shopping center downtown and spotted Joe sitting alone behind the wheel of his car in front of the restaurant. The back windows were open. Victor drove up and double-parked for a moment beside Joe's automobile. Reaching down he took the bank bag and threw it into the back seat of Joe's car and then sped on back to the Meyerland Bank. Joe drove directly to Western Union and wired the money up to Idus Ash.

On Friday, the day after Thanksgiving, Joe was broke, the entire $30,000 blown on the Thanksgiving Day football games. But there were still the Saturday and Sunday pro games left to bet on.

When the Meyerland Bank opened Joe put a call through to Victor. The date was December 2, one he would never forget.

"Victor," he said, "I need some more money."

"How much do you need?" Victor asked.

"I've got to ship twenty thousand up to Dallas by noon."

"All right, you can come by in an hour," Victor replied. "Maybe you'd better call me first, just before you leave."

"Okay, Victor, I'll call you in one hour."

At ten-fifteen Joe called back. He planned to have Victor meet him outside the bank which was just a few minutes away from Joe's house and then dash on down to Western Union.

"Joe," Victor said in a voice hoarse with agony, "the FBI are here."

"I'll be there in ten minutes," Joe replied.

Exactly ten minutes later he walked through the front door of the bank, the first time he'd been inside it in over a month. His float was now back up to $145,000. In six weeks, from September 15 to November 1, he had lost $330,000. Then, between November 1 and Thanksgiving, he had won $215,000 and put it back in the bank, only to lose another $30,000 on Thanksgiving Day football games.

Joe suspected he might be arrested when he arrived at the bank and had taken all his lists of people and institutions to whom he owed money out of his pockets, as well as the numbers of his bookies, and hidden them under the floorboard of his car.

From the moment he walked inside the bank he could feel the tension and hostility as the tellers stared at him from behind their cages. All the officers' desks were empty and the bank guard, recognizing Joe, escorted him to the boardroom. Victor was sitting at the long board table, two FBI agents standing across from him. The chairman of the board and the president of the bank stood at the end of the table, their faces set, regarding Victor angrily.

Victor, his head bowed, his shoulders convulsed with sobs, was trying to give a coherent statement of what had happened in his dealings with Joe H. Hodges from September 15 to the present. Everybody looked up at Joe when he walked in.

Victor's eyes were red and he had tears rolling down his cheeks as he gave Joe a hopeless look and then bowed his head again. The bank guard slipped out of the boardroom and closed the door behind him. A stenographer was taking down Victor's statement as he sobbed out his confession.

The president of the bank walked over to Joe. "Mr. Hodges, we'll want to talk to you in a few minutes. Would you wait outside until Mr. Vermillion finishes giving his statement?"

Joe nodded, let himself out of the boardroom, and stood in the corridor beyond. Ten minutes later the president called Joe back into the room. With Joe standing there he said to Victor, "Didn't you know he was a gambler?"

Victor shook his head and blurted out, "Not until this morning."

The FBI agents turned to Joe and went through the identification process, showing him their badges and cards. "Mr. Hodges," one of the agents asked, "would you care to give a statement?"

"I'm not prepared to give any statement," Joe answered. "Will there be anything else?"

"Surely you must have something to say, Mr. Hodges," the other agent bore in.

"Yes, I want a lawyer," Joe replied. "You can take that down if you want to."

Joe was acting as blasé about the situation as he could. He didn't want to be arrested if he could help it.

"Well, I guess that will be all—for the time being," the agent added ominously.

Joe returned home at 1 P.M., extremely worried, despite his jaunty attitude. He had no bets down so the usual weekend score sweat was eliminated.

He managed to hide his concern from Nancy and Mark over the weekend, acting as though nothing were wrong. He was in no mood to make light conversation with the neighbors and devoted all his attention to Nancy which made her wonder if indeed something were wrong, so unusual was such a show of family feeling on Joe's part these days. On Monday he tried to call Victor Vermillion at home. Victor's wife answered, her voice turning cold when she heard who was on the other end of the line. Victor was not home, she informed him, and Joe asked that he call back when he could. But the next time Joe saw the young banker was in court.

They were going into the Christmas holidays now and Joe tried to keep up the appearance of a normal business routine. Actually he was still borrowing money from such sources as he could locate, betting on the professional football games and going out to another crap game run by Joe Luke. At least he occasionally won at Luke's game which made it better than Bobby Wilks's.

Nancy, very pregnant by now, went with Joe to the Christmas round of parties, and then, on their wedding anniversary, December 27, Harry Newkirk called Joe saying he had a deal in Birmingham. A businessman, Everett Chambliss, wanted to secure the services of a money broker to finance a real estate deal he was in.

Joe was paid some money up front for the services he was asked to render and his first move was to ask Chambliss if he knew a bookmaker in Birmingham. Chambliss, though no gambler himself, did know a bookie and put Joe in touch with him. Joe's advance fee went directly to the bookmaker, bet on the various bowl games New Year's Day.

On New Year's Eve the neighbors on Braeburn Street had a party at the Strobels' house. Joe tried to make a show of enjoying it but he was completely absorbed in trying to devise a solution to his problems.

By now he had confessed to Nancy the full extent of his involvement in the Meyerland Bank scandal and they both knew that some time in the near future there would be serious repercussions.

In the early hours of the morning he took Nancy home from the party; at six o'clock Nancy knew the baby was on the way and Joe took her to the hospital.

He spent New Year's Day at the hospital with Nancy, waiting for the baby to be born. Between the imminent arrival of the baby and the bowl games which Joe was sweating out on television, New Year's Day of 1968 was full of action.

At 2 P.M. Nancy's obstetrician, Dr. Franklin, came out of the delivery room and walked up to Joe who was watching one of the bowl games.

"Well, it's a girl, Joe," the doctor announced.

"It's born?"

"No, but I've seen her rear end. It's a breech birth and all I can see is her rear—but it's a girl!"

"How can you tell by the rear whether it's a boy or a girl?" Joe asked. It was not easy to distract him from the football game on which he had so much riding.

"Don't worry, I know a girl's fanny from a boy's fanny and it's a girl."

Joe's joy at having a daughter was complete when at 6 P.M. he finally saw the nurse carrying that red scaly infant across from the delivery room to the nursery where she was bathed and put in her crib. His elation was increased by the fact that he won the day's bowl games and was now $15,000 ahead. If Tennessee could win the night game, he would have a total of $50,000 in winnings from the bowl games.

He stayed in the hospital in front of the television set all through the evening and saw Tennessee lose. But when he went home that night he was still $15,000 ahead. Two days later, instead of going to the hospital to see Nancy, he took a plane to Birmingham, picked up his money from the bookie there and came home with it.

Although there were no overt signs from the bank or the FBI

that he was in deep trouble, Joe sensed that he'd better make preparations for a difficult siege ahead. While Nancy was still in the hospital he drove down to Corpus Christi, Texas, to see their landlord and paid a year's rent in advance on their house. Then he stopped in at Beaumont to see his father and gave him $3,000 to hold for Nancy if she needed it.

On January 10, 1968, two days after Nancy came home with the baby they named Amy, Joe received a telephone call from Henry Baker, the marshal, who informed him that he had been indicted on thirteen counts of conspiracy and interstate transportation of forged securities, a technical name for hot checks. Baker had a warrant for Joe's arrest. Bond had been set at $5,000.

Joe told the marshal he'd be down at his office as soon as he could make arrangements with the bondsman. He experienced a sickening sense of *déjà vu* as he was fingerprinted and photographed. Bond was posted and he walked out of the marshal's office, still free.

Arraignment was set for January 20. Victor Vermillion was also indicted that day but only for conspiracy, a count that carries five years. In the case of Joe's indictment, the first one, conspiracy, carried five years and a $10,000 fine. All the other counts against him carried ten years each and $10,000 fines. The FBI had tracked down every one of the checks Joe had given to Vermillion, each check amounting to one count in the indictment.

On the day of the arraignment, he had Adrian Carter come down from Dallas to represent him. Petrified, Joe went to court at 2 P.M. with Adrian. He knew the indictment would make the newspapers though until then there had been not a mention of the case. He pleaded not guilty.

Joe hoped that he had a fighting chance to beat this conviction. The United States Attorney in the Southern District of Texas was Anthony T. J. Farris, a close friend of Senator John Tower who had arranged for him to be appointed to the powerful post. Senator Tower's father had been Joe's preacher for eleven years and Joe had been a friend of his sister, Beryl Jo, all during high school.

Sitting in the back of the courtroom was Hugh Mack Johnson, Joe's probation officer, who had been told by Henry Baker, the marshal, that Joe was going to be arraigned. Joe was so involved in the court procedure that he didn't even notice Hugh Mack was there.

After the pleadings, Joe, already out on bond, left the court to prepare for the trial which was set for April. Adrian flew back to Dallas with another lucrative case on his hands. One thing he knew about Joe was that his friend could always pump money when he had to and was particularly adept at the pumping process when he was under the gun.

CHAPTER 36

BANKER AND EX-CONVICT ARRAIGNED cried the evening *Houston Chronicle,* and the following morning's *Post* headline echoed the story: "Victor Vermillion, Vice-President of the Meyerland Bank and Joe H. Hodges, gambler and ex-convict, are charged with embezzling $145,000 from the Meyerland Bank. It is alleged that Hodges was involved in an elaborate check kiting scheme."

The Turk, Tommy Glispen, and Joe's other gambling friends all called to express condolences for his problems. Amy was occupying much of Joe's time if not his thoughts as he changed her diapers and helped to perform the other tasks necessary when a new baby comes home.

On January 28, Joe flew to Dallas to consult with Adrian Carter at his office. He was confident that, with careful preparation and attention to legal details, he and Adrian could win his acquittal.

There was the matter of that phone call to Ben Rogers. Joe had, in effect, warned the optometrist–bank director that he was in trouble with the Meyerland Bank. The director had done nothing about it. Wasn't it incumbent upon Rogers to call the president of the bank and check on Joe's account and question the top executive as to any irregularities that might be in progress? Since he did no such thing, wasn't he considering the check kiting merely an extension of credit? That was one avenue Joe would pursue.

When Joe arrived at Adrian's office, he was told that Nancy had called three times. He immediately called her back.

"What's the matter?" he asked, trying to conceal the apprehension he felt.

"Henry Baker is trying to reach you. He's called several times. He says he needs to talk to you."

"Well okay, I'll call him."

"He didn't tell me anything." There was panic and worry in Nancy's voice. She knew as well as Joe that Henry Baker was the Chief Deputy United States Marshal in the Southern District of Texas.

Joe braced himself and put the call through to the marshal. "Henry," he said when the marshal was on the line, "this is Joe Hodges."

"Yes, Joe, I've been trying to reach you. I've got a warrant for your arrest."

Joe's innards turned cold. "What's that for?" he asked, making an effort to keep his voice steady.

"It's a parole violation. It's an old warrant but I've been asked to execute it."

That old warrant at the time of the Tim Fowler problem, Joe thought. They'd sent it to the marshal from the Justice Department in Washington with a notation on the back *Do Not Execute*. Now, after all this time, they were going to arrest him. He would be in jail, unable to manage his defense. You cannot make bond on a parole violation.

"How long do I have, Henry?"

"Well, you need to be down here. Can you come in today or tomorrow?"

It was Wednesday. "Can you give me until Monday? I'll be down there on Monday."

"Yeah, okay, Monday."

"What time?"

"Monday morning."

"Can you make it Monday afternoon? You've got to give me a chance to make some preparations. I'm not going anywhere, you know that."

"Yeah, let's say one o'clock Monday afternoon," the marshal acquiesced.

"I'll be there," Joe promised, hanging up. Then he turned to Adrian. "Well, I'm going to jail," he said hopelessly. "It's the Fowler business. I'm out on bond on the Meyerland Bank charge. They can't put me back in jail on that. I don't have any hot checks out and there are no other charges pending." He shook his head dejectedly. "That warrant was issued seventy days before my parole would have been over. If Fowler had only waited seventy days I wouldn't have to serve the whole twenty-two months in jail now. Jail is going to hurt me, Adrian. It's really going to hurt my ability to handle this case. I can't defend myself sitting in a prison cell."

"Try not to worry about it, Joe," Adrian soothed. "You better stay here today. Give me all the facts, dictate everything into my machine, every detail. Don't forget anything. What do you think about pleading not guilty because of insanity?"

Joe shook his head. "Adrian, I've gone to several psychologists and psychiatrists. None of them understands this gambling thing."

Adrian knew a psychiatrist, a friend of his from California who was now working in Houston, Dr. Carl Cross. He offered to contact him.

"Well, we'll see," Joe procrastinated. "You know I don't have much faith in that sort of thing. But let's see what happens."

When he had finished dictating all his thoughts onto a tape, Joe gave Adrian most of the money he had to go toward the legal fee and then called Cindy.

He needed a friend now more than ever in his life. He called her, feeling it would be the last time. Thoughts of the horror to come for Nancy froze his spirit. Yet, in his attempt to shield her, he would not be able to communicate with her. Cindy sensed Joe's inner turmoil and restrained herself from asking to see him. He feebly said goodbye to her and called a cab to take him to the airport and the plane which would return him to Houston—and jail.

Nancy took the news that Joe would be going back to jail for an indeterminate period of time stoically. She'd been through so much that one more horrifying occurrence hardly seemed out of the ordinary. Joe did his best to make ready for jail. He had a long talk with Mark who was going on seven and aware of what was happening.

On Monday morning all the neighbors came to see him off, the women hugging and kissing him and crying and the men shaking hands. The stir among the neighbors caused by Joe's going off to jail was considerable. This represented something totally new in their experience.

Henry Baker was waiting for Joe at his office. After the fingerprinting and mug shots and filling out of forms, Joe was taken out to the Harris County Rehabilitation Center in Humble, Texas, an overcrowded, filthy facility where he was to be incarcerated for the next five months. Designed for a thousand men, it contained eighteen hundred criminals crowded into jail tanks, many without beds. They slept on the concrete floor, without even mattresses or blankets. Although the "Rehab" was only four years old at the time Joe went in, it was an indicator of how fast Houston had grown. The criminal element had swelled in proportion with the law-abiders.

Riots and uprisings were commonplace. In one riot that involved Joe, tear gas and mace were used on the rioters and Joe was threatened by a black inmate with a knife for trying to get out of the cell and away from the rioting.

Joe secured a job in the kitchen and then finally a typing job in the booking office where at least he could make phone calls. He ingratiated himself with the prison personnel, the guards, the cooks, and others, by doing legal work for them. It seemed as though everybody was coming to him for a free will. He was also moved from the tank to a smaller cell which made life slightly more bearable.

As the trial approached, Joe was spending more and more time on the telephone trying to organize his defense. He was getting frequent visits now from his parents and from Nancy.

The booking office was where thc people from the free world, as the inmates referred to the outside, came into the jail and it made Joe's visiting arrangements far more pleasant than having to see his visitors through a plate-glass window set in a steel door with little holes below the window. When the inmate wanted to talk to the visitor he had to bend down and talk through the holes, thus being unable to see and talk to his visitor at the same time. Visits were a real ordeal.

The job in the booking office made all the difference to Joe. Being able to call Adrian Carter and Nancy on the phone was of great comfort to him and he could even talk to Mark. Nancy did not think it was good for Mark to go out to the teeming jail to see his father.

Victor Vermillion, who had pleaded guilty, was out of jail on bond and his sentencing had been postponed until after Joe's trial. He was, of course, the chief prosecution witness and he was told that if he did a good job at the trial he would get off without a jail sentence.

In April, Adrian Carter filed a paper with the court stating the intention of the defendant to rely upon the defense of insanity, a gambit to which Joe had finally and reluctantly acceded. The government appointed a psychiatrist, Dr. Carl Voght, to examine Joe. The examination lasted precisely seven minutes.

Adrian's friend Dr. Cross spent hours trying to understand Joe and to uphold the not guilty plea by projecting a sympathetic portrait of a man whose gambling compulsion was a psychological disease, a kind of insanity. Dr. Voght reported that Joe was sociopathic—an antisocial type.

Joe was in a state of chronic depression during the months before his trial which he expressed in writing poetry. His first poem, "Little Faces Fade from Sight," was a dirge expressing his increasing inability to picture his two children's faces in his mind's eye.

He finally came to trial late in April. The trial judge was Joe Ingraham, whom Senator John Tower had asked President Johnson to nominate for service on the Fifth Circuit Court of Appeals. He was about sixty-five and Joe saw him as a highly intelligent man who was very much on the side of the government in the case, although careful not to show it.

The trial lasted fourteen days, with Adrian representing Joe. Adrian had already received $12,000 from Joe in advance of the trial but he was able to get Joe declared a pauper so that the government would pay him for handling the case as well. The government's psychiatrist, Dr. Voght, was an accomplished witness who did an excellent job of convincing the jury that Joe was a psychopathic swindler. Carl Cross, on the other hand, was virtually unintelligible in court and the judge frequently had to tell him to speak out.

Joe later learned that Adrian had not paid Cross his fee of $2,500 that Joe had given to Adrian, which might have been one reason for the doctor's ineffective testimony on the witness stand.

The daily ordeal of the trial started for Joe at four in the morning when he woke up, shaved, put on his suit, and was caged in a small holding cell that gave him just about room to sit down or stand up until the marshal came in to take him to court at eight-thirty. Before the trial, when Joe went to psychiatric examinations or other meetings, he sometimes had to stand or sit in the cage until one or two in the afternoon.

Joe's defense included the plea of not guilty by reason of insanity. He also argued through Adrian that there was no fraud intended but rather that the alleged check kiting was basically no more than a way of getting an extension of credit; and he pointed out that he had pared down his debt at Meyerland from almost $350,000 to $145,000. He mentioned that every day his computerized fluctuating bank account was subject to scrutiny by the president and chairman of the board as well as by Victor Vermillion. Furthermore, Joe affirmed, he had told a director, Ben Rogers, that he was in trouble at the bank and yet his credit extension had continued.

Rogers denied that Joe had ever made that phone call from Las Vegas, but Joe showed on his credit card billing where and on what date he had made it. Joe brought in numerous character witnesses including C. W. Conn, the older brother of George who had been a prosecution witness testifying that Joe had stolen one of his checks and used it fraudulently at another bank.

The jury deliberated for twelve hours which signified to Joe that perhaps they would find him not guilty. The longer a jury is out, the greater the chance of acquittal. However, when the jury returned the foreman announced that it found the defendant, Joe H. Hodges, guilty on all counts.

Right then and there at ten o'clock in the evening Judge

Ingraham called an ashen-faced, shaking defendant up to the bar of justice. He asked if Joe would accept sentencing forthwith. This is a highly unusual procedure. If Judge Ingraham had been following custom he would have made a pre-sentence investigation, discussed the case with Joe's probation officer and tried to learn as much about his background as possible. But Joe, hardly able to stand, his knees quavering, agreed to accept sentencing forthwith.

The judge, obviously pleased with the outcome of the trial, leaned toward Joe and began sentencing him, giving him the maximum on each of the thirteen counts. Partway through he could see that Joe, swaying and sweating profusely, might faint and called for a chair. Joe sank back onto the upright hardwood seat and the judge continued.

The sentence overwhelmed Joe and he had to fight to keep from passing out and falling off the chair. It added up to $65,000 in fines and sixty-five years in the penitentiary, five years on the conspiracy count and ten years on six of the individual fraudulent checks. The judge concluded by ordering that the sentences were to be run concurrently. Thereupon he stood up and, without making clear what he meant, left the courtroom.

Joe was unable to get to his feet and he didn't understand whether he was going to serve sixty-five years or fifteen, or what the sentence actually meant. The young Assistant U. S. Attorney, Donald Stone, pleased with the conviction, came over to Adrian and Joe. What the sentence amounted to, Stone said, was ten years. Bad as ten years sounded, fifteen years was a lot worse and that was what Joe had first thought the sentence meant. But sitting there in his chair, the post-trial confusion whirling around him, he realized that before he could even start serving these ten years he would first have twenty-two months to serve because of his parole violation. The rule was that if a convict was paroled so many months before his jail sentence had been completed and violated his parole on even the last day of that period, the entire period must be served in prison.

The marshal gave Joe time to recover and spend a few minutes with Nancy and his mother and father, and then he was taken back to the Harris County Rehabilitation Center.

In a few days he got his old job at the booking office back

which gave him the use of the phone again. Meanwhile Adrian Carter gave notice of appeal and Joe settled down in the Rehab to await the decision of the Appellate Court.

From the jail Joe called Victor Vermillion's lawyer and volunteered to appear before the judge who would be sentencing Victor. He hoped he could explain that Victor had indeed been taken advantage of and it wasn't his fault the bank was out that $145,000. Vermillion's lawyer accepted the offer and Joe did appear.

Before a stern-faced judge, Joe declared: "Victor Vermillion never asked for, nor did he expect, or even have reason to expect, that he would be getting the first dime of the bank's money. Victor Vermillion never even saw as much as a plate lunch out of the money I got from the bank. In a word, I conned him. He never realized what I was doing."

Joe sat down and the judge called Vermillion to the bar. He looked down at the young former bank vice-president balefully. "You were hired to take care of that money out there at the bank, weren't you?"

"Yes, sir," Victor answered.

"You didn't take care of it, did you?"

"No, sir," came the quiet reply.

Victor was forthwith sentenced to three years in the penitentiary, much to the shock of Donald Stone, the prosecutor at Joe's trial, who had promised him he would do no time if he cooperated.

The next day Victor arrived at the Rehab en route to the Federal Corrections Institution at Texarkana, Texas. Joe tried to help him by showing him some of the pitfalls at the jail, and even stole some fried chicken from the kitchen for him. But Victor wasn't there long. He was soon taken to Texarkana.

Joe did not understand why he was not being sent to a federal prison, but at least here he was able to see his mother and father and Nancy.

On July 3, 1968, the marshals came for Joe to take him to the federal prison where he would be incarcerated. They didn't tell him which prison it would be but they started out in a northeasterly direction. The first night they stopped in Muskogee, Oklahoma, where Joe and two other federal prisoners were put in the female tank. In the next cell were three prostitutes to whom Joe talked all night. Joe had secreted a couple of envelopes and some stationery inside a paperback he was reading. During the night he wrote a letter to Nancy and sealed it. Handcuffed in the back seat of the marshal's car, he had the letter with him, hidden in the paperback book.

They arrived in Kansas City and the marshal took one of the prisoners into the federal building. Joe was left with another guard in the car.

"Can't we get out and stretch our legs a little bit here?" Joe asked.

The guard shrugged and agreed, opening the back door so Joe could get out and walk around. Joe had already spotted the mailbox and he directed his footsteps toward it. When he got up to it he threw the paperback into the mail chute.

"What the hell are you doing?" the guard cried sharply.

Joe looked at the mailbox. "Oh my God, I've been in the joint so long I forgot what these things looked like. I thought it was a trash basket."

The guard gave him a suspicious look. "Come on, you, get back in the vehicle."

Joe followed the guard to the car and climbed inside. It was a small victory but a satisfying one. At least Nancy would get a letter from him expressing some of his innermost feelings. He wanted her to know how very much he cared for her without the letter being censored from inside the prison.

It was with a sinking heart and queasy stomach that Joe once again watched the huge structure of Leavenworth loom up ahead of them. They arrived late in the afternoon of July 4, thus missing the biggest day of the year at the prison. The inmates eat steak and chicken, hear cowboy singers, and generally have a holiday on Independence Day.

As he walked up the steps to the prison door he had no idea how many months or years he was facing in the grim confines of this federal penitentiary. He only knew he had a possible twelve years ahead of him. He tried to blot the prospect from his mind. In prison you take the days one at a time. He went through the now familiar procedure at Admission and Orientation—and four weeks later was classified for a job. He was assigned to the personnel office working for John Allman, an aspiring young officer in the Bureau of Prisons.

Joe soon got used to the prison routine, including the prisoner counts. He became friendly with certain inmates, tried to steer clear of trouble by avoiding the dangerous ones, and typed letters and forms every day for Allman.

To get his parole violation to run concurrently with his sentence, Joe began filing writs. As a result of the writs he received credit for the time he'd spent at the Harris County Rehabilitation Center.

Wisely, he vested little hope in the appeal. He thought there was virtually no chance of its succeeding and left it in Adrian's hands. Once he could start serving the ten-year sentence he had at least a chance of getting out in three years and four months, a third of the sentence, if he could make parole despite his stigma as a parole violator. But the fact that this was his second conviction worked against him.

Joe's deep concern that he might inadvertently become involved in prison trouble made one objective all-important: he must try to get a single cell. With Allman helping him he was finally assigned to one. He might have to do more than the forty months—it was likely that he would—but his only chance of getting out before the full term was to maintain a spotless record.

In the cell next to him he observed what long-term incarceration could do to a person. An Indian who had killed a federal marshal on the Reservation in 1930 was still there in Leavenworth in 1968. He had become virtually a deaf-mute and would not have been able to cope with life on the outside.

It was from Leavenworth that Joe watched the astronaut Neil Armstrong land on the moon. The inmates were allowed to stay up and watch important televised events.

Working in the business office, Joe had access to the officers' mess where a friend of his worked. Occasionally he could steal some ice, put it into a plastic bag and smuggle it back to his cell for a glass of cold Tang before going to bed at night. And every night before lights out at 10 P.M. he wrote his letters and poetry.

The worst part was at night. Eight hundred men all in one room, even though separated by barred cells, could generate a buzz-saw cacophony of snoring. The cell block was a large old cement structure and the primitive acoustics magnified and distorted the already ghastly sounds.

The prisoners were up at 6 A.M. and Joe reported to his job at seven-thirty. If he wasn't on time for work an immediate alarm would go out. The authorities had to know where every inmate was at every moment.

Like Dante's Inferno, there were several circles of the hell that was Leavenworth. Joe's job was in the first circle which meant he had to walk through two gates to get to it. The farther out from the center, the less the security and the better the job. Joe had a special badge with his picture on it which allowed him to pass through the two gates into the outer section where he worked.

Naturally, a great deal of the leisure-time talk was about sex and the sexual experiences the men had had before being thrown into the joint. Joe rather enjoyed listening to the amorous adventures of some of the younger men.

He played some handball for recreation and was a gifted participant in the prison duplicate bridge club. Bridge players from the free world were brought in once or twice a year for a tournament which added to the excitement.

One of Joe's special friends, Jim Massey, also from Houston, was a good handball player and taught Joe some tricks of the court. Massey also played bridge well and was an amusing companion. The younger men in the prison seemed to gravitate to Massey. He was serving ten years for assembling a team of young men, supplying them with fake I.D.s, and giving them forged payroll checks to cash at grocery stores.

Joe was able to keep his tennis game in shape when he secured an old racket and began hitting tennis balls against the prison wall. He also worked out with weights and generally got himself into fine physical shape, taking off all the extra pounds he had acquired over the past two years.

The highlight of his day was the mail call which came right after the four o'clock count. After that the prisoners had supper and went back to their cells. Joe got four and sometimes five letters a day. They always included one from Nancy, his mother and dad, or one of his friends.

The educational department provided a real respite from the drab prison routine. Inmates with special skills taught classes to each other. Joe studied computer programming, was taught by a brilliant prisoner who had robbed the First City National Bank of Houston. Joe himself taught a course in business law.

His best friend in prison, Larry Parker of Decatur, Illinois, was a short, handsome man of about thirty-two with a violent temper who was in Leavenworth with his partner Lucky Sanderlin for bank robbery.

Joe, Larry, and other inmates with whom they were friendly played miniature golf together. The loser had to stand up in the mess hall at supper and scream out at the top of his lungs to the thousand inmates eating there: "Quack quack, I'm a duck, I can't play golf worth a fuck." Depending upon the betting, the loser would have to give five and sometimes ten quack-quacks.

The penitentiary administration allowed good-natured shouting at meals, believing it helped ease tensions. Joe made every effort to keep away from trouble and Larry's partner, Lucky, was a magnet for it. There was a strong Black Muslim element at Leavenworth and Lucky was not hesitant to express his contempt for these sullen, shaven-headed criminals. More than once he ended up in a fight with the Muslims and once was beaten badly.

Joe's lessons in shooting craps were particularly popular. He cut out thirty-six cardboard squares, each square representing a possible combination that could be thrown on a pair of dice. The squares were mixed in a hat and one was drawn out, representing a throw of the dice. Then Joe explained the different ways of betting on a blackboard. Many of these inmates, gamblers all their lives, had never really understood or studied the math of a pair of dice. Joe made up paper money and kept track of the throws and the betting combinations on the blackboard.

At one point, with a $10,000 Monopoly money bankroll, Joe won $116,000. He showed his students his method of shooting craps and many inmates, when they finally left Leavenworth, were far more educated crapshooters than when they had entered.

The most important hazard to avoid in the penitentiary, Joe concluded, was the homosexual element. The second most dangerous activity was gambling. Even though the stakes were meager—cigarettes, candy, and whatever simple possessions a prisoner might have—gambling debts, if not settled, could lead to severe disturbances. Joe saw one prisoner beaten up with a baseball bat in the yard because he hadn't paid a gambling debt. In his first two years at Leavenworth there were five killings of inmates by other inmates.

Joe made every effort to avoid the parties to an inmate "marriage." Becoming friendly with such people, whether they were stud or queen, could easily lead to turmoil. Some of these inmate couples actually considered themselves man and wife and there were such couples in the bridge club. Joe went to great lengths not to become a friend of an inmate's "wife."

The smart prisoners, hoping for parole, were very guarded around these couples, fearing that the old man might think they wanted the old lady or something of that sort. The old ladies knitted socks and sweaters for their men and a regular transvestite colony existed within the prison walls.

Penitentiary life was a balancing act at all times. There was constant trading going on with cigarettes as the medium of currency. "How much do you want for that watch?"

"I want two boxes for it," might be the answer. That would be two cartons of cigarettes. A carton of cigarettes sold for two dollars. Stealing was always a problem, and a good mattress was particularly liable to theft. Most mattresses were flat and worn out but some were comfortable. An inmate works his way up just as in the outside world, acquiring more and better possessions. What would seem to an outsider a ridiculous system of values was very real in the joint. An inmate might have a good pillow but a poor mattress and constantly search for a trade to get a mattress on which he could enjoy sleeping.

It was prudent not to get too close to a guard for fear of seeming to fraternize with the hacks. Yet a sullen or distant attitude could result in undue harassment. So it was a constant spinning of plates, something at which Joe was expert, to try and get through the hours, the days, the weeks, and the months with safety and some degree of comfort.

Prison life was far from egalitarian. It was dominated by trade-offs, compromises, and the need to make friends with the right people. The prizes went to the strong—and the smart.

While Joe was in Leavenworth his gambling friend Idus Ash and the bookie to whom Idus passed Joe's money, Ralph Phalen, found themselves in a huge tax problem with the federal government. As a result of Joe's trial and the large amounts of money which he had taken from the Meyerland Bank and sent up to Ash, the IRS had filed a tax lien on Joe for $340,000, the entire amount he had taken from the Meyerland Bank, ignoring the fact that more than half that money had been repaid. As a result, IRS agents came up to Leavenworth to talk to him about the tax lien on his ill-gotten gains from the bank. At the same time, the IRS agents were taxing Idus Ash and Ralph Phalen on that same money, regarding it as income to them. Since Ash was merely a conduit he maintained that he should not be taxed on what he passed along to the bookie.

Ash hired Adrian Carter to get an affidavit from Joe stating that it was to his specific knowledge that all the money he had sent via Western Union to Idus Ash had immediately been given to Ralph Phalen. The IRS had impounded all of Western Union's records on Joe H. Hodges' remittances. Thus Adrian was motivated to make a trip to Leavenworth to see Joe and get him to sign the affidavit. He would pick up a $5,000 fee from Ash merely by getting Joe's signature on a piece of paper.

Joe agreed to sign the affidavit only if Adrian would give half his fee to Nancy. At first Adrian refused, but Joe was adamant and he finally agreed. In Joe's presence Adrian signed an agreement to send Nancy $2,500 immediately after Joe signed the affidavit. This made Joe feel like a good family provider and greatly boosted his spirits.

Joe had been in Leavenworth about a year when he heard that Charlie Wyche was dead at age eighty. It was a blow to lose this friend who had been so supportive of him for years. Shortly afterward, in the summer of 1969, Adrian wrote him that his appeal had gone to the Fifth Circuit in New Orleans to be argued. The Fifth Circuit extends from Miami all the way across

Texas, the court's home being in New Orleans. It was in Fort Worth that the court heard Adrian argue the appeal for Joe. There had been a famous bank robbery case tried in Miami at the same time Joe was on trial in Houston, the Blake case, and it had ended in acquittal for the defendant on the ground of irresistible impulse.

Adrian and Joe had attempted to get Judge Ingraham to instruct the jury on irresistible impulse, but the judge had declined to do so. The jury was not asked to think about that factor. Adrian wrote Joe that he was going to stress this omission.

Then one day, to Joe's surprise and jubilation, he received a wire from Adrian. The Joe Henry Hodges case was reversed and remanded. That meant it was completely reversed. The sixty-five years and the $65,000 fine were lifted in full in July of 1969. If Joe's case had been reversed and rendered he would have been cut loose entirely. However, remanded meant a new trial. The Appellate Court did not find Joe innocent, they merely reversed the outcome of the trial, finding that the judge had made an error in not having charged the jury with the irresistible impulse type of defense.

Joe would have been let out of prison immediately to go back to Houston and prepare to stand trial a second time on the Meyerland Bank case except that he still hadn't finished serving the time on his previous conviction due to the parole violation. When that had been served in full the Texas marshal came for Joe and brought him from Leavenworth back to the Rehabilitation Center in Houston where he spent one night in the tank before his release at eight-thirty in the morning. Even the horrors of the tank did not daunt his spirits.

Nancy was there at eight-thirty to meet him. She brought him home to Braeburn Street in Bellaire. It was a great day, and Nancy, Mark, and Amy were joyful and hopeful. The Strobels and Fonvilles walked across the street to greet Joe and the other neighbors came by. It was an exhilarating time for Joe despite the little dark cloud that hung above his head and was with him wherever he went.

CHAPTER 37

After the reunion with his friends, Joe had to face the inevitable resolution of the Meyerland case. There was no thought of gambling in his mind now. He was obsessed with one thing: avoiding a return to prison.

He dropped in to see his probation officer, Hugh Mack Johnson. Sympathetically Hugh Mack tried to give him some sense of direction that might help in the days to come as he attempted to plan for the retrial. He had a heavy charge pending and a tough judge, undoubtedly angered at the reversal of the satisfactory results of the first trial.

While Adrian Carter and those representing the government side discussed new trial dates, Joe secured a promise of work as a laborer at Todd Shipyards in the event he was given probation instead of a jail sentence. He hoped that after this lapse of time the government might take a less stringent stand on his case although he didn't have much hope of this.

Harry Newkirk paid Joe's air fares for two flights to Washington where he tried to enlist the aid of Texas senator John Tower. He even visited the Bureau of Prisons in the city, explained his situation, and asked for help when he went to court. He had a perfect prison record and perhaps that might help.

In an effort to secure some leniency for Joe, Senator Tower called Anthony Farris, the Assistant U. S. Attorney in Houston, who had taken over the case. Perhaps as a result of the senator's nudging, the attorney called Adrian and made him an offer. If Joe would plead guilty this time instead of putting the government to the expense of another trial, he would only be sentenced to five years. They would give him credit for two of the five years, including the last year in Leavenworth, if he would agree.

Joe and Adrian discussed the alternatives at great length. He was taking a gamble going back to trial. Judge Ingraham would undoubtedly give him the maximum sentence again. The next time around, if convicted as was likely, Joe could end up with sixty-five years and the judge, out of spite, could make the sentence run consecutively rather than concurrently.

Carl Cross, the psychiatrist who had spent so many hours analyzing Joe, could not be counted upon to do a better job in front of the jury than he had before. Don Stone, the prosecutor in the previous trial, who had shown some sympathy for Joe once he had secured the prosecution, was no longer an Assistant U. S. Attorney. Joe remembered the headlines in the paper during the previous trial when he had pleaded insanity and Stone's remarks to the newspapers had resulted in the headlines: HODGES CRAZY—LIKE A FOX says D.A.

Judge Ingraham was very careful about taking Joe's guilty plea, as Sarah Hughes had been before him. He had made one mistake and was wary of making another that might lead to Joe "walking." He spent a whole hour insisting that Joe reiterate that he was not pleading guilty as a result of promises made to him by the prosecutor, even though the judge and the prosecutor both knew this was the case.

Wearily, the judge allowed Joe and Adrian to present their case for probation. Several of Joe's friends appeared—Harry Newkirk, C. W. Conn, Pat and Robert Strobel; even an executive at Todd Shipyards was there, to confirm that Joe had a job waiting for him. Hugh Mack Johnson said it would serve no purpose for him to be sent back to the penitentiary. Then Adrian handed Ingraham a letter from Senator Tower which said in part, "It is apparent that society will gain nothing by your return to prison," and continued, "I feel confident that you will soon be making the significant contribution to society of which you are capable."

Ingraham reached over the bench and took the letter but didn't glance at it. Staring straight ahead, he simply dropped it to the bailiff a few feet below him.

When Ingraham rejected the letter of character appraisal from the senator who had appointed him to the federal court, Joe knew he was finished. And the judge, in fact, sentenced him to five years in the penitentiary and a $10,000 fine. Joe protested the fine saying that the judge had declared him a pauper and that to fine a pauper $10,000, which could keep him in jail indefinitely since he would have no means of paying it, was just not right. The judge, probably mindful of his previous mistake in not instructing the jury correctly at the trial, recanted and declared that the $10,000 was an uncommitted fine. This meant that when Joe's term was up he could leave the penitentiary even if the fine was not paid.

The harsh ruling from Judge Ingraham rocked Joe, but he asked for a week to get his affairs in order and this was granted.

One afternoon during his respite from prison, after walking the few blocks home from the shopping center where he had gone to buy Mark and Amy a token gift, he walked in and went through the kitchen to the backyard where Nancy and Margie O'Donnell, who had come to be especially close to Nancy, were in the midst of an intimate conversation. He could hear them clearly, and though a little ashamed of himself for eavesdropping, he stood quietly listening.

". . . Yes, Joe is an unusual man," Margie was agreeing. "And you are an unusual woman to be able to live with this situation. Most women wouldn't put up with it. But, Nancy, I honestly believe that if you can get through this bad time things will be different."

"I pray you're right, Margie. Oh, I hope when this is behind us Joe will be able to live like a normal man. We do have a good life sometimes, when Joe is home, when he isn't gambling. The happiest I've ever been in my life were those three years in Irving. We had friends and were a part of the community."

Margie placed an arm around her friend's shoulder. "It will come back. It's just sad that he is not being given a chance now. Don't listen to those people who say you should leave him, Nancy."

Joe could hear Nancy sigh deeply. "I never know from one day to the next where he'll be or what telephone calls I'm going to get from some bank or marshal. I know he doesn't mean to neglect us, but that's what he does. I'm always worried about him, about hot checks, about those places he goes to gamble. But that's all part of his life and I guess I'll never change him."

"Do you ever talk to him about it?" Margie asked.

"Of course. But then we got into those awful fights which leave both of us bitter—hating each other. It's so bad, especially if the children are around. I just let things slide by. It's easier that way. If only it wasn't for the gambling, what it does to him, to me, to the children . . ."

Nancy's mirthless laugh unsettled Joe as he listened to a conversation he wished he wasn't hearing. "Wives who only have to worry about another woman don't know what a vicious mistress gambling can be," Nancy said flatly. Joe slipped away, back into the living room and then out the front door. He was well aware of what he was doing to Nancy and her remarks had now made the pain of it almost unbearable.

During that final week in October, knowing each day was bringing him closer to a return to the penitentiary, Joe almost wished he'd let the marshal take him right from the courtroom back to the Rehab Center. He hoped that at least he'd be sent to the Texarkana penitentiary right in Texas, three hundred miles away from Houston; and parole from places like Seagoville and Texarkana are more easily achieved than from Leavenworth.

Once again he reported to Henry Baker, the marshal, and was taken out to the Rehab Center. There he waited for his assignment to a federal penitentiary praying it would not be Leavenworth again.

Then one day Henry Baker arrived to take him away. Joe asked where they were going but Henry said he couldn't tell him. Later he whispered, "We're going to the Big Top."

"Leavenworth! I can't believe it," Joe replied, stunned. He asked permission to let his wife and parents know where he was going but the marshal couldn't let him make a call. However, Baker said he'd let Nancy and his father know before they got to Leavenworth. The night on the road was spent in the drunk tank at the Oklahoma City jail; the next day it was Kansas City and then that monolithic abode of the dead looming up as the prison van approached. This was the stone tomb in which Joe would be incarcerated for another three years.

He went through the familiar processing at A&O once again, then spoke to the associate warden saying he'd only been away for six weeks and would like to get his old job back. He was fortunate and reported for work at the personnel office in the outer ring a few days later.

Larry Parker had been transferred to the Terre Haute penitentiary which was closer to his home. Joe missed his one really good prison friend, and while he and Larry had kept a no smoking pact between them when they were in prison before, he now started smoking again.

His first task once he had reentered Leavenworth was to try to get himself transferred to the Texarkana facility. About 2 percent of Leavenworth prisoners going before the parole board actually get paroled, whereas would-be parolees at some of the other federal facilities, such as Eglin in Florida and Texarkana, stand a much better chance.

In February of 1970 Joe was transferred to Texarkana and two weeks later his mother and father and Nancy drove up to see him. Now at least it was feasible for friends and family to visit him from time to time.

He was relieved to be in Texarkana, that much closer to home, although there were more youngsters there, more "jitterbugs" as they were called, and there was more contraband inside the institution because it maintained lax security compared to Leavenworth and was not cut off from the outside as much.

While closer association with the free world was morale-lifting in some ways, this very fact made it more difficult for the prisoners to adjust to incarceration.

Joe was able to see Mark and Amy from time to time and watch Amy grow from an infant to a young child. The forbidding building at Texarkana with the big high fence around it and the guards did not have any significance to Amy. To Mark, fast growing up and becoming aware of his surroundings, visiting his father in prison was a disturbing experience.

Joe made some friends at Texarkana and ran into a man he'd known at Seagoville who was now doing "a bit," as prisoners say, at this facility. He made his first appearance before the parole board seven months after his arrival. He had served one third of his five-year sentence. This did not mean that he would be out in a week, a month, or even a year, but at least he was starting on the process of parole.

He found himself a job in the recreation yard working under a corrections officer named John Clark, a football player. Clark was not one of the stereotypic cops that worked at the prison. He was there to have a good time and let the inmates have as good a time as possible, whether playing tag football or softball or participating in any other type of athletic recreation.

Joe worked out lifting weights and taking excess poundage off his body, trimming down for the day when he would finally get out. While he was on his health routine, he met Ernie Hall, former president of Westec, the Houston–New York corporation whose collapse had stripped Tim Fowler of his money and driven him to hounding Joe to the point where he got Joe's parole violated. In a way Joe could have considered Ernie Hall the author of his present jail sentence. If it hadn't been for that parole violation he could have been out on bail during the Meyerland case and perhaps won it in court.

But he spent some good time with Ernie Hall learning how the professionals play the stock market. Hall charted the market while he was at Texarkana, probably thinking of the millions that were lost in the Westec scandal. Joe never questioned him on the specifics of that. Such inquisitiveness was not considered good form in prison.

Inevitably there was homosexuality at Texarkana, and even more danger from it than at Leavenworth. Stabbings were routine. Joe made an effort to keep away from this community.

Joe's months in Texarkana were filled with vivid little episodes of prison life, but his thoughts were concentrated on parole. After his first appearance before the U. S. Board of Parole, he began a program to make every contact possible in order to get out of the place.

Senator Tower's secretary, Carolyn Ely, had kept in correspondence with Joe from time to time and was doing what she could to help. Tower himself wrote an outstandingly sympathetic letter on his behalf to the parole board. Joe's father and his friend Carroll Conn persuaded Judge Joe Fisher, the federal judge in Beaumont, to write a supportive letter. Judge Ingraham was now on the Fifth Circuit Appeal Court and no longer Joe's nemesis.

Nancy and Pat Strobel flew to Washington, D.C., and appeared before the parole board there. They also went up to see John Tower at his offices. Short on money, they took the low-cost all-night tourist flight and checked into their hotel. To their surprise they found themselves in the same elevator as Tower who was going up to the roof restaurant for breakfast.

Unfortunately, Pat and Nancy were too surprised and unprepared to introduce themselves. Just the same, they did go to the senator's office later that day and were promised all the help the senator could give in Joe's case.

On November 15, 1970, six weeks after Joe had first appeared before the parole board, he was called out of his job in the recreation yard by a caseworker handling his parole application. He was sure that his parole had come through and could hardly conceal his excitement when he walked into the office of A. W. Atkinson, an old veteran of the service, with whom he had established cordial relations.

Atkinson, who was on the phone when Joe walked into his office, wordlessly handed him the receiver. It was Nancy on the other end.

The day before, November 14, was the first day of the deer season. Joe's father had gone out on a hunt with his old friend Carroll Conn and several other friends who included a famous heart surgeon from the Denton Cooley Clinic.

From the tone of Nancy's voice Joe sensed what he was going to hear. Joe Hodges, Sr., had killed the first buck of the hunt and, an avid hunter, was highly excited. The doctor and Carroll Conn were about two hundred yards away when they saw him suddenly fall on top of the deer he was stripping. It took thirty or forty seconds for the heart surgeon and Carroll Conn to get to him but they were too late.

No heart specialist could have reached a heart attack victim any quicker. But out there at Hebronville, Texas, Joe's father died. Joe, stunned and heartbroken, could hardly believe it. His father had been out to visit him just two weeks before and seemed in fine health.

Joe's cousin by marriage, Bob Thomas, a Beaumont lawyer who had recently been appointed a judge, arranged with Atkinson for Joe to get a three-day furlough from prison and a plane ticket to Houston.

Nancy and C. W. Conn, Jr., who had also been with Joe's father when he died, drove to the airport, picked up Joe and drove him to Beaumont for the funeral.

Homer Fort, who had succeeded Dr. Tower as the preacher of the First Methodist Church of Beaumont and then gone to Liberty, Texas, returned to conduct the service. The church was full of Joe Sr.'s friends. After the funeral the procession drove to Forest Park Cemetery in Houston where Joe Sr. was interred in a family plot. Joe and Nancy's friends from Houston joined the funeral party after the interment ceremony.

The great tragedy of it all to Joe was that the event occurred while he was in the penitentiary. His father's death at seventy-six was in itself neither sad nor tragic. He died in a wonderful way, Joe thought. He died with his boots on, doing what he did best and elated over having distinguished himself by killing the first buck of the hunting season.

Joe's mother, Florence, a strong woman, took her husband's death with fortitude and dignity. She had never entered a grocery store during their marriage. Joe Sr. had done all the shopping and washed the dishes. He even did the laundry himself. He enjoyed his work around the house and being at home. Now she would have to live without the husband she had depended on for so much.

The loss of his faithful, forgiving father in these circumstances was excruciatingly painful to Joe. He remembered how his father used to brag about him.

Even after the disaster in Beaumont, when Joe got the job with Del Webb, his father was proud of him and talked about him to everybody that would listen. He was an optimist who always felt that given one more chance Joe would achieve the potential he had shown in so many ways.

Joe duly reported back to the Texarkana penitentiary and settled down to waiting for the parole board to give him an answer on his release.

Without a job awaiting him he could not be paroled. He

wrote to a cousin, Jack Gordon Folmer, who owned one of the largest airplane insurance businesses in the country, but Jack declined to give him a job.

Then Joe met Cliff Carling through a friend and fellow convict at Texarkana, Paul Carling, Cliff's brother. Cliff was the head of the Southwestern Business University and promised Joe a minor job as a salesman signing people up to take night courses which were federally sponsored.

In the middle of January 1971 he received the good news that his parole had been granted. The bad news was that it would be effective May 1, 1971, one hundred days away. Atkinson informed Joe of this date in his office and let him call collect to Nancy and tell her of his impending release which she would pass on to his mother and their friends.

A letter from Judge Fisher had been helpful. He wrote the parole board that after the death of Joe H. Hodges, Sr., Joe's mother badly needed her son. The letters from prominent people who knew Joe, including Senator Tower, had also lent weight to his petition. But he had a hundred days more to serve.

Joe wasted no time in putting in a request for transfer to the Community Treatment Center in Houston. These centers, halfway houses for convicts about to be released, are located in fifteen of the major cities in the country. Normally, when a prisoner with a good record gets down to the last three or four months of his sentence he can be transferred to a community center which is much like a large boardinghouse. The inmates at this one had to be in by eleven-thirty at night but were given all day to work at a job. CTC Houston was not a jail. Yet it was a reminder that the sentence was still being served.

A combination of circumstances destroyed Joe's hopes for finishing his sentence in CTC. First, Atkinson was retired and a young, unsympathetic caseworker who was hoping to make a name for himself in the federal prison administration took over Joe's case. Secondly, the Sharpstown bank scandal hit all of Texas politics in February of 1971. Some of the biggest men in Texas banking were indicted.

When Joe came up before the new caseworker his transfer to the CTC was refused. While he had nothing to do with the Sharpstown bank scandal, the caseworker told him that he was just too involved with all those banks to be allowed to walk around the streets of Houston free. Thus two scandals with which he had no connection, the collapse of Westec and the Sharpstown affair, seriously worked to his disadvantage.

Each day was a long and bitter one as he sweated out his sentence in the penitentiary. During his last five weeks he was approved to work outside the prison, coming back after work in the evening. He was given a job with a young man in Texarkana named Heywood Lloyd. Lloyd, with his partner Charles Jones, had formed a small company called Mid-South Oil Company. They were the first to build and operate self-service gasoline stations all over Texas and Arkansas and Joe was given a perfunctory job with the company.

Ernie Hall, the former Westec president, was a driver at the Texarkana prison, trusted to leave the confines of the facility, and it was Ernie who drove Joe and the other twelve inmates from Texarkana out to their jobs. Heywood Lloyd had a new Oldsmobile with a phone in it and he gave Joe carte blanche authority to make phone calls. Joe got an Arkansas driver's license and was able to drive the car around town calling Harry Newkirk, Nancy, Adrian, and his mother.

Lloyd was a sympathetic employer and at times called the prison to say he was going to keep Joe Hodges working a little later that night. Then he would take Joe home to supper and later return him to the prison.

Joe and Heywood became close friends during this period when Joe was so in need of a sympathetic ally in the free world.

By the time Joe's release date came about, he had never been in better physical condition in his life. He played handball and was pressing 220 to 230 pounds of weight ten times. His stomach was flat and muscular and he had acquired a healthy suntan working hard every day. He wanted to return to the world young and virile and try to recapture those days when his future seemed so bright.

In prison he was careful not to get into any type of gambling; he didn't even play in the poker games. He continued his nightly letter writing which was so important to him. And his friends from Dallas came to see him. Even Idus Ash paid him a visit.

The morning of Joe's release, May 1, Heywood picked him up

at the prison gate and took him home for breakfast. Heywood, his wife Jean, and their children all came to see him off on the bus to Houston. Once again Joe was out. Nancy met him at the bus station and that night she and their friends gave a welcome home dinner.

Joe had been let out on a Friday so he was able to enjoy a real weekend celebration. On Monday morning he reported to Hugh Mack Johnson, once again his parole officer. He had exactly two years of parole ahead of him and had made up his mind that this time he was not going to violate it. Hugh Mack did not insist that Joe report to him every month but let him mail in his reports.

Nevertheless, the future Joe faced was uncertain to say the least; he had an old $55,000 debt structure and he badly needed a job.

CHAPTER 38

Nancy Hodges had been supporting herself teaching school all the time Joe was in jail. Joe, with his meager job selling men on improving themselves by taking night business courses, was at last able to contribute to the household expenses.

However, it didn't take long for the business school job to irritate him. In the first place he didn't believe in what he was selling; secondly, the job kept him working at night because that was when his prospective buyers were to be found at home. As a result, he was always on the alert for another job opportunity.

Every day he visited insurance companies and lending institutions, seeking a job as an investigator. He told them frankly of his background and criminal record but stressed these would make him a particularly astute investigator. Unfortunately, nobody wanted to hire an ex-convict.

A friend from law school, Tom Arnold, recommended him for a job at the Institute of Behavioral Sciences which specialized in criminology and white collar fraud. Even here, where Joe could have been valuable, he was rejected for a job.

The inevitable happened. As one job after another failed to materialize, he began building up bankrolls for Las Vegas. This seemed his only recourse if he was to liquidate his debts and support his family. He went to a friend of his who had been released from the Texarkana prison, Jerry Gordon, and borrowed a total of $5,500 in two weeks. He borrowed from everybody he knew, fattening the bank account which he started in the Houston Citizens Bank.

A friend in Irving lent him $6,000. Charlie Wyche's family lent him $10,000. An acquaintance of his in Houston was in the advertising agency business and he had a backer interested in financing the agency. Joe arranged a loan for the backer and made a $6,000 commission on that.

As fast as he was able to make these loans he lost them in Las Vegas, raising his debt structure still higher. When he ran out of cash he reverted to beating the casinos on hot checks. A typical trip to Vegas occurred while he was selling the self-improvement business course. Because his wife was a schoolteacher Joe was able to join the Houston area's Teachers Credit Union from which he borrowed $8,000 without telling Nancy. He borrowed another $4,000 from friends who sympathized with his efforts to make a living while just out of prison.

With a $10,000 bankroll he called his old prison friend Larry Parker who had also just been released on parole. They met at the Houston airport and together enplaned for Las Vegas.

Arriving at 8 P.M., Joe and Larry proceeded directly to the Desert Inn casino. By three the following morning Joe had blown his $10,000. He had played hard and extravagantly. His bankroll had gone up and down before he finally lost the last of it. As Larry Parker watched in surprise, Joe turned to the crap table banker. "Let me have five thousand," he demanded. The dealer looked at him hesitantly.

"Give it to him," the pit boss behind the dealer assented. The chips were slid across to Joe and he started gambling again. As he was laying his bets the pit boss walked up to him.

"Do you have a credit line with us?" he asked.

"No, I don't have any credit with you. My name is Henry Hodges from Houston. I'll give you a check when I get through." Joe summoned up his righteous indignation act. It was three in the morning and while they couldn't call Houston, they might be able to discover the various bogus checks he had laid along the Strip over the past twenty-odd years.

He continued to gamble under the watchful eye of the pit boss and finally, when he was back up to $10,000, he took $5,000 worth of chips from his rack and slid them across the table to the dealer, extinguishing the loan. The pit boss's constant stare made Joe nervous so, having already taken a successful swing at the casino, he cashed in his other $5,000 worth of chips and left the Desert Inn for more congenial surroundings.

Down the Strip at the Dunes, Joe and Larry settled down to another crap table and Joe began his usual bold betting. Despite his skill, betting with the most advantageous mathematics, he soon lost the $5,000 and was broke again. Once more he asked the bank dealer at the table for $5,000 worth of chips. This time the pit boss confronted him directly. "Do you have a credit line with us?"

"No, I don't," Joe growled. "My name is Henry Hodges from Houston."

"I'm afraid we can't take a check until morning, Mr. Hodges," the pit boss replied apologetically. "We have a policy on checks that we clear them immediately."

"Well I'll be a sonofabitch," Joe began his routine. "I've been coming out here for twenty-five years and I've never asked you for a dime's worth of credit and I'm not now. I've always cashed checks here."

Joe needed that $5,000 badly. The action was waiting and he knew he could win. The more desperate he felt the more brazen he became and finally the pit boss, resignedly, motioned for the dealer to give him $5,000 worth of chips. Joe took a check from his pocket and began writing it out. "While I'm at it, I might as well make it for ten thousand. I'm not going to get much action for five."

The pit boss shrugged and nodded to the dealer again. Another $5,000 worth of $100 chips were slid across the table to him. Joe handed the $10,000 check to the pit boss. It was two hours later in Houston, so it would not be until 7 A.M. in Las Vegas that they could contact the bank. That gave him plenty of time.

Once again Joe plunged into the crap game. Fiercely he attacked all the numbers as a shooter stepped up and began rolling the dice. With his debt structure now at $55,000, he hoped to be able to pay at least half of it off. His goal was $27,500. No, he had to win $37,500. Ten thousand would have to be used to make the check good.

Larry Parker, a skilled gambler himself, felt his heartbeat quicken as Joe fought his bankroll upward toward his goal. He hit his $27,000 and then the $30,000 mark. He turned to Larry and gave him a wan smile. "Seventy-five hundred to go. Then we get out of here."

Anxiously Larry watched as Joe continued to pile up the chips in front of him—up two thousand, down a thousand, up a thousand, down three, then up again. By six o'clock in the morning the pit boss, who had cashed the check for him, went off duty and a new crew came in. Joe was back down below $30,000 now and had no intention of quitting until he made his goal. His mind could not accept what he knew to be the truth: that he would be well advised to take his winnings, make the bad check good, and walk out of Las Vegas ahead. That $37,500 had become an *idée fixe*. And he had to win and get out before the banks opened in Houston.

Larry marveled at both Joe's stamina and his skill. How could a man keep going so long, his mind constantly attuned to the odds, and hold his own, even win, in an intricate betting process that favored the house? As the clock moved toward six-thirty Joe became more desperate. He well knew that on the stroke of seven the casino manager would be on the phone to the bank in Houston checking on him. Going to another casino wouldn't solve the problem. The word would flash up and down the Strip like lightning. In his efforts to win fast he doubled his bets, pressing, continuing to press—and then, in a matter of ten minutes, his last chip was raked in by the dealer and he was broke again.

Beaten, busted, he walked out of the casino, Larry Parker beside him, and they took a cab out to the airport where they split up, Larry going back home to Illinois, Joe working his way through Denver back to Houston.

Well, Joe thought, sitting on the plane, getting over the depression of his loss, he still had spots open at home and of course he could always try some sort of credit deal with the Las Vegas casinos. There were scores of casinos out there, he reckoned; and even if he couldn't go to the Dunes, there were plenty of other places he could go.

Every day Joe was in his car driving around the greater Houston area, particularly out along the Gulf Freeway on the way to Galveston, selling the business course. Wherever he looked along the Freeway he saw "For Sale" signs on plots of land. As he drove here and there, seeking potential students for the business college and borrowing money, he began to conceive a real estate venture.

He noted the phone numbers of the sellers of the roadside tracts he thought were particularly valuable. Houston was in an enormous boom. Everything was moving ahead in 1971. Land speculators were making fortunes, new oil discoveries were being made, and the city was becoming the medical center of the world, with an army of doctors earning between $150,000 and $250,000 a year on the average. Everybody was making money, and none more so than the promoters and the speculators.

There was certainly room for a Joe Hodges to make money as well. He decided that he would get into the fringe real estate market in Houston. He began calling the sellers he had noted. Prices ranged from $2.75 per square foot down to 25¢ a square foot.

He investigated one of the tracts owned by a company called Fairlane Corporation. Calling the phone number at Fairlane, he was put in contact with John Howard, chairman of the board of the company. Howard told Joe the price was $15,000 an acre but that if he was interested to come by the company's offices and speak to Jess Brown, the company's real estate officer.

Fifteen thousand dollars an acre was close to 35¢ a foot and that turned Joe on. He felt that there was leverage there. He went over to Fairlane's offices and met with Jess Brown. Joe was dressed up in his vested suit, carrying his attaché case and looking every inch the prosperous business executive.

The property Joe was interested in was part of the city of Houston but way out on the fringe, almost into the city of Pasadena on the Gulf Freeway and in the direction of Del Webb's Clear Lake City. Joe knew that this was a good piece of property in a good area. Jess Brown gave him a set of plats—maps showing the property for sale—which revealed that it was a long strip between four hundred and five hundred feet deep along the Gulf Freeway stretching from one intersection of an interchange to another. This, of course, made for easy access to the property.

There certainly seemed to be a great deal of promise for this land. While Joe was calling on the sellers, he also renewed his relationship with Bill Robinson, whom he'd met while in Texarkana and who was now a promoter of dinner theaters. Joe felt that the dinner theater business could be very lucrative in Houston. It was the glamor type of investment that many Houston big earners would like to get into as a relief from the rather mundane if highly lucrative businesses in which they were working. It seemed to him that this piece of property out on the edge of Pasadena, which itself had a population of 150,000 people, was an ideal site for a dinner theater. A dinner theater could be sold and promoted as an entertainment bargain. For $8.50 a patron could have a good roast beef dinner and see a New York play with a New York road company cast. Seventeen dollars was a bargain price for a couple to enjoy a fine evening of entertainment.

Joe took the plats of the property to Ben Kostial who was immediately impressed with its possibilities. He also showed Ben the plans for the dinner theater and introduced him to Bill Robinson, a brassy young showman type who wore white alligator cowboy boots and highly styled suits with ruffled shirts and a string tie. Naturally, a ten-gallon hat went with the outfit.

Using the dinner theater idea as a basis for developing the property, Joe felt that they could buy it and, with some dazzling development propositions thrown in, resell it immediately at a profit. However, he knew that another gimmick was necessary to make a fast turnover of such property. He was intent on selling the sizzle rather than the steak, something at which he had always been adept.

In 1971 and 1972 investors were disillusioned with the stock market and looking for a safe place to put their money. Investments in savings and loan associations, insurance companies, and other types of financing institutions were rocketing, keeping pace with the success of Houston. As a result, the lending corporations in Texas found themselves inundated with money and anxious to get it out and working. Joe and Ben studied the property on the Gulf Freeway which Joe had checked on and approached John Howard directly, securing a price of $85,000 for the six-acre-plus tract.

Ben called his friend Howard Hamilton in Dallas who represented the Modern Security Life Insurance Company out of Springfield, Missouri. Hamilton was adept at putting together loans. Joe called on Mrs. Marguerite Taylor at the Guardian Title Company to examine the title to a six-acre tract of land. Satisfied, he gave her a check for $1,000, on an account in which he had no money, as earnest money on the purchase until he could arrange for the cash to purchase it.

Then Ben and Joe went up to Dallas to see Hamilton with plats of the property and aerial photographs. They also took with them a new appraisal showing a value of $300,000 on the property. In Dallas, with Hamilton's help, they arranged for a loan of $195,000 secured by the property. Wayne Henson, president of the insurance company, would have had to go to the board of directors if they'd asked for any more than that amount. It took about two weeks to close the deal, the loan having been made by Modern Security Life. The key was the appraisal which they got from Roger Boswell, a past president of the Society for Real Estate Appraisers. With the money in hand from the loan Joe went back to the lawyer, John Howard, and Mrs. Taylor who had held the earnest money Joe had given her to bind the deal. They paid the $85,000 in cash from the proceeds of the loan, purchased the property, and then split $110,000 of the overloan with Howard Hamilton who had arranged the loan. Half went to Joe and Ben and half to Hamilton.

When Joe and Ben split their proceeds they had $27,500 each in cash plus the land itself. Modern Security Life had given them ten years to pay off the loan, the first payment due one year from the date that the financing was closed. Now Joe was onto a good thing and riding again. He and Ben had discovered a new way to make a lot of money fast.

Reducing the potential real estate deals down to their essentials, Joe evolved a formula which worked. Confidence in land was far stronger than it was in business and the lending institutions were flush with funds and actively seeking to make loans. There were three elements to a deal. First was the land itself, second was the purchaser of the land, and third was the lending institution. The trick was to get a piece of property appraised for two or three times its cost, and it was not hard to do this in

Houston. As the future proved, all land in and around Houston was increasing in value 300 and 400 percent in just a few years, certainly less than the life of a loan.

John Howard and Fairlane Corporation, which owned tracts of land up and down the Gulf Freeway, quickly analyzed the first deal Joe and Ben had made and realized they could have charged more. When Joe came back to buy a ten-acre tract of property, the price had gone from $15,000 to $20,000 an acre. Thus, the second tract cost them $200,000 and they needed to find a buyer with a strong-enough financial statement so that he could be given a loan for $400,000. Then the buyer not only owned the land on an equitable financing basis, but the other $200,000 was split between the buyer, Joe and Ben.

Joe went actively seeking new life insurance companies and savings and loan institutions that were making loans. Once Howard Hamilton at Modern Security Life had seen how easily the first deal went through, he realized what a lucrative position he was in. Naturally Ben and Joe wanted to circumvent him if they could, and they looked for key men who could swing loans within their company and take a smaller piece from the overloan profits.

Part of the sizzle in increasing the value of a tract of land along the Gulf Freeway was the intention of building a dinner theater. Joe and Bill Robinson put together elaborate plans for the theater and surrounding parking area, and these plans were incorporated with the plats and aerial photos in making an appraisal presentation to the lending institutions.

The next important facet of the situation was to create the owner borrower. With doctors making so much money Ben and Joe put together small syndicates of doctors, whose aggregate worth would be three, four, or five times the amount of the loan being sought. With the borrower firmly emplaced and his net worth statement prepared through Joe's competent handling of figures, the next step was to go to the lending institutions with the financial statements and appraisals and get the loan set up. This involved a double closing. Simultaneously with the loan being made to the final purchaser, Joe and Ben purchased the land from the original owner, Joe keeping the two parties apart though close together in an office so that all checks could be exchanged simultaneously. This took considerable juggling, and while on the surface it might have appeared unorthodox, in the long run everybody won. That was Houston.

For Joe it was a curious and most joyous phenomenon that as his legitimate earnings increased so did his luck in gambling. His trips to Las Vegas in 1972 invariably ended up with comfortable wins. He was still getting beaten in Bobby Wilks's crap games and still couldn't handicap basketball, but what he lost consistently to the Houston bookmakers, he always made up in Las Vegas.

Many individuals, particularly doctors, wanted to buy land for investment purposes and at the same time put into their bank accounts $50,000 or $100,000 cash as a result of the overloan. Joe was handling the owners of the land tracts such as John Howard and making the deals at the lending institutions. Ben was providing those of his friends and acquaintances whose statements of personal worth could be used where it was possible to make the loans to buy the land.

From the beginning of his real estate transactions in partnership with Ben in the late fall of 1971, until his parole was extinguished on May 1, 1973, Joe profited handsomely on his side of the deals. Meantime he was flying out to Las Vegas where he scored twelve consecutive times, winning from $40,000 to $70,000 a trip playing baccarat and craps. He was in one of those streaks where he couldn't lose for winning.

Joe's credit rating was triple A now and he could easily make a loan at the Houston Citizens Bank. Joel Taylor, the senior vice-president, was liberal with him when he came in and explained he needed a loan to make a real estate deal. He was building up a large supply of cash, and he had $510,000 hidden in the attic of his house.

CHAPTER 39

The end of Joe's winning streak coincided almost exactly with that happy first of May when his parole was terminated and he was free of all legal encumbrances. Everything had been winners for him except the annoying losses to the Houston bookies and the Bobby Wilks crap game.

To celebrate the end of his parole, Joe decided to go out to Las Vegas with a group of his Houston gambling pals and enter the annual gin rummy tournament. Before leaving he called the commodity exchange room at the prestigious brokerage firm of Paine Webber and got a new young broker on the line, Mike Fields.

"What's interesting today?" Joe asked.

"Well, you can get into the wheat-corn spread," Mike replied.

"What's that?" He'd bought wheat and he'd bought corn but he didn't understand the spread.

"You buy wheat long—we're sure it will go up; and you buy corn short—looks like the price of corn futures will go down tomorrow. They'll balance each other off in any case, so you can't lose and you'll probably be sitting with a big profit."

"What's the price?"

"Two hundred dollars a contract," Mike replied.

"Sounds good. Give me sixty contracts. I'll be down with a check at noon." Joe was ebullient. He was winning, he was heading for Las Vegas with his action-loving crowd, and he had a reasonable bet going on corn and wheat which he didn't completely understand but which sounded solid. He went to his bank and picked up a certified check for $12,000 which he took to the commodity room and presented to Mike who gave him an anguished look.

"I made a mistake, Mr. Hodges. Those contracts are selling for two thousand, not two hundred dollars." Then he added brightly. "But I went ahead and bought you your sixty contracts."

"Hold on a minute, son. Now you're talking about a one hundred twenty thousand investment." Joe looked up at the board. "How's it doing?"

"Oh, wheat's way down and corn's gone up. I'm afraid you're a bad loser at the moment. Of course it can all change tomorrow." Joe had arrived at twelve fifty-five and he watched the board fix the prices at the one o'clock closing.

He was shocked at the loss but said nothing. "Well here, I brought you this." He dropped the $12,000 check on the counter in front of the young broker. "I've got a meeting to go to." Disgruntled, he left the brokerage office and went directly to the airport to get the flight for Las Vegas. By the time he was in the air with Larry Parker, who had flown in from Decatur, Illinois, to join him, he was back in a jovial mood again, putting aside the commodity fiasco for the time being.

He was still in high spirits when they arrived in Vegas, and he and Larry headed straight for the Stardust casino.

The gin rummy tournament opened the next day at noon and Joe wanted to get in some advance action. He hit the Stardust with a run of luck which he exploited for everything he was worth. He had arrived in Vegas with a $30,000 bankroll so he had plenty of money to ride out the rough spots as he shot craps until, at midnight, he was a $90,000 winner. It had been a marvelous play. He turned in his winnings plus his bankroll, $120,000, for safekeeping at the cashier's cage and went upstairs to his room and slept soundly.

At seven-ten the next morning, nine-ten in Houston, he knew the commodity market was open. He decided to check on the opening prices of his wheat-corn spread, but instead of calling Paine Webber he called Merrill Lynch.

"What's December corn doing?" he asked, only to be told it was up strong. "And December wheat?" Way down. The broker quoted the figures and Joe hung up. He did some figuring and discovered that he was a $140,000 loser on yesterday's commodity transaction. He was furious. A little old twelve-grand plunge had cost him a hundred and forty big ones.

Joe was mad, both at the broker and himself. But he didn't call Mike at Paine Webber, thinking perhaps the situation would correct itself as the day went on. But in his gambler's mind he had suddenly changed from a $90,000 winner to a $50,000 loser. Even though it was the broker's mistake, Joe had let the bet ride, so to speak, not calling him on the $1,800 difference on the contracts, and he fully intended to pay.

At seven-thirty, without even bothering to stop for orange juice and coffee, he hit the crap tables and recklessly gambled for four hours. Before noon he had lost his entire $120,000. He went home furious, enraged at himself and the broker, without even checking in at the gin rummy tournament.

The next day he appeared at Paine Webber where a frantic Mike Fields said he'd been trying to locate him for two days. By the end of the week the market had corrected itself to a point where the broker sold Joe out for a loss of $40,000. Joe refused to pay and the broker ended up only with the check for $12,000. But the incident had precipitated the downslide. As if to seal the termination of Joe's Houston high, two days later he went up to his attic, took another $30,000 from the half million cash horde, went out to Las Vegas and lost it in thirty-two minutes.

CHAPTER 40

The wheat-corn spread and the ensuing large loss in Vegas developed into a losing streak that seemed to have a malicious will of its own. The bookies, Wilks, and Vegas all began snatching back the fruits of Joe's glorious wins.

Slowly the stacks of $100 bills stashed in his attic dwindled, and as they did, so did Joe's ability to relate to Nancy. It was not that he didn't love her. Rather, he was so consumed with his losing that nothing else, no one else could enter his private world.

Normally a compulsive gambler loses all interest in sex when he is at the table. So possessive a mistress is gambling that even when the play is finished, the need to plan the logistics of the next play leaves no room for other thoughts, other drives. He seldom takes a female companion to Las Vegas, nor does he avail himself of the beautiful girls at the casinos. This lack of interest in sex is perhaps the most constant behavioral phenomenon that an enlightened psychiatrist looks for in determining whether or not he is dealing with a compulsive gambler.

Week after week Joe took Bill Robinson to Las Vegas with him. Though deeply in the trough of a losing streak, he was certain on each trip that he would win. But even his skill at betting the baseball games seemed to have deserted him.

After losing $60,000 between Bobby Wilks and the bookies in one week, he flew to Las Vegas with $10,000 in his pocket, resolved to leave with $70,000—his $10,000 bankroll plus the $60,000 he had lost. Bill followed him to the baccarat table.

"Who was the last winner?" Joe asked.

"The players," the dealer answered.

Joe took out a $5,000 stack of $100 bills, broke the wrapper and put it beside him to help him keep track of how much he was betting. "Three hundred dollars on the players," he announced, placing the bet on the players' square in front of him. He had decided to use a system called "following" on this trip to the baccarat table. Hopefully in baccarat, either the players or the bank have a prolonged winning streak, and Joe's strategy now was to stay with the players as long as they were winning, then slide over to the bank the first time they lost and slide back again the first time the bank lost. Betting on the bank entailed a 5 percent commission to the house.

He hit it lucky. The players were in a winning streak and hand after hand Joe doubled his bets, pressing until he was betting the limit of $4,000 on a turn of the cards. There were eight decks of cards in the shoe which meant about twelve minutes of playing time before the cards were shuffled again and put back in the shoe for a new deal. After four hours of play, when he calculated he had hit his $70,000 goal, Joe cashed in his chips.

With Bill Robinson, who had won $3,000 or $4,000 following Joe's play, he walked over to the cashier's cage, turned in his chips and asked that the money be given to him in $5,000 increments wrapped in a bank seal. He left $50,000 in the cage and took the other $20,000 up to his room. The house sent a girl to visit him, to tire him out, or perhaps to get him excited so that he would come down and bet some more.

Wearily, Joe passed the girl over to Bill and slept for a few hours. Having reached his goal, his only desire was to get back to Houston. He felt triumphant that he had broken the losing streak that had dogged him through May and June, but he was unable to sleep any longer than the period of time required to erase his exhaustion. He was anxious to get home.

After showering and putting on a clean shirt, he was ready to go out to the airport. He called Bill's room and told his companion to meet him downstairs. Then he counted his money again. Joe was meticulous about knowing to the last penny how much cash was in his bankroll. To his surprise he counted $19,500. He was $500 short of his goal. For a few moments he wondered if

Bill had helped himself to $500, but he knew Bill wouldn't have done that. Somehow he had miscounted. Five hundred dollars short of his goal. Well, he'd soon cure that.

He went directly to the baccarat table and without sitting down asked the dealer, "Who won the last hand?"

"The players," the dealer replied.

"Five hundred dollars on the players," Joe cried, throwing five $100 bills onto the players' square. The players lost. Now Joe was $1,000 short of his goal. "One thousand on the bank," he said, throwing the money onto the table. Instinctively he had felt that the cards were "chopping" now, going aimlessly from bank to player with no winning streaks occurring. He would have bet the first $500 on the bank, as his gut instinct had told him to do, but that would have required a $25 commission and even if he won he would still be $25 short of his $70,000 goal. This time the bank lost, the players won. He was down $1,500.

Grimly he sat down at the table to win back the $1,500, managing his money more effectively, he thought. Now his bets were $100 and $200. But the cards in the baccarat shoe were chopping up his bankroll. He opened up a new wrapper of $5,000. He began to win. And with the winning came a more reckless betting system. Back to $300 and $500 bets on each turn of the cards. In a matter of fifteen minutes, with an anxious Bill looking on, he sat with three wrappers in front of him and no cash. He'd lost $19,500.

"Give me five thousand in chips," he commanded. The chips were slid across the table to him. The baccarat boss was well aware that $50,000 was sitting safely in the cashier's cage credited to Joe H. Hodges' account. The game went on, Bill canceling flights as Joe doggedly fought to regain his goal.

He was still feeling invincible because of his win the night before and continued to play. When he lost the first $5,000, he considered himself a $5,000 loser, not a $64,500 winner. All the gambler could think was, "Oh my God, I'm a five grand loser. I've got to get it back."

He was losing ten or twelve bets before winning one and the money was flowing away from him. He tried to manage his money more carefully, cutting down to smaller bets—$200, $300, $400, sometimes $600 a pop. Then he'd win once again, become encouraged, think he'd turned it around as he had so many times before in the past year.

He won three $2,000 bets in a row and kept going, fighting to get back to $70,000. The cards were chopping him, hitting, missing, hitting, missing. But he couldn't stop chasing after the goal. His thoughts occasionally turned to Bache & Company, Paine Webber, Jackson and Curtis, and E. F. Hutton. He was fast blowing the small fortune in his attic and this time he was not going to go home without making some of it back. Wheat, corn, pork bellies, sugar, cocoa, copper—the commodities were draining him.

Suddenly, he was surprised and shocked to be told by the baccarat pit boss that he had used up all the money credited to him in the cashier's cage. He had gone through $69,500 in the grip of a mad compulsion to win $500. Stunned, he pushed his chair back from the baccarat table. Silently he left the casino, with an equally silent Bill.

At the airport Joe bought a newspaper and on the way back to Houston picked out the ball games he would bet on as soon as he got there. There was still a comfortable $150,000 cash left up in the attic. He had no debts, he was clean at the banks, his borrowing power was strong. By the time he had picked out his bets and the plane was nearing Houston, he was once again relaxed and cheerful. He knew he had the winners.

It was hard for Bill Robinson to understand the change of mood. What he didn't know was that once a compulsive gambler has conceived his plan for the next big win, he is back in control of his emotions.

Five minutes after the plane landed, Joe was on the phone calling in an ambitious $20,000 combination on the baseball games for that afternoon and evening. Then he took a cab directly to E. F. Hutton's commodity room. He had a hunch on soybeans that would surely extinguish his losing streak.

As the summer of 1973 moved into the fall, Joe's losses continued. All of the $100 bills in his attic seemed to be melting away. His deals continued and a trip to Chicago to secure a loan for a group of investors put together by Adrian Carter was a success. His commission on that was $25,000 which he split with Adrian.

Nancy was as steadfast as always though she could see the dark clouds gathering that would signal another cycle of debts and trouble with the law. But Joe, after the years of horror his gambling had wrought, could not talk to her about his fears and shortcomings. He and she were becoming strangers.

Nor would Joe go to Cindy, even though she was the only person in the world in whom he could confide. Sex seemed to have dropped out of his life.

CHAPTER 41

Joe had never been out of touch with Harry Newkirk, and Harry had been pleading with him to come to Pensacola to take over the financial aspects of a gravel pit he and a group of his associates owned.

Well, Joe had run out of borrowing spots in Houston and he needed to try something new.

For several months Nancy had seen the inevitable coming. She had seen it before and recognized the signs. In the fall of 1973 people began calling Joe about the money he owed them.

In early September, Nancy realized she had to get a job again and applied for a teaching position. Five days after her classes began, her mother suffered a fatal stroke as she was sitting in a cafeteria. She was kept alive artificially for ten days, although she had suffered instant brain death. It was a blessing when she died.

With Nancy's school-teaching money they had acquired their first home, but early in October of 1973, when Joe had gone through the last of the cash he had stashed in the attic and all his other assets, he sold his bookie Art Cohan a lien on the house for $20,000. Art gave Joe the money but neglected to go down to the courthouse and register his lien. As a result, this mortgage did not show up in the real estate records of Harris County.

Knowing he was going to have to move out of Houston, Joe took steps to sell the house. When he found a buyer, the latter drew up a contract under whose terms Joe and Nancy would sell the house and receive $51,000 in equity from the sale. No mention of the unregistered lien was made so the bookie was not paid.

Possessed of a contract for the sale of their house, Joe found it easy to make loans against the closing. Finally, the day before Thanksgiving, he closed the sale. Being unable to make the payments on his and Nancy's cars, he had returned the vehicles to the respective mortgagees. Joe, Nancy, Mark, and Amy left Houston and drove in a rented car to Pensacola where Joe, with the help of Harry Newkirk, rented a small house on the north side of town. Joe had $30,000 in cash with him from the sale of the house when they left Houston.

Harry Newkirk, musician, music teacher, and deal promoter, had assembled a small group of friends who had borrowed $300,000 to buy and mine a large gravel pit in Atmore, Alabama, fifty-two miles north of Pensacola, Florida. Gravel is the stuff of which great buildings are made and the whole area around these two towns was booming. Construction was at an all-time high and the demand for quality gravel, cement, and other building supplies was insatiable. It looked like a surefire deal.

In his previous trips to Pensacola, Joe had put together a nine-page report analyzing Aggregate Developers, Inc., the name Newkirk's associates had chosen for their gravel mining operations. All the partners had been impressed with the acumen Joe showed in his analysis and with the recommendations he made. The group which put the money into the gravel mine did not contain one businessman. There was Frank Tugwell, a surgeon, Tommy Thompson, who owned a large motel in Pensacola and lived partly off the income from his wife Harriet's considerable estate, Winston Reynolds, a senior officer of the Pensacola Loan and Savings, and Louis Barrow, a dentist.

Soon after Joe arrived in Pensacola he began taking charge. He wanted no title in the company but he was, after a unanimous vote of the directors, the only officer of the company who could write checks. All money from this point on would funnel through Joe H. Hodges. Once more he was settling in, getting his roots into a new situation. Mark and Amy went off to school and liked Pensacola. The furniture was en route to their rented house, on which Joe had signed a six months' lease at $200 a month, paying the whole six months in advance.

Although Joe had $30,000, he wanted to get solidly into a banking situation in Pensacola and he knew the best way to do that was to borrow money and then pay it back. Winston Reynolds, who was well respected in the community as well as in the banking sector of Pensacola business, took him into the Charter Bank and introduced him to an officer named Lonny Gilmore. Joe showed Gilmore the contract to sell his house, not mentioning that the deal had already been closed and the money received. He told the banker he would be getting the money in about three or four weeks but he needed a little money in a bank account right then.

When Winston Reynolds told Lonny Gilmore that Joe was the new de facto treasurer of their gravel business, throwing in a hearty endorsement of his character at the same time, Gilmore immediately loaned Joe $10,000 on an unsecured note at the Charter National Bank in Pensacola. Joe promptly opened a bank account at the Charter Bank with the money. He was just getting his position consolidated and wasn't planning to catch a plane to Las Vegas. At the moment, his whole thrust was to establish himself in Pensacola.

Although Joe had written a glowing report on the future possibilities of the gravel mining business, he had private reservations about them. Nevertheless, Winston Reynolds was extremely effective in pumping money for the enterprise and this made him one of the most important owners of the company. He could go to the Barnett Bank or the Bank of Pensacola and secure loans. After all, he'd been the treasurer of the biggest and oldest savings and loan association in the state for over twenty-five years.

Winston and Harry between them had pumped almost $300,000 into the gravel pit, and already, as Joe studied the situation on the spot, he began to wish he had told Harry something like, "Okay, I'll join you in Pensacola but let's get into something like real estate where we can make some money."

Joe lived to regret not following his instincts. Before he was finished he would pump a total of $686,000 down the pit.

There was great demand all over southern Florida for gravel. Mountains of it are required to construct an office building, and it was needed for the new roads that were going in all over the two-state area. But it only sold for $3 a cubic yard, a cubic yard weighing a little more than a ton, and none of the partners in ADI knew how to mine it. Joe Hodges was working strictly on the financial end of the business, and the expertise of Harry Newkirk, who ran the mine when he was there, lay in other directions.

Harry had gone up to Milwaukee and bought $200,000 worth of heavy equipment, big draglines, and dredges to get the gravel out of the pit. The existing dredge had created its own lake from its digging operations and was floating on the water that had flooded the pit from the water table.

Joe had walked into a situation where a music teacher, a doctor, a dentist, a savings and loan association officer due for retirement, and a motel owner were using heavy technical equipment under adverse circumstances with the aid of a single engineer whose main purpose was to get money from the partners and run.

He soon determined that the heavy equipment Harry had purchased in Milwaukee was obsolete, the $200,000 the partners had spent, a loss. They were in debt $300,000 when Joe came into the picture.

Joe told Nancy after they'd been in Pensacola for only a few weeks that the gravel deal was no good. She disagreed. She had met the partners and was fond of them all. If they thought it was good, who was Joe to say it wasn't?

"Nancy, I don't know anything about the gravel business but I can smell that this deal is not going to work." Nevertheless, Joe had sound reasons for staying in Pensacola, one being that it was a fair distance from Houston.

There were a lot of people looking for Joe in Houston and he was not anxious that they should find him. He had given as his forwarding address the construction office of the gravel pit in Atmore, Alabama. Sometimes as many as ten or fifteen dunning letters and payment-overdue notices arrived there in a single day. But nobody could find him in Atmore—he had built a successful shield for Nancy, Mark, and Amy. Art Cohan by now had discovered that his $20,000 cash against Joe's house was irredeemable, and he and the other creditors were on the warpath.

A few weeks after Joe had made the loan, he went back to Lonny Gilmore at the bank and paid the $10,000 note. Now his credit was established. He was in business.

He discovered that the gravel company owed the IRS $23,000. Of course he had a $300,000 indebtedness to the IRS himself, but this was in Houston and there was no connecting the Joe H. Hodges of Houston with the J. Henry Hodges of Pensacola.

Meantime the gravel pit was swallowing money as fast as they could pump it, though there was always the promise of big gravel sales ahead. A $45,000 loan was arranged in Chicago and a $60,000 loan in Mobile. The group already owed Pensacola Loan and Savings $168,000, the Barnett Bank $25,000, and other banks and lending institutions, including IT&T, $190,000.

Joe and Harry moved doggedly forward trying to make the gravel pit work, but over the next year the company lost $686,000 in additional borrowed funds. Joe and the partners signed personal notes of responsibility for the loans, all in the name of ADI, and their wives had to be on the notes as well.

With the heavy equipment virtually useless, Joe got in touch with the sellers of the equipment in Milwaukee, Bob Brauer and his partner Bill O'Brien. By now all the money that came into ADI went into an ADI account with only Joe Hodges as the signator.

Joe was concerned about his Houston lists. Joel Taylor, president of the Houston Citizens Bank, found his address in Pensacola and Joe had to fly back and see him. He owed Houston Citizens almost $20,000. He had put most of the $30,000 he brought to Pensacola into ADI. He felt that he must show his faith in the operation even though he had serious misgivings about it.

Harry's engineer, Mark Brockston, had left the gravel mine and gone down to Mexico. From there he called Harry and Winston Reynolds and convinced them that he had discovered a silver mine he could buy for them.

Harry and Winston insisted that Joe send Brockston $16,000, which he did against his better judgment. This was after they'd already sent $20,000 before Joe knew about it. Brockston soon arrived in Pensacola from Mexico with a box of gold and silver coins which he said had been minted from the same vein that went through the mine he had found. Harry, Winston, and the others were impressed despite Joe's warnings.

As it became obvious the pit was a loser, Joe began flying to Las Vegas once again, his trips made possible by the money that was coming through ADI and Joe's personal account. He discovered that flying via Atlanta was the best route, but it was a six-hour flight and very tiring.

His luck seemed to have turned. On his second venture, for which he had Tommy Thompson as a companion, he won $80,000. Elated, once again vindicated as a man who could save the day for his friends, he brought the whole sum back to Pensacola. On a super high he paid back the money he owed in Pensacola, as well as some he owed in Houston, and put the balance in the ADI account.

Perhaps the most positive step Joe was able to take in trying to turn the gravel pit into a healthy operation was to get Bob Brauer and his partner involved in the company. They knew heavy equipment and, equally to the point, they did not at first see the weakness in the gravel operation, even though they were good businessmen. Joe was paying off individual owners' personal loans out of company receipts; Harry Newkirk had taken a loan out on one of his cars and it was always threatened with repossession . . . ADI was falling into worse financial shape daily.

Fortunately, or perhaps unfortunately, ADI got a new lease on life when Bob Brauer and his partner came into the company, bringing in new equipment and taking 50 percent ownership. None of the Pensacola group was let off the hook when this occurred, however. They all had their personal guarantees for the many loans that had been taken out.

At this point Las Vegas became once again a big part of Joe's life. He would go to Winston Reynolds whom he knew had borrowed money for the gravel pit from several people and give him a company check to pay off one of the loans. Then, using Winston's prestige, he would get a loan at another bank and take off for Vegas with Harry or another ADI partner.

He was now gambling at the new MGM Grand Hotel and once, when he went broke in the casino with Tommy Thompson beside him, he showed Tommy how to get a $5,000 credit there. Joe by then already owed the casino $32,000 and was out of credit. He lost the $5,000 and Tommy was suddenly a nervous wreck—he was convinced that hit men would be sent to get him. As soon as they returned to Pensacola Joe pumped up the $5,000 and secured a cashier's check for Tommy, which the latter sent to the MGM Grand.

At the Charter Bank, Lonny Gilmore introduced Joe to another officer, Bob Gilmore, no relation of his. Bob Gilmore was more of a swinger, Joe thought. He wore a jaunty mustache and less conservative suits. With Bob handling his account Joe found it easier to borrow money when he needed it.

Bob Brauer was becoming concerned about the way the company was being run. He trusted Joe, having no idea he was gambling in Las Vegas at this time, but was worried about Harry Newkirk and the others.

Bill Robinson came to Pensacola, stayed a few days with Joe and then flew with him out to Las Vegas. This time Joe was a winner by $88,000. He had the sense to take the money home with him in his briefcase. They came back through Shreveport where Joe was beginning to put together a real estate deal with Bill's help.

Bill had an interest in the local dinner theater in Shreveport, and when they got back from Las Vegas they went to the theater where Bill had some girls waiting. After the show, Bill, Joe, and three of the girls were sitting around Bill's apartment when Bill told the girls about Joe's big win. One of them insisted that nobody won in Las Vegas and refused to believe that Joe had come away with $88,000.

Joe went upstairs and in an unprecedented act of braggadocio unwrapped the money and brought it all down in the briefcase. Equally uncharacteristically, he emptied all the loose cash on top of the girl's head. As the $100 bills fluttered about the room, he asked with sardonic pride, "What do you think about that?"

He instantly regretted this piece of tasteless behavior, but the young women screamed at the sight of this leaf storm of money. Before they could get their hands on it, Bill and Joe hastily gathered it up and stuffed it back into the briefcase.

The next morning Joe headed back for Pensacola where he repaid some personal loans and put all the rest of the money directly into the bottomless pit that was ADI, the enterprise that was gobbling them all up alive.

CHAPTER 42

Joe's next trip to Las Vegas was a far cry from the last lucrative sally. He was, in fact, almost prepared for a loss since he felt there had to be some divine retribution in store for him as a result of his display in Shreveport.

He had first flown to Milwaukee to meet with Bob Brauer and Bill O'Brien. They decided he should open a bank account in Pensacola upon which he could draw checks to make the payments necessary to keep the gravel pit operating.

With a check made out to him for $20,000, Joe took the next flight from Milwaukee to Las Vegas.

From McCarran Airport he headed for the Sahara Hotel and settled into the casino to shoot craps. But there was to be no authentication of Joe Hodges as a man of parts on this trip.

As the $15,000 bankroll he had brought to the tables dwindled and he pressed his bets trying to recover, the big win slipped further from his grasp. Finally, at three in the morning, he had run out of money. But he was in no mood to stop gambling. He felt certain he could overcome this loss if he had another $10,000. Then he remembered the check for $20,000 in his pocket. Well, he rationalized, he was just going to double the money he would bring back and put into the system.

He approached the pit boss with the check, and since he had very conspicuously lost $15,000, the casino manager agreed to give him $5,000 in exchange for the check. The manager promised him the rest of the cash in the morning when the check could be cleared. By 4 A.M. Joe had lost the $5,000 and he asked for another $5,000 on the check. This, the credit manager refused. It would only be a few more hours before they could verify the check with the bank in Milwaukee.

But Joe was in no mood to hang around the casino without money to gamble. He headed for the airport and over the course of that day worked his way back to Pensacola. At nine-thirty Milwaukee time he was on the telephone to Bob Brauer telling him to stop payment on the check. It was late in the afternoon when Joe finally got back to Pensacola, and the next day he was contemplating the shambles of ADI in his office.

Brauer and O'Brien, consummate heavy equipment and construction experts that they were, did not know how to run a gravel mine, and there was just no way they'd learn in time, Joe realized. For him, the most important thing at the moment was to get together another bankroll and go back to Las Vegas.

The dredge had sunk to the bottom of the man-made lake in the middle of the gravel pit and there was little hope that Joe could get money out of ADI. He began making the rounds. The Charter Bank, to which he already owed money, seemed his most likely prospect. He went to Bob Gilmore who was finally persuaded to cash a check for him. Joe was well aware that the check would be coming back but he knew he could get to Las Vegas and win and pay off before the check landed.

He continued the rounds, scrounging up his bankroll. This time he wanted enough money to carry him through a losing streak. Then, just as he was getting close to his goal, two neatly dressed men with "law" written all over them surprised him by walking into his office. They had to be FBI men, Joe thought, and indeed they identified themselves as such.

"We're here in response to a complaint from Nevada that you cashed a bad check in Las Vegas," one of the agents stated flatly.

"I didn't cash a bad check, I stopped payment on a check," Joe snapped back.

"In any case, you're charged with transporting stolen securities across state lines."

"If by stolen securities you mean money, I didn't transport it anywhere," Joe replied hotly. "I lost all my money in Las Vegas. I didn't bring any back with me."

"This is a very serious charge, Mr. Hodges," one of the young men contributed.

"Is it? Well, what are you going to do about it?"

"The U. S. Attorney will seek an indictment against you."

"Let him do what he wants," Joe retorted. "What is it you're here for?"

"Perhaps you would prefer to repay the twenty thousand dollars to the Sahara Hotel," the same agent suggested.

"No way! In the first place I gave them a check for twenty thousand and they only gave me five thousand. What are you anyway? Bill collectors for the Mafia? Is that what the FBI has come to?"

"You had better take this matter more seriously," the agent replied weakly.

"You do what you want to do. Tell the U. S. Attorney he's welcome to go out and seek an indictment. He'll certainly do a lot of seeking and damn little indicting."

The two agents, realizing Joe would not be intimidated, left the office. They hadn't been gone more than thirty minutes before the phone rang. It was Bob Brauer calling from Milwaukee. "Joe," he said, coming straight to the point, "The FBI have been in to see me."

"I know, Bob, I talked to them just now myself."

"They tried to make me pay back the whole twenty thousand," Brauer cried.

"Bob, keep a tight asshole," Joe counseled. "There's nothing they can do. Hell, I only got five thousand on the check. They wouldn't give it back to me so what could we do?"

"We've got to clear this up somehow."

"The best way to clear it up is to sit on it. They're not going to do anything out at the Sahara. They know damn well they didn't cash that check for me, they just lent me five thousand. Just try to forget it, Bob. I tell you, nothing's going to happen."

After Brauer hung up Joe was well aware that even though the whole thing was basically a mistake, the most damaging blow to him was the harm it did to his relationship with Bob Brauer. If nothing else, Brauer knew that he had tried to cash the check in order to gamble instead of bringing it back to Pensacola to use for payments that had to be made.

As always, there was only one answer: back to Las Vegas. Joe called Bill Robinson in Shreveport and they made arrangements to fly out together. By the time they arrived, Joe had four bad checks out and the Charter Bank was screaming at him to repay some of his outstanding personal notes.

In Vegas, Joe and Bill headed for the Stardust, Joe's favorite casino. Certainly he would give the Sahara a wide berth.

As Bill watched him play craps, baccarat, then craps again, Joe felt excitement coursing through him. He pounded along on a winning streak, gambling fast and furiously. Buying the numbers, he hit one winning hand after another and the chips piled up in front of him.

After twelve hours of nonstop gambling, Joe walked away from the cashier's cage with $125,000 in $100 bills. It was truly a big win, and no experience, no sensation that Joe could imagine approached the exaltation of such a stunning victory. It was worth all the losses, all the leaden-eyed retreats from "Fun City" to hit a big one like this. Such ecstasy could only be matched by paying off loans and redeeming bad checks. Together they were what made life worthwhile. The big win to the gambler was what sex was to the adolescent.

As Joe walked away from the cashier's cage, his briefcase bulging with neatly stacked $100 bills wrapped in $5,000 packages, he began thinking of the spots he had to cover, and cover fast. By nine the following morning bad checks would be coming in, notes overdue, people looking for him. He wanted to be there in Pensacola first and pay off everything he could. The best flight from Las Vegas to Pensacola was via National Airlines, landing at New Orleans en route.

Joe and Bill Robinson exuberantly boarded the flight, plumped themselves down in the first-class section, and asked the stewardess to bring them bourbon and water.

Joe glanced at his watch and, when the stewardess brought them their drinks, commented that the plane was late leaving Las Vegas. He asked if it would land in Pensacola on time.

"I don't know, sir. We've been advised that the airline is going on strike, perhaps before we get to Pensacola." Joe looked at her in concern. "What do you mean?"

"The strike is called for midnight tonight Eastern standard

time," the stewardess replied. "That means that this flight might terminate in New Orleans."

"How are we going to get to Pensacola then?" Joe asked in alarm.

"I don't know, sir." Joe gave Bill a helpless look and began to drink his bourbon.

One hour out of New Orleans the pilot announced that the airline was now on strike. Joe had already studied the Official Airline Guide in the magazine rack and discovered that there was no commercial airline that would get him to Pensacola in time to make the requisite payoffs before the banks called the sheriff.

The strike notwithstanding, Joe and Bill were still in their euphoric state when they deplaned in New Orleans. There was only one way they could make it into Pensacola by the time the banks opened. They would have to charter a plane. At the airport, in the middle of the night, they began making phone calls and trying to contact a charter service. Finally, at six in the morning, they contacted one. They got the pilot out of bed with promises of double the ordinary charter fare and soon were bundled into a single-engine Cessna, Joe holding his briefcase on his lap.

As the sun came up they discovered they were flying into heavy fog, and the youngster flying the plane was hard put to conceal his nervousness. As they approached Pensacola, the pilot staring pale-faced at his instruments, a voice crackled over the radio from the control tower at Pensacola.

"Hello, four five poppa. This is Pensacola tower. We have you on approach control radar. No use in me telling you what's around you, you're right in a hornet's nest!"

Joe, Bill, and the pilot peered out the windows. This was the home of naval aviation. There might be as many as twenty Navy fighter planes flying around them in the dense fog.

Joe clutched his briefcase. Here he had all this money and he was going to be killed and the money would be scattered over the countryside. It would be like his ashes being scattered. If he had been coming back a loser, depressed and broke, with the sheriff looking for him, he wouldn't have cared. But now he heard himself praying softly, "Oh my God, Lord, please let me get back so I can pay this money; then I don't give a damn."

The plane came over the outer marker of the Pensacola airport and the marker beacon lit up on the cockpit instrument panel. The pilot put the plane into a nose dive. Joe felt his heart shoot up into his throat and his stomach turn to concrete as he clutched his briefcase to his chest.

"Just let me pay this money, Lord," he heard himself mumbling. He was sitting beside the pilot who suddenly pulled back on the yoke and the plane leveled off. They had broken through the fog and the runway was directly in front of them. The pilot wasted no time putting the plane down and taxiing over to the terminal.

Accompanied by Bill, Joe took a cab directly to the Charter Bank where he arrived at 9 A.M. just as the doors were opened. Bob Gilmore was sitting at his desk behind the railing when Joe walked in. He looked up, a sigh of relief escaping him. It would have been no fun for Gilmore to have to explain to the president of the bank why he had allowed Joe Hodges to lay off two bad checks and not pay up his note.

Joe sat down at the desk beside Gilmore and triumphantly snapped open his briefcase. Gilmore glanced inside and drew a sharp breath.

"All right, Bob, what does it all come to? By the way, I just discovered there wasn't enough money in the account to cover that check I gave you. Anyway, it's all here."

Flushed with joy, a man of substance and authority again, Joe began counting out the stacks of $5,000 until the banker had been paid off. Then he hurried on to the next bank that was harboring one of his hot checks.

CHAPTER 43

It was six o'clock in the morning and the sun was just coming up over the desert to the east when Jon Roberts, defeated, shambled out of the California Club blinking in the pale light outdoors. It would be eight o'clock in the morning Central time, nine o'clock Eastern time.

He possessed $28. Now he needed to get on the telephone again, but whom could he call? He was not sure what day in the week it was. Probably it was Saturday or Sunday, though it might be Monday.

Once again, as though his footsteps knew better than he where to point, he found himself standing in front of the 4 Queens. He had to get on the phone and call somebody. Somebody who would send him more money. Who would that be?

He thought of an old gambling buddy from Lufkin, Texas, Jim Zack. Jim had been out to Las Vegas with him once. He ought to be able to catch him at home before he left for the office. Jon looked through his list of phone numbers. Then he went to the slot machine cashier's booth and turned $8 into quarters. The same phone on which he'd called Three Finger Pat was available. It had brought him luck once, maybe it would again. He dialed the home number direct and fed in the quarters.

Jim Zack's wife answered and Jon asked for Jim, saying it was important. Jim picked up the phone. "Yeah, Jon, what is it?" He didn't sound happy to hear from his old gambling buddy, Jon noted.

"I'm out here in Las Vegas, Jim. Remember when we were here a couple of months ago?"

"Yeah, yeah, yeah, Jon. What do you want?"

"Look, can you send me three thousand Western Union?"

"Are you crazy, Jon. It's Sunday morning, eight o'clock. I don't keep that kind of money around the house. Banks are closed, the office is closed, and even if I had it why would I want to send it out to you in Las Vegas? You'd just blow it anyway."

"Please, Jim, if you can help me I'd appreciate it."

"Jon, I like you, we're friends, and as a friend I've got to tell you—no! Why don't you get on a plane and get out of there?"

"I already cashed in my ticket."

"Look, if you're really stuck out there call me tomorrow morning at the office—the office, you get it? I'll see if I can at least send air fare to get you home. That's the best I can do. Goodbye, Jon." Jon heard the line click and counted $3.50 wasted on a phone call.

So it *was* Sunday. Now what was he going to do? Who did he know that kept cash around the house? He put a call through to Fort Walton Beach, Florida, and another one to Chicago. Irate friends reminded him it was Sunday; they didn't keep big cash around the house and even if they did they weren't sending it to him in Las Vegas.

A feeling of panic began to envelop him but he fought it off. There was one more call he could make. He braced himself for the ordeal and then dialed the number and counted in the quarters as he heard the familiar voice answering on the other end.

"Hi, Mom." He put on his most cheerful tone. "I've been meaning to call you."

"Where are you?" his mother asked, her voice betraying the worry she felt at getting a call from a pay station—she had heard the last of the change trickle into the coin box as she picked up the phone.

"I'm in Las Vegas, Mom. No, I'm not here gambling. I had to meet two men from New York who were coming out to close that big real estate deal I was telling you about."

"Oh, I hope it works out for you, son."

"It will, Mom." Jon tried to sound confident. "But I've got a problem. It's Sunday out here, I can't cash a check, I ran out of money. I wonder if you could get down to the Western Union there and send me five hundred dollars."

"But son, I don't have that kind of money around the house. I'd have to go to the bank and it's closed today."

"Go see Uncle Ethan, he always keeps a thousand dollars at home. In his business he has to, you know."

"Oh, son," she said with a stricken tone, "I hate to bother Uncle Ethan on Sunday."

"I wouldn't ask you if it wasn't an emergency, Mom. I'll get it back to you Tuesday at the latest. It's just that I got in this jam out here and I can't come home until these men arrive. This is the deal I've been trying to make for six months and I know that if I can just take them to lunch and dinner and pay the hotel bills we'll close and I'll probably get a check right here."

"Well, son, I'll do my best. I'll run over and see Uncle Ethan. I hope he'll give it to me." There was a doubtful timbre in her voice.

"Of course he will if you ask him, Mom. He's your brother and you know he's got it."

"I'll do it, son," she said with sudden resolution.

"It'll cost twenty dollars to send it to me, Mom," Jon continued.

"Twenty dollars? Oh my. Twenty dollars, that's a lot of money."

"You'll have to borrow five hundred twenty from Uncle Ethan, and please, do it right now and get the money off to me. I'm in a real jam. All right, Mom? Also, tell Western Union there to use A-L-A-N for a code to identify me. Okay, Mom?"

There was a long pause on the other end of the line, then, "Well, all right, son. I'll do it."

"Right now, Mom?" Jon wheedled.

"Right now, son," she replied. "Are you all right?"

"Yes, I'm fine, Mom. As soon as that five hundred comes I'll be all right. I'm sure I'll be able to put the deal together."

"Don't worry, son," his mother said soothingly. "I'll get this money down to the Western Union before I go to church. It's a good thing you called me early. Call me later today when you get the money. Goodbye, son."

It was like a stab in the gut for him to have to do this, especially after his father's death and all the other things that had happened. But with that $500 he knew he could recoup everything. All he needed was to get started again.

He walked about downtown Las Vegas, sweating out the Western Union money order. He knew better than to go to Western Union for another two or three hours; probably four hours would be more like it. If the money came in at twelve noon he would be in fine shape again. That was six hours from now. He had $13 left in his pockets after the phone calls and wandered back to the counter for some orange juice and a cup of coffee. His stomach just wouldn't accept solid food.

He thought of going to the 25¢ crap game and trying to build up the $10 he had left, but discarded the idea. When the $500 came through he'd go out and really do some good.

To while away the time he fed nickels into slot machines here and there, staying clear of Binion's and the El Cortez. He thought of going up to the room at the Golden Nugget. It should still be there. Now that he had a plan of action, now that money was on the way and he could go back to the crap tables, he might just as well have a little rest, take a shower, even buy a clean shirt. He had just enough money to get one at the shirt store on the street. It would cost about $4, less than if he bought one at the men's shop in the hotel. Even though it was Sunday, the shops were open in Las Vegas; nothing closed here. He bought the shirt and with $1 left went back to the Golden Nugget and took the elevator up to his room.

After showering, shaving, and brushing his teeth he fell into an exhausted slumber which lasted until some inner alarm woke him with a start at exactly twelve noon. The money should be at the Western Union office now.

Another old man was behind the counter at Western Union, wearing the green eyeshade that seemed to be the trademark of the clerks there.

"Have you got anything for Jonathan Alan Roberts?" he asked. Once again he looked reasonably presentable.

The clerk looked at him. "You Roberts?"

"Yes, sir, I am."

"You got any I. D. on you?"

"No, I don't have it with me. You have a code, don't you?"

"What is it?"

"The middle name is Alan, A-L-A-N."

"That's right. I'll make out the check now."

"Can you cash it for me? It's only five hundred."

"Yeah, I guess so. Any more than that I'd have to send you over to the El Cortez Hotel."

It was one o'clock and Jonathan Alan Roberts walked out on the street again with $501 in his pocket. Good old Mom, she'd come through. She wouldn't be sorry. He'd make this money really move and get it back to her so she could pay Uncle Ethan. Now he wanted to get out of downtown Las Vegas and play on the Strip. He took a cab out to the Riviera and, putting $41 in his pocket, set $460 aside as playing money and bought into the first crap table he came to. He played carefully now; there'd be no reckless betting. In two hours he had won $1,500 on the crap table and he then sauntered over to the baccarat game. In another hour he'd won $2,175 more. Now he had $3,675 besides the $500 his mother had sent him and was feeling in high spirits once again. He was ready to launch the main drive for the big win.

At a new crap table he started buying the numbers again at $100 a number and watched his bankroll grow. Suddenly he had an urge to make the win fast and get out of Las Vegas. It was his turn to roll. With the chips in front of him he bet $200 on the pass line and threw a five. It was a lucky point to catch, he decided.

"Five hundred across on the numbers!" he ordered imperiously. He threw the dice again. Impossible! This couldn't happen to him. The old six-ace—seven—stared up at him from the table.

"Seven out, seven and out!" The croupier raked in $3,000 plus the $200 on the pass line. Jon was back to the original $500 again.

Moving aside for the next shooter, he once again began to bet carefully, babying his remaining bankroll which lasted him another hour before he was down to $50—$91 counting the $41 he had stashed in his pocket. In a state akin to shell shock, he asked to see the casino manager. The manager was by his side almost instantly.

"I need about five thousand dollars credit," Jon announced.

The casino manager shrugged. "I'll go over to the credit manager and check with him." Jon watched the casino manager walk over to the cashier's cage. He did not want to go with him and have to personally confront the credit manager. The casino manager returned all too quickly.

"Sorry, Mr. Roberts, we can't let you have any money."

"I have a check right here," Jon blustered.

"We'll have to wait until Monday when we can verify with the bank." The casino manager was implacable.

"I don't understand this," Jon cried indignantly. "All the money I've lost here and you can't give me a few thousand dollars credit."

"Come back Monday morning, we'll help you then." There was obviously no profit now in one of Jon's displays of righteous indignation. He turned and stalked out of the casino with $91 in his pocket. He wasn't going to pass any of this along to a cab driver and he began walking down the Strip toward town.

It was the middle of the night, and almost a mile to the Foxy Lady which featured 25¢ crap games. Somehow he had to work the $91 back up again.

He felt a surge of confidence and optimism as he bought $60 worth of $5 chips. He began playing $5 on the pass line and $5 behind it on the odds. The blowsy woman shooting, who looked like a third-rate whore on her day off, was hot. Rapidly he scored six hits and got off just before the blowsy lady tossed a seven.

Now the dice were his. He bet $10 on the pass line and threw a four. "Five dollars across on the numbers," he instructed the dealer, banging down the chips to cover the call bet. He threw the dice again. This time he came up with a six. He threw four more rolls, each time hitting one of the numbers he had bought before he threw the four again, making his point. Once again Jon's bankroll was building.

With confidence he bet $25 on the front line and caught a six. He backed his bet with $25 odds and raised his place bets to $25 each and began throwing fervently.

For one incredible fifteen-minute period he tattooed the four and five, repeatedly hitting those numbers which were paying him two to one and seven to five. Repeatedly he hit the trey deuce and trey ace, pressing the bets each time until he built them up to the house limit of $100 on both the four and the five.

Finally, to top off the hand, he rolled a six, winning on the pass line. He was moving now and two of the housemen from the Foxy Lady came over to watch him play. They had seen him win the $1,000 and, to this low-stakes gambling emporium, that was a lot of money. Jon felt the battle lines being drawn against him and, after three hours at the Foxy Lady, he cashed out with $2,870, a big win against his $60 buy-in.

He walked over to the cashier and asked for the money in $20 bills. As he was waiting for the count to be made and the cash to be pushed back to him under the grille, he was aware of the hooker who had been standing near him as he gambled. She had made a few remarks indicating that she would be available as she watched him win. Now, as he picked up his sheaf of $20 bills, she renewed the offer. But there was nothing on Jon's mind but gambling—running his stake up to the big win again.

CHAPTER 44

There wasn't a shadow of doubt in Joe's mind that the gravel pit was doomed. Everyone in the venture who had written a personal guarantee was bound to find himself levied against sooner or later. Yet Joe's high regard for Bob Brauer and Bill O'Brien, and his friendship with the Pensacola group, compelled him to struggle on.

In the fall of 1974, while Joe was looking around for an alternative business situation, as he had been forced to do, Bill Robinson called him and asked him to come to Shreveport to look at a piece of property that might be developed. This was an opportunity Joe simply must not miss, Bill enthused. Joe responded by immediately going off to inspect 102 acres of property outside Shreveport that had frontage on the major highways. It was indeed a startling opportunity. A group of promoters were about to build a large racetrack nearby to be known as Louisiana Downs. Bossier City had for many years been known as the sin city of northern Louisiana. Right along the main highway, a two-and-a-half-hour drive from Dallas, close to where the racetrack would be built, were 102 acres of land eminently suitable for almost any sort of development.

Bossier City was in fact the Texas trap. From all over Texas fun seekers and gamblers flocked in to enjoy the scene. Now, with the finest racetrack between Florida and Hollywood Park, California, about to be constructed, there was no limit to its possibilities. Joe was excited. Bill had come on a gusher.

The price was $11,000 an acre or $1,122,000 to purchase the

land. The owner of the land, Sandy Ferguson, had asked $50,000 for a twenty-day option to buy. As Joe structured the deal, the joint venture which he presented to Brauer and O'Brien would buy the 102 acres for $14,000 an acre or a total consideration of $1,428,000. Since Joe was buying it for $1,122,000 and selling it to Brauer and the joint venture for $1,428,000, he would make himself $306,000 on the deal and still be part of the joint venture, enough to get ADI and its partners at least partially solvent.

The property had been appraised for $17,000 an acre so he was still offering it to Brauer and the joint venture for $3,000 an acre less than its appraised value. Everybody was getting a good deal. His problem was to raise $50,000 for the option.

Joe went to his old partners in the gravel pit and explained the whole scheme to them. If they could put it together, the $306,000 immediate profit would pay a large portion of the ADI debts, he explained.

To help Joe pull the deal together, and to show good faith, Brauer wired him $15,000. It was a long way from being enough and the tight money market made it difficult for Joe to find the $1,500,000 loan to purchase the property.

The land was not ready for development yet. That was several years away. First the race track had to be built and operating. But certainly within two years the property would be worth 50¢ a foot or $22,000 an acre, a substantial profit for the joint venture partners. While Joe felt that Bob Brauer would probably come up with the other money for the twenty-day option, he was equally convinced that in the prevailing money market it would be extremely difficult to get the $1,500,000 loan. Nevertheless, he had developed an enticing real estate project, one that would interest any promoter. If he couldn't get the $50,000 for the option, he doubted if anybody else could either, and the property would sit there for some time.

Rather than risk Brauer's money, he returned $7,500 of the first $15,000 Bob had sent him. He kept the other $7,500 on the basis that there was still a deal and he needed the money if the opportunity arose to clinch it quickly.

From Milwaukee where he had gone to give Bob half the $15,000, Joe flew directly to Las Vegas hoping to run the $7,500 up to $25,000 and then talk Bob into risking another $25,000 with him to buy the option. In just a few hours he lost the $7,500, and flew back to Pensacola.

A week later Joe called Bob in Milwaukee again and said he still wanted a shot at the Bossier City land deal. Brauer sent him $30,000. Within hours of the time the money reached Joe's bank, he was on his way to Vegas. In one night of heavy gambling at baccarat and craps he lost Brauer's $30,000 and limped home.

The next week Joe called Bob yet again and asked him for $28,000 more. Bob had a bank partner sufficiently interested in the Bossier deal to make a loan of the $28,000 to Brauer and O'Brien on their signature. Joe had sent copies of the option agreement up to Bob and the banker-lawyer was impressed. When the money arrived Joe immediately caught a plane for Las Vegas, returning a day later, broke again.

It wasn't long before Brauer knew Joe was in trouble. He called Tommy Thompson at his motel and asked him to look into it. Joe convinced Tommy that he had almost put the Louisiana land deal together and that if they could get a bankroll of $20,000 or $25,000 they could run it up in Las Vegas to the amount needed for the deal. Tommy gave Joe the $25,000—which they lost at the Vegas crap tables.

At the Charter Bank, Bob Gilmore had been watching the money coming in from Brauer to Joe's account and was impressed. He and a group of investors had purchased an island just off Pensacola and were interested in selling it at a profit. Joe, eager to ingratiate himself at the bank, agreed to Gilmore's request to introduce him to Brauer and O'Brien with the thought that they might be interested in buying Gilmore's island property.

Joe was keeping Tommy and Harriet Thompson assuaged, despite the $25,000 he had borrowed and lost in Las Vegas, on the basis that he would sell their motel for them at a large profit. As usual, he had plates spinning in all directions. Joe did introduce Bob Gilmore to Brauer and O'Brien, and as the reward he felt he deserved, he persuaded Gilmore to cash two hot checks for him amounting to $12,000, even though he already owed the bank $28,000 on personal loans.

With the $12,000 Joe made another desperate foray to Las Vegas in an effort to win enough money to at least partially straighten out his finances. In hours he had lost the whole amount and was on his way back to Pensacola, drained, exhausted, approaching desperation.

He was trying to put the sale of Tommy Thompson's motel together when he got a call from Bob Gilmore at the bank. The checks had come back and something had to be done about that $12,000 in hot checks.

"Joe, we're going to have to talk about this," Gilmore said ominously.

An hour later Joe was at the bank in a meeting with the executive vice-president, Bob McKay, and Gilmore. Joe laid out his situation. "I've got these two hot checks for a total of twelve thousand dollars, and I've got these unsecured notes that amount to twenty-eight thousand. As you know, I've lost heavily in this gravel deal but I'll pay you."

"I'm afraid that's not good enough, Joe. You're going to have to get us this money," Gilmore replied.

"I can't do it right now," Joe protested.

McKay shrugged his shoulders. "Let's go in and talk to Mr. Crona." The executive vice-president escorted Joe and Gilmore into the large corner office of the bank's president. Crona was in an angry mood and wasted no time attacking Joe. "What it comes down to, Mr. Hodges, is that you've defrauded the bank." Inwardly Joe shuddered as his thoughts turned to Leavenworth. Bank fraud equaled time in the joint. In Joe's case it equaled a lot of time for a third conviction.

"I can understand," he began, "why you would be angry at the way things have turned out. Obviously when I came to Pensacola and became associated with the group of businessmen whom you have known for many years, it wasn't with the idea of defrauding anybody, certainly not your bank." As he talked, Joe thought fast. Crona was a dangerous man. His financial power stretched far and wide. He was no small-time banker. This was a situation that had to be handled, and handled right away.

But Joe was at his best in these situations, his computerlike mind able to offer battle plans of offensive and defensive ploys when under threat of danger that would demoralize or paralyze a lesser man. A bold plan, its chances of success uncertain, formulated in his mind.

"Mr. Crona, I'll get this money secured." The tone of assurance he brought to his voice was a far cry from the fear he felt deep within himself.

Joe was recalling his efforts to sell the motel for Tommy Thompson. While seeking new equipment for the gravel pit he had met "Pop" Johnson and his son Jack. They were in the construction business in St. Louis and owned some heavy equipment which the gravel pit operation needed. During discussions Joe learned that Jack was anxious to move to Pensacola and that Pop was willing to let his son use the heavy equipment they owned in St. Louis as collateral against loans to purchase the motel in Pensacola.

Since Tommy was deeply involved in the gravel pit, Joe had introduced the possibilities of selling their dragline, a valuable piece of heavy equipment worth about $125,000, to ADI as a down payment on the motel. Both Pop and Jack were so anxious to move their family to the Sun Belt they were willing to make all sorts of deals on heavy equipment.

"Mr. Crona," Joe went on, "I've got some people who will put up a quarter-million-dollar dragline as collateral against the unsecured loans. I need Bob Gilmore to fly to St. Louis with me and we'll get the title to the dragline. I'll give you a note for twelve thousand dollars to cover the bad checks and that note will also be secured."

Crona looked at Joe balefully. He was not the type of banker who dealt in loans secured by heavy equipment or anything else that couldn't immediately be turned into cash. His glance moved from Joe to his vice-president, Bob Gilmore. It was the bad judgment, the weakness of this executive that had caused the bank to come to its present unfortunate situation with Hodges and the whole ADI deal. At the moment there wasn't much Crona could do except agree to let his executive go with Hodges and try to get title to something that would pass for security. He grunted assent and waved Gilmore, Joe, and Bob McKay out of his presence.

In St. Louis, Gilmore and Joe met with Pop Johnson and Jack. They accepted a $50,000 note from Joe which, they were convinced, they could immediately use as a down payment on the motel in return for giving Joe and the Charter Bank of Pensacola title to the dragline under the Uniform Bill of Sale Act. With the bill of sale to the dragline in hand, Joe and Gilmore flew to Milwaukee where they asked Bob Brauer to verify the ownership of the dragline from the serial numbers on the bill of sale.

It took one call for Brauer to assure Gilmore that the dragline was owned by Jack Johnson and his father and that it was a very fine piece of equipment. Armed with this verification Joe and Bob returned to the bank and met with Crona and McKay again. With the dragline as security Joe was permitted to sign a note to the bank for $40,000 on December 8, 1974.

Joe asked for his two hot checks to be returned but the bank president gave him a nasty look. "We'll just keep those checks as further security until the loan is paid," Crona snarled.

The day after Joe signed the note he got a call from McKay. "What have you got that's worth anything, Joe?" McKay asked. "We've got to start getting some payments made against that note."

"I don't own anything but my car," Joe replied.

"Well, we want that car down here, right now."

"Look out your window in ten minutes," Joe said. He drove down to the bank, parked his car in front of it and walked inside, handing the keys to McKay. Joe took a taxi home and called Bob Brauer in Milwaukee. "Bob, they're keeping my car," he said when he got Brauer on the phone.

"How are you going to get it released, Joe?" Bob asked.

"Well, they want four thousand five hundred and all I've got is five hundred."

"I'll send them the four thousand. You can make over the title to me but at least you'll have wheels."

The next day, good as his word, Brauer sent the $4,000 to the bank and they let Joe take back his car, reducing his $40,000 note by $4,500.

Joe had $1,100 in his Charter Bank account and told Gilmore to tap his account, take it and put it against the note. He closed a small brokerage account totaling $1,500 and he applied that against the note too.

In the meantime the Johnsons moved to Pensacola and Joe

persuaded them to open an account for $60,000 in the Charter Bank, hoping that Crona would appreciate Joe's efforts on the bank's behalf.

At Christmastime, Joe, Nancy, Mark, and Amy went to Houston for the Christmas dance which some of their friends would be attending. The $40,000 note at the Charter Bank was for three and a half months and would be due April 1, 1975.

By the time Joe and Nancy left for Houston, he had whittled the $40,000 note down to $32,800. Just before he left, Bob Gilmore came around to talk to him. "Well, I guess I won't be with the bank when you get back from Houston, Joe."

"Crona fired you?" Joe asked incredulously.

"Not yet, but I'm expecting it. I divorced a cousin of his about four months ago and"—Gilmore nervously fingered his mustache—"Crona doesn't like this adornment and told me to shave it off. I told him I wouldn't do it."

Early in January, after Joe and Nancy and the children had returned from Houston, Joe went to see Harry Newkirk. He tried to lay out all the problems they had and how they might cope with them. The notes were crashing in on them from all sides. Lawsuits were being filed. Every member of the Pensacola group was being levied against. Joe didn't even have a bank account in Pensacola since Charter had closed down his account. But that morning Harry did not care to understand what Joe was saying.

Joe turned on his heel, walked out of Harry's house, and went back to Nancy. They were returning to Houston, he announced. They hated to leave Pensacola. They all loved it, the children particularly, but there was no viable alternative.

Through Bill Robinson, Joe had also met an attractive young woman, Joy Wilson, who was an executive of the Rapides Savings and Loan in Alexandria, Louisiana. Although Joe was little more than an acquaintance of Joy's, he never forgot her.

The day after he had confronted Harry Newkirk, Joe was in his car driving alone back to Houston, having decided to leave Nancy and the kids in Pensacola while he was getting resettled. On the way he remembered Joy Wilson and stopped by Alexandria, Louisiana. He carried with him a bogus check on his closed bank account at the Charter Bank in Pensacola. Joy felt she knew Joe well and was aware that he and Bill Robinson were working financial deals together. It was her emotional involvement with Bill that threw her off guard with Bill's old friend and colleague.

After some spirited conversation, Joe mentioned that he would like to favor her bank with a savings account. He only had a check for $20,000 on his Charter Bank account in Pensacola, he explained, and he needed $13,500 for Bill Robinson to close a deal on which they were working.

Joy was glad to help and opened a $20,000 savings account for him. She gave him a check for $13,500 and a passbook showing an account of $6,500. Cashier's check in hand he raced his car to Shreveport and caught a flight to Las Vegas. He blew the $13,500 that same night shooting craps and playing baccarat.

Always when Joe lost his bankroll he had to develop a plan to acquire the money he needed to pay off the heat and get him back to the tables. This was a psychological necessity, almost a physical compulsion. He couldn't function without the plan.

It was Saturday morning when he flew back to Houston. He had already smashed his first hot check of 1975. He went out to the Oak Forest Bank on the northwest side of town. This had been one of the banks where he had cashed a check for $7,500 and made it good before it was returned. An officer at the bank remembered how Joe had covered the check a few years before and, after some conversation and a quick examination of Joe's identification, cashed a $15,000 check on the Charter Bank in Pensacola which was closed Saturday.

Joe caught the 1 P.M. plane that day back to Las Vegas. There were not many casinos left that he had not bilked. One of the few he could visit safely was the Frontier. He walked into a lucky streak there and won $35,000 in just over two hours. At that point he stopped rolling the dice, retired from the table, and assessed his situation.

He had to pay Joy Wilson $13,500 before his hot check from the Charter Bank hit the Rapides Savings and Loan. Then there was the $15,000 hot check at the Oak Forest Bank in Houston. That made $28,500. And he needed $33,000 to pay off the Charter Bank, which brought the addition up to $61,500;

too, he wanted to do something for Brauer. He also needed a bankroll to give him some moving-around money. As he figured it, he was $30,000 shy of his immediate needs. Determined to win that sum, he hit the tables again and after three hours of furious crap shooting had blown the entire $50,000. At least the ostentatious high-rolling enabled him to cash a $10,000 check on his nonexistent account in Pensacola, Florida, with the casino manager, Sam Hogan.

An hour later he blew the last $10,000 and dragged himself back to Shreveport. On Monday he drove out to Alexandria and went to see Joy Wilson at her house. He didn't waste time in inconsequential conversation.

"Joy, I've got a lot of problems with that check I gave you to open my savings and loan account."

"Tell me about them, Joe. If I can help you I will," she answered sympathetically.

"The truth is, Joy, I can't cover it. You see, Bill and I are in a land deal in Bossier City."

"Yes, the hundred and two acres close to where the racetrack is going in. It certainly is a fantastic opportunity."

"Right, that's what I figured. Anyway, I guess in my enthusiasm to help Bill make the deal I overdrew my account. And furthermore I've got to go down and meet Bill this afternoon with another eighty-five hundred to close the deal. The minute it's closed, I've got the developers ready to step in."

"I can't cash a check for eighty-five hundred for you even if I wanted to, Joe," Joy replied. "You know a savings and loan is not a bank. We can't cash checks. We write them."

"Could you—" Joe began.

Joy looked at him and smiled. "I suppose so. Come on down to the Rapides with me. I'll take your check and write you one that you can cash."

At the savings and loan Joy gave Joe a check for $8,500 and called the president of the Alexandria Bank & Trust asking him to cash the check for Joe H. Hodges when he came over.

Thanking Joy profusely, Joe took the check, hurried to the other bank, cashed it, then drove frantically back to Shreveport and caught the flight to Las Vegas. This was his third trip to Vegas in a three-and-a-half-day span. Now even the Frontier would be looking for him. It had been more than fifteen years since he'd given the Freemont casino a bogus cashier's check so he took a chance on hitting it.

In three hours he lost the $8,500 he had obtained through Joy Wilson's good offices. Now he owed her $22,000. Broke again, he flew to Shreveport and telephoned Joy to tell her that he would soon cover all the checks and to ask for just a little time. He was getting to the end of his "borrowing" capacity. Where could he go? The compulsive gambler must have his plan before he can go to bed at night, talk sensibly, or relax in any way.

Joe thought of his mother and Beaumont.

CHAPTER 45

Florence Hodges was delighted to see her son again. It had been a long time since she'd even heard from him, much less had him come to her house. After an hour of talk about how happy he and Nancy were to be coming back to Houston where he would be able to see more of her, Joe got down to business. "Mother, I'm in the deal of a lifetime in Shreveport." Briefly he explained the land deal and how he would be a partner and make $500,000. Florence didn't really understand what Joe was telling her but she did recognize his enthusiasm and succumbed to the urgency of his need to put his business transaction together.

"Mother," Joe importuned. "it will only take me another two months to close this deal." Florence looked at him helplessly as he went on. "Look, I only need twenty-two thousand. If you'll let me get a short-term mortgage on the house for that amount, I'll be able to make the deal and pay off the mortgage in just another two months. Will you help me?"

"Of course I will. How do we get the mortgage?"

"Leave that to me. I'll be back in just a few hours."

Joe left and went to the offices of his first cousin, Gene Van Meter. Gene was a prosperous electrical contractor with a high credit rating at the Beaumont banks. For two hours Joe showed Gene the pitch kit he had developed on the land deal in Bossier City. Gene was skeptical and well aware that Joe had been in constant financial troubles since he had graduated from Texas University.

"Look, Gene," Joe went on urgently, "I'll put you into this

deal. I'll even get you the electrical contracting for the development and I can give you ironclad security on the money I need to borrow from you, twenty-two thousand."

"Now look, Joe," Gene said in exasperation, "I told you when you came in here I wasn't going for any of your deals."

Joe could see that Gene was interested despite his first refusal. "Gene, my mother wants to mortgage her house for that amount," he persisted. "I'll give you the deed made out to you and if in three months you don't get the money back, you own Mother's house. What could be better than that? You've got security, and it's never going to come to that anyway. You'll get your money, you'll be a partner in the deal, and you'll get a lot of business when we start developing those hundred and two acres."

After another thirty minutes of Joe's persuasive talk Gene Van Meter acquiesced. Joe rushed back to his mother's home, had her make over the deed to her nephew, took the deed back to Gene. They went down to the bank, where Gene borrowed $22,000, handed the money to Joe, and took the deed back to his aunt's home. After all it was a short-term agreement—only three months. There was no way *he* could go wrong on it.

Joe thanked his mother and then, with a cashier's check for $22,000 in his pocket, caught a bus for Shreveport. Early the next morning he jumped in his car and sped out to Alexandria to see Joy Wilson.

By now the full extent of Joe's manipulations with bogus checks had dawned upon Joy and the president of the Rapides Savings and Loan for whom Joy worked, as well as the bank's lawyer who was advising immediate legal action against Joe H. Hodges.

Joy took Joe to meet Jack Sommes, the attorney.

"How much more time can you give me, Jack, before you have to go to the district attorney?" Joe asked the lawyer. "I know I can settle this matter. It's just a question of when Bill Robinson and I"—he flashed a smile at Joy Wilson—"can put this deal to bed."

For ten or fifteen minutes Joe explained to the lawyer what it was that he and Bill were trying to do. He brought out his plats of the land and the development program already underway in the area. Nobody could doubt that the 102 acres would be one of the most valuable land acquisitions in Louisiana when it was pulled off. Joe showed the lawyer the personal worth statements of Bob Brauer and Bill O'Brien, also the latest balance sheet of their Milwaukee corporation and correspondence which indicated they would be going along with him as soon as the option was signed over.

As Joe watched the lawyer and Joy succumbing to his persuasiveness, he had a flashback to the day when the sheriff of Montgomery County along with the vice-president of the Conroe bank had picked him up in front of his house and threatened him with jail and criminal prosecution if he didn't immediately make good the hot check he'd smashed that morning. He could easily have obtained the money from Turk but that would have meant nullifying the bets which he was so positive were going to be winners. He knew how crazy it was to go through the same idiocy again but the compulsion was too overpowering. He had $22,000 in his pocket, was in grave jeopardy, and could have settled the whole problem immediately. But the gambler, desperate to get back to the casinos, slyly reminded Joe that he didn't have enough to pay off the Oak Forest Bank and the balance of the fearsome $40,000 note outstanding at Crona's Charter Bank. Still, Joe could have squared things for Joy Wilson and dispelled some of the heat on him if he paid up right away.

The bank attorney looked at Joe squarely. "I can't help you borrow the money you need to finish off the deal but I'll give you until the end of the week before I call in the district attorney." Joe left the lawyer's penthouse office, drove to Shreveport, and caught the next flight for Las Vegas.

The Sands Hotel out on the Strip was one of the last of the class casinos that Joe had not in one way or another defrauded. He took his cashier's check to the casino credit manager who verified it and gave Joe $22,000 in cash with which he attacked the first crap table he could find.

Joe made the money last ten hours, and then he had blown his mother's house.

Suffering the most acute psychic pain and the deepest feelings of guilt he had ever known, he waited at the airport for a plane that would take him back to Texas. He had just enough cash left to buy a double bourbon and consider the next plan of action. He couldn't exist without some reasonably plausible scheme to replenish his bankroll and try again.

But the plan wouldn't materialize. The next flight out to Texas was nonstop to Dallas. There he would have to find a flight to Houston. He thought about the dire straits he was in. Suddenly a thought flashed through his mind. He strode to the bank of telephones and put through a collect call to his refuge, his sanctuary in times of trouble when there was nobody else he could turn to.

CHAPTER 46

Cindy Bramlet ran down the concourse and threw her arms around Joe. He still had no plan and the strain showed on his face. Cindy took his arm and led him out of the airport.

They stopped for breakfast and talk at the first coffee shop and she listened to him tell her about the problems he was facing. "How can I help, Joe?" she asked, her pretty face working in concern.

Joe shook his head hopelessly. "I don't know, unless you can think of someone who will lend me the money I need." Seeing her obvious worry, he smiled.

"There's a man I know in Houston now, he used to live here in Dallas," she began hesitantly. Joe looked at her expectantly. "I know he makes a lot of money and has his own business. Maybe he would help us."

"Do you think he would?"

"I'll call right now. He gets into his office early. Then we'll both fly to Houston and see him. I don't think he would have any trouble lending you the twenty-two thousand dollars you need for the bank in Alexandria."

Now that a plan of action lay before him, no matter how frail, Joe could relax. Cindy had listened to the latest chapter of his descent into the vortex of uncontrollable gambling and together they had worked out a tactic that could extricate him from it.

Jerrel Sullivan was half owner and chief executive officer of Century Hardware, Inc. Century sold such mundane but lucrative items as doorknobs, door locks, doorjambs, and the entire hardware involved in mechanical security for the construction companies putting up the large office buildings, hospitals, and apartment houses that were fast changing the greater Houston skylines.

As president of the company, the thirty-five-year-old Jerrel earned a handsome yearly salary as well as bonuses and dividends.

While not possessed of great wealth, he had access to funds when and if he needed them. Joe was immediately drawn to Jerrel Sullivan and his tasteful, structured life-style as evidenced by his large, elegantly appointed office.

Jerrel was almost Hollywood good-looking, with his finely groomed mustache and curly brown hair, his fitted three-piece suit and amiable though perceptive eyes.

Any friend of Cindy's was a friend of his, Jerrel began the conversation. Once again Joe was at his confidence-inspiring best. With Cindy's encouragement he launched into a description of the Shreveport–Bossier City strip of property near the new racetrack complex that was being built, and of the deal he was trying to put together. He told Jerrel honestly that he had gambled away in Las Vegas the money he had succeeded in raising. He made a clean breast of his troubles with the Rapides Savings and Loan and the Oak Forest Bank of Houston. Within a few days at the most his hot check would be back at the Oak Forest Bank and he would be subject to criminal prosecution. He had only a few more days to make good on the Rapides Savings and Loan situation or they would turn it over to the district attorney.

"As I've told you, Jerrel," Joe said earnestly, leaning across the wide, polished wood desk, "I've been in the joint twice now. The third time is for keeps."

Jerrel listened attentively, refusing all phone calls and interruptions until he completely understood what Joe was saying. Then he turned to Cindy, a warm smile taking the reproof from his words, "You certainly have interesting friends, Cindy." That said, he again turned his attention to the land deal in Bossier City. "This sort of thing is way out of my line," he remarked. "Oh, I can see that it could be a highly profitable venture, but it is in a field I don't really understand." He held up a hand at Joe's crestfallen look. "I'm not saying I won't try to help you, Joe. I will. Let me think about the situation a couple of days and we'll get together again. They're not going to jail you right away." He turned to Cindy. "Let's see, it's Tuesday. Come in Thursday, okay?"

Cindy and Joe thanked Jerrel and left his office. In a cab back to the airport they reviewed the meeting. Both agreed that Jerrel Sullivan intended to help, and Joe decided he'd better telephone his mother after he put Cindy on her flight back to Dallas.

By the time Joe reached his mother that evening a local banker had already called her regarding the Rapides Savings and Loan case. She was worried but Joe was able to calm her fears.

The next day Joy Wilson herself called Joe's mother. Florence did not tell her that Joe was in Houston but assured Joy that she would locate her son and have him take care of the matter. Joe also called his cousin Gene Van Meter, assuring him that the loan would be repaid before it was necessary for him to take possession of his aunt's house.

Joe sweated each hour until the next meeting with Jerrel Sullivan. Now his fate lay in Jerrel's hands. Between Oak Forest and Alexandria there was no doubt that he was facing virtual life imprisonment.

When he went back to Jerrel Sullivan's office he was struggling to conceal the anxiety that was gnawing at him. He frankly told Jerrel that his days were numbered if he didn't take care of Rapides Savings and Loan immediately. Jerrel nodded and called in his bookkeeper, an older lady who had been with him since his business career had begun.

"Betty, how much have we got in the bank?"

"About thirty-five thousand dollars, Mr. Sullivan," she replied.

"Write me out a check for twenty-two thousand," Jerrel said firmly. She gave him a questioning look and walked out the door, returning a few moments later with the check which she proffered, frowning, to Jerrel. Jerrel grinned at his bookkeeper's obvious disapproval and waited till she'd left the office before handing the check to Joe. "My bank's downtown, Joe. You can get a cashier's check and that should take the heat off you in

Alexandria. Come back tomorrow and we'll talk about what to do over at the Oak Forest Bank."

Joe hurried downtown to the Cullen Bank and got the cashier's check for $22,000.

He glanced down at his watch. It was two-twenty. He started walking toward the First City National Bank in Houston. There was a plane leaving for Las Vegas in one hour. He knew that this time he could run the $22,000 up to the $60,000 or $70,000 it would take to get him out of trouble. He also had exactly thirty minutes to get to the First City National Bank and have the money transferred to the Rapides Savings and Loan.

Desperately though he wanted to take the money out to Vegas and run it up at the crap tables and the baccarat game, there just wasn't time. The money had to be in Alexandria today. If only he could have had until tomorrow to get the money to Joy Wilson he would have been on that plane. He found himself standing in front of the bank at ten minutes before three. An empty cab came by and he actually started to hail it. Surely they would give him another day.

Suddenly, reason overcame him. No. They weren't kidding. The district attorney in Alexandria would move against him tomorrow morning at nine o'clock. Joe let the cab go. He walked into the bank, strode deliberately to the transfer department, and by three o'clock the money was on its way to Alexandria.

He was broke and had missed his chance to go to Las Vegas, but at least the heat was off at the Rapides Savings and Loan. Of course he owed the Oak Forest Bank, but the $22,000 would liquidate the Alexandria debt and he had a day or so left before the Oak Forest Bank pressed charges against him.

Joe walked out of First City National and headed for the nearest phone booth. He called Cindy to tell her what had happened and both of them sighed in relief. He had a meeting scheduled with Jerrel the following morning at eleven o'clock, he told Cindy, and would report what happened.

Promptly at eleven Joe arrived at Jerrel Sullivan's office. "Joe, I'm going to level with you," Jerrel said. "I own fifty percent of Century. The other fifty percent is owned by my partner and very close friend. He's old enough to be my father and I guess he thinks of me as a son. You and I are going over to see him.

I'm taking my stock certificates with me and I'm going to borrow some money from Dick, using my half of the company for security. Are you ready to go?" he ended briskly.

Dick Price did indeed treat Jerrel like a son. He was expecting him and had a check for $30,000 written out for him. Jerrel handed over the stock certificates and then he and Joe took the check to Century's bank. Jerrel put $15,000 back into the company account to cover part of the money he'd given Joe to pay off the Rapides Savings and Loan obligation, then, with another check for $15,000, he and Joe drove to the Oak Forest Bank. Jerrel gave Joe the certified check and stayed in his car while Joe went into the bank.

Joe went up to the vice-president who had okayed the check almost two weeks before. The vice-president looked up at him, a mixture of surprise and relief on his face. Before he could say anything Joe went into his hoary spiel. "I just discovered that while I was traveling on that deal I told you about, my bank back in Pensacola mistakenly closed out my account. But here's a certified check for fifteen thousand to cover the check you okayed for me."

The bank officer nodded, giving Joe a strange look. "Yes, Mr. Hodges, the check was returned to us just this morning."

Joe felt he could breathe again. The banking system was really slow, he thought. It had taken two weeks from the time he'd cashed the check for it to come back. The bank manager examined the $15,000 certified check, telephoned Jerrel Sullivan's bank and was told that the check was indeed good: it had been certified by them less than an hour before. Now the bank manager was all smiles.

"I wish everyone we did business with was as conscientious as you, Mr. Hodges."

Joe walked out of the bank and stepped into Jerrel's car, feeling as though the cares of the world had been lifted from his shoulders.

"What are you going to do now, Joe?" Jerrel asked.

"I'm going back to Pensacola, then I'm going to get this Shreveport deal put together and pay you back."

"You're busted now, Joe," Jerrel said. "Here, take this." He handed Joe an envelope. Joe opened it and found $2,000 cash inside. "You've got to have some walking-around money. Keep in touch. You can take your time about paying me the money but in the meantime maybe we can do some things together."

Joe was too choked with emotion to frame an adequate reply for this almost total stranger who had just saved his hide.

"Where do you want me to drop you off, Joe?" Jerrel asked.

"Take me to the bus station. I'll go to Shreveport and pick up my car, then drive to Pensacola and get all that behind me. Oh, and Jerrel?—thanks."

CHAPTER 47

Joe arrived at the bus station in Shreveport to pick up his car where it had been parked during the three frantic trips he had made to Las Vegas. He called Nancy in Pensacola and told her to get packed up: he'd be there late the next day and they were going to get out of town. Nancy told him that Wally Odom was looking for him. He had a lawyer now and, close church friend of the Hodgeses though he was, he wanted the $15,000 Joe owed him. He needed it. As usual, Joe had not told Nancy that he had gotten $15,000 from Wally on the Shreveport deal.

"Just be packed up, Nancy. I'll take care of that. We're coming back to Houston." Joe had called Pat Strobel and asked her to find a small rental house they could move into on February 1.

At nine o'clock on the morning after Joe returned to Pensacola, he called on Wally Odom. Wally apologized for getting a lawyer to collect the money but said he just had to have it. With all their furniture and belongings stowed in a U-Haul trailer, Mark, Amy, Nancy, and Joe were ready to leave Pensacola behind them. Unfortunately, Wally's lawyer had threatened to get a warrant for Joe's arrest if he tried to leave town before paying. Joe's family had already moved out of the house and were at the motel waiting for Joe to drive them home to Houston. Now Joe had to persuade Wally and his lawyer to let them go.

Joe met Wally and the lawyer at Wally's house. Wally had given the money to Joe to get in on the Shreveport deal which his lawyer characterized as a fraud. For four hours, from nine in the morning until one in the afternoon, Joe tried to convince Wally and his lawyer to let them go on to Houston. He would pay Wally back as soon as he could get the money but he couldn't make any money in Pensacola. Keeping him there did nobody any good.

Finally, despite his lawyer's angry remonstrances, Wally agreed to let Joe leave town. Joe hurried back to the motel and at two in the afternoon he and his family were on their way home to Houston. Flashes of *déjà vu* came to his mind's eye: the flights with Nancy from Zanesville, Midland, and Irving; angry creditors left behind again and again; he and his family speeding off toward what they hoped would be a new life.

Pat and Robert Strobel invited the Hodgeses to stay at their home until their rental house, only three blocks away, was ready on February 4. Joe had no idea how he was going to earn a living and he had the debts in Pensacola hanging over him. But he did have a friend and ally in Jerrel Sullivan. He began his old real estate transactions, trying to make some money for Jerrel and himself.

For a while Las Vegas was far from his mind. Jerrel gave Joe a small room and desk in his company offices in Houston and once again Joe was in business looking for opportunities. He kept in touch with Harry Newkirk, although he felt guilty about leaving the gravel pit mess behind him with all its impending lawsuits and judgments.

But even in Houston, Joe could not get away from the Pensacola problems. McKay, the executive vice-president of the Charter Bank, called him frequently. The bank also wrote him registered letters reminding him that he had to pay the $32,800 at the Charter Bank by April 1. Joe did not try to dodge his responsibilities and certainly was not hiding from creditors. He borrowed another $2,500 from Jerrel and reduced his loan at the Charter to just over $30,000. McKay informed Joe that they had allowed the Johnsons to withdraw the dragline as collateral for the loan so once again it was an unsecured loan and the bank was holding his hot checks. Joe did not understand the reason for this at first. He had long since paid back the money to cover them.

By March Joe had the loan down to $28,000. This was considerably over the amount owing on the bad checks but the bank was applying the money Joe sent in against the loan, not payment against the bad checks. Now he realized that the hot checks were being held as evidence for possible criminal prosecution.

Bob Gilmore was long gone from the Charter Bank and was working for, ironically, the Johnsons. He called Joe and so did Tommy Thompson, who was depressed about his motel which he still couldn't sell and the fact that the creditors of the gravel pit company were coming against him with a lien on the only property that Tommy and Harriet Thompson owned.

All Joe could do was tell Tommy to keep the faith. Curiously enough, he got a pleasant letter from Bob Brauer telling him the same thing.

Nancy, realizing the depth of their new troubles, once again wanted to go back to teaching school but had no car. Jerrel Sullivan stepped in and helped them out. Buying his faithful secretary-bookkeeper a new Pontiac, he let Joe take her old car, giving him title to it and telling him he could pay for it when he could afford it.

Joe's bad angel, Bobby Wilks, was still exerting his destructive attraction. Whenever Joe did get his hands on money he took it immediately to Bobby Wilks's crap game and lost it.

Finally, Joe was able to put together one of his real estate package deals out on a new freeway to the south of Houston and showed Jerrel how to joint-venture a real estate deal.

Early in May of 1975, while Jerrel was on vacation, Joe heard from Wally Odom in Pensacola that the Charter Bank had caused an indictment to be handed down against Joe for the bad checks they had been holding. Joe had been unable to pay off the loan and this was the bank's answer to his request for an extension of time.

Joe's response to the indictment was characteristic. With Jerrel on vacation he persuaded Carol, Jerrel's secretary, to call the bank used by Century Hardware and okay a check that Joe wanted to cash for $12,500. Naturally the check was hot, written on his nonexistent account at the Pensacola bank. On the basis of Carol's call the bank cashed his bogus check and Joe was off for Las Vegas to win the money he needed to get out of all his problems. As might have been expected, he blew it in one night, returning to Houston broke.

Needless to say, Jerrel Sullivan was livid when he found out what Joe had done. It wasn't a question of the money so much as Joe using Century Hardware's bank. Joe knew he had to pay the bank and decided to try to borrow some money on his two cars. Even though Bob Brauer had already loaned him $4,000 on one car, he had not asked for the title, which Joe still had. And Joe had title to the car that Jerrel had given him for Nancy, although he hadn't paid Jerrel for the car yet.

Joe slightly knew the president of a small bank, the Ashford Bank in a Houston suburb, and called on him. Mason Webster, president of the bank, loaned him $7,500 on the titles to the two cars. Now Joe had a relationship with a bank and was able to take the money from the loan and pay off part of what he owed at Jerrel's bank on the hot check.

Jerrel continued to be patient, even indulgent with Joe. Joe had made one successful land deal and the Shreveport racetrack land looked as though it might yet come through. But now he was back in the hot check business. His chief interest was getting the money for Vegas where he would try to gamble his way out of his myriad difficulties. Between unsecured notes and hot checks, he took $24,500 from the Ashford Bank after having made his car loan, all of this money going to Las Vegas and not coming back. He now owed Jerrel Sullivan $45,000. Jerrel had signed a note for Joe at the Ashford Bank and had allowed him to present the Sullivan financial statement to Mason Webster as some security that the loans would be repaid. Meantime Joe continued to reassure Jerrel, saying that the Shreveport deal would be coming through momentarily.

At last Jerrel became so discouraged with Joe's financial drain on him that in desperation he gave him $3,000 cash. "Take it out to Wilks's. Maybe you can hit a lick."

Joe took it to Bobby Wilks's and blew it. Then he got into a gin rummy game with some old friends and lost a further $1,800 which he was unable to pay. He stiffed them and that really hurt him. There was nothing worse for a gambler than playing gin rummy with friends, losing, and not paying off.

Joe was so obsessed with winning big at Las Vegas that all his energies were concentrated on pumping money and trying to make the big win. He'd made them before, he knew he could make them again.

It was becoming increasingly difficult for him to cash checks at banks. Mason Webster, who had been president of the Ashford Bank, was no longer employed there. This was a blow to Joe who had just convinced Webster to consolidate his hot checks into an overall unsecured loan with Jerrel's help. Jim Kelly, the vice-president, was handling the collection of the money Joe owed.

In his customary manner, Joe ingratiated himself with Jim Kelly, who was impressed with Jerrel Sullivan's financial statement, and of course he made an active effort to get Jerrel to switch the Century account from the Cullen Center Bank to the Ashford Bank. Jim Kelly, despite Joe's indebtedness, would remain indulgent for a while.

When Joe went to Jim Kelly desperately in need of money, Jim called a friend of his at the Jacinto City Bank in a suburb of Houston. He even loaned Joe a certificate of deposit in the amount of $2,500 which he could use to establish credit at the Jacinto City Bank. With Jim Kelly's introduction and the CD, Joe was able to borrow $4,000 at the bank which of course he took right to Las Vegas where he lost it in a matter of hours.

A week later he went back to the Jacinto City Bank and again, because he'd been set up by Jim Kelly, smashed a $6,500 hot check and was on his way to Las Vegas. Again, he lost it all.

Before the hot check could come through, Joe went back to the Jacinto City Bank with a bogus check for $17,000 which he deposited into his account, withdrawing $6,600 against it. On Friday night he blew it at the crap tables of Vegas and flew back to Houston, showing up at the Jacinto City Bank Saturday morning to cash yet another check since he knew that the $17,000 bogus deposit could not have come back by then.

Joe had arrived from Las Vegas at 6 A.M. He drove out to Jacinto City where he found an old washroom and shaved and made himself presentable. At nine-thirty he went up to the cashier's window and made some conversation with the girl behind the teller's cage. He handed her a check on his account for $6,000.

"Just a minute, Mr. Hodges," the girl said. "It's just routine, I've got to check in back." Joe waited at the teller's desk for a few minutes wondering why it was taking the girl so long to clear his check. He began to get nervous and instinctively started to turn and get out of the bank when suddenly a police officer was standing there with a shotgun pointing at him. "Joe H. Hodges, you're under arrest."

"For what?" Joe snapped. He knew that the check he had opened his account with could not possibly have gotten back to the bank in two days.

"There is a warrant for your arrest for flight to avoid prosecution. It's a federal warrant out of Florida." The police officer took Joe to the Jacinto City jail. Joe was completely taken by surprise. He knew that he had been indicted, because his friends in Pensacola had told him. But flight to avoid prosecution? Everybody knew where he was, he had not been hiding from anyone. He'd been on the phone constantly to the Charter Bank and had even made more payments against the loan which, of course, was overdue.

At the jail they let Joe make one phone call and he caught Nancy at home. He asked her to get hold of a lawyer friend of his, Earl Lilly, whom he had run into in Las Vegas on his last trip.

Earl and Nancy went out to the Jacinto City jail to see Joe but they could not get him out on bond; that would have to wait until Monday when a hearing was scheduled. So Joe spent the weekend in Jacinto City jail and on Monday was taken before a federal magistrate in Houston. When he arrived in Houston he was turned over to the U.S. marshal who, of course, was his old friend Henry Baker.

"Henry," Joe began, "I'm not guilty of this charge. I don't expect you to believe that but they've got a ten-thousand-dollar federal bond sitting on me and I can't make it."

"I'll help you if I can, Joe," Henry promised. At the hearing, to which Earl and Nancy had come along to lend Joe their support, the magistrate listened to the charges. Then Henry Baker spoke up. "I know this man, your honor, he won't run."

The magistrate released Joe on his own recognizance on the $10,000 bond. Joe immediately borrowed $500 from his Greek friend Jimmy Demeris and $500 from Turk and flew to Pensacola. He paid the bondsman in Pensacola $1,000 to put up the $10,000 state of Florida bond and Winston Reynolds signed for it along with Joe. Then Joe hired a lawyer, Calvin Wilson, to handle the matter.

The Pensacola indictment and the arrest so unnerved Joe, so demoralized him, that he saw no option but to continue smashing hot checks and trying to score big in Las Vegas.

He no longer stayed at home but lived at various motels, visiting Nancy and the children but never making himself easy to find. At any time the hot checks would be coming back to the Jacinto City Bank which would file against him, adding to his Pensacola woes. He also had a hot check at the Cullen Center Bank which still carried Jerrel's account. Some raw instinct of animal survival had taken over as he struggled to win his way out of trouble.

As luck would have it, he ran into an old gambler and thief he had known who gave him a set of checks on the First Security Bank of Utah printed with the name of Cedrick Hoover. Another friend of Joe's, one of those he still hadn't paid back for the gin rummy game, Tim Smith, gave him an introduction to the Colonial Savings and Loan Association.

On Saturday morning in May, Joe used a Cedrick Hoover check to open a savings account at the Colonial and at the same time took a check for $3,500 back from them so he could "wire some money to his partner on a deal." Unfortunately for Joe, the Colonial's bank was the Fannin Bank which he had beaten out of $20,000 ten years before. The Fannin Bank immediately warned Colonial which stopped the check that they'd given Joe on Saturday. Joe had already presented the check at the Oak Forest Bank to take some of the heat off him and now had to go around and pump the $3,500 to pay Oak Forest for the check that Colonial had so prudently stopped just in time.

It was cut and slash now as Joe went after the bankroll that would give him another shot at Las Vegas and the win that would save him. On a Wednesday in May he went down to the main branch of the Houston First Federal Savings and Loan and opened up a large savings account, depositing checks on a Pensacola bank and, of course, one of his Utah checks printed with the name of a depositor, Cedrick Hoover. He made a total deposit of $25,000 and received a passbook in return indicating his deposit.

The following Saturday he went to one of the branches of the Houston First Federal Savings and Loan with another Cedrick Hoover check, this time made out for $16,500. He approached the manager of the branch and took out his passbook.

"Perhaps you can help me," Joe began in his usual polite manner. "I have a check here for sixteen thousand five hundred dollars and I need to put eight thousand of this money into my account and wire eighty-five hundred to my partner on a real estate deal we're closing Monday morning."

"We can't wire money on a Saturday, Mr. Hodges," the branch manager informed him. Naturally Joe knew this. The transfer department of any bank is closed on Saturday.

"Oh, I'm certainly sorry about that," Joe said in mock chagrin.

"What we can do is give you our check for eighty-five hundred and deposit the other eight thousand into your account," the manager said cheerfully.

"Oh well, I think that would work out just fine." Joe beamed. "Do you have a bank that is open?"

"Oh yes, we bank over at the Galleria Bank just across the way. You can cash the check there. I'll call over and tell them you're coming."

"Oh would you please? I'd sure appreciate that."

The bank manager took Joe's passbook which showed a balance of $25,000. He upped the balance to $33,000 and gave him a check for $8,500. Then, obligingly, he called over to the bank at the Galleria and informed them that Mr. Hodges would be coming over with a check just issued by them and would they cash it please.

Joe walked over to the Galleria complex where he cashed the check. Well before noontime he was on a flight for Las Vegas. Today he wouldn't have too much time. His son, Mark, was the catcher of his little league team and they had a big game that night at seven. Robert and Pat Strobel and Hugh and Nelda Fonville would be there, along with Nancy and some of their other friends, to cheer Mark and their sons on to victory.

Joe arrived at McCarran Airport at about noon Las Vegas

time and took a cab over to the Sands casino, his favorite now. In two hours he had won $28,000 above the $8,500 he'd gone out with. He felt that he was in a winning streak and could have gone anywhere, but he knew he had to get back to the little league game. If he put anything in front of gambling it was his son.

Reluctantly he cashed in the $28,000 worth of chips, knowing he was walking out on a winning streak. He was back in Houston at five after seven that evening and turned up at the little league game just in time for the opening of the first inning. He smiled at Nancy and their friends and sat down beside them.

The $28,000 was not enough to cover his checks at Houston First Federal or make much of a dent in his other debts and hot checks. He felt he should not have come back when he did but stayed and run his winning streak as high as he could. Returning was foolish, he told himself. But then, watching Mark out on the little league diamond, he realized he had done what he had to do.

Nevertheless, on Monday he took the $28,000 plus the $8,500 he had extracted from the bank, went back to Las Vegas, and lost it all overnight.

On Tuesday morning when he arrived back from Las Vegas broke, he went to the main office of the Houston First Federal Savings and Loan to draw more money from his $33,000 account. Ordinarily, he knew the bank put a hold into the computer on out-of-state checks for fifteen days until the checks had cleared. But thinking back four days to the previous Saturday, it occurred to Joe that when he had deposited one check in the branch bank and received a check despite the hold that should have been on his account, the computer may have been thrown off and not registered a hold on the deposit he had made the Wednesday before. That transaction turned it all into real money!

In the main office of the bank on Tuesday morning Joe went up to one of the windows and said he wanted to withdraw $12,500 from his $33,000 account, leaving in it a balance, or an apparent balance, of $20,500. The teller put the request into the computer and out came the check for $12,500. For one reason or another there was no hold on the money.

Joe dashed from the savings and loan to a bank where he could cash the check and then made a direct run to the airport and was airborne for Las Vegas less than an hour after he had pocketed the stacks of $100 bills.

At the Sands casino he hit a streak and ran the $12,500 up to $50,000. The old excitement swept over him at this win and he toyed with walking out a winner. But this win was not enough to square all his problems. He would go for $20,000 more and then quit. He tried baccarat, betting on players and bank depending on who was the last winner, but the cards chopped down his pile of chips drastically and he returned to the crap table. The streak had deserted him. He went through all his winnings and then dropped the last of his bankroll on the crap table and slunk out of Las Vegas, again defeated.

Joe was now afraid of the Houston First Savings. He was on the run, living in motels; but compulsive gambler that he was, already he had evolved the new "plan."

Fate seemed to have him in a stranglehold. Nevertheless, on Wednesday he went to two savings and loan banks in Houston, Southwestern Savings and Gibraltar Savings. He opened up accounts with each one using a fictitious address, 4600 Westheimer. Just J. H. Hodges. There were still no charges of a criminal nature against him. He was safe on the Florida charge for the time being, having bailed himself out. And there was nothing pending against him in Houston.

With his Utah and Pensacola checks he opened up $32,000 accounts at each of the two savings and loans and received his passbooks back indicating the amounts.

It seemed he had bought himself a short breathing space.

CHAPTER 48

Late the following Saturday morning, Joe went back to a small branch of the Southwestern Savings and Loan and stood in the line waiting for the services of the young woman behind the teller's cage. He had picked the smallest branch he could find and made himself last in line so that he would be alone with the teller. He began his usual pitch. He wanted to make a deposit, and he had to wire some money to a business partner.

He handed the girl a $15,000 check, on the nonexistent Cedrick Hoover account in Utah. She added $10,000 to his savings account and gave him a check for $5,000. "You can't wire money today, I'm sorry."

"Oh, I didn't realize that," Joe said innocently. "Is there a bank you deal with that will cash this for me?" The teller called a small bank nearby and asked them to cash the $5,000 check she had just given to Joe.

Less than an hour later he was at the airport on his way to Vegas. Gambling all Saturday night and on till noon on Sunday, he ran the $5,000 up and down. By early Sunday afternoon he had blown it all and he took a flight back to Houston.

That Sunday night he was champing at the bit waiting for Southwestern Savings to open the next morning. He was back at the same small Southwestern branch first thing, opening a friendly conversation with the same girl behind the window who had given him the check on Saturday. Joe was good at building rapport with bank employees.

This time he gave her another of his Cedrick Hoover Utah

checks made out to Joe H. Hodges for $25,000 and withdrew $17,000, increasing his balance in the savings account by $8,000.

Monday afternoon he was back at the Las Vegas tables in mortal combat with the craps dealers; and by Tuesday morning, after fifteen hours of struggle, he had blown the $17,000 and was on a plane home again, broke. He had been getting very little sleep recently, going to Vegas almost every night. But what could he do? Pull up and quit now? At this stage there was no quitting. The big win which kept eluding him, he knew, would be his if he could just stick things out.

His private war against the banks and casinos intensified. Although he was frightened even to enter any of the savings institutions, he had to get money for the next attack on the tables. He went to a different Southwestern Savings branch and tried to make a withdrawal, but this time the computer beat him. There was a fifteen-day hold on the account until the checks cleared.

"Oh, my goodness, I need to wire this money to my partner. We've got a big real estate deal working." Joe's worried, almost pleading tone had no effect on the lady behind the teller's cage.

"I'm sorry, Mr. Hodges, there's nothing we can do about it. There's a hold on the account until the check clears."

Joe drove to another branch of the Southwestern Savings and Loan and walked up to a woman office manager who also worked as a teller.

He handed her his passbook. "A few days ago they had a hold on my account. I was told it was taken off. Maybe there's some way you can help me. I have to wire this money to my partner who's closing a real estate deal up in Dallas."

The woman pressed buttons on the computer and then looked up at Joe. "No, the hold is still on there. But I'm sure it should be off by now. It's been eleven days. We ought to be able to help you, Mr. Hodges." She gave him a sincere business smile.

"I need to send some of this money by wire," Joe said, handing her a check for $18,500. "I want to deposit this with you and take out ten thousand eight hundred so that I can get it off to my partner. Can you handle that for me?"

"I think so." Her voice was reassuring. "We'll issue you a check."

"Fine, I sure do appreciate that, ma'am. I'm right in the middle of putting together this real estate deal and then it will all be going in and none coming out." He gave the woman branch manager a friendly smile, got the money, and left for the airport.

Thirty-six hours later, broke once more, he presented himself to a Gibraltar Savings teller. Again he traded a bogus Utah check, this time for $9,600, and took $5,000 from his passbook. Back in Las Vegas he lost the entire bankroll out of which he had defrauded Gibraltar. The following Saturday he went back to Southwestern Savings and Loan one last time and drew out everything in his passbook in one of the small branches, leaving $200 in the account. When the Southwestern "account" was extinguished he continued with Gibraltar until his account there was bled dry too. Over a two-week period, which included eleven trips to Nevada, the total was over $60,000!

In June, Joe's mother had to move out of her house when the $22,000 payment to her nephew Gene came due. The house was sold. A terrible pang of guilt and self-loathing assaulted Joe, but all he could do was continue trying to solve his problems at the tables. Gene got his $22,000—and Southwestern had finally caught up with Joe H. Hodges.

When the vice-president of Southwestern threatened to prosecute him, Joe borrowed $1,000 each from Judge Bob Thomas in Beaumont, who was married to his first cousin Dolores, his cousin Gene Van Meter and another cousin, Ronny Van Meter, having them write checks directly to Southwestern Savings. He then dashed back to Houston and with the $3,000 delayed the bank opening criminal charges against him.

Southwestern turned the account over to its bonding company and was paid all but $5,000 of the money Joe had taken.

To keep his Las Vegas excursions going Joe went to Lake Charles, Louisiana, to try once again to use the Bossier City land package to extract money from possible investors. In July he had found Ed Godwin, who gave him $24,500 to get into the land deal. Now, on another trip to Lake Charles, he approached Godwin again and told him he needed another $15,000 to cement it. Godwin gave him the money, whereupon Joe flew directly to Las Vegas and lost it at the Aladdin. Now he owed Houston First Savings, Southwestern Savings, Gibraltar Savings, and Ed Godwin a total of $100,000.

Joe's next move was to stall the Gibraltar Savings and Loan. The checks had all come back and it was only a matter of time before Gibraltar would file a criminal complaint against him.

Forthrightly he picked up his phone and called the president of Gibraltar, identifying himself as J. H. Hodges. He heard a surprised gasp on the other end of the line.

"I'd like to come down and talk to you about the situation I have with your bank," Joe said.

"You want to come down here?" the bank president replied, hardly able to believe his ears.

"Yes sir, I'd like to come down and talk to you."

"Well fine," the president boomed back heartily, having recovered from his shock. "Come in at ten a.m. tomorrow."

"Fine, sir. I'll be there."

The next morning Joe put on his best suit and asked his friend Rudy Flato to go down to the bank with him. He had a premonition that something untoward was going to happen. He walked up to the president's desk. "I know we have a problem and I am here to discuss how we can take care of it. I have a check for five thousand dollars I can bring in to you tomorrow." He was expecting a check against Nancy's retirement to come in the mail. "And I'd like to work out a repayment schedule with you."

The bank president stood up. "I'll have to talk to our lawyers about it. Why don't you gentlemen have a seat over there." He gestured toward a leather sofa. "I'll be back in just a few minutes."

Five minutes later a police officer arrived with a warrant for Joe's arrest. Resignedly Joe handed his car keys and briefcase to Rudy and the police officer escorted him to the Houston jail. Bond was set at $50,000, an impossible amount for Joe to raise. The first person to visit him in jail was Jerrel Sullivan. Joe greatly appreciated his friend's thoughtfulness.

"Joe, I'll help you all I can but I don't see any way you're going to get out of this. They're certainly not going to turn you loose until you make that fifty-thousand bond. I can't do it. Nancy can't do it. But somehow we'll keep trying."

Joe had asked Rudy Flato to call Nancy and tell her to get in touch with a bondsman friend of Joe's, Scott Templeton. With Nancy anxiously directing the operation, Templeton found a small-time lawyer friend of his and they went before a justice of the peace to get a reduction in bail. Fortunately for Joe, the justice of the peace who had set the $50,000 bond was away on a fishing trip and another justice reduced the bond to $10,000.

Nancy scraped together $1,000 and gave it to Scott Templeton. They made the bond. Joe had been in jail for three days before Nancy succeeded in getting him out.

Joe went home with Nancy just long enough to pick up the clothes he would need and to see Mark and Amy. By now Mark knew that his father was out of jail on bond and understood that he would make himself hard to find from now on.

The gambling, far from coming to a halt, was more frenzied than ever. After Joe got out of jail he went to Pensacola where he and Harry Newkirk obtained $12,000 from two investors in Panama City for the Shreveport land deal.

Joe went immediately from Pensacola to Atlanta and from Atlanta to Las Vegas, losing the whole sum in two hours.

As Joe flew back from Vegas after losing the Panama City contribution, he as usual began putting together the new plan. He remembered his old friend Heywood Lloyd out in Texarkana who had given him the work release job when his sentence at the penitentiary was coming to an end. Heywood and his wife had been good friends so Joe flew to Texarkana and spent a day with them, ending up borrowing $8,000.

Next stop, of course, Las Vegas.

He ran the $8,000 up to $80,000 at craps and baccarat. Why not take it back to Houston with him and try and buy out of his criminal problems? He stopped gambling long enough to total up the debts that amounted to intense heat. They came to $279,000, and were exclusive of personal loans.

Joe had been gambling hard for one and a half days to win the $80,000 but he was still a long way from overcoming the heat waiting for him in Texas and Florida. "My God!" the gambler thought. "What else can I do?"

Back to the crap tables he went for another spate of hard, aggressive gambling. It only took half a day for him to lose the entire $80,000. Now he was really panicking. He arrived back in Houston on a rainy Thursday afternoon and stayed hidden, although he and Nancy kept in touch by pay phone. He never knew when the law would descend upon him.

Sitting in his hotel room Joe noticed a newspaper ad. The University Savings and Loan had opened a new branch on Beechnut, not far from Bellaire where Nancy was living. Joe put on his suit again, took up his leather attaché case and headed for the new bank, arriving about 3 P.M. There were two women in charge of the branch when Joe walked in. He went up to the one behind a desk, nodding and smiling at the other who was handling the teller's cage.

He paused at the desk, looking down at the branch manager. "Good afternoon. How are you, ma'am? I want to start a savings account. I just read in the paper that University Savings has opened its new branch here, and since it's near my home, I thought this would be a convenient savings bank."

"We'd be glad to have you with us." The manager smiled cheerfully. "Here are the forms. If you'll just fill them out we'll get you started with us."

"Thank you, ma'am. I've got these checks. I want to put them into my savings account and wire some money to my partner. We're trying to close a big real estate deal up near Dallas."

"You need to wire some money?" the woman asked sharply. From the tone of her voice Joe smelled trouble.

"No, I'm thinking about wiring some money but first I'd better call my partner and see how much he'll need. I probably ought to have him on this account with me. Can I make a local call?"

"Certainly," the manager invited. Joe picked up the phone, faked a call and hung up.

"I'll tell you what I'd like to do. I'll get my associate and we'll be back at four o'clock if you're open that late."

"Oh, don't you want to do it now?" She seemed to be pushing him.

"No, I've got to go. I'll be back later." His eyes—wary now—

covered the bank, the sidewalk and the street outside as he left the savings and loan. There was big trouble brewing here—but he had escaped it!

He got back into his car and drove out to Gulfgate where the main office of the Buffalo Savings and Loan was located. He had been to this bank before when he'd made loans with Ben Kostial. Now what used to be the main office was a branch in the shopping center.

Joe walked into the bank and again there were two women, both standing behind the tellers' cages.

"Good afternoon," Joe opened. "I need to wire some money and I've got these checks. Perhaps you can help me."

"We can't wire any money," one of the girls said.

"Could you give me your check back if I start an account here? I really need a savings account."

"Even if you start an account with us today we can't give you a withdrawal check until the checks you give us clear."

Joe realized he wasn't going to get any money here and there was no use pursuing it. He felt totally deflated and asked if he could use the phone. By now it was almost 4 P.M. and Nancy was at home waiting to hear from him.

"Joe, where are you?" She sounded distraught. "The Ashford Bank is desperately trying to get hold of you. Jim Kelly says to call him, it's an emergency. And a man at the Cullen Bank is trying to reach you. Also somebody from Southwestern Savings, a Mr. Schlar, called."

"Thanks. I'll take care of them and I'll call you in a little bit." He hung up the phone, thanked the teller for letting him make the call, and then proceeded out of the bank and down the shopping center to the Walgreen's drugstore. He needed to make some phone calls in privacy.

As he walked down the sidewalk he saw a car drive up to the Buffalo Savings and Loan and park right in front of it in a "no parking" zone. A gray-haired man in a blue suit briskly stepped out of the car and hurried into the bank. Joe went into the drugstore and searched about for a phone that was reasonably private.

He had to talk to the Ashford Bank. He was stalling—spinning plates—trying to avoid indictment and prosecution. He was already out on bond with the Gibraltar so they couldn't do anything to him. He was also on bond in Florida on the Charter Bank bad checks. But the Ashford Bank—he had to talk to Jim Kelly and he had to stave off the Cullen Bank, Southwestern Savings, and Houston First Savings.

He found a phone and called Jim Kelly at the Ashford Bank. Kelly urgently importuned Joe to do something about their $17,000 in bad checks. "We're carrying that as cash out here, but it's been a couple of months, Joe. I don't know how much longer I can wait. You've got to do something."

"Jim, I'm working on this deal; I should have some money for you within two weeks. Can't you hold off for a couple more weeks?" Kelly didn't have much choice; prosecuting Joe wouldn't have helped his own banking career. He gave Joe another two weeks to raise the money.

Joe hung up and started to call Schlar at the Southwestern Savings. He didn't know what to tell him. He had taken the $3,000 he'd borrowed from his cousins and some of Nancy's teacher retirement money and paid back some of what he'd fraudulently withdrawn. But he still owed the bank $23,000.

Just as Joe dialed the last digit of the number of Southwestern Savings he noticed the man he had seen going into the Buffalo Savings coming down the hall toward him with a uniformed armed security guard. A sense of foreboding gripped him. No one but he was in the corridor or at the phones. His heart pounded furiously as the two men passed by him. The phone was ringing at Southwestern. Suddenly the men turned on their heels and each one grabbed Joe by an arm.

Joe looked around and stared at them. "What's this all about?" In anger born of terror he hung up the phone, taking his dime back out of the slot. "Now just what's this all about?" Righteous indignation arose as fear tore at his guts.

"Were you just over there in the Buffalo Savings Bank?" asked the man in the blue suit.

"I sure was. Why?" Joe could see the monolithic stone structure of Leavenworth in his mind's eye.

"Did you have some checks there to open a savings account and ask to wire some money?"

"Yes, but they couldn't wire the money." Somehow he had to

brazen it out. "I was just calling my associates. They're going out to your main office. We've got a real estate deal we're trying to close. I've done a lot of business with Buffalo. What's the trouble?"

The executive identified himself. "I'm Angelo Fortunato, president of Buffalo Savings."

Before the banker could go on, Joe hid his panic behind outrage and said icily, "I don't know what you want of me. You certainly have no right to accost me this way." He could see his indignant protests were having some effect. The security guard seemed doubtful and even Fortunato was unsure of his next move. They let go of Joe.

"Is your name Hodges?" Fortunato demanded.

"What? No. My name is Rogers."

"Do you have identification?" the bank president asked.

"I sure do." It took enormous control to inject the right pitch of confidence into his tone. "Why?"

"I'd like to see it."

"Well, you're not going to see it," Joe stormed. "Now what is this? I want to know exactly what you're trying to do." This approach was his only chance.

The bank president started to back off. "Well, perhaps I've made a mistake. A letter has gone out to all the savings and loans in Houston about a man named Hodges. All the banks are looking for him. Perhaps I've made a mistake."

"I can guarantee you've made a mistake, sir. If there's anything else, I'll be glad to meet you with my lawyers at your main office on Monday."

"No, that won't be necessary," the bank president replied. Joe flashed an aggrieved look, straightened out his suit coat, turned and walked away from the two men. He could feel them watching him and he took his time getting to the car. He drove out of the shopping center, taking devious routes, which wasn't hard because he had no idea where he wanted to go.

When he was well away from the bank he slumped weakly behind the wheel and sighed deeply in relief. It was the closest call yet. No wonder the woman at the University Savings had tried to hold him in the branch. She had undoubtedly called for a security guard before he left.

CHAPTER 49

His spirits at the zenith from beating the Foxy Lady, his breast pocket brimming with $20 bills, Jonathan Alan Roberts once again heard the siren call of the large casinos.

He walked out onto Las Vegas Boulevard and took a cab to the Dunes Hotel. At the Dunes he went to the men's room where he washed his face, straightened his tie, and smoothed his hair. By now it was 3 A.M. and only a skeleton shift was manning the casino, although the baccarat table was more than half full.

Jon sat down and began betting $100 on each turn of the cards. Encouraged by a few wins, he advanced his bets to $200 and $400 on each play. But the shoe was mixed and no streak appeared for either the bank or the players. Jon's system of going with the players as long as they won, then shifting to the bank was rendered ineffective and the hard-earned $20 bills from the Foxy Lady soon dwindled.

He walked away from the baccarat table with only $9 left in his pocket. Asking for the shift manager, he requested that the house cash a $1,000 check for him. The shift manager gave him the stock reply: "We'll have to wait until Monday morning when we can verify it with your bank."

Jon's vociferous protests were to no avail so he left the casino. Now unable to use a cab, he started walking. After almost a three-mile hike he found himself in front of the blinking lights at the Jolly Trolley.

He began betting 25¢ chips across on all the numbers at this lowest of low-limit games and after winning some and then losing he moved on to another penny-ante-type joint, Slots of Fun. He got $8 in change for the $1 bills he had left and started feeding the slot machines. He watched which ones were played for a long period of time without hitting and then tried to coax jackpots from them.

At 7 A.M. with eighteen nickels in his hand, he staggered out into the Monday morning sunlight, startled at its brilliance. He stank of alcohol, smoke, and sweat. He weaved downtown looking at the $250,000 Keno signs, the storefronts advertising beautiful models, girls, and escort services. But of real life there was nothing. The town was dead, a ghost town.

A cab driver paused. "Give you a lift, buddy?" Jon looked up at him wearily and shook his head. He had emerged from some subterranean world a bum, a thin shell of the Jonathan Alan Roberts who had been riding so high with $140,000 in the rack in front of him for a short while at Binion's, when was it—yesterday? The day before? There were no outs left for him, nobody he could call. He was broke. He shambled over to the bus station, dropped onto a bench and stared at the buses coming and going. He was shell-shocked.

Well after darkness fell, with the lights glittering and the action popping all over Las Vegas, Jonathan Alan Roberts was still sitting on that bench staring straight ahead.

CHAPTER 50

Twisting, turning, looking for some hiding place, Joe had located the son of his old gambling friend Sid Wright from Irving, Texas. Sid was dead now but his son Jim had become a friend of Joe's and was protecting him, letting him stay in his apartment in Houston. Joe's other friend and lawyer, Earl Lilly, was trying to stall off indictments against him by the banks, assuring them that Joe would be paying them if they'd just hold off a little longer.

In his frenetic search for money Joe had hit most of the regular banks within a twenty-mile radius of the center of Houston. There were eighty-four of them but he was beginning to run out. Each time he scored off a bank he was on the next flight to Las Vegas, staying there until the money was gone. He was now passing checks from all over the country. He had a collection of Florida instruments and was still using the Cedrick Hoover checks and even some of Jim Wright's to raise a bankroll for Las Vegas.

Things were getting so hot he no longer dared go through the Houston Airport. He even took his bogus checks to his hometown of Beaumont early one week and opened up a $25,000 savings account with a savings association there. Then on Saturday he made a $15,000 withdrawal and flew from Beaumont to Dallas to Las Vegas deliberately avoiding Houston. By September law enforcement officers were coming around to Joe's house looking for him, asking Nancy and even Mark questions. In Beaumont, Joe did not stay at the apartment his mother rented although he did go over to see her. They were looking for him there as well. Four times he flew between Las Vegas and Beaumont, each time tapping the Beaumont Savings and Loan for more money as he gave them bogus checks.

By the fourth trip he had hit Beaumont for $41,000. He was using his Utah checks because he knew it would take a minimum of two weeks for them to be returned unpaid from Salt Lake City. That fourth trip to the Beaumont bank was on the twelfth day after he'd opened the account and he knew he was getting close to the time when the checks would come crashing back.

Most of the money from the Beaumont bank was going into the Sands casino but finally, on his last trip, after losing so regularly at the Sands, he went to the Stardust. By now the criminal heat on him had reached $400,000. Then at last, after so many disastrous trips, he cashed the Beaumont check with the casino cashier and ran into a lucky streak, playing all night, building up his bankroll to where be was betting with the white $500 chips. He built up racks of them and won $125,000 shooting dice.

In ecstasy he retired, at least temporarily, from the crap tables. Feeling as though he had put the electric surge into Frankenstein's monster and brought it back to life, he deposited the $125,000 in the credit cage and went back up to his room with the $8,000 he'd started with. This was the $8,000 that had moved his deficit on the Beaumont Savings and Loan from $33,000 to $41,000. Upstairs he took a shower and telephoned Earl Lilly. He told Earl he had done well and had just scored in a big way. Not enough to pay off all the heat, but certainly enough to make substantial down payments to the banks he had defrauded. "How much do you have, Joe?" Earl asked.

"It doesn't matter, you don't know how much I owe. But I don't have enough."

"Well, those checks to the banks, you're going to have to pay them all."

"I'll see you when I get back, Earl," Joe promised.

Joe thought about the $400,000 or more that he owed and the $125,000 that he now possessed. There was no way $125,000 was going to get him out of the trouble he was in. He went back down to the casino and started gambling again. When he was down to $60,000 his anger at himself and the casinos suddenly rammed some sense into his mind. He stopped gambling and went home with $60,000 plus his $8,000 from the Beaumont Savings and Loan.

On September 23, 1975, he gave Earl Lilly $34,700 and handed him the Beaumont Savings and Loan check which he had won back. He also gave Earl a list of the banks to which he wanted to make partial restitution in exchange for an undertaking from them that they would not prosecute him. At the top of the list was the Beaumont Savings and Loan, followed by banks to which he was indebted for lesser amounts. There was no way he could handle Gibraltar or Southwestern which he owed $28,700 and $23,000 respectively.

Earl telephoned the various banks and then the district attorney's office. The assistant D.A. told Lilly that he had Joe Hodges' case before the Special Crimes Division of the Harris County D.A.'s office. No restitution would be accepted in return for dropping criminal prosecution. "We don't want the money," the district attorney informed Earl Lilly in no uncertain manner. "We want Joe Hodges in jail. Permanently."

Earl reported the discouraging news to Joe at a meeting in his office the next day. "I guess there's nothing we can do. Even if you make full restitution they're going to prosecute you. And this is a series of cases you can't win."

"All right, Earl, let me have my money back." Earl took out his checkbook and started to write a check. "My God! What in blazes can I do with a check even if it's good. I've got to have the cash."

"I deposited it in my account when you brought it to me, Joe," Earl said. "I don't keep a lot of cash around the office."

"How am I going to cash a check? The FBI has an all-points bulletin on me, the sheriff and the police are looking too."

Joe thought about the problem for a few minutes and remembered the banker who had helped him before, Pat Hamilton. Lilly's check was written on Pat's bank. Joe owed him no money. He called Pat and asked if he could come in to his private office and cash a check. "It's a good one, Pat," Joe said hastily when he heard the intake of breath over the wire. "I'll bring the maker of the check, Earl Lilly, with me."

Joe and Earl drove out to the bank in Bellaire just a few blocks from where Nancy, Mark, and Amy were living. Joe was certain every car he saw had FBI or plainclothes detectives looking for him. Joe walked into the bank hesitantly, his eyes darting around, Earl Lilly behind him, and proceeded to the gate behind which was Pat Hamilton's office. He presented Earl's check and Pat sent the check out with a bank officer who soon brought back the $34,700 in cash.

Joe thanked Pat and left the bank with Earl. Outside in the shopping center he telephoned Nancy and asked her to meet him. When she arrived, her face a mask of anxiety, Joe said he was going to have to leave Houston for a while. He gave Nancy $1,000 and told her he'd keep in touch by telephone. Then with $33,700 and the additional $25,000 from his last Vegas trip, he flew back to Las Vegas and in one night blew the whole $58,700 at the Dunes.

Trapped and desperate, Joe still had to come up with "the plan" before he could rest or think of anything else. Houston, of course, was out. He decided to try the American Bank in Huntsville, Texas, about seventy miles north of Houston. He'd never been in Huntsville although he knew it was the location of the state penitentiary. "I might as well get used to the town," he told himself grimly. The American Bank was not a savings and loan but a regular bank. With one of his Utah checks he put $27,000 into a savings account there. The banker gave him a passbook and he gave his name as Henry Hodges leaving out the J. He also gave a Conroe, Texas, address. It was in fact the address of a barbershop.

Following his usual pattern with savings accounts, Joe made his first withdrawal from the Huntsville Bank on October 1. On October 3 he was back from Las Vegas broke. His first withdrawal was for $15,000. On October 3 he took out $9,000 and was back again on October 8 when he withdrew $8,700. Back once more from Las Vegas on October 10 he withdrew another $5,400, depositing bogus checks as he accepted the cash. Even as he took money out, the account balance indicated in the passbook was going up.

And so on October 10, with the money he had withdrawn from his account, Joe returned to the casino of the Sands Hotel. The $5,400 lasted two hours. He had lost over $300,000 at the Sands in just over three weeks and everybody knew him well. The credit manager, Bucky Walters, extended him $2,000 credit. Joe still had two bogus checks he had made out previously. He gave one for $8,000 to Bucky. "I've got this check, Bucky, and I have two more in my wallet. I know you'll be getting off work in an hour."

"That's all right, Joe. Come with me." Followed by Joe he walked over to the cage and said, "Let Mr. Hodges have his eight thousand." In forty-five minutes of rash playing Joe had lost the $8,000. By now it was after 4 A.M. and Bucky would have left. Joe went back to the cashier's cage to talk to the young man whom Bucky had directed to cash his first check. "Remember, Bucky said I'd have more checks?"

Joe pulled out another bogus check for $11,100 and handed it under the cage to the cashier. "How much of it do you want now?" the teller asked.

"Just give me about three thousand and leave the rest on deposit." Joe didn't dare ask for it all. He probably would have been given the money but he was scared. As he turned from the cage he saw another pit boss coming over to the cashier. Casually Joe edged toward the door with the $3,000 as the public address system blared, "Paging Mr. Bucky Walters." Joe knew very well why they were paging him. They wanted to see if he'd really approved the $11,100 check.

Joe eased himself out the door of the casino and then walked down the Strip to the Holiday Inn casino where he played the rest of the night. He ran the $3,000 up and down, trying to hang on, punishing himself, hoping against hope, even though by now he realized his struggle was useless. Nevertheless, with that last $3,000 he fought the odds, playing $20 a time, even $10 and $5, trying to make the dice behave for him. He played through the sunrise and all day. Late in the afternoon the casino finally beat him out of the last dollar.

He walked to the airport having only some change and his airline ticket. He had no destination. He only knew he had to get out of Las Vegas. He was tired, disheveled, dejected, and like a man at the bottom of a well who doesn't cry out because he knows his cries will go unheard.

Walking through the airport, past the security guards who are always on duty, wondering what plane to take, his eyes met those of one of the guards. The guard stared back at him and then beckoned him over. Joe approached. "Yes, sir?" Suddenly he was worried.

"What's your name?"

"Rogers. Why?"

"You ever go down to the Sands?"

"Yeah, I go down to the Sands. Why?" Joe answered. Terror gripped him.

"You got some I.D. on you?"

Joe's eyes darted across the airport concourse to a row of lockers.

"I've got it up here, in my locker," Joe replied.

"Well, go get it," the guard directed.

"All right," Joe said. "But right now I've got to go to the bathroom something awful."

"Go ahead, the men's room is right across there." The guard pointed. Joe walked into the men's room which fortunately was empty. He reached into his right breast pocket and pulled out his wallet with all his identification and credit cards. Looking around he spotted a wire disposal basket which was full of used paper towels. He threw the wallet deep into the towels and walked out of the men's room and across the concourse directly to the lockers, the security guard ambling after him. When he reached the bank of lockers he stopped at one, allowing a perplexed look to come across his face as he turned around toward the guard.

"Got your I.D.?" the guard asked.

"I don't know why I forgot, but my partner took it with him. He flew out of here earlier with all my I.D."

The security guard pulled a notebook and pencil from his pocket. "Let's have your name and address, right now."

Joe knew the officer didn't have a warrant for his arrest or he already would have been grabbed.

"What's this all about, officer?" Joe asked innocently.

"Down at the Sands some high roller from Texas came in

there and slapped a bad eleven-thousand-one-hundred-dollar check on them last night."

Joe knew they had him. That was the exact amount of the bogus check he had passed. He gulped and covered up by saying, "Oh, I'm afraid I don't gamble with that kind of dough."

"Well give me your name."

"John A. Rogers, 2939 Turtleneck Boulevard, Dallas." The guard made note of the address and then, a dubious look on his face, walked away.

Joe could hardly contain his fear and anger. In the last three weeks the Sands had beaten him out of $400,000; he had beaten them out of a lousy $3,000 and they were trying to do a number on him. The vindictiveness of his adversaries, the casino bosses, seemed almost unbelievable. As the security officer went back to patrolling the airport, Joe edged toward the bathroom again. There was no money in his wallet, but he desperately wanted all the information on his debts and his credit cards which were tucked inside. Once inside the bathroom he upended the wire basket and found his wallet at the bottom. Then he strode out, his thoughts now on how he was going to get away from Las Vegas. A tough proposition on a Sunday afternoon.

As he tried to get a flight to anywhere, he kept crossing paths with the security guard who each time regarded him with considerable interest. Joe was sure that if he couldn't leave the airport the guard would call for a warrant and arrest him. Finally, he got the last seat on a plane that would take him to Denver, with trepidation as he used his credit card with his name on it to pay the larger fare. Escape was imperative. He had gambled steadily for almost two and a half days and was emotionally, physically, and mentally drained. As soon as the plane arrived in Denver he grabbed the next flight to Houston.

For the next few days Joe borrowed several hundred dollars—just to eat, to keep going—from friends like Turk and Jimmy Demeris. Then he headed for Baton Rouge, Louisiana, where Bill Robinson let him stay in his apartment. There was nobody left to pump, he had exhausted his banking resources, and by now he had no idea how many warrants were out on him.

CHAPTER 51

Joe Hodges had reached the nadir of his career. He had no idea where to go or what to do. The incident with the Buffalo Savings and Loan had clearly indicated that the banks were on the lookout for him. His efforts to save himself by gambling were over. He no longer had the strength to go out and cash a check. It was all over. The gambler was stymied—out of business—because Joe was emotionally incapable of providing another dollar for another pass at another casino.

But where could he go? There just didn't seem any refuge.

Bill Robinson had a town house in Baton Rouge with two bedrooms upstairs and a downstairs living room and kitchen. Joe moved in with him while he attempted to sort out his life.

Bill operated a dinner theater in the town, and Joe, who stayed in Bill's house all day, went to see the performances at night, soon getting to know them by heart. After doing nothing for a month, he called his old friend from Leavenworth, Larry Parker, and inmediately accepted Larry's invitation to visit him and his new young wife in Decatur, Illinois.

Larry gave his prison pal a warm welcome and even bought him an old secondhand Buick to drive. It was a heartening period for Joe, being with a real friend, but at the end of three weeks he felt he was outstaying his welcome. After all, Larry and his wife were just getting adjusted themselves.

Joe drove back to Baton Rouge for another stay with Bill Robinson. He kept in telephone contact with Nancy, calling her at a prearranged pay station near her Houston house. Nancy told him she had mailed him a copy of the *Reader's Digest* with a special article she wanted him to read. The magazine arrived the next day and he carefully read "The Gambler Who Must" by Steve Cady which was largely about the work of psychiatrist Dr. Robert Custer. Custer, a Veterans Administration specialist in alcoholism and narcotics, had made the first definitive studies of compulsive gambling.

For the first time, with the insight he gained from Custer's studies, Joe was able to focus on his problem. At the same time he was struck by what seemed a promising thought. He and Bill had been discussing what he might do, and Joe suggested that if a writer could tell his story, perhaps it would generate understanding of the disease, as Custer called it, which afflicted him. Perhaps when the day of reckoning could no longer be staved off, such a book might even persuade the courts of law that there were mitigating circumstances which must be considered.

Joe decided to try to reach the author, Robin Moore. Bill Robinson called Moore's agent in New York who said he would pass the information along to his client. But the call was not returned.

On an impulse Joe called Dr. Custer who he knew from the article was located in the Washington, D.C., area.

Custer's office informed Joe that the doctor was in St. Louis for a four-day medical convention and gave him the telephone number of his hotel.

Joe called and, to his surprise, the hotel operator put him through to Custer's room.

Joe turned to Bill. "He's going to come on. Hey! Who do I tell him I am? I can't give him my name with all the heat on me out there."

"Give him a phony name," Bill suggested. "You can explain later."

Suddenly Joe heard a low-keyed, cultured voice on the other end of the line. "This is Dr. Custer. Can I help you?"

"Dr. Custer, you don't know me but I've read the article in the *Reader's Digest* and I need to see you," Joe began in a rush. "My name is—" he paused. "This is Jonathan Alan Roberts calling," he blurted out.

Custer put Joe at ease and then listened as he explained some of his problems.

"Mr. Roberts, if you can come to St. Louis I'll be here two more days and I'd be glad to see you and try to help."

"Thank you, Doctor," Joe replied fervently. "I'll be there tomorrow."

When Joe arrived, Custer put all other work aside and talked with him until 3 A.M. Before unburdening himself, Joe had told Custer his real name and gave him his résumé.

As Joe told his story the psychiatrist studied him attentively. Finally, when Joe was finished, Custer looked at him in deep sympathy. "My God! They think you're a criminal and you're not."

Nobody had ever said that to Joe before. Chills went up and down his back and tears came to his eyes. At last he had found a man who could understand him, and that was an immense comfort no matter what might happen in the future.

The following day Dr. Custer invited Joe to come to Washington and discuss his case further. He said he would introduce Joe to the G.A. (Gamblers Anonymous) chapter in the Washington area. He'd be known as Jon Roberts and would be protected until some plan of action could be evolved and Joe could be treated for his compulsion. Joe said he had no money but Custer promised to try and find him some sort of work.

Joe went back to Larry Parker in Illinois but kept in touch with Custer by phone, making plans for the Washington visit.

Larry loaned Joe the money for a flight to Houston where he stayed on the outskirts of town a few days, furtively seeing Nancy and the children at his motel, not daring to show up at home where either the FBI or the sheriff would be looking for him.

Then, back in Decatur, Illinois, he drove his old Buick to Washington to see Dr. Custer.

What he really needed was a job that would pay him $100 or $200 a week so he could live in the Washington area and have regular consultations with the psychiatrist. Joe, or "Jon" as the others knew him, joined the G.A. chapter in Fairfax, Virginia. He told his story to a G.A. meeting, and a fellow gambler, also almost broke, forced $100 on him to help him out.

Joe discovered that the fraternity of hopeless gamblers was a close one. Only they could understand each other—they and Dr. Robert Custer. Nobody in society at large seemed to know what a compulsive gambler was.

Custer tried to help Joe in every way he could, but the job he had hoped to provide simply wasn't forthcoming. Although Joe was not gambling, he was a compulsive gambler and could not relax or address himself to any issue unless he had projected a plan of action to remedy his fortunes. Between Dr. Custer's treatment, conversational probings inducing him to uncover the sources of his aberration, and the G.A. meetings in Fairfax, Joe began to feel he could beat the compulsion. But he felt instinctively that there was a further move he could make to purge himself of the poisonous craving that permeated his mind and soul and had reduced his life to a shambles.

He thought of Dostoevski's classic short novel *The Gambler*. Reputedly the great author had purged himself of his own guilts and compulsions by writing that account of the horrors of a degenerate gambler's life. Joe decided to make another attempt to reach Robin Moore.

Moore had not responded to the messages he and Bill had left with the writer's agent. Most authors, Joe reasoned, lived in and around New York. By the simple expedient of calling New York Information he got Moore's listed phone number which he called for several days with no answer. Then finally, almost a week after he had first called, a woman's voice with a slight trace of Irish brogue answered. "Robin Moore's residence."

"I need to speak to Mr. Moore." Contact at last. Joe sighed.

"He's not here," the voice replied.

"Do you know where I can reach him?"

"I'm not allowed to give out the number," was the answer.

Joe correctly deduced that he was talking to the housemaid. "Mr. Moore is expecting my call," he assured her in his most imperious tone. "He will be very upset if he doesn't hear from me. It's about a multimillion-dollar movie deal." This last elicited a gasp from the maid and produced Moore's home phone number in Westport, Connecticut. Joe dialed the number and a woman answered. "Robin Moore's office."

Louise Webb, Moore's secretary, was accustomed to phone

calls from people who had great ideas for a book that Moore should write. Sensing this, Joe nevertheless persuaded her that what he had to say would be interesting and convinced her she should at least ask her boss if he'd consider talking to a man with a compelling story. "I've been trying to reach Mr. Moore for several weeks," he added plaintively.

Louise put Joe on hold and he waited in suspense. Suddenly Moore was on the line. After exchanging pleasantries, they arranged to meet in Kansas City, Missouri, where Moore was going to give a speech.

Joe hung up and called Bill Robinson. "Good news. I'm seeing Moore next week at the Muehlebach Hotel in Kansas City. I need you to meet me there next Tuesday at noon."

The drive from Washington, D.C., to Kansas City was a long and dangerous one. Wanted in four states, and with the FBI looking for him, he was taking a tremendous risk. But as he saw it there was no choice. After three weeks of G.A. meetings and treatment with Dr. Custer, he was ready for his interview with the author.

Joe had hardly begun his trip when it almost became a disaster. Driving through Pennsylvania at fifty-five miles an hour he crested a hill and hit a long, steep decline. The car picked up speed and was doing sixty-three when the sound of a siren froze Joe's stomach.

The police car made him pull to the side and a local town cop swaggered over. Joe produced his license and the car's registration which the policeman studied. "Guess I'd better call this information in." Obviously the downward slope increased a car's speed unless the driver were careful and this cop was obviously out collecting fines to help pay for the town government.

"Officer, I'm late for a very important meeting," Joe pleaded. "Can't I just drive into town and pay the fine?" He thought of the computer hits that his name would return when put on the network and felt sick, barely suppressing a shudder.

"Sure. A couple of miles straight ahead," the officer replied cheerfully. "You could send it in, if you want," he went on helpfully. "Of course if you don't we notify the authorities in"—he paused and looked at the carbon of the ticket he had made out —"Harris County, Texas."

"I'll stop ahead," Joe promised.

"You can't miss the Town Hall." The officer walked away and a shaken Joe drove on into town and paid the fine. That was the end of his lunch and dinner money but he didn't want any trace of his whereabouts revealed back in Houston.

The most direct route from Washington to Kansas City led Joe through Zanesville, Ohio. From the elevated highway running along the edge of town he could actually see Carl's Cafe where he had done so much of his gambling with the local bookmaker. He was tempted to veer off at the next exit, drive into Zanesville and see Carl. How many years ago was it? Twenty. If Carl was alive he probably wouldn't remember him.

Joe drove all night toward Kansas City. He wanted to be early. He was very careful not to allow the speedometer to go even one point above fifty-five miles an hour as he headed toward what he sensed might be salvation of a sort. Driving along, he remembered the days just before he met Dr. Custer when he used to think how easy it would be to make his car veer a little off to the right and crash it into an abutment or through the guardrails of a high bridge.

His mind reverted to the television show he had watched a few nights before in the motel room in Alexandria, Virginia, where he had been seeing Dr. Custer every day. *Eleanor and Franklin* had been on. At the end of the show he had envied the peace Roosevelt finally found when he died and was put in the casket. Certainly thoughts of killing himself had passed through his mind from time to time, but the warning about suicide that Dr. Passaro had given him in Leavenworth reached out to him and helped to hold him back. Now, as he pushed through the night to Kansas City, a plan started to unfold. The book might bring him enough money to at least pay partial restitution. Further, it would present mitigating circumstances that would buttress Custer's contention that, like an alcoholic, he was suffering from a disease. It might even help him win acquittal in the various trials he would inevitably have to face.

If the book could be written before the law finally caught up with him, just maybe he would have one more chance in life.

He arrived in Kansas City at 10 A.M. and went to the hotel. He was wearing his vested suit and carrying his briefcase, as though walking into a bank to cash a hot check. He sensed this might be the most important meeting of his life. At forty-seven, he had very little hope left. What he wanted more than anything was to be at home with Nancy, Mark, and Amy. But he had destroyed that chance over and over again. How many reprieves had he been given—only to gamble them away?

When he entered the lobby of the Muehlebach Hotel the first person he saw was Bill Robinson, wearing alligator-skin boots, western-cut jacket and pants, a loud tie, and a cowboy hat at a rakish angle on his head.

Joe hoped Bill's appearance would not have an adverse effect on Moore. By now he had learned quite a lot about the author: that he'd gone to Harvard, that he'd been born in Boston, that his real name was Robert Lowell Moore, Jr., that he was a conservative despite the frequently lurid books he wrote. He had also learned that Moore, like himself, was a Scorpio, born on Halloween, the day before Joe's birthday on November 1. Moore was three years older than Joe.

Outwardly cool and collected, Joe and Bill sat on the sofa facing the registration desk. In a bookstore Joe had found a copy of Moore's latest novel, *Dubai*, on the back of which was a photograph of the author. He couldn't afford the ten-dollar cover price but he fixed Moore's image in his mind.

Joe spotted him coming up to the reception desk carrying an attaché case. He nudged Bill who walked over, introduced himself, and waited for Moore to present his credit card at the reception desk and check in. After giving his attaché case to a bellman to take upstairs, Moore came up to Joe.

"Mr. Moore, this is Jon Roberts," Bill said.

Moore shook hands with Joe, a warm smile on his face. "You had a long way to come," he began. "I hope it turns out to be worth your while."

You don't know half how long, Joe thought as the writer sat down on the sofa beside him and said, "Okay, why don't you start telling me the story."

"Well, I guess I'd better tell you right off, Mr. Moore, that I am a fugitive from justice."

Moore looked at Joe and then at Bill Robinson. Joe could sense his thoughts. Bill looked more like a fugitive than Joe did.

To Joe, Moore said, "Well, Jon, that makes it interesting already. You wouldn't be the first one I've worked with." He glanced at his watch. "Look, it's about twelve-thirty. Why don't we go into the dining room and have some lunch."

Joe was famished and felt at ease with the writer already. In the dining room they found a quiet corner table. "How about a drink?" Joe ordered a bourbon on the rocks; Bill and Moore followed suit.

Over their drinks, Joe and Bill took turns telling the story of Jonathan Alan Roberts. They still were not ready to give the author Joe's real name. One phone call and it could be all over for Joe. It was not that they thought Moore would do such a thing, just that Joe couldn't afford to take any more chances. They ordered lunch and the saga continued.

Joe could see that the writer was truly interested in his story. When they'd finished lunch, Moore asked his first question. "If I do write this book with you, if we tell the whole story, get it out to the public, are you prepared to give yourself up?"

"Yes," Joe replied steadily. "I have always intended to surrender myself. Once the book is out there's nothing more I can do. If we can make some money perhaps I'll be able to afford a lawyer to handle all that must be done."

For the next two hours they continued their conversation. By now Joe had trust in the man he was confiding his story to. "I've been using the name Jonathan Alan Roberts but my real name is Joe Henry Hodges."

"Okay, Joe. But I'll get used to calling you Jon Roberts. No point in any of us having a slip of the tongue at the wrong time. I'd certainly be interested in talking to Dr. Custer."

Joe placed the call, but Custer would be out for the rest of the day so he spoke to his secretary. She and Custer were apparently worried about Joe and where he had gone.

"I just had to get out of the motel, Martha. I didn't have any money. They would have thrown me out and then I could have been in real trouble."

Joe said he would call back the next day, and Moore left to take care of some business.

The next morning they put through the call to Washington.

"I recognized Joe as a desperately sick man," Custer told

Moore after the phone introduction. "I would have considered him almost terminally ill if his disease had been physical. If you decide to take on this project you'll be doing a great service. Only a few psychiatrists have specialized in compulsive gambling. There is a crying need for more understanding of the disease."

"I told Jon I'd seriously consider doing the book with him if he agreed to give himself up when the book was finished," Moore put in.

"Yes, and he will have to make restitution," the doctor said.

"From what I can gather Jon will require over six hundred fifty thousand dollars to pay off just the criminal counts against him. On top of that there seem to be a lot of people in his life he should pay even if it doesn't involve criminal action."

"That's correct," Custer affirmed. "It may take him the rest of his life but it has to be done. That is the fundamental concept in treating compulsive gamblers. Restitution must be made."

After the conversation with Custer, Moore turned to Joe. "Look, I can start working early next year. I can fix you up with a small studio in the building where I keep an apartment in New York. We'll work out a weekly allowance to keep you going."

Joe smiled and nodded. "I'll be in touch." He had no trouble making up his mind. With a safe place to live and food to eat, of course he would go to New York. Even if the book didn't work out, it was his only chance.

CHAPTER 52

After Robin Moore left Kansas City, Bill Robinson took a flight back to Baton Rouge and Joe drove there in his battered Buick since he had nowhere else to go. He felt he could not return to Washington, D.C., without any money. Once again he settled in at Bill's town house apartment where he would wait out the time till he could go to New York. He had no plan other than to keep clear of the police, the FBI, and the sheriff.

He had been back with Bill a week when, during breakfast, they were startled to hear imperious knocks on the front door. They stole across the living room to the door and first Bill, then Joe peered out through the peephole. Two beefy men, obviously plainclothes policemen, were standing outside. Softly Joe and Bill beat a retreat up the carpeted staircase to the second-floor bedroom where they waited until the cops went away. Joe was already gathering up his few possessions. If the law had tracked him down to Baton Rouge, he would have to get out of Bill's house.

Giving the police an hour to leave the vicinity, Joe said goodbye to Bill, stole out the back door to where his car was parked, dumped his belongings into the rear seat, and started out for destination anywhere.

For several days he drove aimlessly through Louisiana and Texas, sleeping in the car at night, until finally, during the Christmas season, he arrived in Houston. His friends J.D. and Pat Robb took him into their house where Nancy could come see him with the children. It was a harrowing time. The sheriff of

Harris County was most anxious to apprehend him, and every time a police car cruised by the Robbs' house Joe trembled in fear.

A few days before Christmas, Joe walked into a drugstore not far from the rented house occupied by Nancy, Amy, and Mark. He was looking for Christmas cards for them when he was surprised and shocked to see Jim Lindsay, the vice-president of Century Hardware, who had spotted him at the same instant, ducking behind a counter.

It was not to be wondered at that Jerrel Sullivan's patience, strained beyond the breaking point, had been replaced by a desire to see Joe prosecuted and jailed. When Jim slid into a telephone booth Joe hurriedly left the store, jumped into his car, and headed away from the shopping center.

Joe was really alarmed. Now the sheriff would certainly be looking for him at Nancy's house. Bill Robinson had been in touch with him and suggested that they meet in Dallas. He was no longer with the dinner theater and the police outside the door had been looking for him, not Joe, Bill confessed. A small matter of some hot checks that had come home to roost.

Joe arranged to meet him in a seafood restaurant in Dallas on Christmas Day, but on Christmas Eve, Hugh and Nelda Fonville gave a party which Joe and Nancy attended. Uncomfortable, Joe asked that the curtains be drawn so the merrymakers would be invisible from the street.

At five o'clock on Christmas morning Joe left the Robbs' home and drove up to Dallas. Both he and Bill were penniless and, two lost souls on Christmas Day, they wondered what to do.

After some hesitation Joe went to the telephone booth and called Cindy Bramlet. He hadn't seen her since the Pensacola troubles started and was almost afraid to try and reach her. He located her at her mother's home and she immediately insisted that Joe and Bill come out for Christmas dinner. Gratefully Joe accepted the invitation.

On the way he stopped by a Western Union and wrote out a long, sentimental poem which he had been composing on the drive from Houston to Dallas. He sent it off to Nancy and the children and then he and Bill ate Christmas dinner with Cindy and her mother.

Late that afternoon, after a long, heartfelt talk, Cindy gave Joe $200. "It's not much, Joe, but I hope it helps. Merry Christmas!" Cindy's $200 at that moment seemed like $2 million, and Joe was deeply touched. They said goodbye for the last time. Joe headed back to Houston late that night feeling that with Christmas over the danger in Houston would have lessened.

He sold the Buick for $400 and, after another couple of nights with the Robbs, moved into a motel on the outskirts of Houston where Nancy and he could visit on her birthday and their wedding anniversary. For New Year's Eve, Joe and Nancy went with Robert and Pat Strobel and Hugh and Nelda Fonville to the house the Strobels owned at Lake Forest Falls, north of Houston.

Joe's friends wished him well on the eve of his new venture in New York which they all fervently hoped would bring an end to his troubles. Two days later Joe flew to Shreveport where he and Bill Robinson set out in Bill's car for New York City.

They arrived and moved into Robin Moore's apartment. A few days later when the interviews on tape began, Bill drove back to his home in Shreveport.

It was a difficult time for Joe, away from home, only able to talk to Nancy and the children at set times on certain days at a pay phone near their small rental house.

Late in April, Dr. Custer and his wife Lil came up to spend a weekend in Westport with Robin and Mary Olga Moore and Joe and Nancy Hodges. It was the first time Moore had met Nancy although by now he knew a lot about her. Dr. Custer was pleased with the progress Joe was making. The very interviews in which Joe poured out his entire story effected a healing catharsis.

Over that weekend Custer, Moore, and Joe retired to Robin's studio and discussed forming a restitution fund once the book was finished.

"What do you think Joe would do if he had, say, fifteen thousand dollars right this minute?" Moore asked.

"He'd head for Las Vegas," Custer said with confidence. "He's got a long way to go before he's cured." They both looked at Joe questioningly.

"I don't think so, Bob," Joe replied. "I think I could handle it now. I really want to make restitution and get busy on my defense."

Altogether it was a valuable weekend. Custer, for the first time, had a chance to talk at length to Nancy and help her understand the compulsion that had held Joe in thrall for more than thirty years. Sunday afternoon Nancy returned to Houston, Custer went back to Washington, and Joe and Robin drove into New York City where the next morning the interviews would resume. It was an exhaustive process, but the painful memories that he was forced to dredge up would give necessary weight to the book. The daily probing of his reluctant memory forced Joe to reexamine the roles of Jonathan Alan Roberts, compulsive gambler, and Joe Henry Hodges, provider of funds and credit. Thus he had to come to grips with both his compulsion and its results. There was no escape.

But he was constantly aware of the grim shadow of the law. The sheriff and district attorney of Harris County, Texas, the district attorneys of Beaumont and Huntsville in Texas, of Lake Charles, Louisiana, of Pensacola, Florida, all were eagerly awaiting the opportunity to prosecute Joe Hodges. It was the FBI that concerned him most, however.

As he had learned in Pensacola when he had stopped payment on a check at the Sahara Hotel, the FBI were undoubtedly the most effective bill collectors that the big gambling entrepreneurs in Las Vegas had at their disposal.

After one of the interviews in May, Robin Moore left a thick envelope on the desk. "Read this, Jon. You've been telling me about the real estate packages that you and Ben Kostial sold, and of course there was the package you sold a hundred times on the Bossier City deal. Here's a package my New York lawyers and accountants have put together with some big-time brokerage firms."

Alone, Joe studied the material Robin had left him. Thanks to the professional treatments with Dr. Custer and the agonizing daily scrutiny of his life with Robin, his mind had cleared considerably. If he was mortally ill mentally when Custer first met him, now he was merely unstable. But his keen business mind had absorbed every detail, the entire thrust of the presentation Robin had given him.

Paperback publishing companies were looking for books with strong movie possibilities, books that had the potential of earning large revenues. An investment in a potentially successful book would have considerable tax advantages for investors. It was one way the government could help writers to develop, much as the oil depletion allowance encouraged investment in oil wells. One requirement for such a book to qualify in this category was that the author or a coauthor have a track record of successful books behind him which would justify the valuation put on the work.

It was an ingenious plan, Joe recognized. Indeed, as a profitable package it overshadowed the real estate deals he and Ben Kostial had been involved in, even Shreveport. Its profit potential was considerable for the promoter who sold a book package to an investor interested in being associated with a literary property that had tax-related benefits.

The following day Joe learned that Robin and his associates had sold four such packages and had two left.

He immediately put a call through to Pensacola and told Harry Newkirk about the venture. With the gravel mine a thoroughgoing mess, Harry was interested in finding some new form of promotion and asked Joe to send him a copy of the book investment package forthwith.

With Robin's permission Joe had the presentation mimeographed and sent to Harry. Now he had found another exciting challenge. But this time he was resolved that any and all money he made would go toward his restitution campaign. There'd be no more running out to Las Vegas. He must now concentrate unswervingly on building up a fund to repay the individuals and institutions he and his nemesis, Jonathan Alan Roberts, had bilked out of so much money.

He wished he didn't have to use Jonathan Alan Roberts' name while he was fighting off his degenerate influence on what Joe liked to think was the real Joe Hodges. Ironically, though, it was not Roberts that the Feds, the sheriff of Harris County, and others were looking for.

Finally Harry Newkirk got back to him. Harry was excited by the package and had already found some interest in the project. Joe relayed the news to Robin who enthusiastically helped Joe retailor the package to fit the needs of Harry's clients. Under the name of Jon Roberts, Joe had been a guest at Robin's country club. There, he encountered an investment counselor who mentioned a colleague in New York City who might be interested in the book investments.

Once again, as had happened so many times before in his life, Joe found a vacuum existing that he could fill, and fill profitably, not only for himself but for a lot of other people. He wasted no time in calling on the investment counselors and personal management firms in New York City and its neighboring New Jersey and New England. He walked in cold, introducing himself and presenting the investment package. The accountants, lawyers, brokers, and many management firms were interested, even enthusiastic. It seemed a great method for clients to invest in an exciting project and gain the tax-related benefits.

In early September, Joe closed his first book investment sale. He had learned the technique. He knew how to put the entire package together according to the existing tax laws and make an attractive presentation. His story was temporarily postponed while Moore and his writing staff put out paperback original books for publishing companies and Joe made the contact and sales with potential investors.

It was a difficult but exciting fall and winter for Moore and Joe. Moore cranked out book after book and the publishers were producing the books in a matter of ten days or two weeks after the manuscripts had been submitted.

Joe had seldom worked harder than during those months toward the end of 1976. Day in and day out he called on investors in New York, New Jersey, and New England. He also went down to Houston at enormous risk, making contacts with potential investors there.

Each sale to an investor netted Joe Hodges in the vicinity of $25,000. Although the money was not forthcoming all at once, Joe's restitution fund was building rapidly. He put aside his own book project in his zeal to sell literary properties to investors. Cash was coming in fast but this time Joe was keeping it from Jon Roberts. Frequent steadying trips to see Dr. Custer in Washington helped.

There is no complete cure for the compulsive gambler, any

more than there is for an alcoholic. But Joe now knew he could kick the habit, and was therefore able to face the future with new excitement and hope. His life was turning around. Yes, the debts were all there—they would not go away until he made full restitution but he was on his way, going in the right direction.

In November, Joe and Robin were working on a book presentation in Westport when two FBI agents came up to the house. Joe made for the balcony above Robin's writing studio while Robin went to meet the agents in his living room. The agents claimed at first to be looking for Bill Robinson and Robin could tell them with a clear conscience that he knew Bill but didn't know how to reach him at the time. Then, just as they were leaving, they whipped out a photograph and asked Robin if he recognized this man, a friend of Robinson's.

Moore looked at the unmistakable mug shot of Joe H. Hodges. He shook his head and, escorting the agents outside, asked why they were looking for this man. Did they have a warrant for his arrest?

"No, we don't have a warrant," one of the agents replied.

"Then technically he's not a fugitive, is he?" Robin asked.

"If we could find him we'd have an arrest warrant from Bridgeport in a day," the other agent declared. By now Robin was of Joe's frame of mind. The FBI had indeed become bill collectors for Las Vegas casinos. He had no qualms about heading them off.

Joe climbed down from the balcony.

"Jon, I think that's a warning we should heed. There must be some way they know you're here, working with me."

But Joe was in the throes of an exciting finish to the year. There were new investors from Chicago, Miami, and California wanting to buy the literary and movie properties. There was no way he could do anything but continue his efforts to sell every book Robin Moore could produce before the end of 1976.

On December 6, Joe and Robin went to LaGuardia Airport. Joe had $6,000 in cash in his hip pocket and carried a laden briefcase which contained lists of all his debts. He had also written an exhaustive letter to his old friend Paul Smith, a lawyer in San Antonio, Texas. He outlined for Paul all the criminal acts he had committed and listed all the warrants that were out for his arrest. He also enumerated his newfound assets, the money he was putting up for restitution. The letter had gone out that morning.

Arriving at LaGuardia, Robin went to the American Airlines counter to buy the tickets while Joe waited for him some distance away. As Robin turned from the counter, he saw Joe with two young men wearing short, Navy-style pea jackets. Joe walked toward Moore.

"These two men are from the FBI," he announced. "They're looking for a Jon Roberts." By now the two men were right behind Joe.

"What's the problem?" Robin asked the agents.

"We're looking for Mr. Joe H. Hodges who is using the alias Jon Roberts and we think this is him," one of the agents answered simply. "We're taking him to headquarters with us."

Robin wrote down the names of the two special agents and where they could be reached at FBI headquarters and glumly watched them take Joe to a car and speed away from the airport.

Back in the city he found a lawyer specializing in criminal matters and that night the attorney was up at FBI headquarters trying to get Joe out. But for the moment Joe was beyond help. The FBI agents had studied the contents of his briefcase and found a copy of the self-incriminating letter to his lawyer Paul Smith which admitted everything. In short order they found out he was wanted in Houston, Beaumont, and Huntsville, Texas; Lake Charles, Lousiana; and Pensacola, Florida.

They also discovered he was wanted on the Las Vegas casino federal rap which accused him of transporting stolen securities across state lines. Translated, this meant that he had cashed a fraudulent check and taken the money with him out of Nevada. Although he had lost every penny and had taken none of the money out of the state, that was no defense.

For the next few days the lawyer made every effort to get Joe out on bail, but his record for jumping bond forestalled this effort. Joe was placed in the Manhattan Federal House of Detention and allowed to make a phone call or two every day.

Soon Joe was transferred to the Clark County jail in Las Vegas to await the determination of his case. Meanwhile Robin kept in touch with Paul Smith in San Antonio and a defense strategy was worked out.

Smith went to work on his old friend's case on a priority basis. He contacted the finest criminal lawyer in Las Vegas, Oscar B. Goodman. The first important step was to try to get Joe bailed out of the Las Vegas jail. However, detaining notices were coming in from Texas, Florida, and Louisiana. To get him out on bail was almost impossible.

It required seventy days and all of the renowned Oscar Goodman's expertise and connections to finally get Joe out of the Clark County jail on a $100,000 cash bond—by now Joe's restitution fund had grown appreciably thanks to the payments coming in on the book investments he had sold. Once he was out on bail, his next problem was to avoid extradition. The sheriff of Harris County was particularly anxious to get him back into his jurisdiction and send him to prison for life.

Fortunately, Oscar Goodman was able to stave off all extradition efforts. Free of the Clark County jail, Joe was able to work with Oscar to direct his own defense in the federal trial coming up.

Dr. Custer had testified previously in trials of compulsive gamblers, contending that compulsive gambling was a disease, but none of these men had been acquitted. He now prepared, with his associate Dr. Jule Moravec, to defend Joe in the federal court.

Joe was now extensively tested by Custer and Moravec, both for treatment purposes and because the resultant psychological profile of his compulsive gambling would be important for his defense. The hours of testing gave Dr. Custer and Nancy a chance to discuss her feelings about Joe and pathological gambling. It was clear to Custer that Nancy had been hurt deeply and nursed some deep resentments. He asked her why she had stayed with Joe. Nancy hated this question since she had asked it of herself a thousand times and had in fact been advised to leave her husband by friends and family. She responded that she didn't know. She indicated that she had a hostile "gut reaction" to Joe when he was gambling, especially to his lying.

Although Nancy had been the first to suggest treatment for Joe with Dr. Custer, she felt this was also an opportunity to break with him. It seemed as if once she was sure that Joe was under treatment, she could escape his control emotionally and spiritually and be free. But she was caught up in the world of compulsive gambling. She was not free. The spouse of the compulsive or pathological gambler becomes confused. Nancy's decision not to walk away could have been either the result of an unconscious desire to be dependent and controlled or an expression of the fact that her desire to help was stronger than her desire for independence. Nancy was a victim. Compulsive gambling had disoriented her. She was in love, but hurt by her love. She had difficulty separating the spouse she loved from the gambler for whom she felt antipathy. She had no idea that she was reflecting the confusion and ambivalence of society in general regarding compulsive gambling.

Nancy had been bitterly disappointed by Joe while genuinely impressed by his accomplishments. If only he had been a *total* disappointment, a decision on her part would have been easy. But, at times, Joe was caring, sensitive, loving, and understanding. Who was he really? She wasn't sure. She loved the kind Joe, she hated the cold Joe—the gambler. Why did she stay with him? How could she answer this exasperating question? She was tired, painfully tired.

Dr. Custer could not help but admire her. She had suffered but she was still strong. At least she was trying to understand. The real test of coping was to have a severe test with which to cope. She had had such a severe test.

By April of 1977 Joe had found an apartment in Las Vegas. Here he was, a compulsive gambler who had been only partially treated for the disorder, in the very midst of the most compelling temptations. Joe called Nancy in Houston and suggested that Mark come to stay with him. He wanted to recapture the father-son companionship that had been missing in Mark's life for so long.

Custer felt that Mark and Joe would have a steadying influence on each other. Though it was with some misgivings, Nancy put Mark on a plane to Las Vegas where Joe joyfully met him and took him to his apartment.

Despite the fact that Joe had, in an electrifying blitz, honestly earned the money to make full restitution and retain Nevada's top lawyer, he was unable to shrug off the depressions that assailed him. All his previous trips to Vegas had ended in two or three days, and sometimes he was there only a few hours. Now he was in the midst of the casinos and their humming action day after day. It was becoming increasingly difficult for him to concentrate on his defense for the coming trial.

Oscar Goodman made frequent flights out of Las Vegas to meet with Paul Smith and the various authorities involved in the case. He tried to persuade the latter to allow Joe to make restitution, which he hoped would mean having the charges dropped or at least reduced so he would avoid prison.

The district attorney in Houston assured Oscar that Joe would go to prison for life. His guilt, he averred, was a foregone conclusion.

"But what if Mr. Hodges makes full restitution and gives himself up?" Oscar asked. "How long would he have to serve?"

"Life!" the assistant district attorney snapped.

"Yes, but how long is that? Parole after five to seven years? How long?"

"Life!" the assistant district attorney reiterated.

No chance of compromise here, Oscar realized. Discouraged, he returned to Las Vegas to report his lack of success in Houston. Even if the banks wanted to drop the charges they could not, because the alleged crimes were felonies, making restitution inadequate.

The Pensacola authorities also maintained the same intractable attitude. They all wanted to convict Joe H. Hodges and send him up for a long period of incarceration. Joe's cause seemed hopeless. Even in the unlikely event that he could win his case in Las Vegas, once that trial was over he would immediately be subject to extradition. At least until the trial came up he had a sanctuary in Nevada, thanks to Oscar Goodman's intercession with the governor himself.

The extradition papers were on the governor's desk but so far he had refrained from signing them. Perhaps there was the glimmering of a chance that in Las Vegas federal court Joe would be acquitted; yet it was a pale glimmer indeed, despite Dr. Custer's vigorous assertions that compulsive gamblers should be treated and restored to the useful segment of society.

Finally, by May, the temptation was too great for Joe, and he began shooting craps again, this time at the El Cortez downtown. It didn't take him long to lose $10,000 and he quickly slipped into the old habit of pumping.

There was only one source he could go to now, Robin Moore, who was still collecting income from the investors in the literary properties Joe had sold. However, after months of interviews with Joe and frequent conversations with Dr. Custer, Moore was well aware of all the symptoms of degenerate gambling.

Custer was not in the least surprised by this turn of events since he knew that without either himself or Moore, the two major anti-gambling influences on Joe's life, Joe would almost inevitably drift back to the crap tables. He asked Joe to come to Washington, D.C., to continue his psychiatric treatments, but before Joe made this dangerous trip beyond the sanctuary of Nevada he had lost $35,000 at the tables.

In the meantime the prosecution and defense were preparing their cases. The U. S. Attorney was forced to hold off the FBI which was seeking an indictment against Moore for harboring a fugitive from justice. However, because the government had failed to prosecute Angela Davis for harboring murderers, fearing this might touch off racial disturbances, it was now hard to convict anybody for harboring a criminal.

The arguments put forth by Drs. Custer and Moravec were certainly telling ones and the U. S. Attorney decided to retain a psychiatrist for the government and one who would be conversant with compulsive gambling. A psychiatric evaluation of Joe Hodges was ordered by Judge Foley who would be trying the case.

Joe was fortunate that the man chosen by Foley to conduct the evaluation was Dr. C. F. Mynatt, one of the most prominent psychiatrists in Nevada. Unlike the psychiatrist years before who had talked to him for less than ten minutes and pronounced him a psychological malingerer, Mynatt spent many hours of personal contact with Joe and read the extensive psychiatric evaluation by Robert Custer and Jule Moravec.

On December 19, 1977, Dr. Mynatt wrote a letter to Richard Wright, Assistant U. S. Attorney, giving him the gist of a psychiatric evaluation which would follow. It was Dr. Mynatt's evaluation that would turn the tide for Joe. This was the government-retained psychiatrist, not the defense psychiatrist, presenting the psychiatric facts as he saw them to the government prosecutor.

Dr. Mynatt wrote in a report that would become a legal precedent:

> In my opinion, Mr. Hodges appreciated and intellectually accepted the wrongfulness of his conduct on each occasion, including an awareness of the wrongfulness of his action during the alleged wrongdoing. However, I feel that in each instance this awareness was overruled by a powerful and primitive psychological motivation that enabled him to rationalize his actions as psychologically acceptable to himself. An earthy comparison one could psychologically equate this to is the man in the midst of lovemaking being surprised and yet unable to discontinue his activity. The common statement that "an erect penis has no conscience" might be an analytic summation of his situation.

Dr. Mynatt went on to write:

> My personal opinion, which apparently agrees with Dr. Custer's, who examined Mr. Hodges in July 1977, is that outright imprisonment is of no value in rehabilitation.

In the lengthy evaluation itself Dr. Mynatt summed up his in-depth study as follows:

> Although by legal criteria, Mr. Hodges has been and is mentally competent, his judgment and response to reality are overwhelmed by the elemental psychological needs he finds temporarily satisfied by the gambling process. The starving person who breaks the window to get a loaf of bread to satisfy his hunger might be a moral and respected individual, but the primitive hunger overrides his intellectual awareness of the illegality of his actions.

On January 19, 1978, in the case of United States of America versus Joe Henry Hodges, an order requesting dismissal of all charges was filed. It was signed by Richard A. Wright, Assistant United States Attorney. Judge Foley dismissed the case the following day. It was a triumph for the psychiatrists who had studied compulsive gambling for so many years. But this, of course, was only a very strong beginning. The extraditions were out for Joe from Pensacola, Houston, Beaumont, Huntsville, and Louisiana.

Together this time, Oscar Goodman and Paul Smith revisited the various district attorneys involved. They were armed with the order for dismissal from Nevada and Dr. Mynatt's letter and psychiatric evaluation. The district attorneys in each case were extremely reluctant to drop charges. However, Joe was prepared to make full restitution, and the banks involved were pressing to get their money. They were certainly more interested in being paid than in a conviction.

Meantime Joe took another risk and flew down to Houston. There he contacted Ben Kostial and asked him to arrange to have Jerrel Sullivan meet him on a side street.

Ben was able to deliver Jerrel to the area where Joe was waiting. Before Jerrel could say anything, Joe began, "Jerrel, I'm making full restitution on everything. To the banks, the bonding companies, and most of all you. Will you take this ten thousand in cash now and let me pay you the rest when my lawyers get me straightened out here? It won't be long."

Jerrel looked at Joe, the man he had worked so hard to save, and had lent so much money, and the hostility drained from his face. He smiled as he accepted the money.

"Jerrel, this is just the beginning. I need to give it all to you. I will soon."

Jerrel shook his head wonderingly. "I always believed in you, Joe. My God, you did it."

The two men shook hands warmly. "Now I've got to get out of here before the sheriff catches up with me, or my old friend Marshal Henry Baker and I get together again under adverse circumstances. I'll see you when it's all over."

Ben drove Joe to the airport and he caught the next plane to

Las Vegas, this time not to gamble but to sit in his only safe retreat until the cases were settled and the extradition requests rescinded.

The federal court's dismissal, the government psychiatrist's report, restitution made to all parties involved—surely no jury would convict Joe under those circumstances. One by one the district attorneys were persuaded that it would be futile to bring Joe's case to trial. Joe Hodges was a free man, albeit he had agreed with the authorities in Houston to serve ten years on probation. However, probation was vastly preferable to imprisonment. Joe had, for the last time, extricated himself from circumstances that would have overwhelmed and destroyed a lesser man.

In December of 1978, just two years from the date on which Joe was arrested by the FBI at LaGuardia Airport, he became the star performer at the American Medical Association Convention in Las Vegas. The most heralded seminar of the entire AMA Convention was that on compulsive gambling chaired by Dr. Robert Custer. Doctors all over the country were becoming increasingly aware of compulsive gambling as a pernicious mental aberration and it was the convention goal of Drs. Custer, Moravec, and Mynatt to secure a consensus from the medical profession that would declare compulsive gambling a disease like alcoholism.

For Joe's many friends who came from all over the country to be with him in his hour of triumph it was one of the most moving events of their lives. They had seen him through two periods of incarceration followed by rapid backsliding into compulsive gambling. Then he had jumped bail, becoming a fugitive from justice. Prosecutors from Texas to Las Vegas were determined to put him in prison for life when they found him. The medical men, absorbed though they were in Joe's story, could have little understanding of how profoundly affecting the session really was for the men and women who had known Joe so well.

Robin and Mary Olga Moore were there, along with Paul and Anne Smith, Pat and Robert Strobel, Hugh and Nelda Fonville, and Margie O'Donnell. Of course Nancy was beside him. Everybody he had known over the last thirty years who had been supportive of him, who had suffered with him, who had tried to help him pull out, was there. Larry Parker and his wife Pam came from Decatur, Illinois, to be present to see the ending of Joe's struggle with the malign forces that had hitherto dominated his life. C. W. Conn and his brother George, who had figured prominently in Joe's life, came to Las Vegas with their wives Dorothy Ann and Renada. Pat and Frankie Smith and Bonnie and Jim Wright came up from Houston, Charles and Margie White from Longview, and from Weston, Connecticut, Nelle Hayes, who had been Joe's landlady and friend while he was a fugitive using the name Jonathan Alan Roberts. These were only some of the people from Joe's past who submitted to the magnetic pull of the occasion.

Dr. Custer introduced Joe and he stepped up to the microphone. A hush fell over the crowded auditorium. For the next thirty minutes, while the doctors and friends listened spellbound, Joe recreated a day in the life of a compulsive gambler, modulating his voice so as to convey the expectancy, elation, or despair of a given moment.

The day began at 6 A.M. with Joe impatiently awaiting the newsboy. Then came the race to the bathroom and the ritual with the sports page: Joe's hand covering the scores on the ball games, inching downward, revealing them one by one, while his nerves tightened to the snapping point.

"Oh my, they all lost, every damn one of them," he cried into the microphone in a hollow rasp. "That makes forty thousand dollars I owe them now."

His voice took on an optimistic tone. "Well, let's see. There must be *some* way I can get it back. I'll try that bank up in Conroe. That's it, they don't know me up there. I can't go to any bank in Houston, I've tried them all. Yes, I'll go up there. Then if I can just hit five teams I'll be okay."

He continued to relive that day, almost oblivious of his audience now, describing by tone and gesture as much as by words his exultation at having the bank vice-president cash his check, the exhilaration of placing the action on the five teams he knew had to win—the shock at finding the banker and the sheriff waiting for him outside his door. He recalled his inability to phone Turk, his bookie, and ask him for the money back so he could repay the banker and avoid jail, since that would have involved withdrawing the bets he had put down. Nothing he had said up to now gave his listeners so deep an insight into compulsive gambling as this.

The doctors' faces reflected their amazement that after a day of such stress Joe could spend a calm evening with his wife and children, one ear cocked to the radio for the baseball game results, and be ready at six the next morning to repeat the whole ordeal.

Joe concluded his speech with a vignette of himself once more standing on the sidewalk in the chill of dawn waiting for the newsboy.

It was perhaps the greatest day of Joe's life. It was the day he could drop his alias of Jonathan Alan Roberts. Furthermore, Dr. Custer was highly optimistic that as a result of this convention the American Medical Association would recognize compulsive gambling as a disease and treat its victims rather than jail them. This would make the occasion Joe's biggest-ever Las Vegas win!

So the joint saga of Joe Henry Hodges and his nemesis Jonathan Alan Roberts ended where it had begun in earnest, Las Vegas. As Dr. Custer, Oscar Goodman, Dr. Mynatt, and the state prosecutor noted before the assembly, not many compulsive gamblers resolve their virtually unresolvable problems as satisfactorily as Joe Hodges had.

The prosecutor, with a touch of wistfulness in his voice, cited numerous cases where the gambler ended up in prison for a long stretch, even for life. He also told of suicides and totally destroyed lives in compulsive gambling's wake.

Within a year the American Psychiatric Association did indeed proclaim compulsive gambling a disease. In 1980 Joe Hodges, along with Drs. Custer and Moravec and other people who knew its ravages at firsthand, started The National Foundation for the Study and Treatment of Pathological Gambling, with Paul Smith's law firm, Cox-Smith of San Antonio, Texas, as legal counsel.

Stephen Wynn, chairman of the board of the Golden Nugget, the scene of some of Joe's most nightmarish moments in 1974, was an early and generous contributor, as were other casino owners. Indeed, some of the very people who were trying to put Joe in jail in the sixties and seventies are now giving him contributions toward the foundation, which will also be supported by state and federal sources as well as private individuals.

Oscar Goodman, who worked so diligently on Joe's behalf, and Stephen Wynn have both agreed to serve as members of the board of directors of the National Foundation. So have Richard Olson if Washington, D.C., and Arnold Wexler of New York City. The first office of the nonprofit foundation has been established and its first address is Post Office Box 1052, Waldorf, Maryland 20601.

In light of the work being done by the National Foundation, it can be said that Joe's harrowing experiences as a compulsive gambler were not entirely fruitless or destructive. He himself did not emerge from them unscathed. Yet it seems something of a miracle that he emerged at all.

EPILOGUE

How do you possibly explain such a bewildering story? You have read about a healthy and lively young boy who later has a lonely struggle to walk again without braces, about a young man who is terrorized by the underworld before becoming a city attorney. He receives a Phi Beta Kappa key and later a prison number. Within a few years of being a fugitive he is a guest speaker at a national medical meeting. How do you go from success to handcuffs to honors? It has to be fiction. It isn't. Ask those whose lives were touched by Joe. To some he appeared generous and considerate, to others greedy and insensitive. Still others saw him as an incomprehensible mixture—ruthless and kind, calculating and warm, foolish and brilliant. Who and what was he, really?

Robin Moore, in *Compulsion*, has described a man as son, student, husband, father, attorney, entrepreneur, prisoner. He has also portrayed a compulsive gambler. Joe was all of these, but it was the compulsive gambling that introduced the negative and destructive elements into his life. It brought him closer to death than did the polio. Insidiously, it robbed him of his judgment, his ability to relate to those he loved, and ultimately his capacity to function. Few of those who knew him realized that once Joe crossed that invisible line into pathological gambling almost his every moment was spent thinking about gambling—about previous wins or near wins, bets placed or to be placed, how to pump money, how to hide his gambling behavior. He could not stop thinking about gambling or resist the impulse to gamble, and the more he gambled the more intense the preoccupation and the impulse became. Few knew he had these consuming thoughts. He hid them well. No wonder others were confused.

When did Joe become a pathological gambler? When did he *have* to gamble? His loss of control can first be pinpointed clearly with the Zanesville episode; it becomes even more evident shortly thereafter with the Midland episode. By this time, gambling had damaged Joe's relationship with his wife, father, and in-laws. He had been rescued from two serious financial predicaments by his father. His first bailouts. He had been arrested both times. He had borrowed money from illegal sources. He was defaulting on debts. He lost two good jobs. All of this turmoil as a result of gambling. He had become a classical compulsive or pathological gambler. Incidentally, Joe crossed the border into compulsive gambling four years before the birth of Gamblers Anonymous in 1957 and twenty-eight years before it was officially recognized by the American Psychiatric Association in 1979 as a mental disorder.

What occurred after the Zanesville and Midland episodes were repetitions of the same pattern with the stakes higher, the alienations wider, the crimes more serious, and the ability to function more impaired. Inevitably, danger and psychic destruction were being woven into the fabric of Joe's life. He could not stop, alone. He had reached out for help a few times. Unfortunately, it wasn't there. Besides, the pathological gambler typically denies he has the problem. He believes another big win will solve any difficulty he might have.

How did Joe become a compulsive gambler? First, he showed many of the personality characteristics of a potential pathological gambler before he ever made a wager. He was unusually bright and industrious. He was intensely competitive and had the ability to endure because of a high energy level which could sustain his fierce desire to win in any situation. Next, he encountered a series of shocks above and beyond the usual stresses of adolescence. Joe's first life shock was polio. Thereafter, the life he had known would never be the same. The polio experience left him a legacy of frightening realities. He had learned he could die, like "Little Boy Blue." More significantly, he had learned that he could suddenly and unexpectedly be confronted with the unfamiliar, the unpredictable, and the dangerous. This knowledge and its attendant feelings were reinforced when he was sent to New Orleans for his physical therapy. He entered an unfamiliar world which seemed indifferent to his needs while also being painful and uncertain. As a result of these experiences, he realized that environmental forces, physical or social, could not be relied upon to be supportive.

All this forced Joe into over-reliance on himself. He began to keep others at what he perceived as a safe distance. For example, his first serious romantic involvement with Genie was unusually cautious. His dread of the unpredictable kept their relationship distant. He craved closeness but avoided it. He sacrificed his needs in order to keep control, avoid the unexpected. It was also during this time that he decided to leave Boston and not even begin his law scholarship at Harvard. Boston created feelings of loneliness and isolation similar to those experienced in New Orleans. He had to return to the more supportive and familiar environment of Texas. A pattern was emerging, its key note avoidance. The life shocks were taking their toll—a characteristic precondition of compulsive gambling.

Another necessary ingredient in the making of the compulsive gambler is the opportunity to gamble. Joe had found such opportunities among his peers and in illegal establishments. It is highly significant that his early gambling was characterized by winning. Remember, Joe was skillful enough at gambling virtually to finance his college education. As is typical of the developing compulsive gambler, he continued to win and win big. He had taken the bait and the gambling was beginning to make him feel important, powerful, influential, and confident. Gambling made him feel alive. *Not* gambling was beginning to give him a feeling of emptiness—an emptiness not unlike that felt during his adolescent life shocks. Gambling also provided Joe with an activity which could substitute for the competitive and athletic needs that were denied him because of his residual paralysis from polio.

In spite of the increased gambling, Joe was succeeding in his academic pursuits and in establishing closer personal relationships with his peers, especially with Nancy for whom his feelings were warm and romantic. Then came rejection by the law firm he had dreamed of joining, his next psychological bomb burst. The unexpected had struck again. He was deeply hurt. His self-confidence was damaged, as evidenced by the fact that he attributed the firm's rejection to their ability to see he had style but no substance. This interpretation was incorrect but reflected Joe's misperception of himself. He was soon to discover that even this pain could be soothed by gambling. It wasn't too long after this episode that he won an amount on a baseball parlay which exceeded his annual salary in his private law practice. The first really "big" win.

Now Joe was becoming unreasonably optimistic about his ability to win at gambling. This is another classical feature of the gambler whose addiction is becoming pathological. Inevitably Joe began to lose and lose heavily. He committed the cardinal sin of gambling by "chasing," betting more to recover his losses. Eventually this leads to the need for a bailout. It is at this point that the anatomy of the pathological gambler becomes complete. There follow endless and desperate and futile attempts to regain or preserve his image, his sanity, his very existence. The end of the road is disaster, not only for the gambler but, in varying degrees, for his family, his friends, sometimes even his community.

As Joe's life became more consumed by gambling, so he had to adjust his value system drastically in order to survive. He would do things he would have considered unthinkable as a youth or as a non-gambler. Pathological gambling always impairs judgment which, in turn, compromises life values which, in turn, allows for gambling to continue. The cycle goes on and it accelerates. Notice how Joe's gambling had a nearly mathematical progression in the amounts of money wagered and the time spent on it. More importantly, note how his judgment and values progressively diminished. Ultimately, he lost almost everything in life that he had once treasured. When he did genuinely reach out for help he did not know if he could survive.

Has Joe survived? If you were to see him today, you would not see all the painful scars. You would see his smile, his liveliness, and his enthusiasm. You would feel his warmth, concern, and intensity. Closer scrutiny would give you glimpses of his hurt, his distress, and his sadness. One cannot "die" as many times as Joe did and be free of fleeting moments of agonizing fear, intense remorse, and burning humiliation. He can still present that imperturbable "poker face" but he can't continuously hide the memories of the past. He must think of the time when the polio virus introduced him to the real threat of death; of his academic successes which lost their luster when the pride taken in them by his parents, wife, and friends faded as he failed to live up to them; of his inability to maintain the standards of his profession; of his successful business enterprises which so often came to naught; of his desperate attempts to salvage his losses and the innocent people he may have hurt. But he is determined that he will not burden others with his past. He is trying to enjoy every moment of his non-gambling existence.

In many ways, however, Joe's conversion from pathological gambler to non-gambler has been the most painful phase of his life. Gambling became no longer an option, but the thirst to gamble returned on occasions. He had to face the unknown outcome of his legal entanglements, to endure the long separations from his family and his home. He lived with loneliness and guilt. He was in pain and he was vulnerable. The many days of dictating his life story for Robin Moore were therapeutic. He had never stopped to look at his life so thoroughly. His judgment was returning. He had goals again. He wanted to be free. He wanted to make full restitution. He wanted to regain control of his impulses. And he was willing to work at it. But it was an exasperatingly slow process for Joe who had always been fiercely impatient. He liked prompt action. He did not like to accept help. But he knew he had to change. This was the agony of recovery. It takes courage to look at yourself and struggle to change. Courage is one of Joe's strengths and he desperately needed it.

There is another whose courage was significantly responsible for Joe's survival—his wife Nancy. She was the person most victimized by his compulsive gambling. With what you now know she had to endure, it would be easy to relegate her to the role of the martyr or the chronically insecure—even of the fool. This would be wrong. She did not feel she deserved her suffering, nor did she enjoy it. She knew she could function in the world independently since she had been forced to do so many times.

Nancy tried to help Joe—but when she mentioned his gambling he invariably became cold and angry. She wanted to get help for him—but she didn't know whom to turn to. She had a deep sense of loyalty and she took her commitments seriously. She also loved Joe. Compulsive gamblers are alike in their passion for gambling and its consistent defining complications; in other respects they differ from one another as non-gamblers do. Joe had been loving toward Nancy. He had also treated her, at times, with consideration, concern, and affection. Perhaps those times were enough to balance out the neglect, the deceptions, the many embarrassments. Nancy has her scars but she too has survived. She has also become a far happier person.

The compulsive gambler in this book is not seeking to excuse his behavior. He has told his whole story—the good and the bad, the successes and the failures, the achievements and the humiliations, the pleasure and the pain—in the hope that he will be understood and, more importantly, in the hope that compulsive gambling will be understood and so avoided by others. Joe would like to think he is not as bad as he suspects he is. He isn't!

R. L. C.